Shinobi Life

Vol. 4

Created by
Shoko Conami

HAMBURG // LONDON // LOS ANGELES // TOKYO

Shinobi Life 4
Created by Shoko Conami

Translation - Lori Riser
English Adaptation - Ysabet Reinhardt MacFarlane
Retouch and Lettering - Star Print Brokers
Production Artist - Michael Paolilli
Graphic Designer - Chelsea Windlinger

Editor - Lillian Diaz-Przybyl
Print Production Manager - Lucas Rivera
Managing Editor - Vy Nguyen
Senior Designer - Louis Csontos
Art Director - Al-Insan Lashley
Director of Sales and Manufacturing - Allyson De Simone
Associate Publisher - Marco F. Pavia
President and C.O.O. - John Parker
C.E.O. and Chief Creative Officer - Stu Levy

A ⊙ TOKYOPOP® Manga

TOKYOPOP and ⊙ are trademarks or registered trademarks of TOKYOPOP Inc.

TOKYOPOP Inc.
5900 Wilshire Blvd. Suite 2000
Los Angeles, CA 90036

E-mail: info@TOKYOPOP.com
Come visit us online at www.TOKYOPOP.com

ISBN: 978-1-4278-1539-2

First TOKYOPOP printing: Feburary 2010
10 9 8 7 6 5 4 3 2 1
Printed in the USA

Shoko Conami

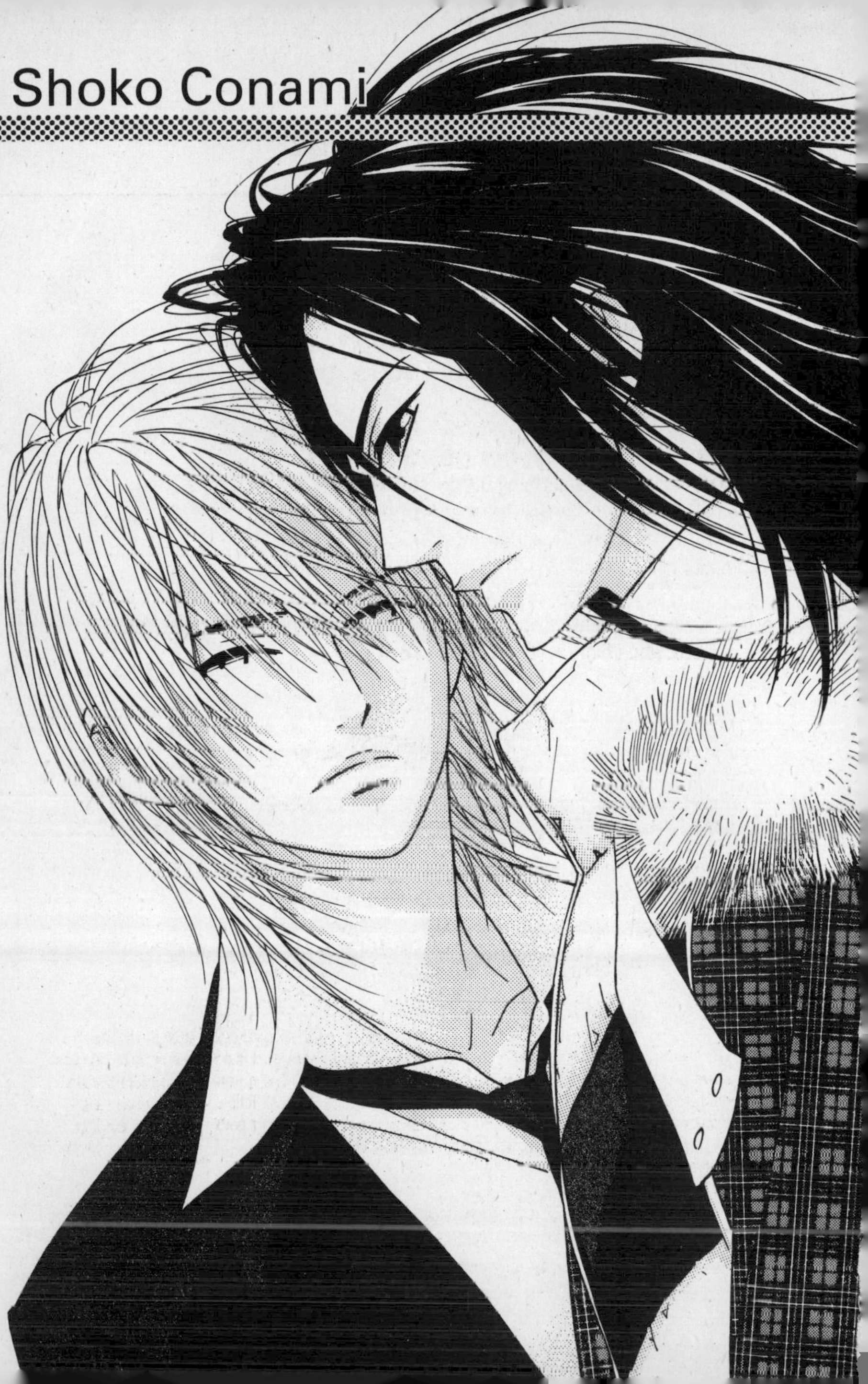

Summary & Character Introduction

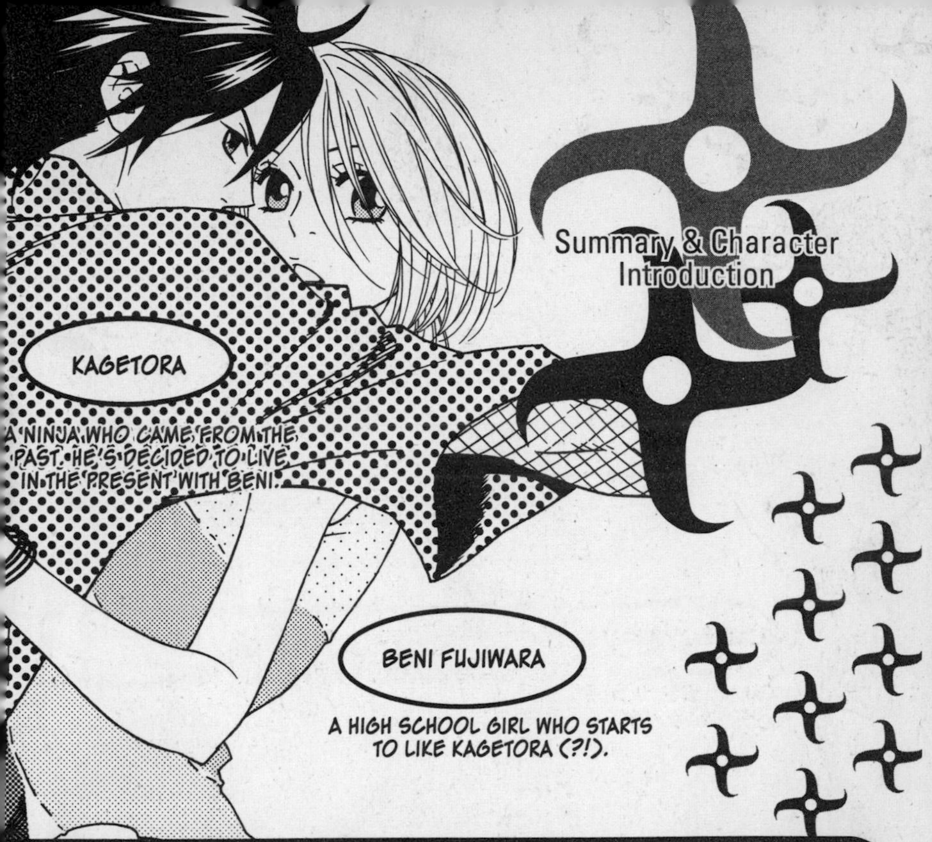
KAGETORA
A NINJA WHO CAME FROM THE PAST. HE'S DECIDED TO LIVE IN THE PRESENT WITH BENI.
BENI FUJIWARA
A HIGH SCHOOL GIRL WHO STARTS TO LIKE KAGETORA (?!).

BENI FUJIWARA, A HIGH SCHOOL GIRL WHO WANTED TO DIE TO GET BACK AT HER ARROGANT FATHER, WAS UNEXPECTEDLY RESCUED WHEN SHE FELL OFF A BUILDING ONE DAY. HER SAVIOR? A NINJA NAMED KAGETORA, WHO HAPPENED TO FALL OUT OF THE SKY AT THE RIGHT MOMENT. KAGETORA CALLS BENI "BENI HIME," AND HE DEVOTES HIMSELF TO PROTECTING HER LIFE AT ANY COST...BECAUSE HE'S MISTAKEN HER FOR HER OWN ANCESTOR, WHO LOOKED EXACTLY LIKE HER. YES, KAGETORA IS A NINJA WHO HAS TRAVELED THROUGH TIME FROM THE PAST! BENI GRADUALLY BECOMES FOND OF KAGETORA AS HE REPEATEDLY SAVES HER FROM DANGER AND PLEDGES HIS ETERNAL LOYALTY. SHE TRIES TO PRETEND TO BE BENI HIME FOR HIM, AND THEY SLOWLY BECOME CLOSER AND CLOSER.

RIHITO IWATSURU
BENI'S CLASSMATE AND FIANCÉ.
HITAKI
KAGETORA'S NINJA FRIEND. HE WANTS TO TAKE KAGETORA'S LIFE.
BENI'S FATHER
A COLD MAN, UNINTERESTED IN HIS DAUGHTER.

BUT WHEN THE PAIR UNEXPECTEDLY TRAVELS BACK TO KAGETORA'S TIME, HE RUNS INTO THE REAL BENI HIME AND REALIZES THAT THE TWO WOMEN ARE NOT THE SAME PERSON. AFTER BENI HIME TELLS KAGETORA THAT SHE WANTS TO LIVE AS A NORMAL VILLAGER, HE LOSES HIS PURPOSE IN LIFE. WHEN A FELLOW NINJA, HITAKI, BRANDS HIM A TRAITOR AND TRIES TO KILL HIM, KAGETORA DECIDES TO RETURN TO THE PRESENT WITH BENI AND LIVE WITH HER. THINGS SEEM TO BE GOING SMOOTHLY FOR BENI AND KAGETORA'S FLEDGLING ROMANCE, BUT THAT COMES TO AN ABRUPT END WHEN BENI'S FATHER REVEALS THAT BENI ALREADY HAS A FIANCÉ--RIHITO IWATSURU! AND WHAT'S MORE, RIHITO SEEMS TO BE CONNECTED TO HITAKI, WHO HAS ALSO JOURNEYED FROM THE PAST. RIHITO REPEATEDLY TRIES TO WIN BENI OVER BY FORCE, AND AT FIRST SHE AGREES TO GO ALONG WITH HIM TO PROTECT KAGETORA, BUT HER FEELINGS FOR KAGETORA WON'T BE DENIED...

CONTENTS

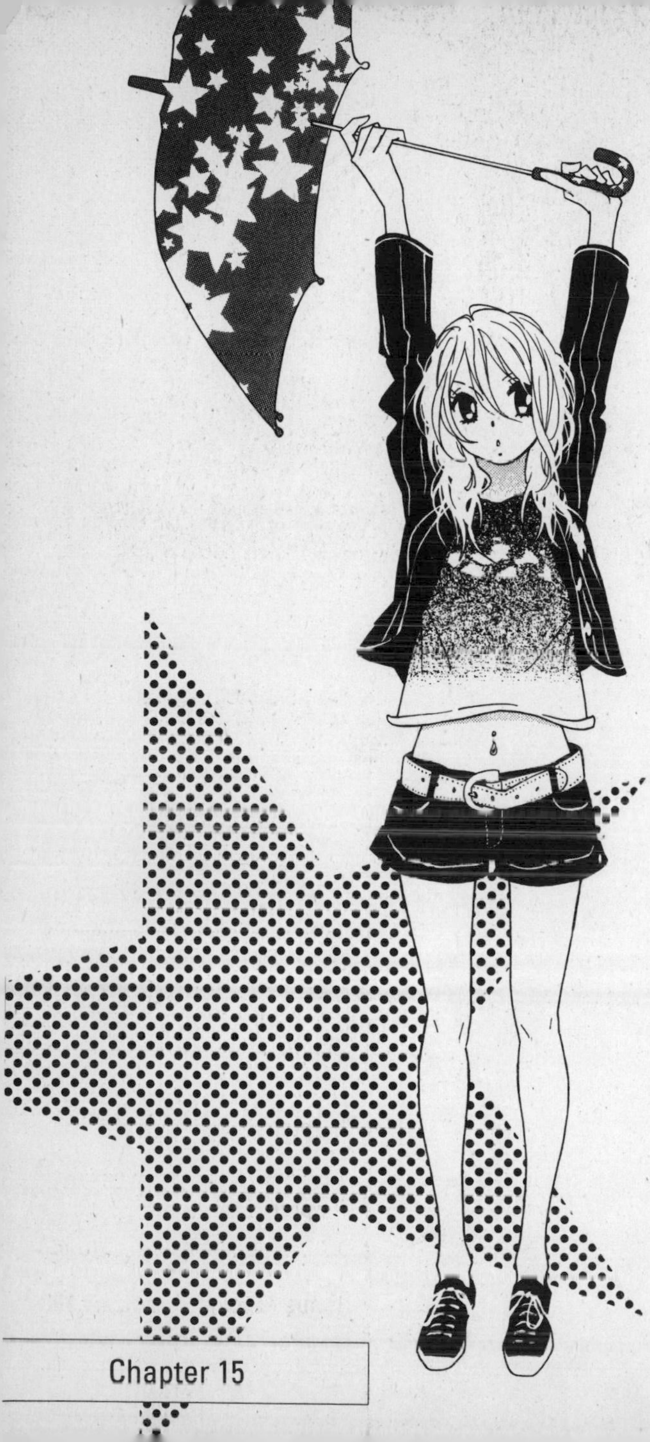

Chapter 15

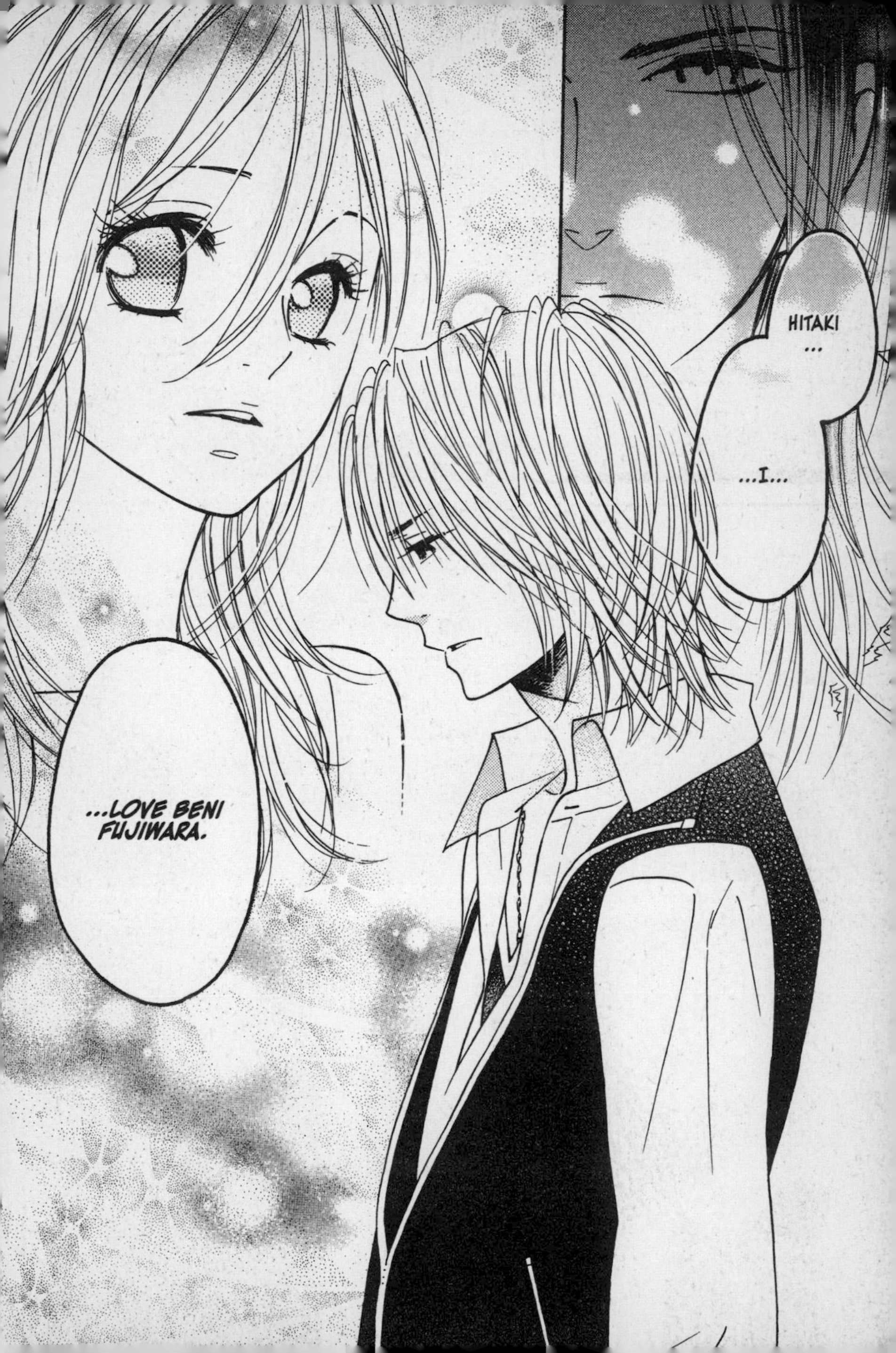
HITAKI ...
...I...
...LOVE BENI FUJIWARA.

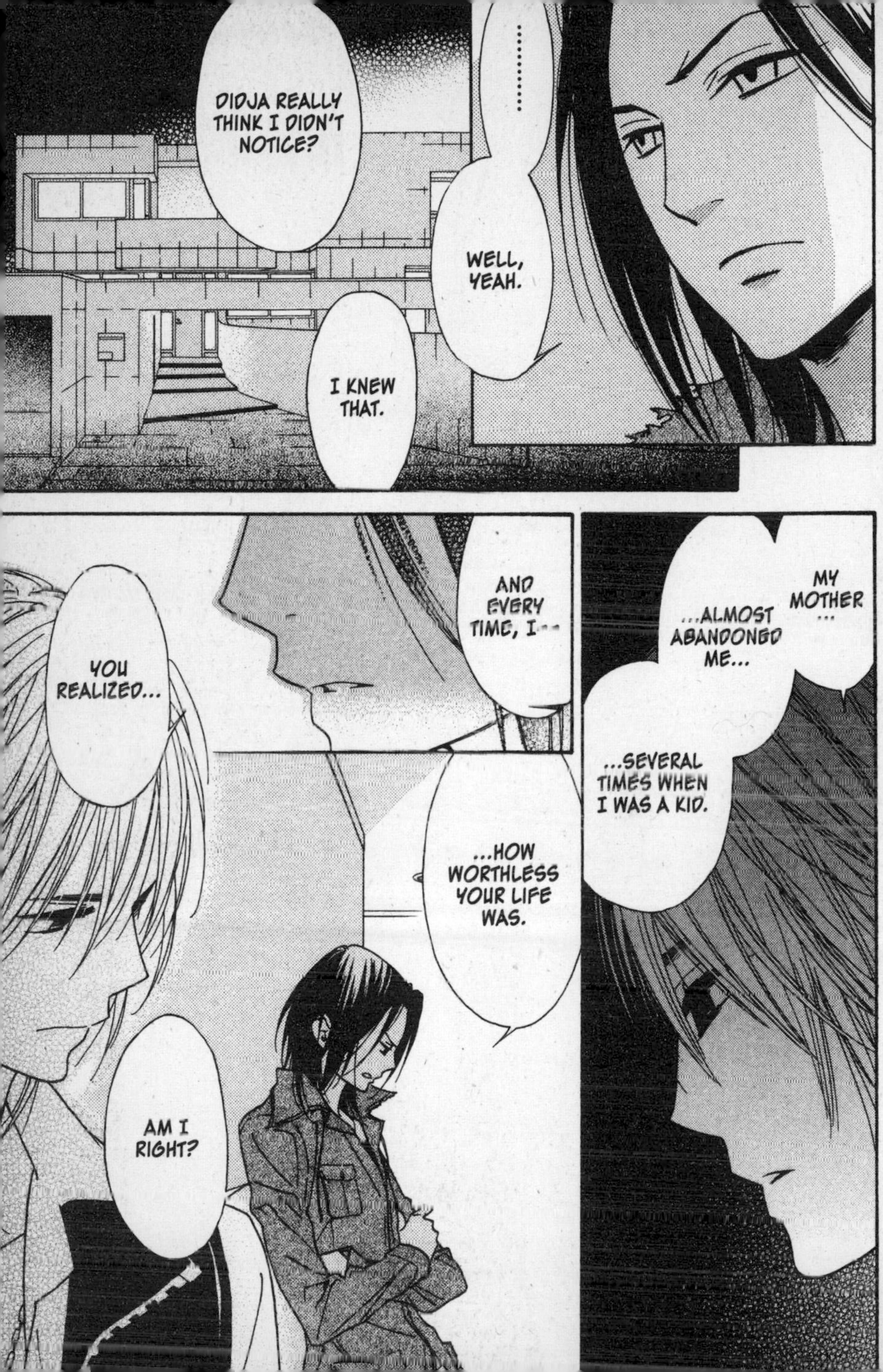
......
DIDJA REALLY THINK I DIDN'T NOTICE?
WELL, YEAH.
I KNEW THAT.
MY MOTHER...
...ALMOST ABANDONED ME...
...SEVERAL TIMES WHEN I WAS A KID.
AND EVERY TIME, I--
YOU REALIZED...
...HOW WORTHLESS YOUR LIFE WAS.
AM I RIGHT?

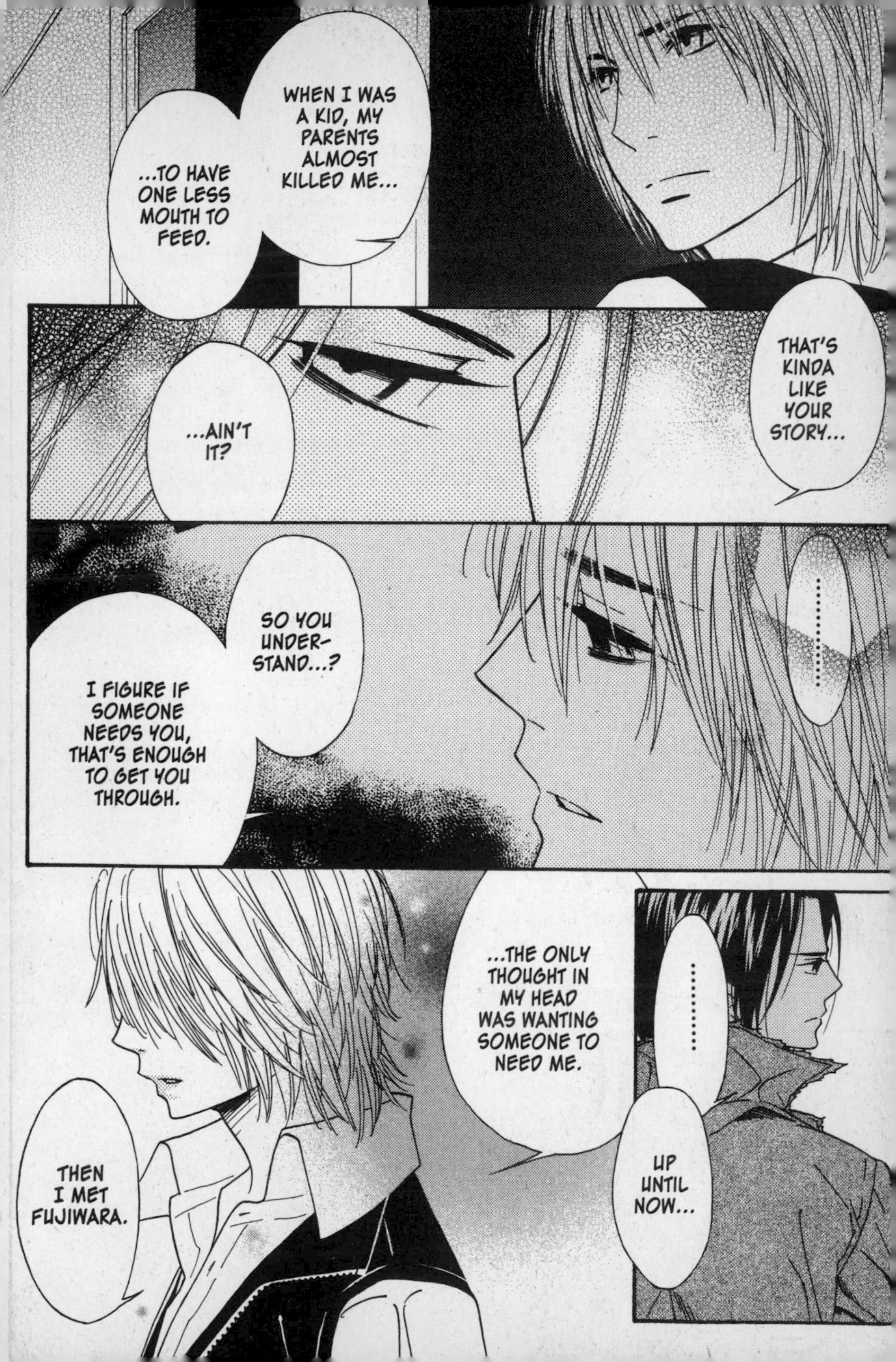

WHEN I WAS A KID, MY PARENTS ALMOST KILLED ME...
...TO HAVE ONE LESS MOUTH TO FEED.
THAT'S KINDA LIKE YOUR STORY...
...AIN'T IT?
......
SO YOU UNDER-STAND...?
I FIGURE IF SOMEONE NEEDS YOU, THAT'S ENOUGH TO GET YOU THROUGH.
......
UP UNTIL NOW...
...THE ONLY THOUGHT IN MY HEAD WAS WANTING SOMEONE TO NEED ME.
THEN I MET FUJIWARA.

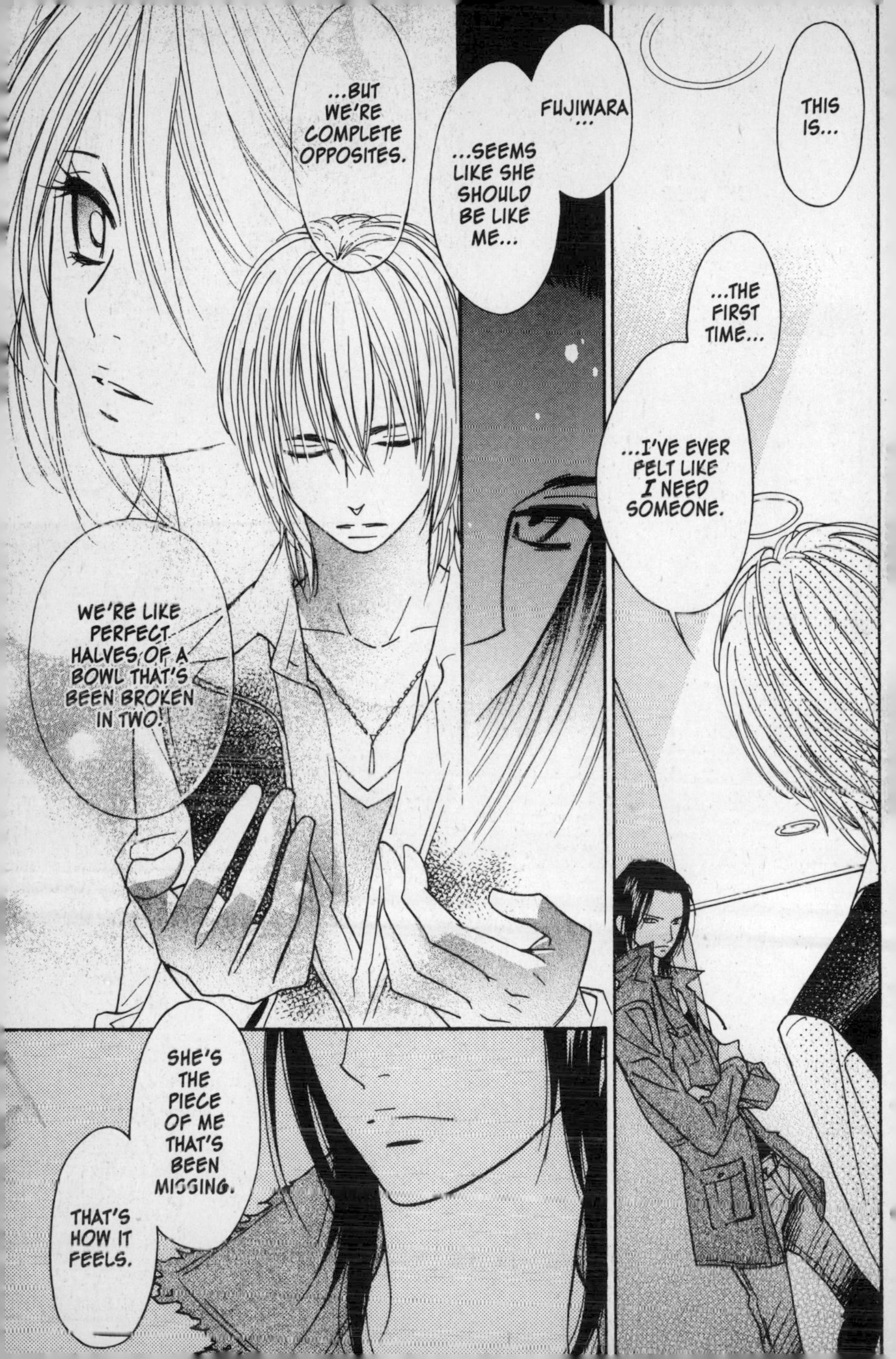
THIS IS...
...THE FIRST TIME...
...I'VE EVER FELT LIKE I NEED SOMEONE.
FUJIWARA...
...SEEMS LIKE SHE SHOULD BE LIKE ME...
...BUT WE'RE COMPLETE OPPOSITES.
WE'RE LIKE PERFECT HALVES OF A BOWL THAT'S BEEN BROKEN IN TWO.
SHE'S THE PIECE OF ME THAT'S BEEN MISSING.
THAT'S HOW IT FEELS.

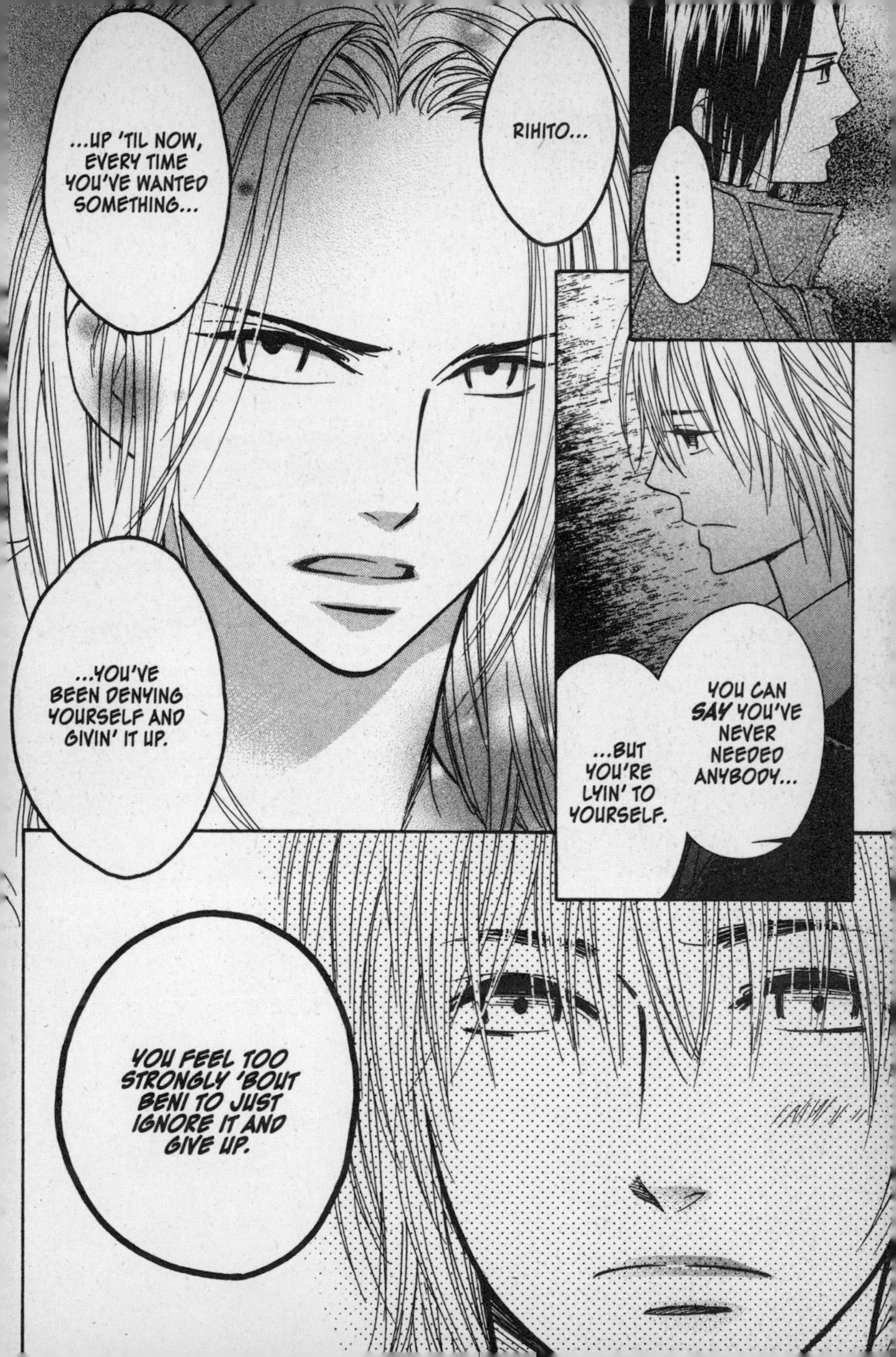

……
YOU CAN SAY YOU'VE NEVER NEEDED ANYBODY...
...BUT YOU'RE LYIN' TO YOURSELF.
RIHITO...
...UP 'TIL NOW, EVERY TIME YOU'VE WANTED SOMETHING...
...YOU'VE BEEN DENYING YOURSELF AND GIVIN' IT UP.
YOU FEEL TOO STRONGLY 'BOUT BENI TO JUST IGNORE IT AND GIVE UP.

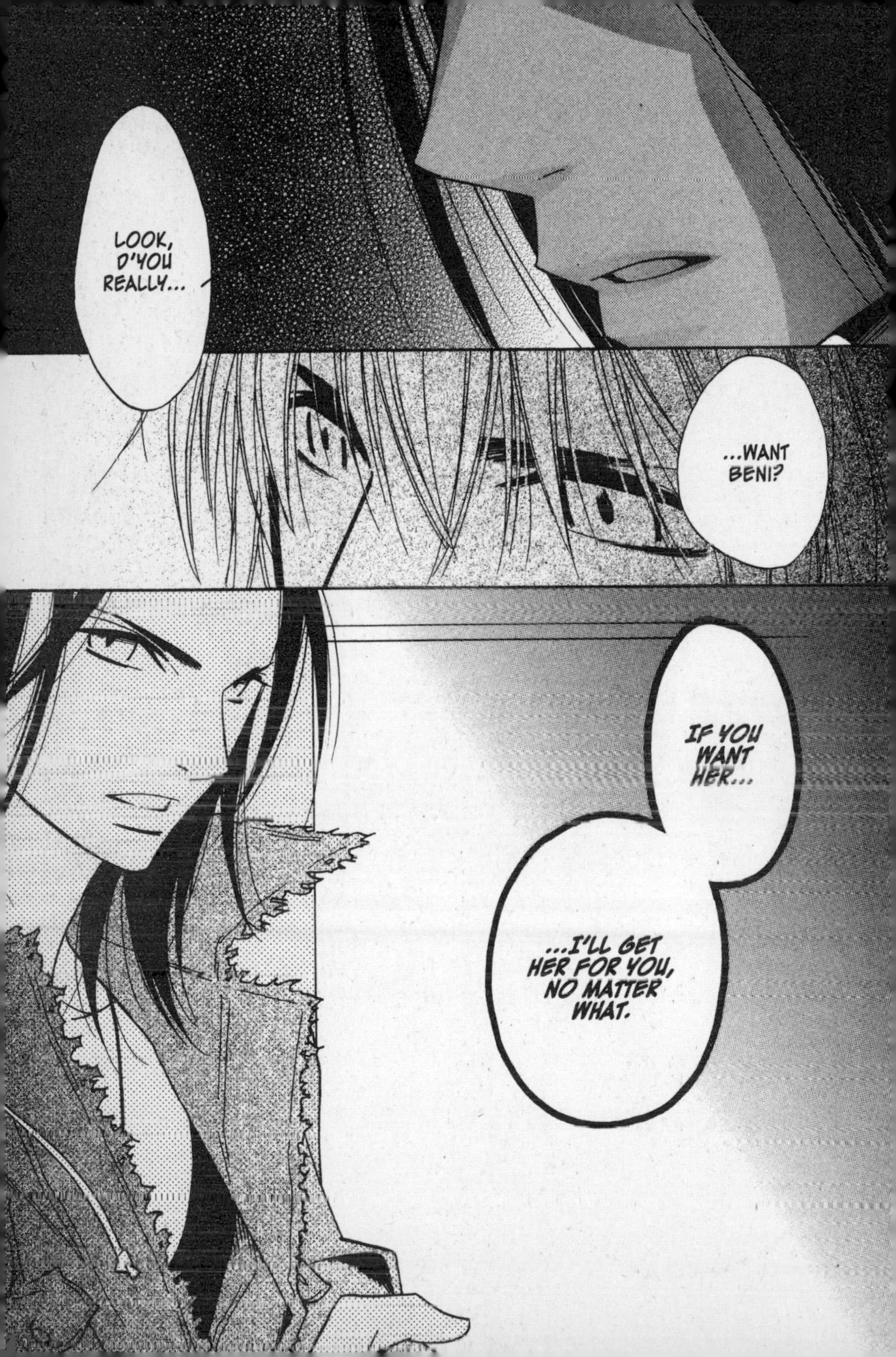
LOOK, D'YOU REALLY...
...WANT BENI?
IF YOU WANT HER...
...I'LL GET HER FOR YOU, NO MATTER WHAT.

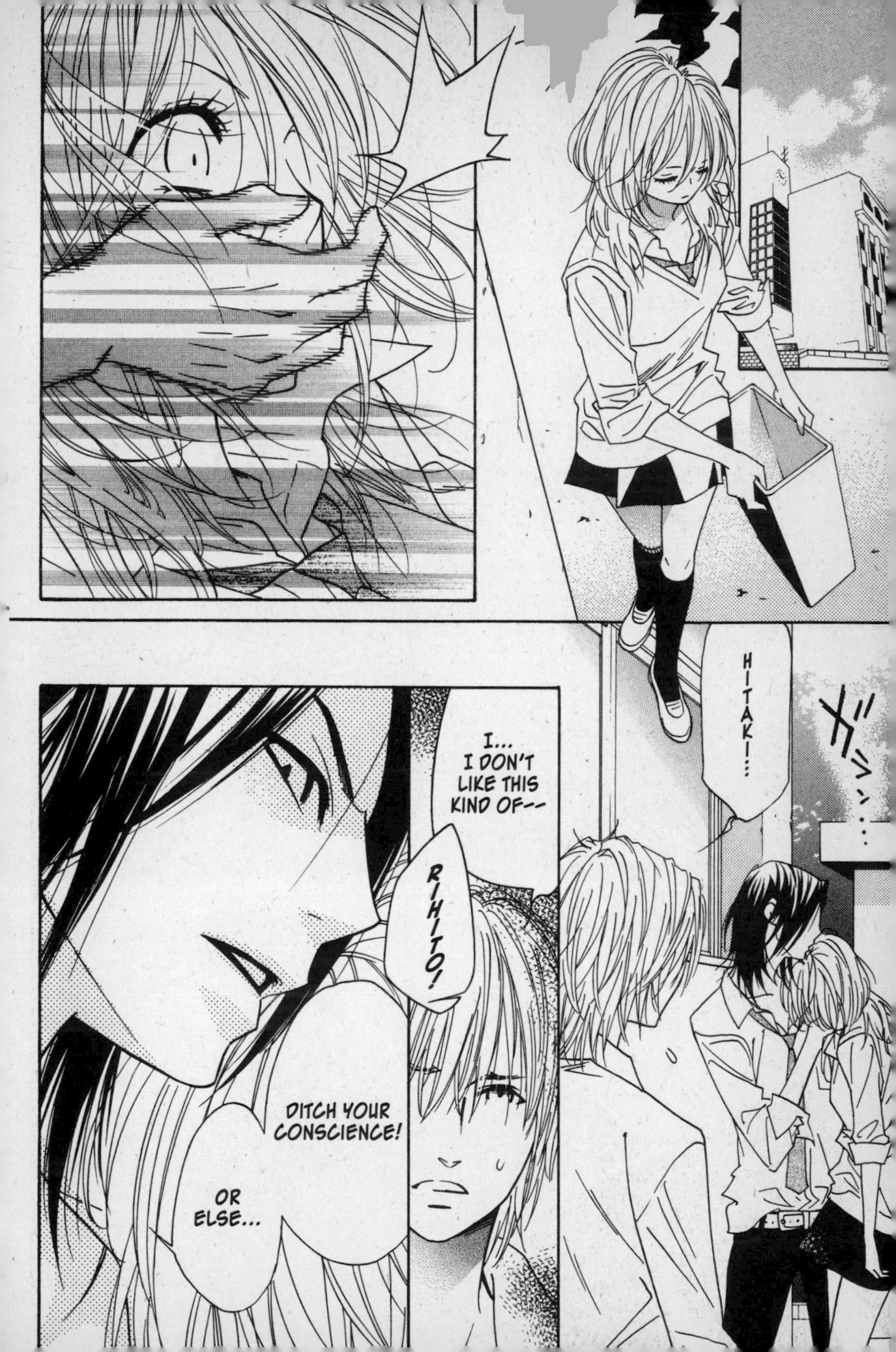

HITAKI...!
ガラ...
I... I DON'T LIKE THIS KIND OF--
RIHITO!
DITCH YOUR CONSCIENCE!
OR ELSE...

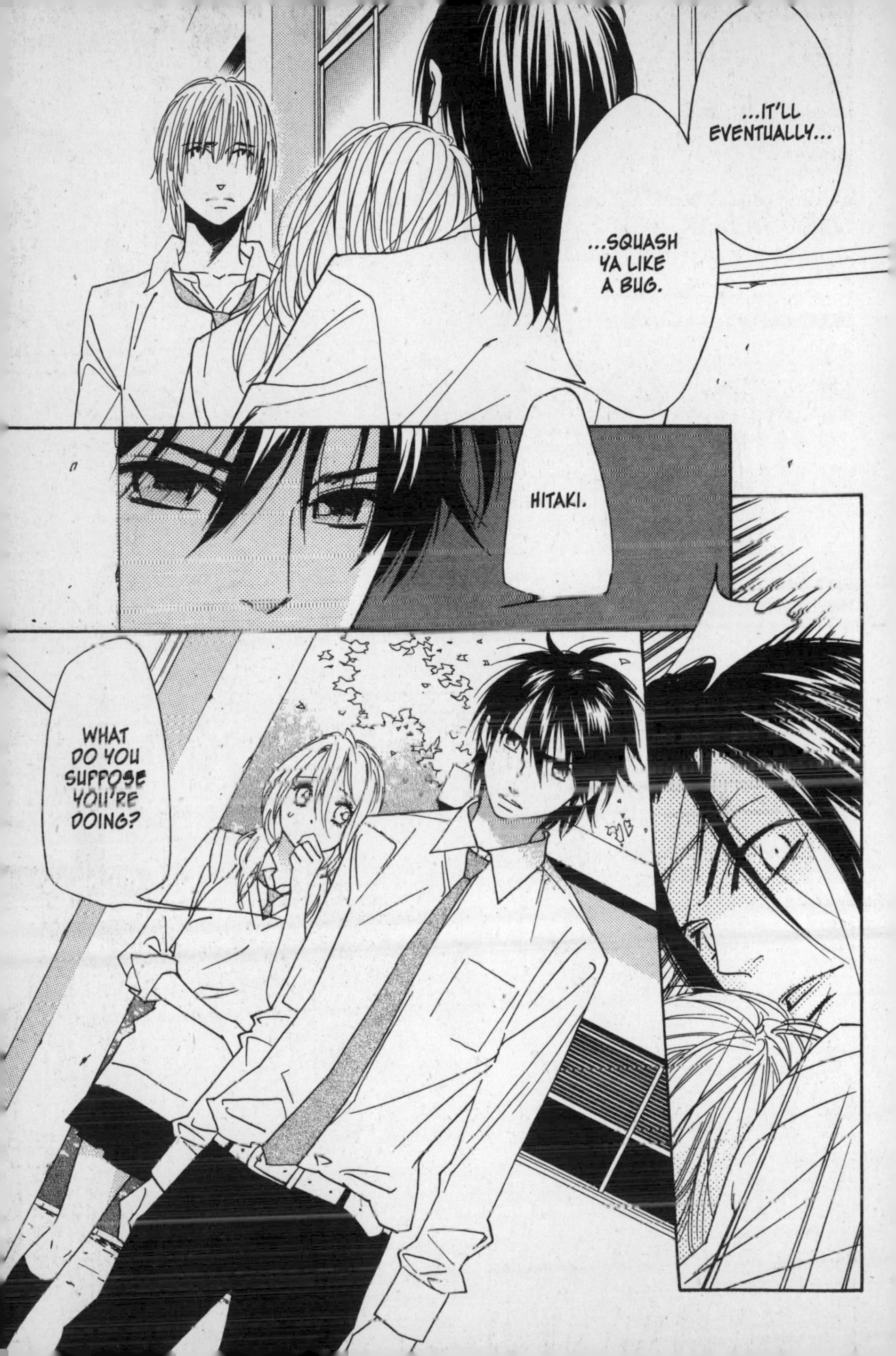
...IT'LL EVENTUALLY...
...SQUASH YA LIKE A BUG.
HITAKI.
WHAT DO YOU SUPPOSE YOU'RE DOING?

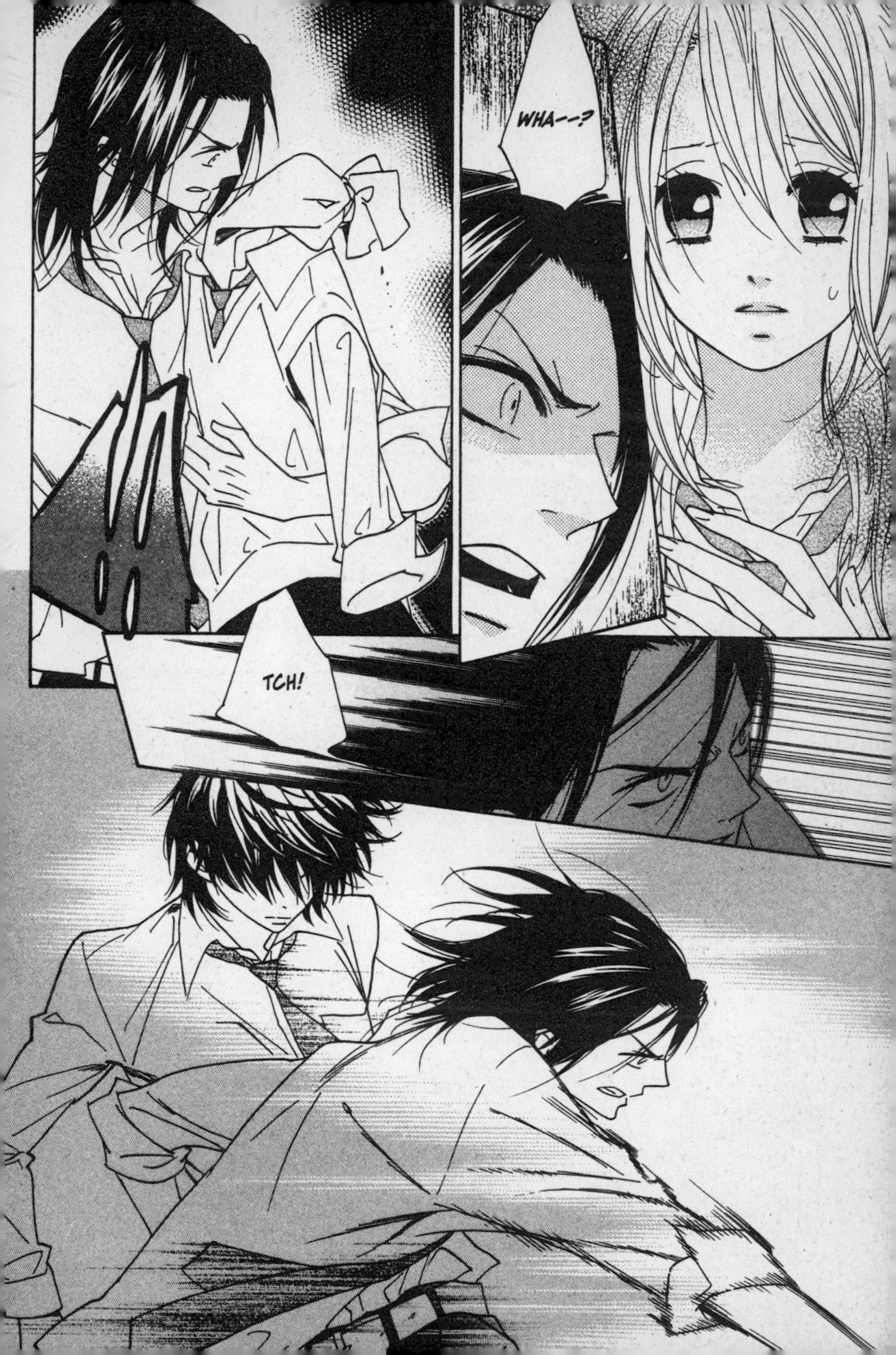
WHA--?
TCH!

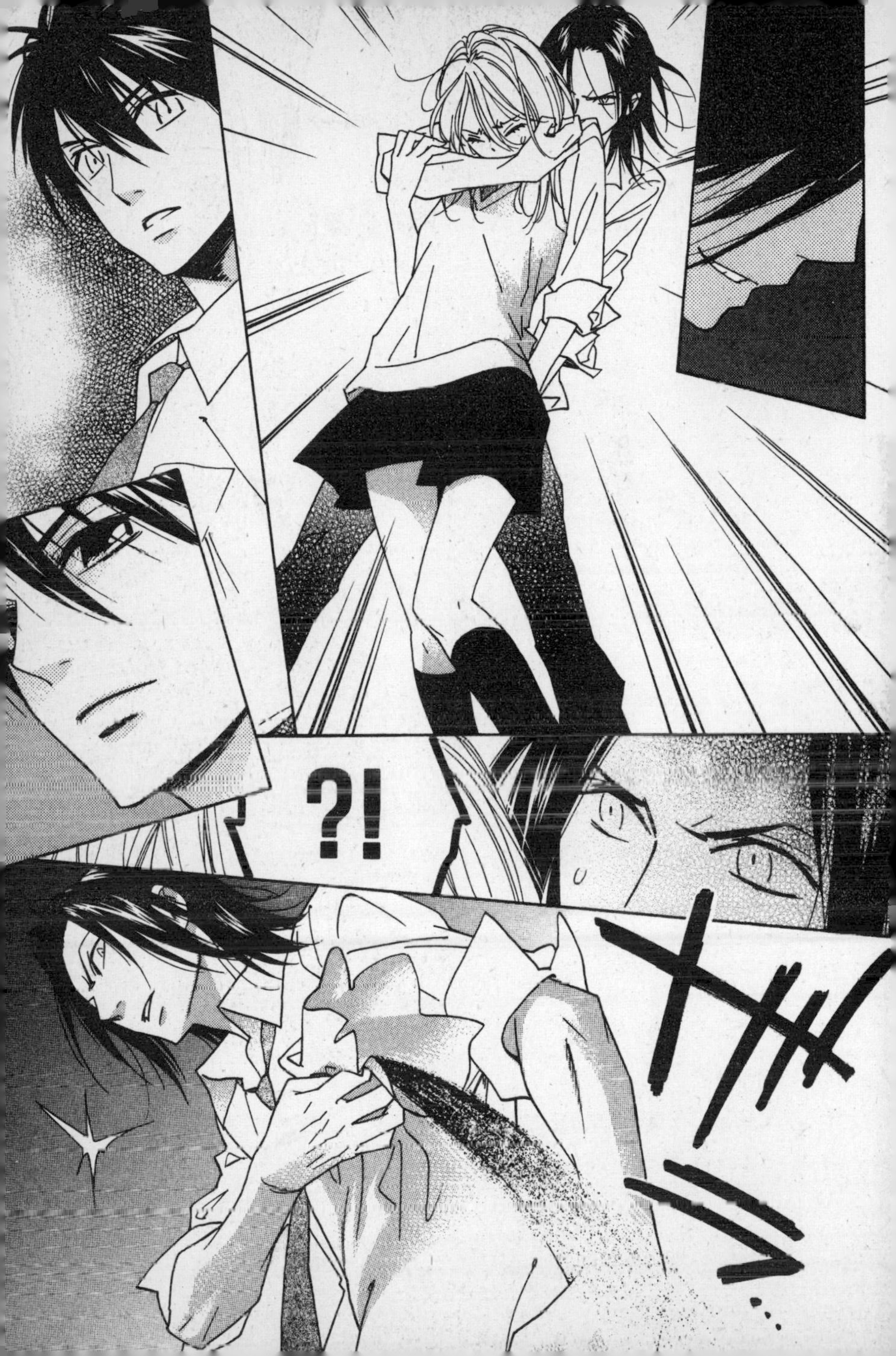
?!

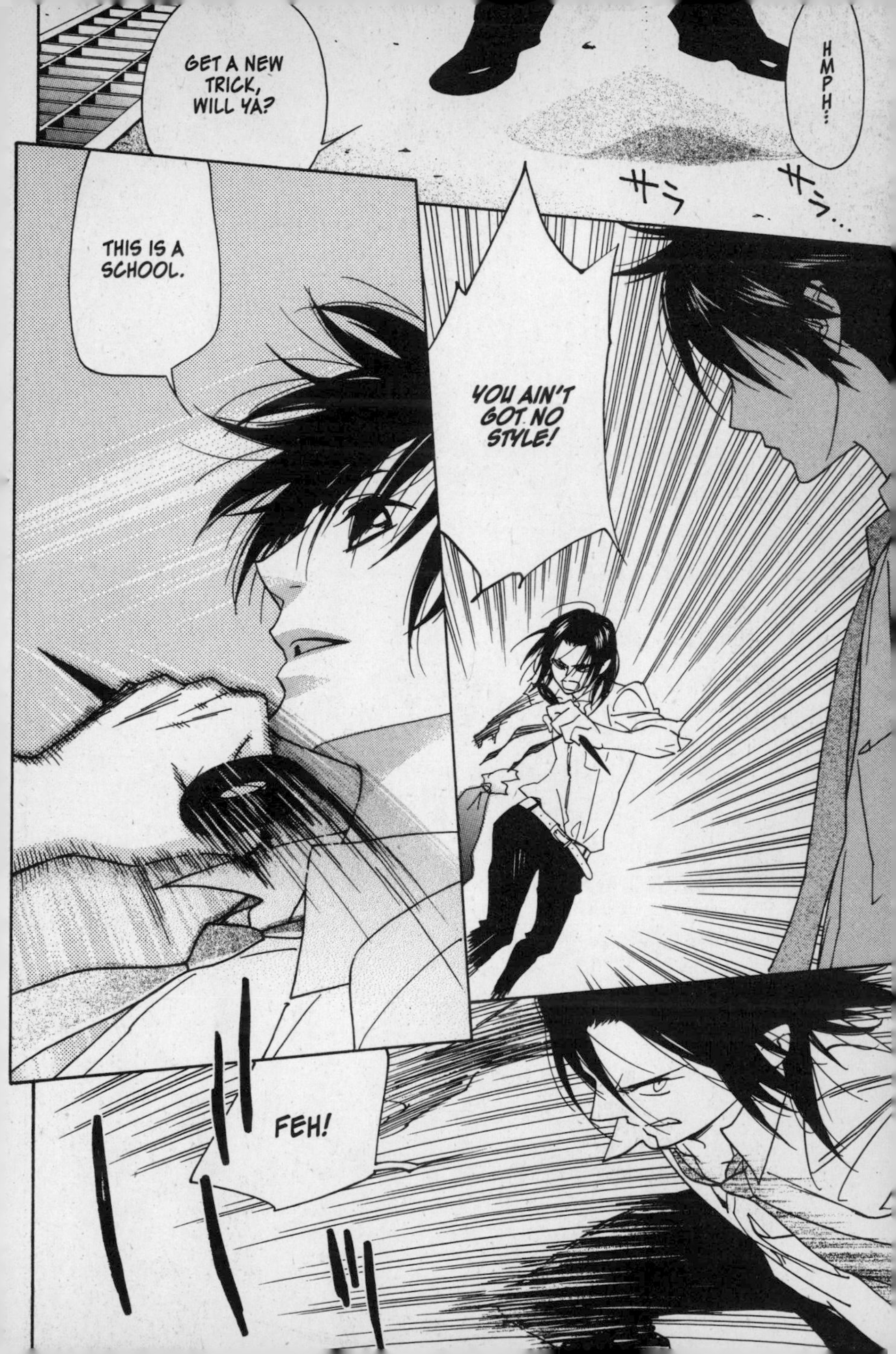
HMPH...
GET A NEW TRICK, WILL YA?
サラ サラ...
YOU AIN'T GOT NO STYLE!
THIS IS A SCHOOL.
FEH!

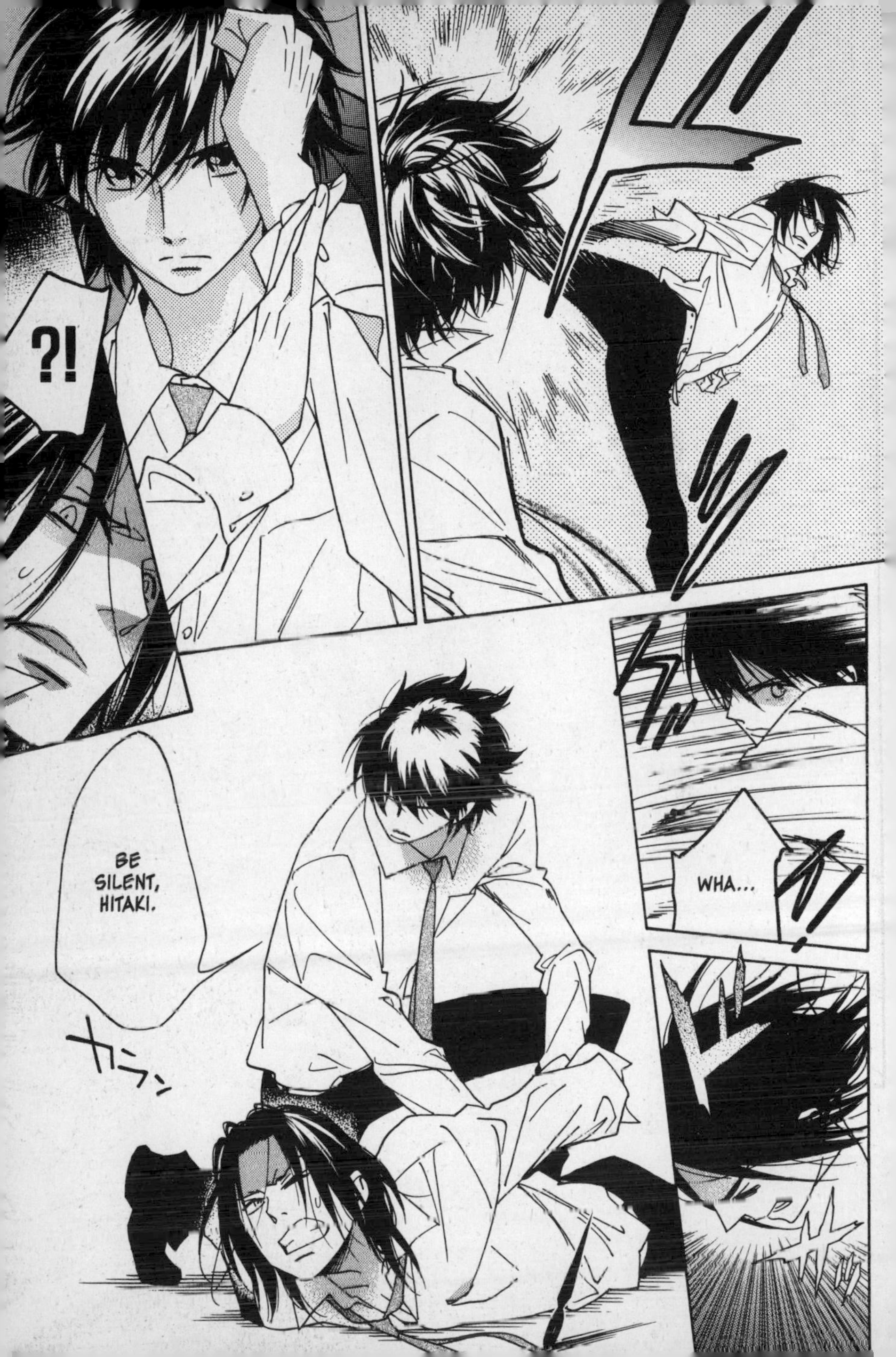
?!
WHA...
BE SILENT, HITAKI.

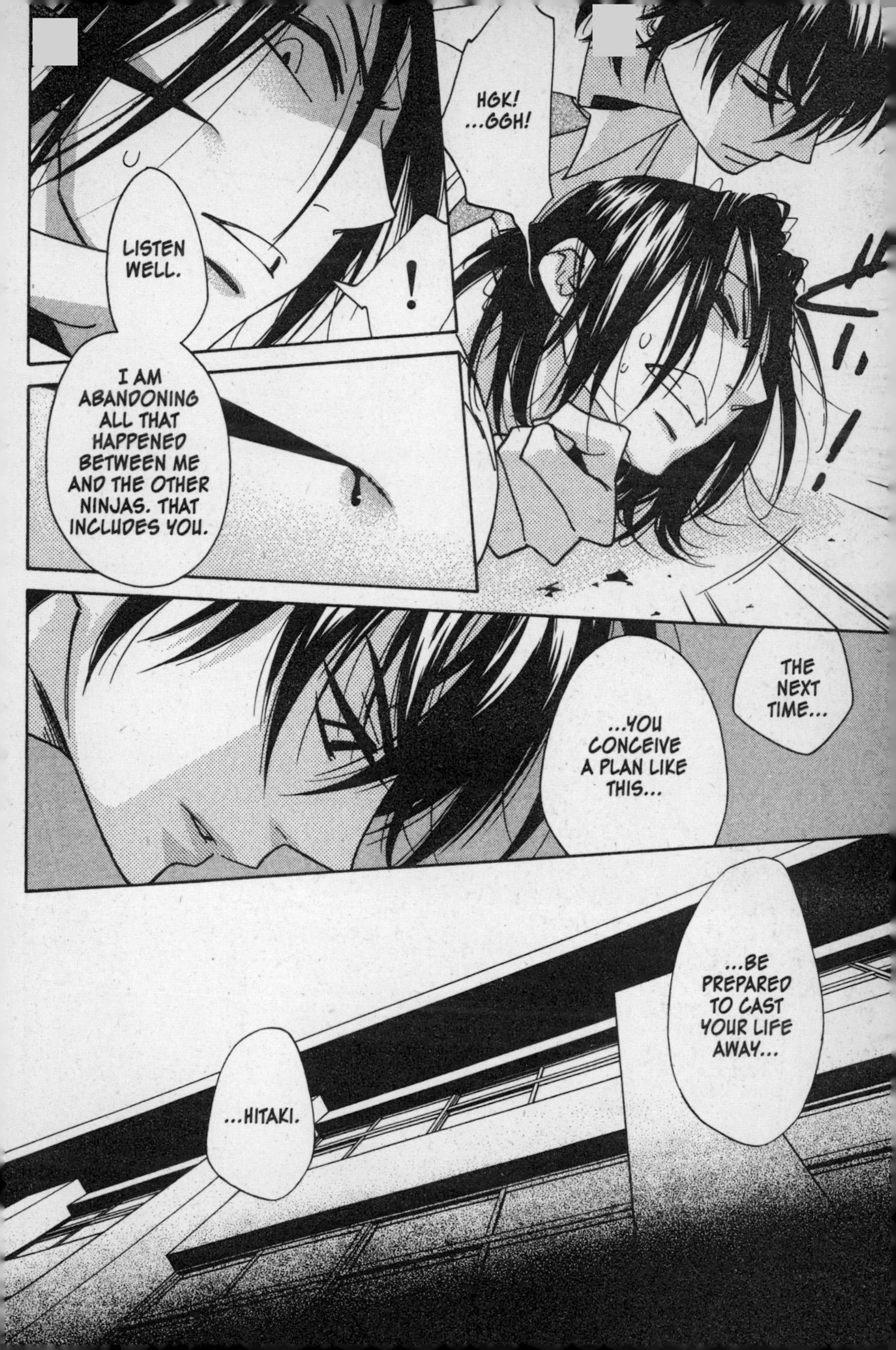
HGK! ...GGH!
!
LISTEN WELL.
I AM ABANDONING ALL THAT HAPPENED BETWEEN ME AND THE OTHER NINJAS. THAT INCLUDES YOU.
THE NEXT TIME...
...YOU CONCEIVE A PLAN LIKE THIS...
...BE PREPARED TO CAST YOUR LIFE AWAY...
...HITAKI.

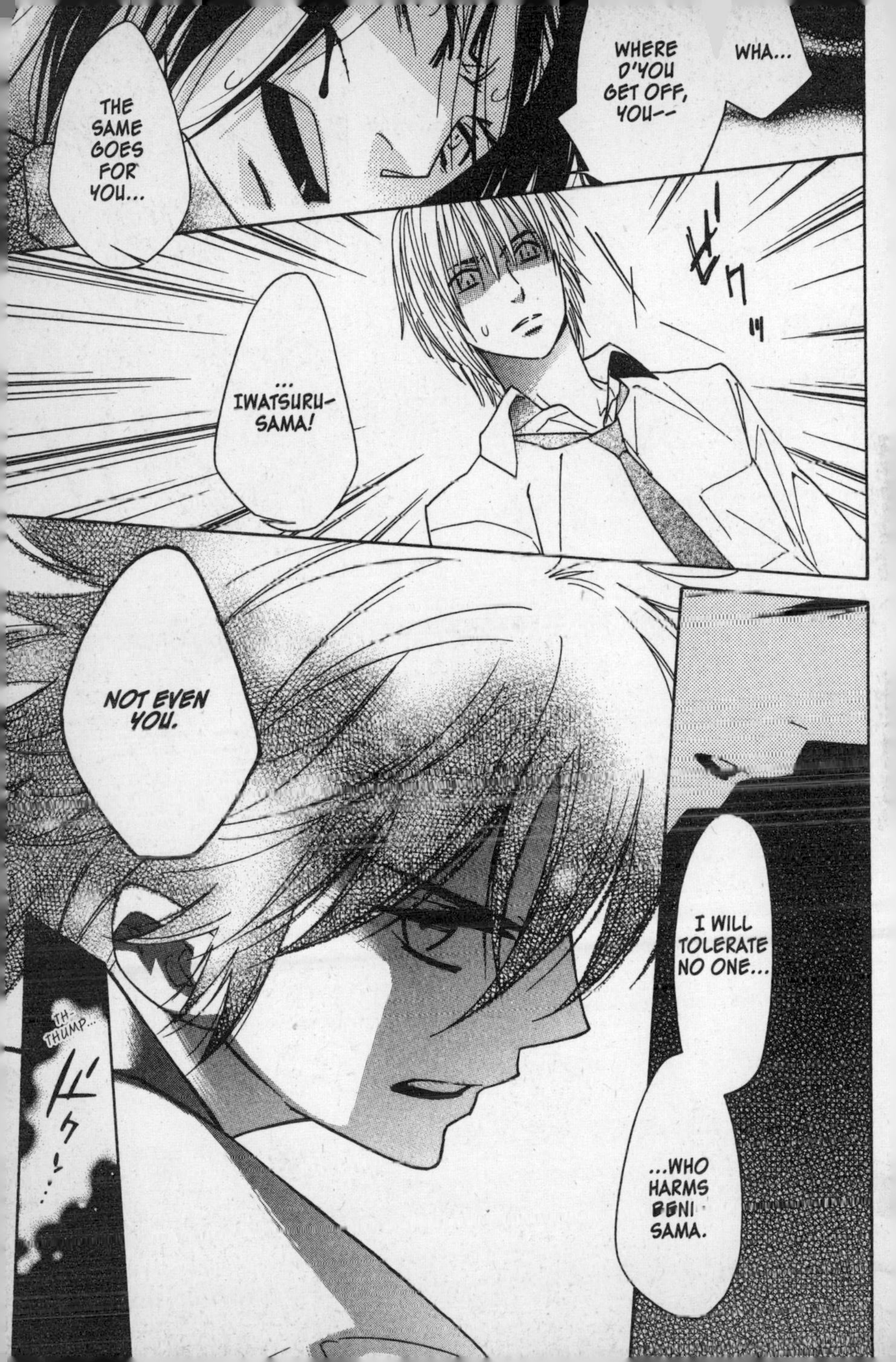
WHA...
WHERE D'YOU GET OFF, YOU--
THE SAME GOES FOR YOU...
...IWATSURU-SAMA!
I WILL TOLERATE NO ONE...
...WHO HARMS BENI SAMA.
NOT EVEN YOU.
TH-THUMP...

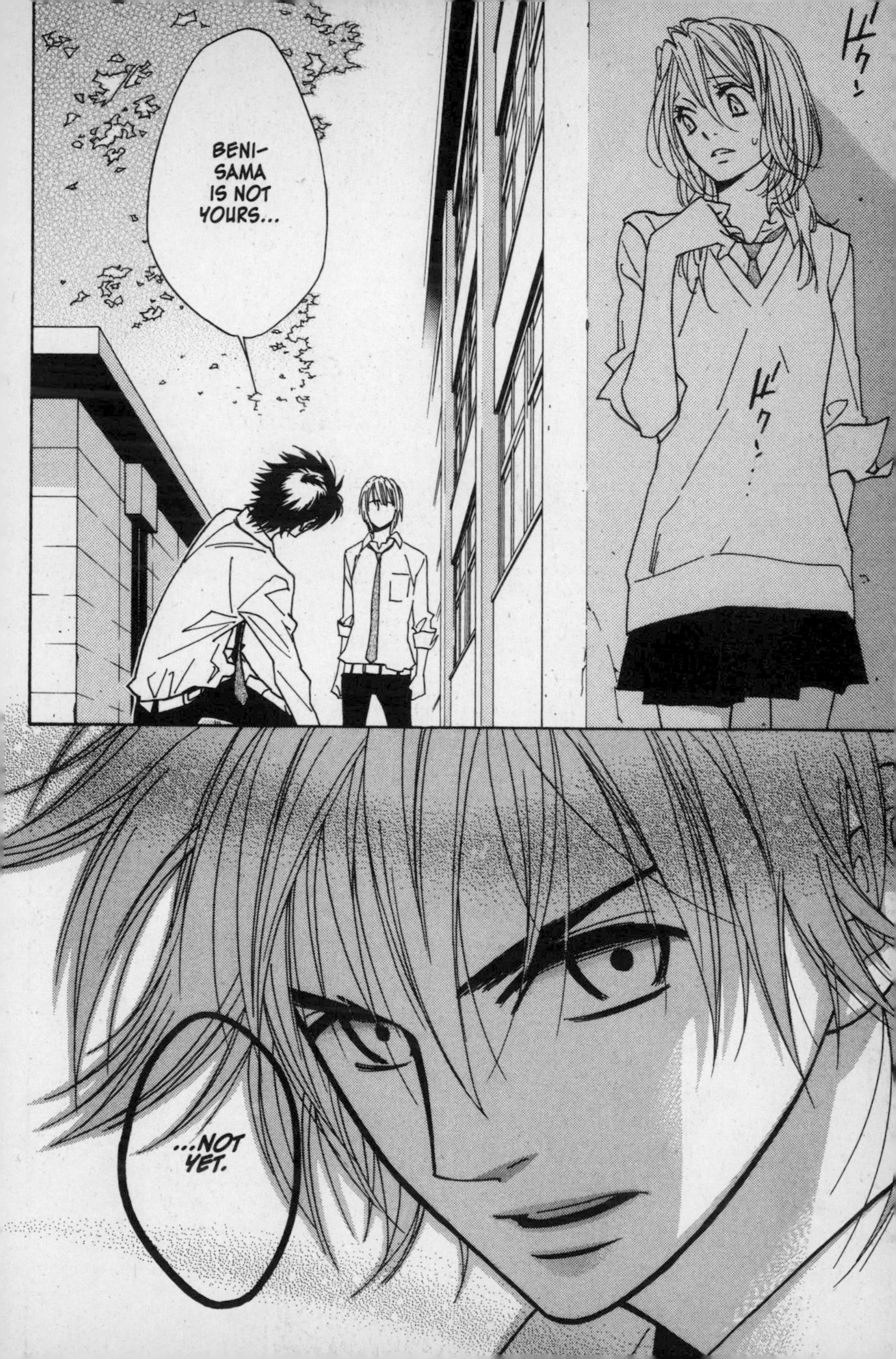
ドクン
ドクン…
BENI-SAMA IS NOT YOURS...
...NOT YET.

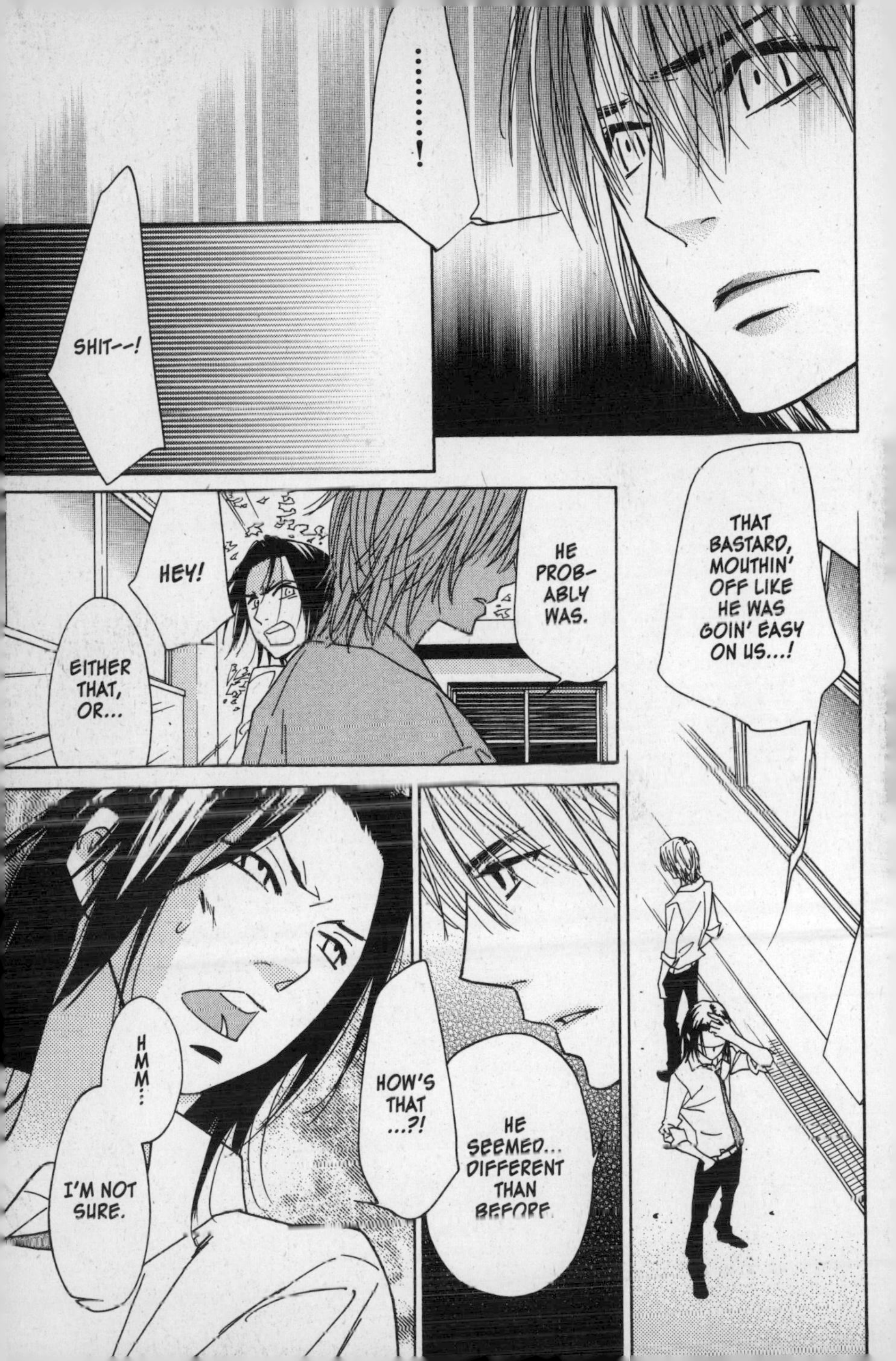
……!
SHIT--!
THAT BASTARD, MOUTHIN' OFF LIKE HE WAS GOIN' EASY ON US...!
HE PROBABLY WAS.
HEY!
EITHER THAT, OR...
HOW'S THAT ...?!
HE SEEMED... DIFFERENT THAN BEFORE.
HMM...
I'M NOT SURE.

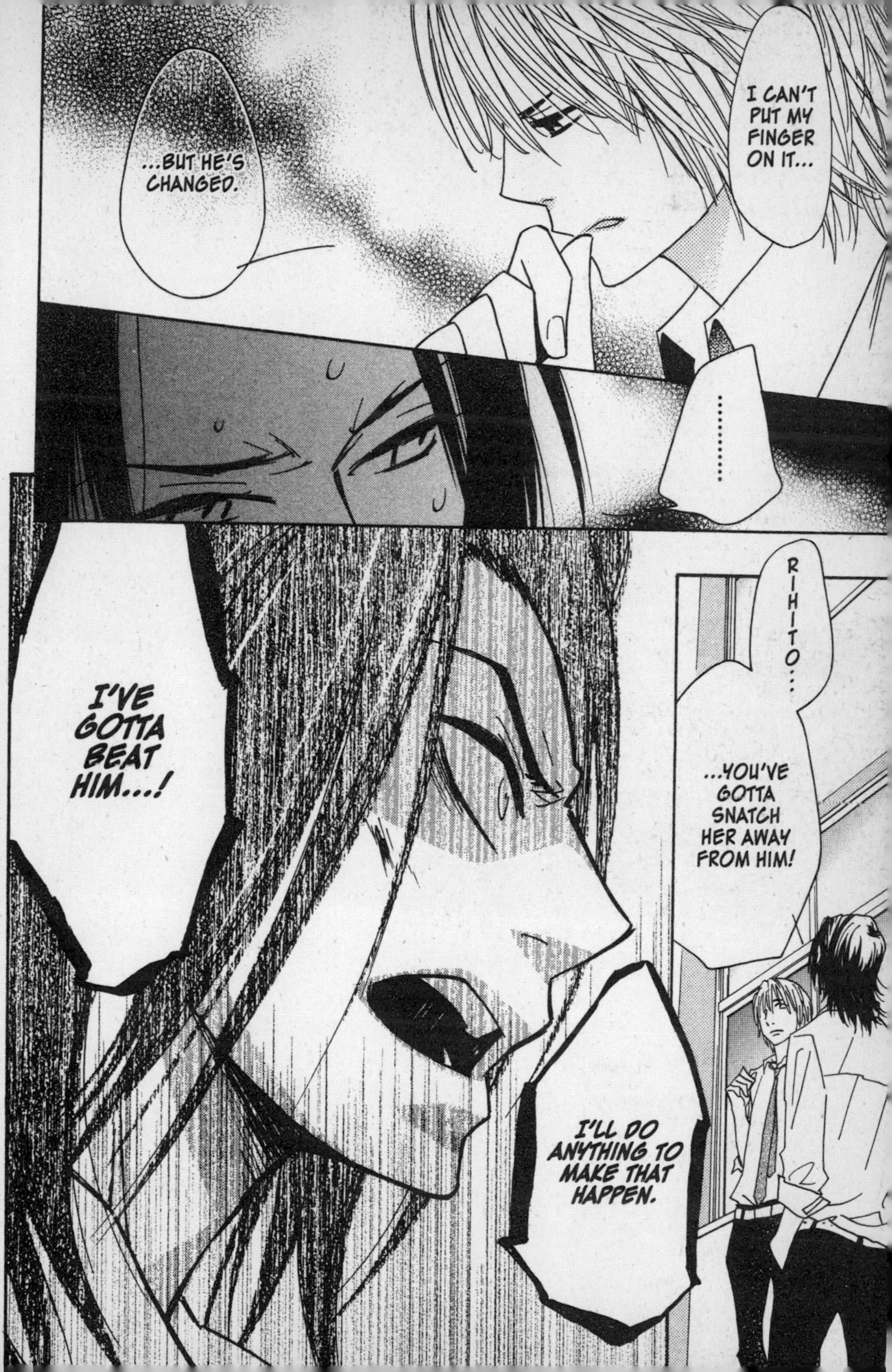
I CAN'T PUT MY FINGER ON IT...
...BUT HE'S CHANGED.
......
RIHITO...
...YOU'VE GOTTA SNATCH HER AWAY FROM HIM!
I'VE GOTTA BEAT HIM...!
I'LL DO ANYTHING TO MAKE THAT HAPPEN.

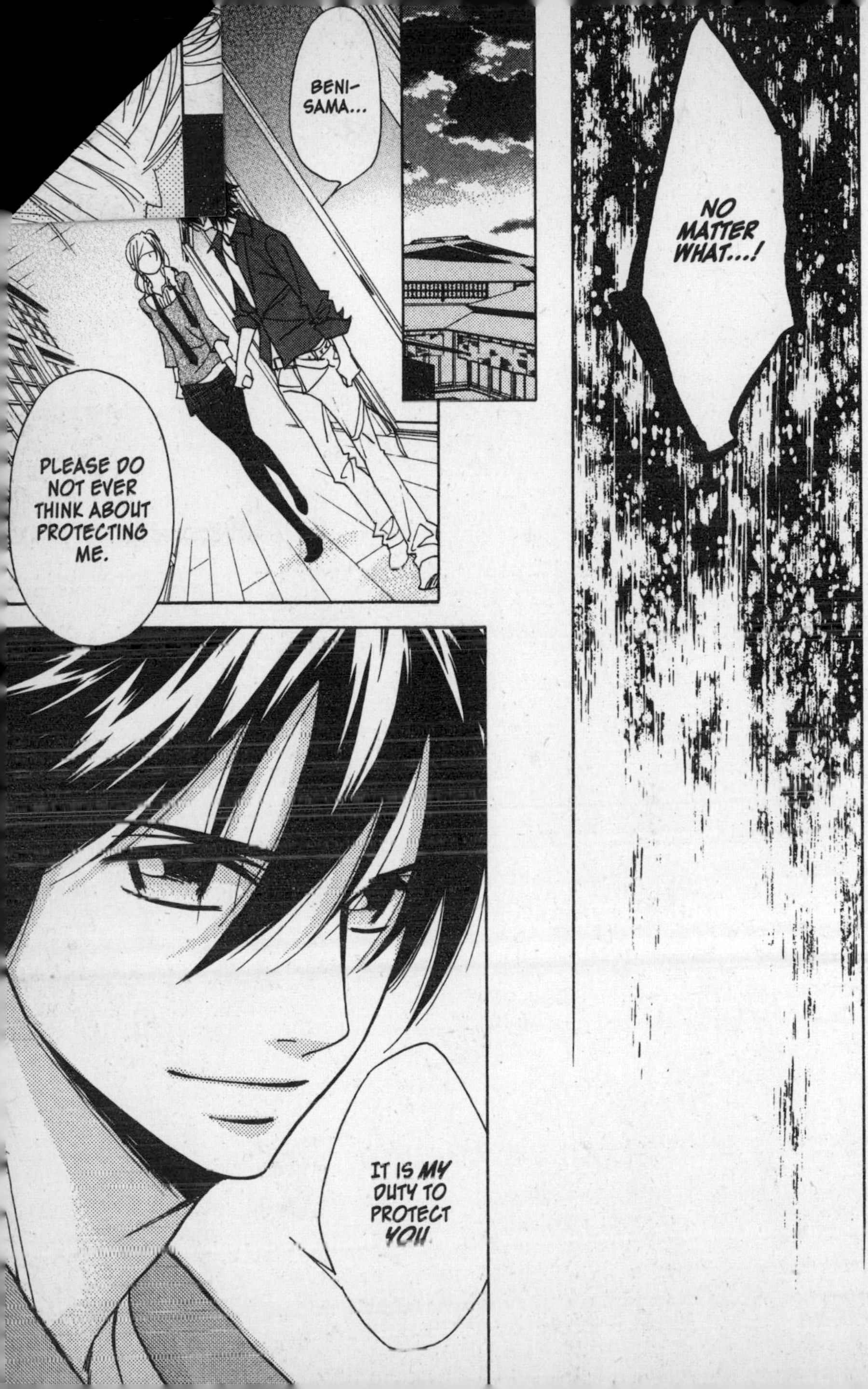
NO MATTER WHAT...!
BENI-SAMA...
PLEASE DO NOT EVER THINK ABOUT PROTECTING ME.
IT IS MY DUTY TO PROTECT YOU.

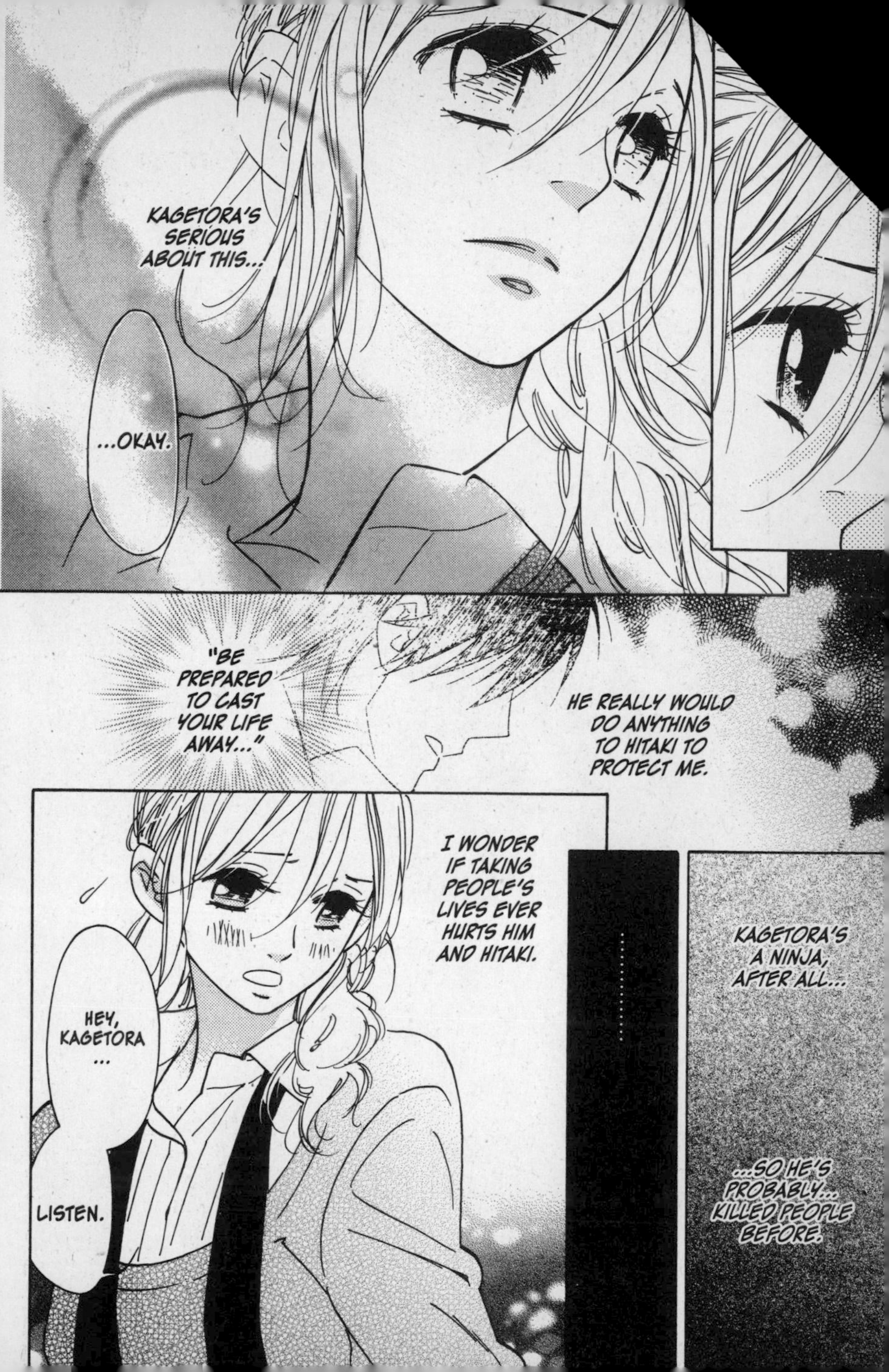
KAGETORA'S SERIOUS ABOUT THIS...
...OKAY.
HE REALLY WOULD DO ANYTHING TO HITAKI TO PROTECT ME.
"BE PREPARED TO CAST YOUR LIFE AWAY..."
KAGETORA'S A NINJA, AFTER ALL...
...SO HE'S PROBABLY... KILLED PEOPLE BEFORE.
......
I WONDER IF TAKING PEOPLE'S LIVES EVER HURTS HIM AND HITAKI.
HEY, KAGETORA ...
LISTEN.

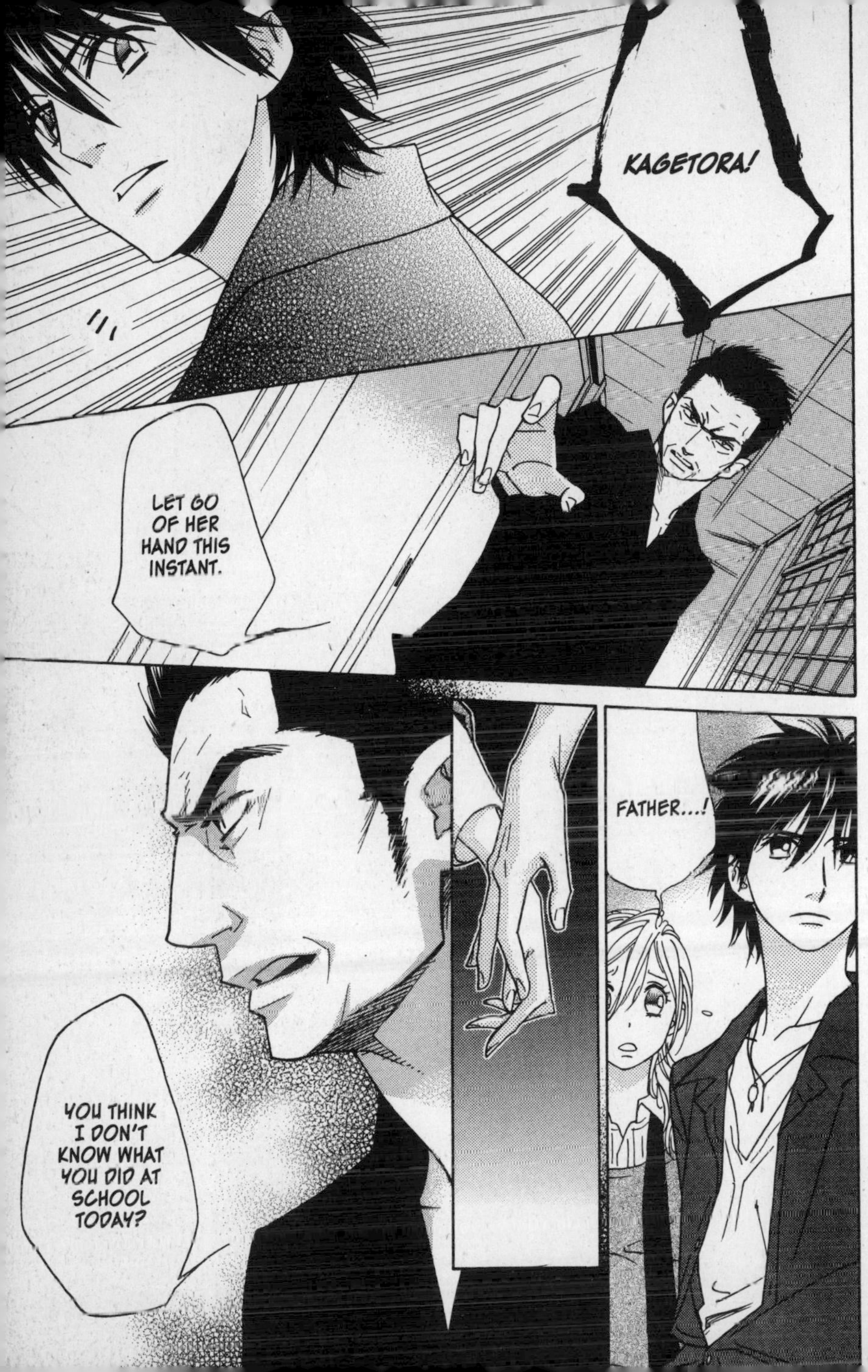
KAGETORA!
LET GO OF HER HAND THIS INSTANT.
FATHER...!
YOU THINK I DON'T KNOW WHAT YOU DID AT SCHOOL TODAY?

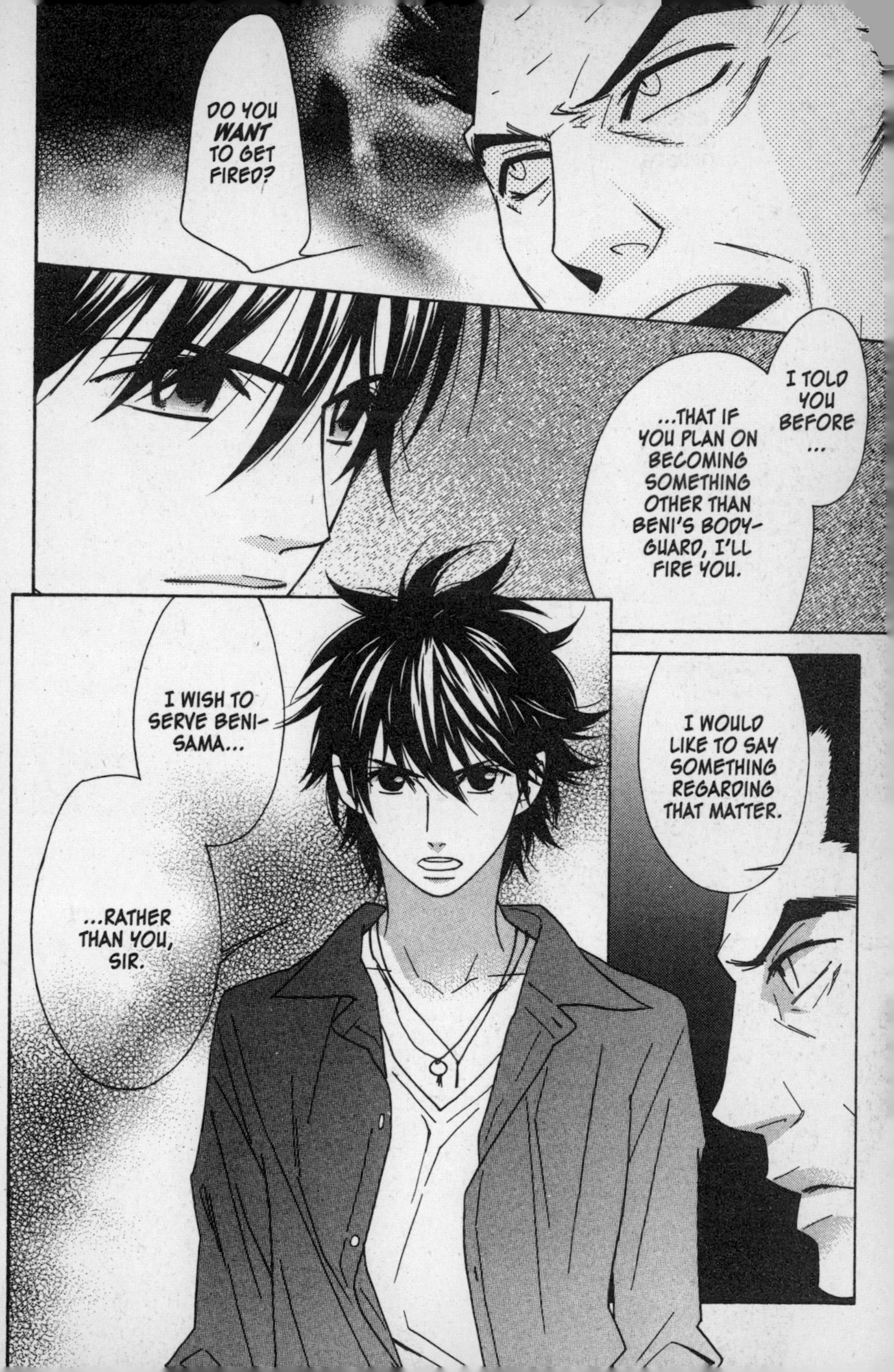
DO YOU ***WANT*** TO GET FIRED?
I TOLD YOU BEFORE...
...THAT IF YOU PLAN ON BECOMING SOMETHING OTHER THAN BENI'S BODY-GUARD, I'LL FIRE YOU.
I WOULD LIKE TO SAY SOMETHING REGARDING THAT MATTER.
I WISH TO SERVE BENI-SAMA...
...RATHER THAN YOU, SIR.

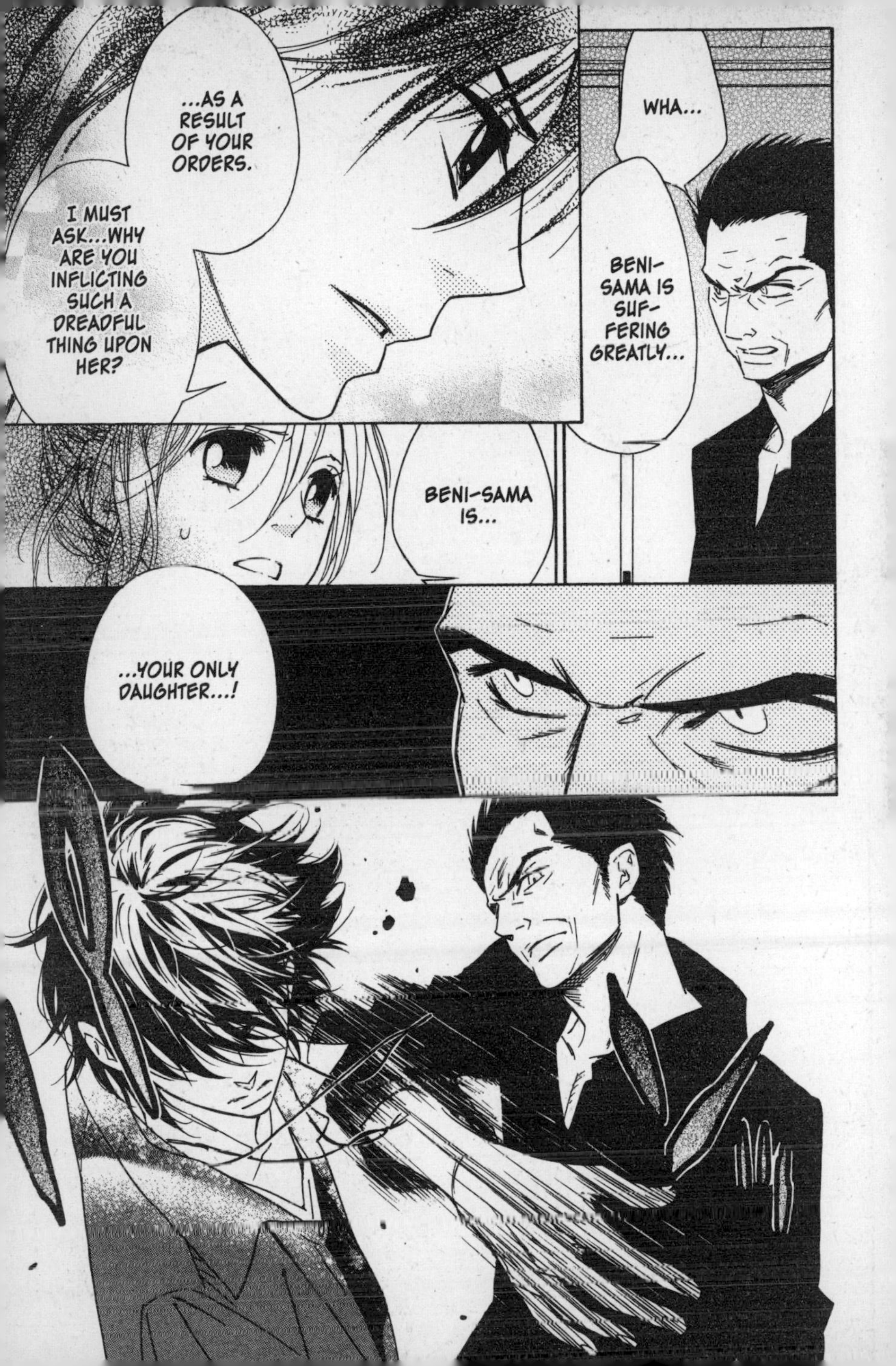
WHA...
BENI-SAMA IS SUF-FERING GREATLY...
...AS A RESULT OF YOUR ORDERS.
I MUST ASK...WHY ARE YOU INFLICTING SUCH A DREADFUL THING UPON HER?
BENI-SAMA IS...
...YOUR ONLY DAUGHTER...!

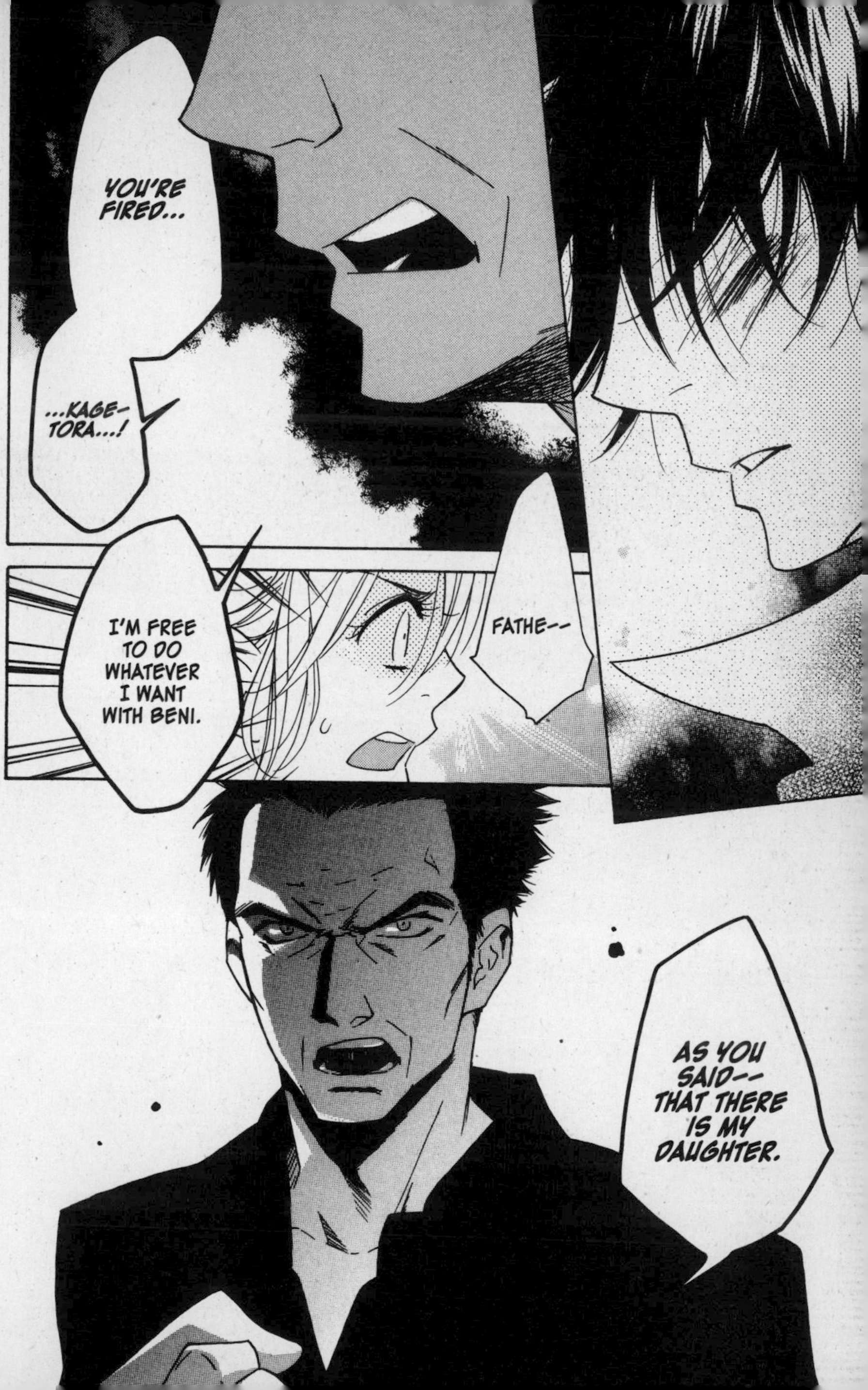
YOU'RE FIRED...
...KAGE-TORA...!
FATHE--
I'M FREE TO DO WHATEVER I WANT WITH BENI.
AS YOU SAID-- THAT THERE IS MY DAUGHTER.

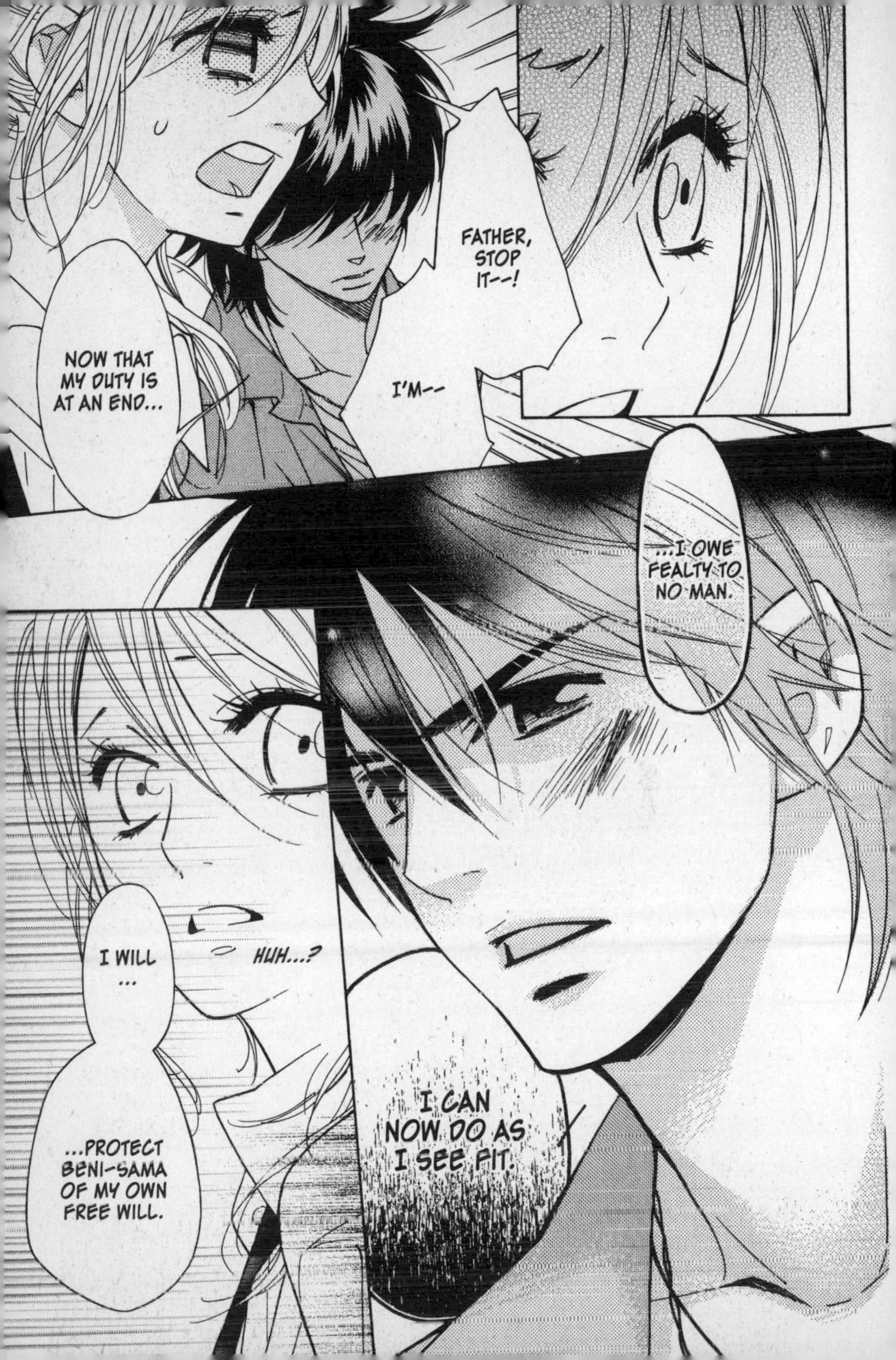
FATHER, STOP IT--!
I'M--
NOW THAT MY DUTY IS AT AN END...
...I OWE FEALTY TO NO MAN.
I CAN NOW DO AS I SEE FIT.
HUH...?
I WILL ...
...PROTECT BENI-SAMA OF MY OWN FREE WILL.

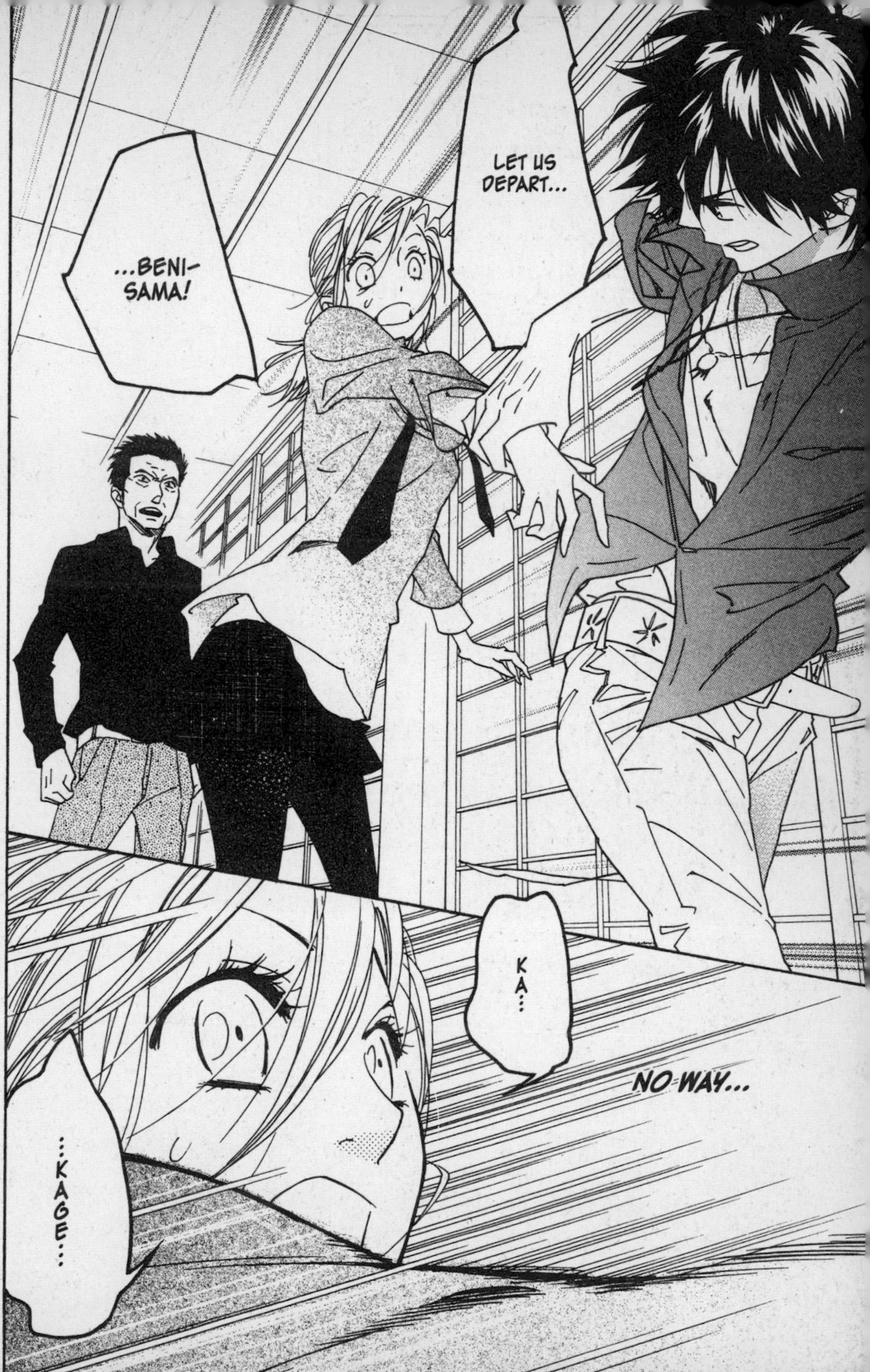
LET US DEPART...
...BENI-SAMA!
KA...
NO WAY...
...KAGE...

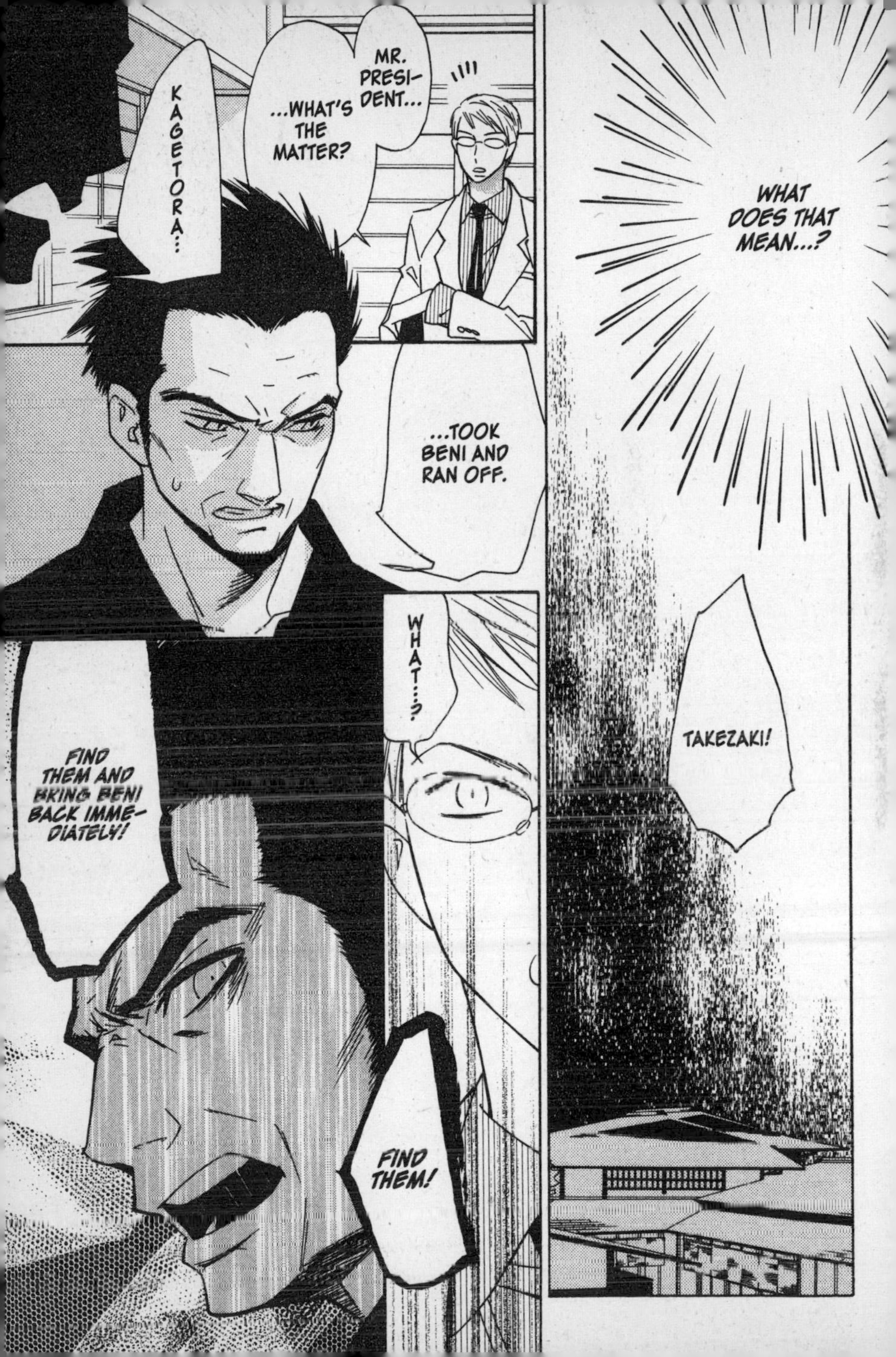
WHAT DOES THAT MEAN...?
TAKEZAKI!
MR. PRESI-DENT...
...WHAT'S THE MATTER?
KAGETORA...
...TOOK BENI AND RAN OFF.
WHAT...?
FIND THEM AND BRING BENI BACK IMME-DIATELY!
FIND THEM!

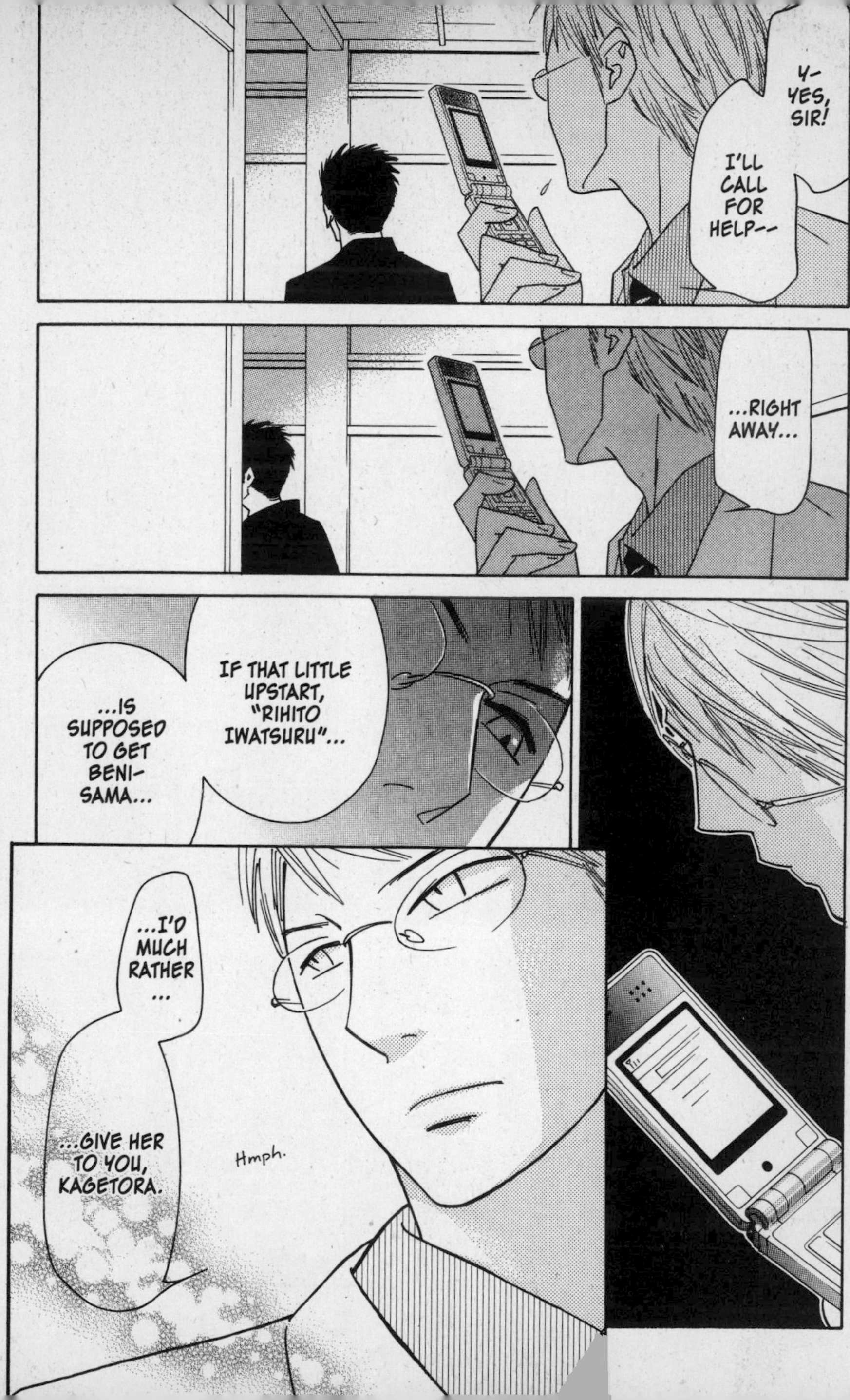
Y-YES, SIR!
I'LL CALL FOR HELP--
...RIGHT AWAY...
IF THAT LITTLE UPSTART, "RIHITO IWATSURU"...
...IS SUPPOSED TO GET BENI-SAMA...
...I'D MUCH RATHER ...
...GIVE HER TO YOU, KAGETORA.
Hmph.

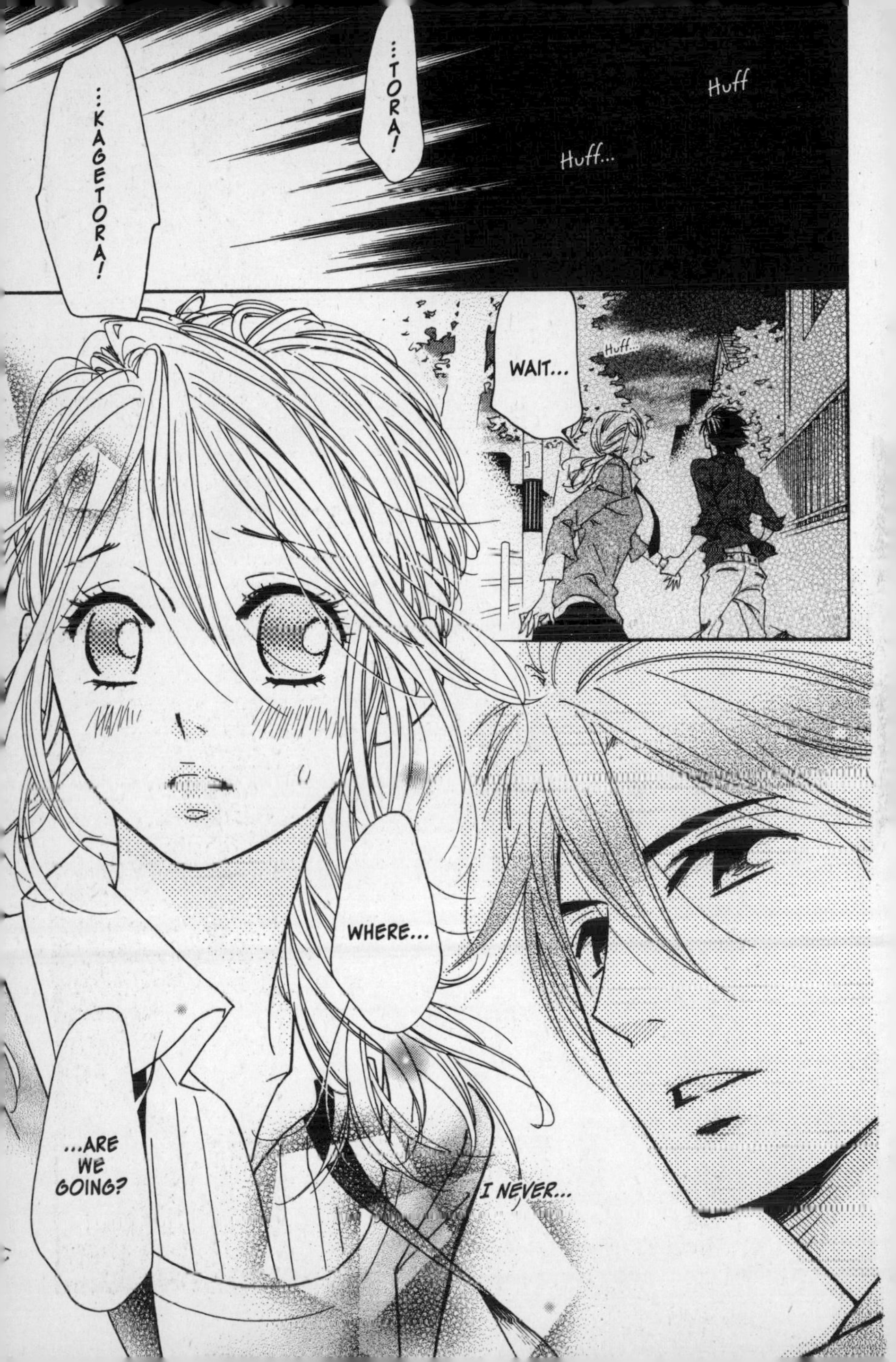
Huff
Huff...
...TORA!
...KAGETORA!
Huff...
WAIT...
WHERE...
...ARE WE GOING?
I NEVER...

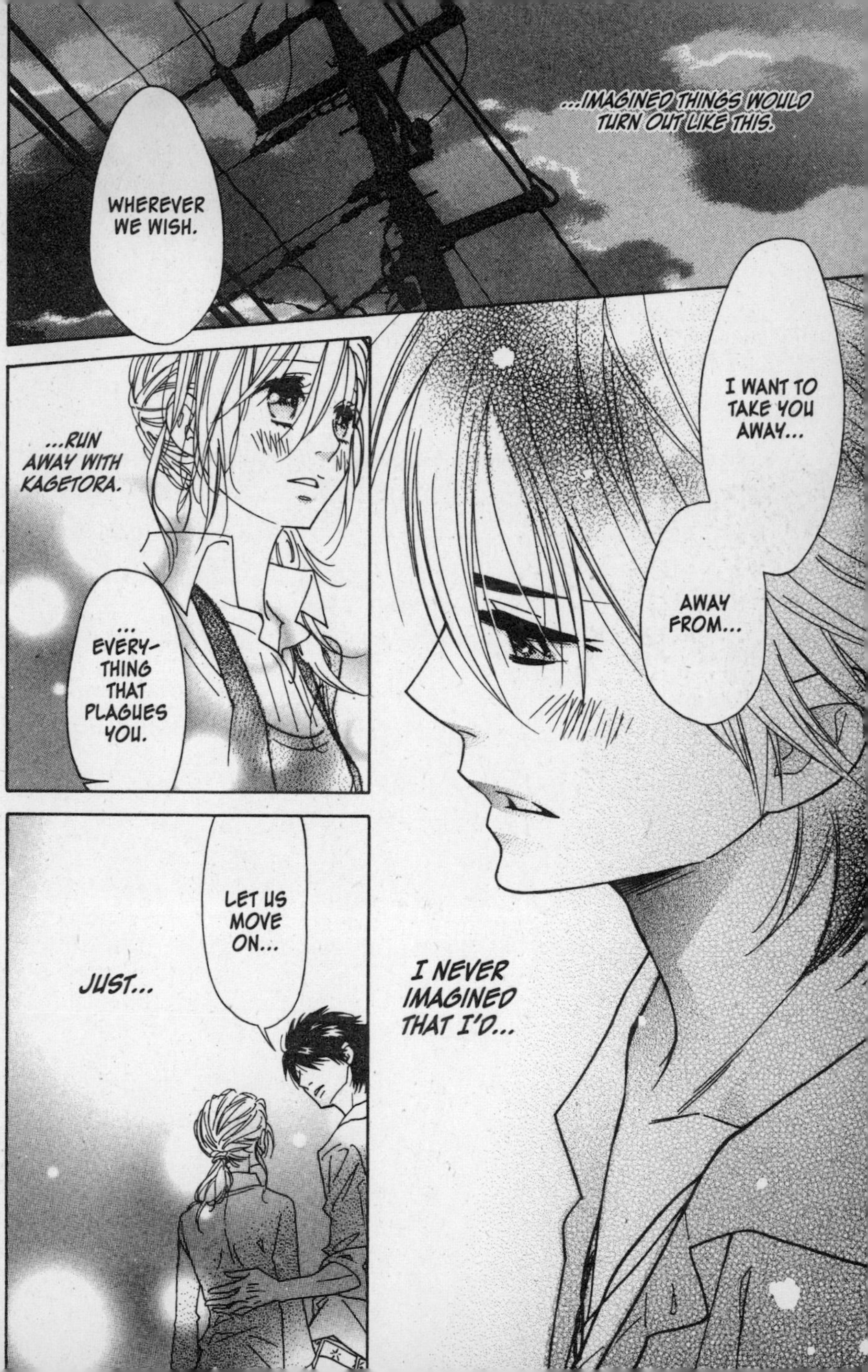
...IMAGINED THINGS WOULD TURN OUT LIKE THIS.
WHEREVER WE WISH.
I WANT TO TAKE YOU AWAY...
AWAY FROM...
I NEVER IMAGINED THAT I'D...
...RUN AWAY WITH KAGETORA.
... EVERYTHING THAT PLAGUES YOU.
LET US MOVE ON...
JUST...

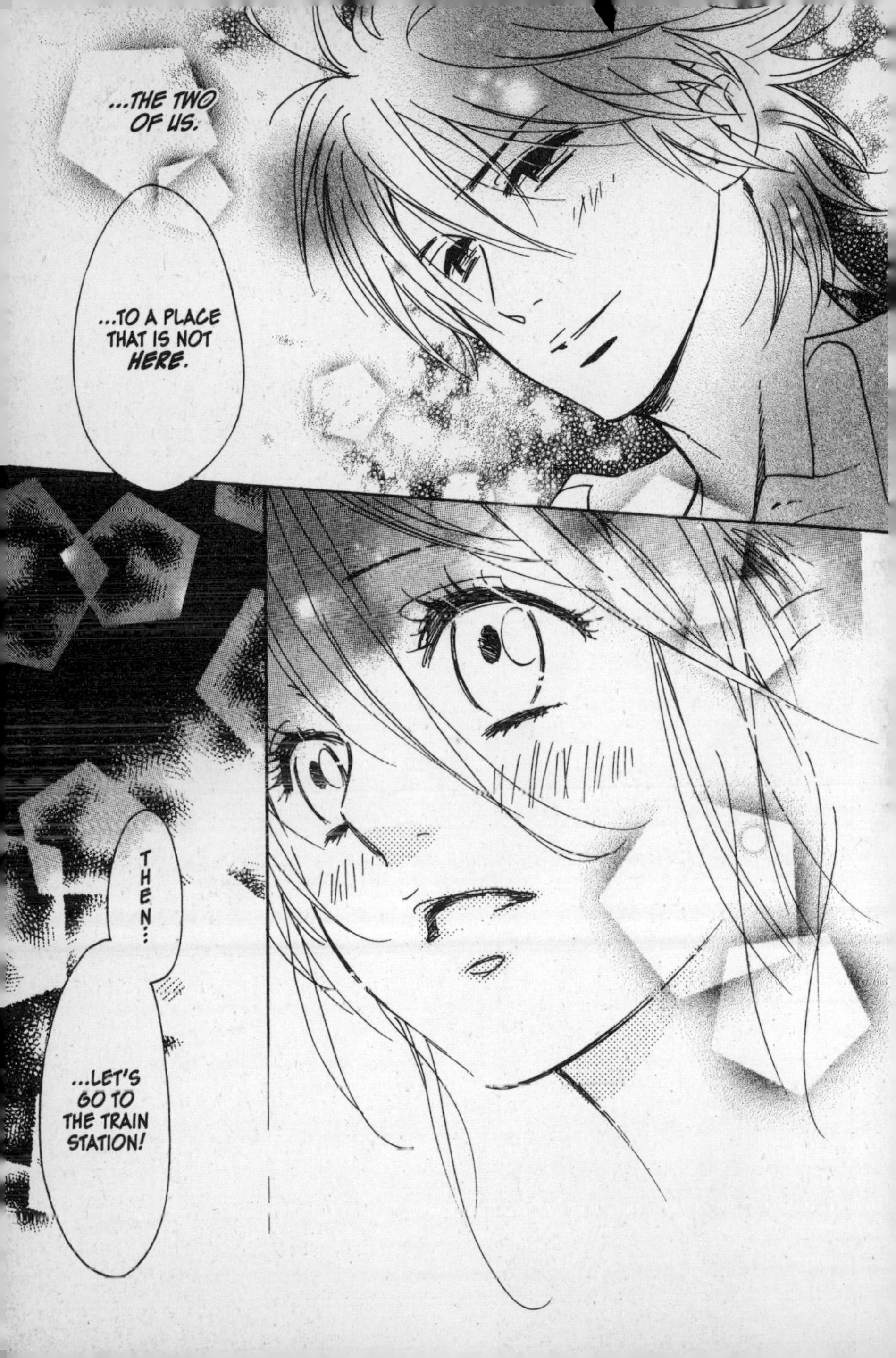
...THE TWO OF US.
...TO A PLACE THAT IS NOT HERE.
THEN...
...LET'S GO TO THE TRAIN STATION!

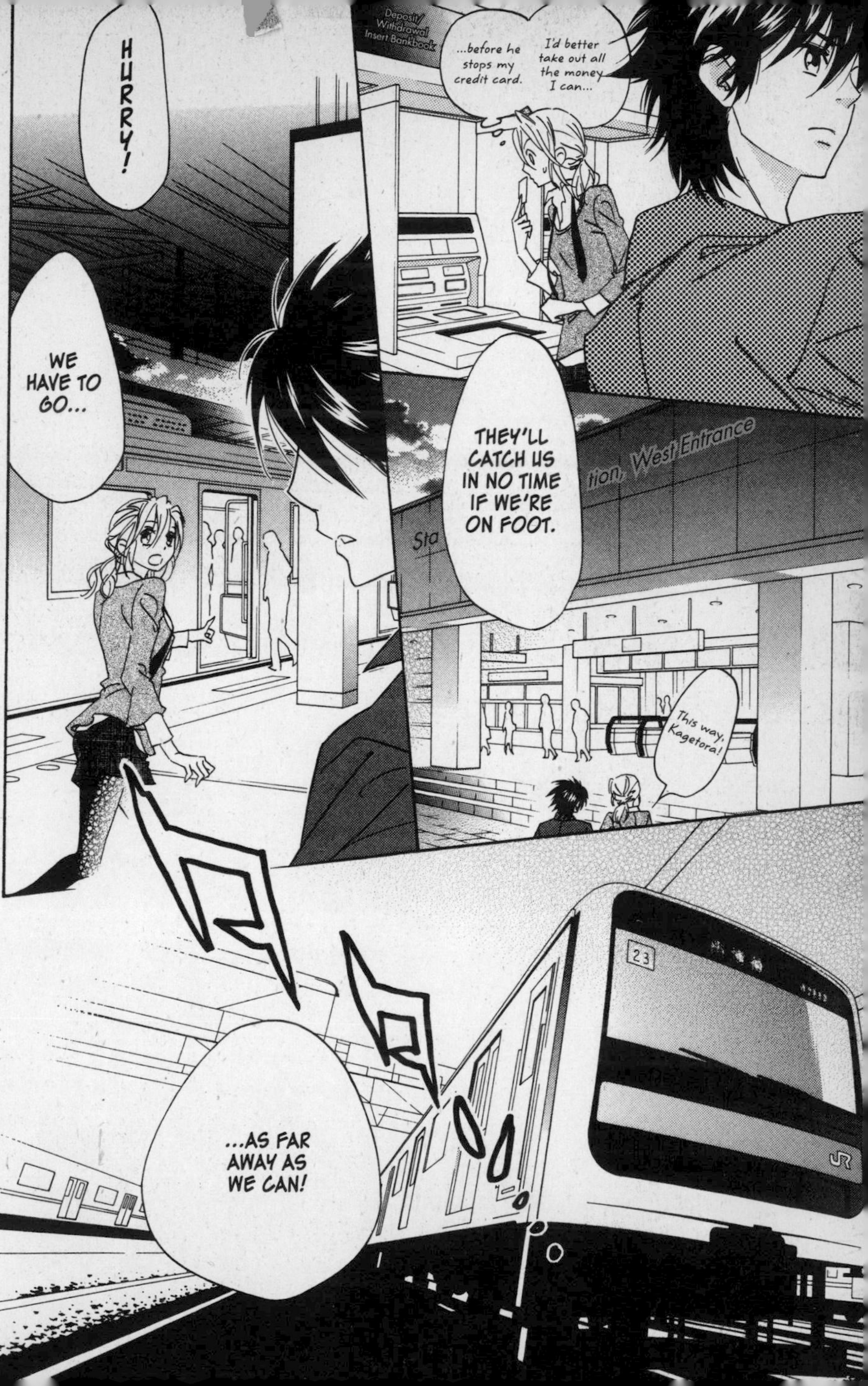
Deposit/ Withdrawal/ Insert Bankbook
I'd better take out all the money I can...
...before he stops my credit card.
THEY'LL CATCH US IN NO TIME IF WE'RE ON FOOT.
Sta
tion, West Entrance
This way, Kagetora!
HURRY!
WE HAVE TO GO...
...AS FAR AWAY AS WE CAN!

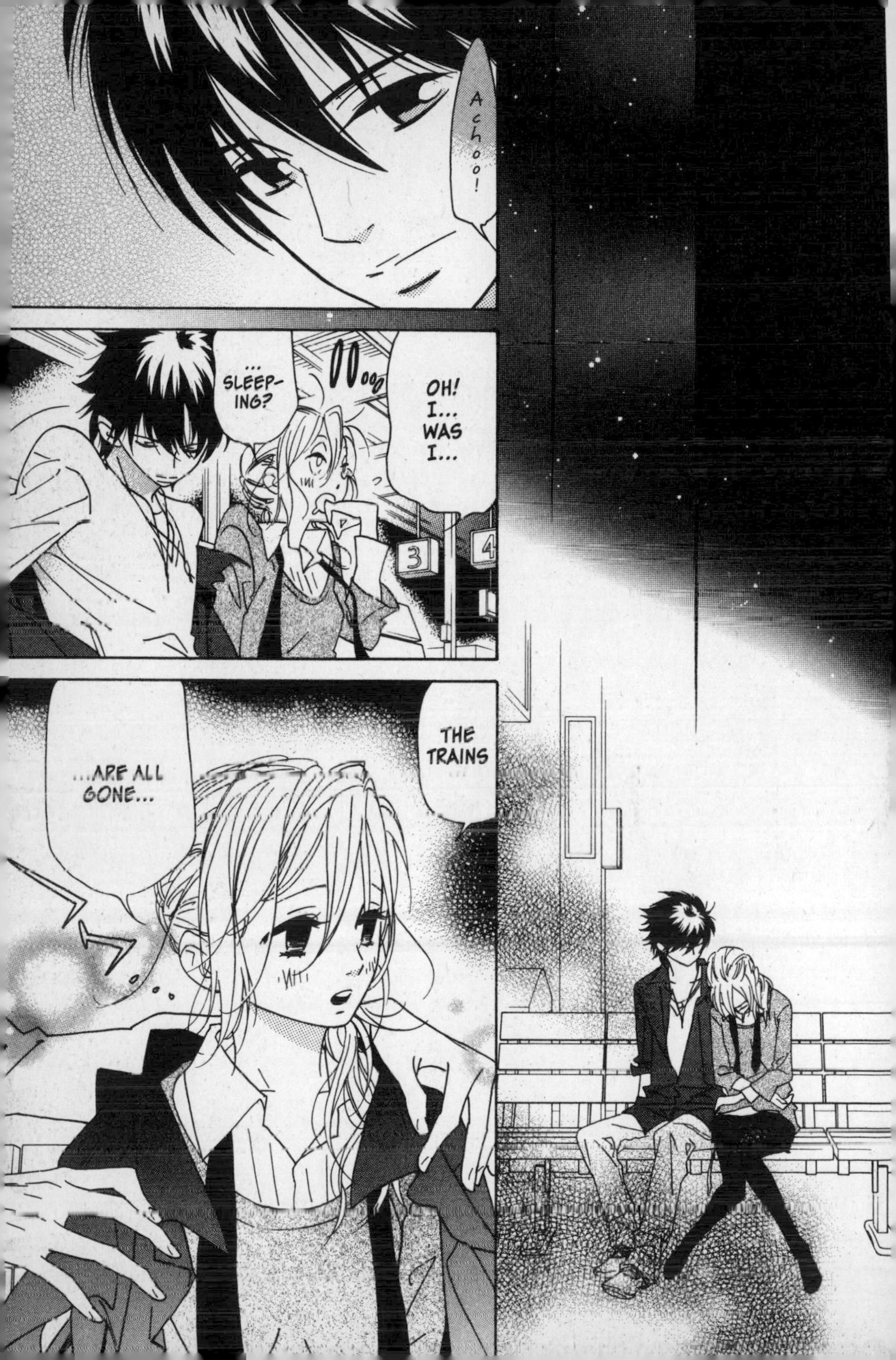
Achoo!
OH! I... WAS I...
...SLEEP-ING?
THE TRAINS
...ARE ALL GONE...

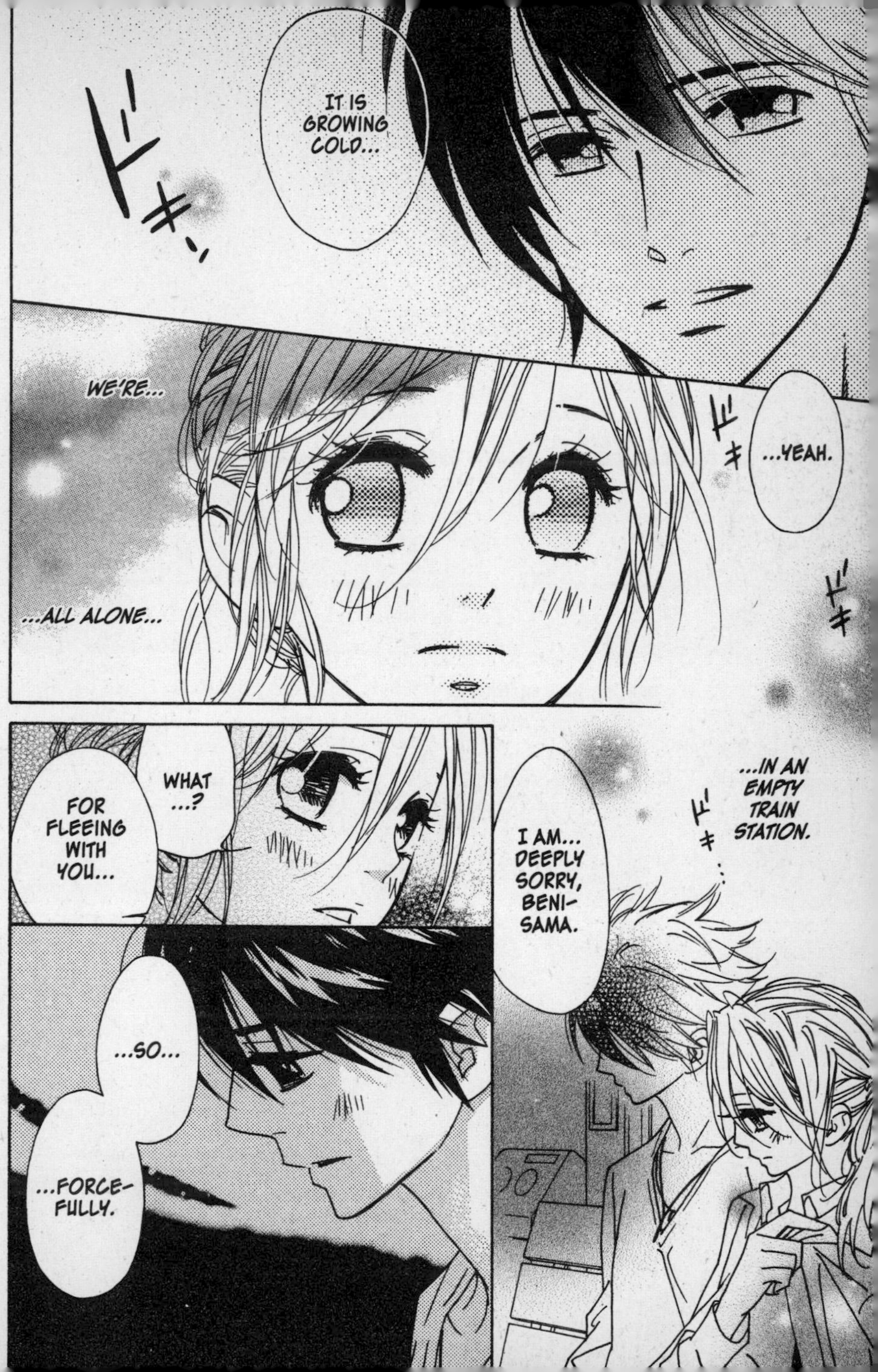
IT IS GROWING COLD...
ドキ…
ドキ
...YEAH.
WE'RE...
...ALL ALONE...
ドキ
...IN AN EMPTY TRAIN STATION.
ドキ…
I AM... DEEPLY SORRY, BENI-SAMA.
WHAT ...?
FOR FLEEING WITH YOU...
...SO...
...FORCE-FULLY.

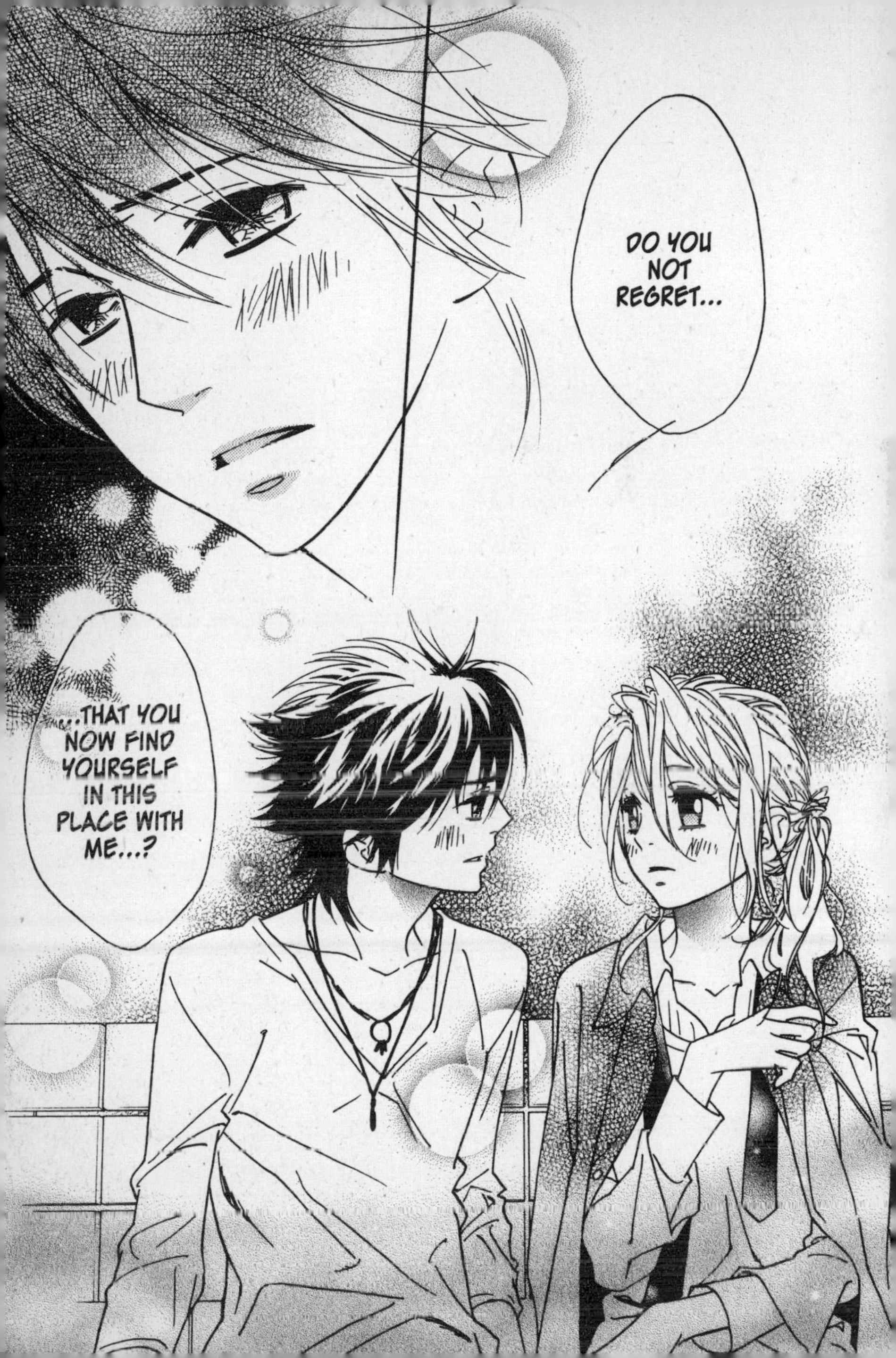
DO YOU NOT REGRET...
...THAT YOU NOW FIND YOURSELF IN THIS PLACE WITH ME...?

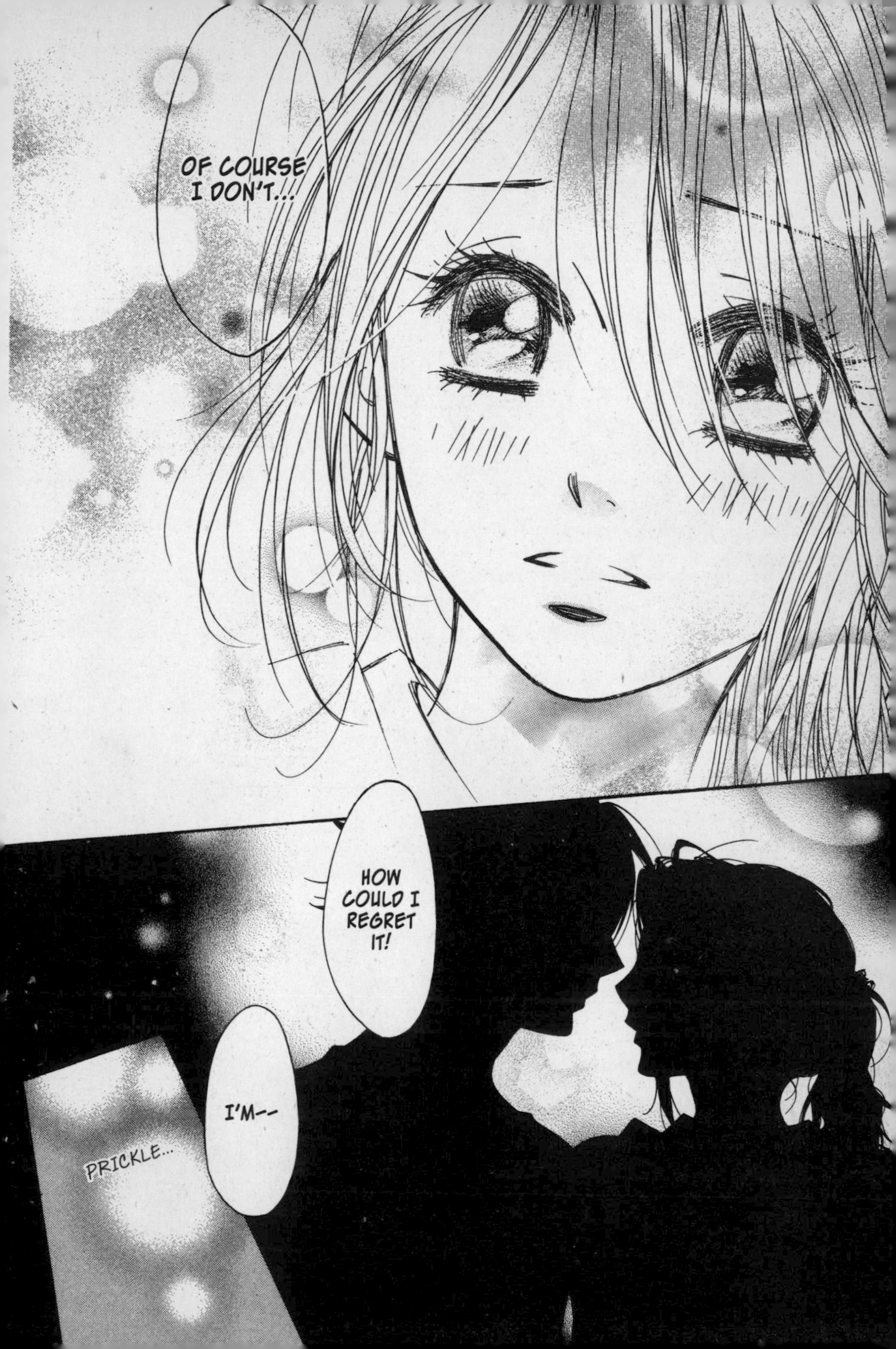
OF COURSE I DON'T...
HOW COULD I REGRET IT!
I'M--
PRICKLE...

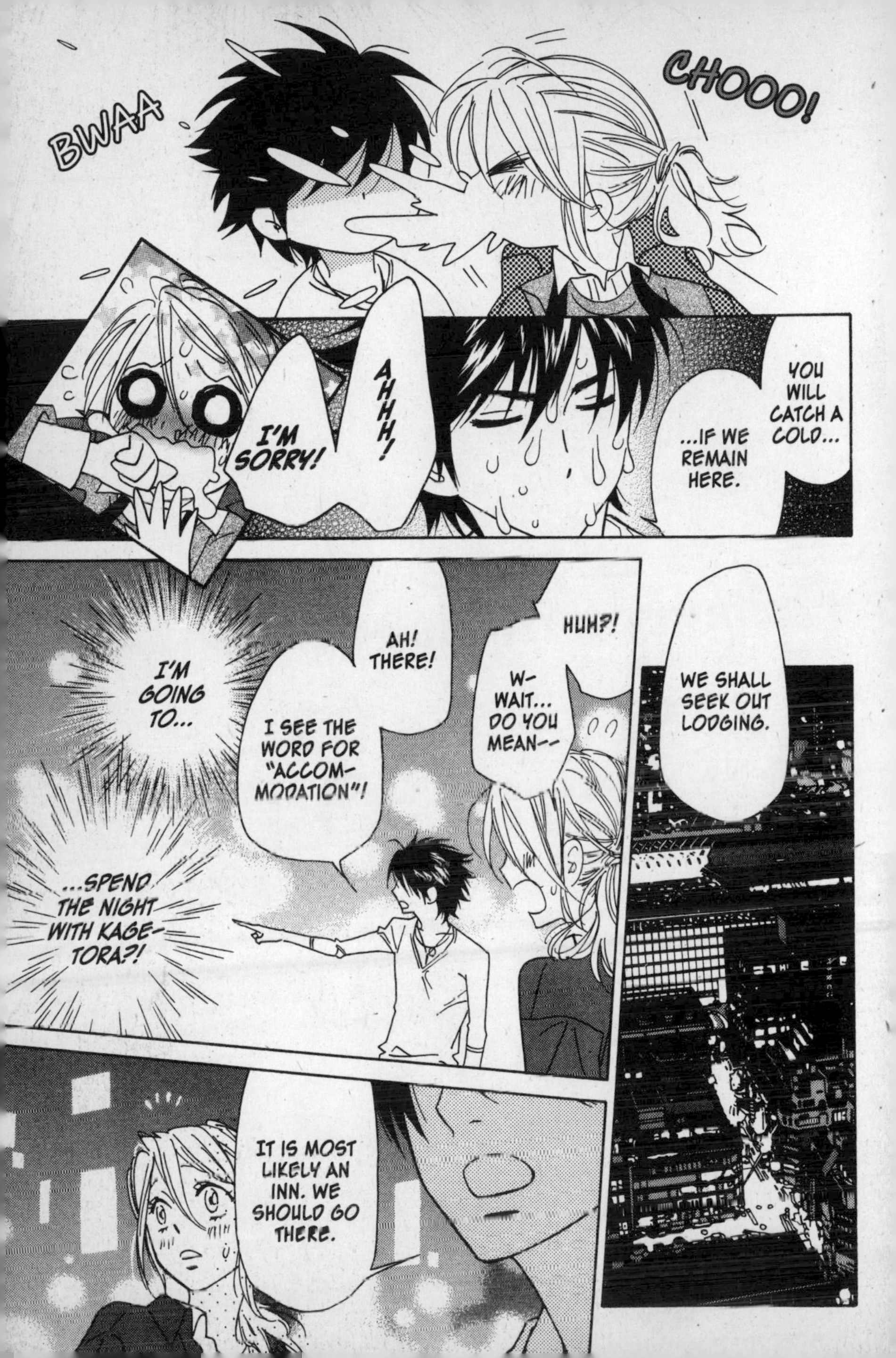
CHOOO!
BWAA
YOU WILL CATCH A COLD...
...IF WE REMAIN HERE.
AHHH!
I'M SORRY!
WE SHALL SEEK OUT LODGING.
HUH?!
W-WAIT... DO YOU MEAN--
AH! THERE!
I SEE THE WORD FOR "ACCOM-MODATION"!
I'M GOING TO...
...SPEND THE NIGHT WITH KAGE-TORA?!
IT IS MOST LIKELY AN INN. WE SHOULD GO THERE.

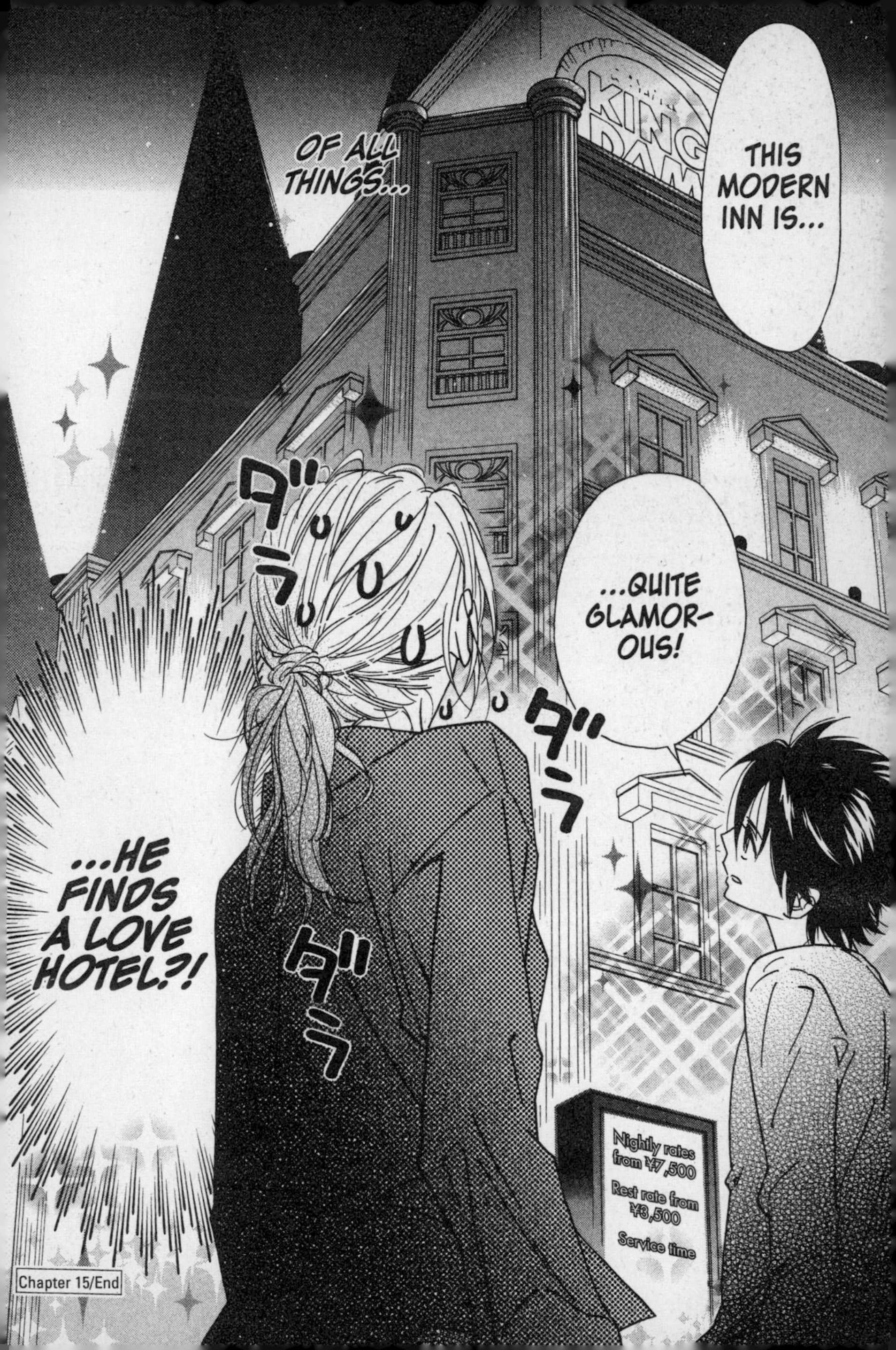
THIS MODERN INN IS...
...QUITE GLAMOROUS!
OF ALL THINGS...
...HE FINDS A LOVE HOTEL?!
Nighily rates from ¥7,500
Rest rate from ¥3,500
Service time
Chapter 15/End

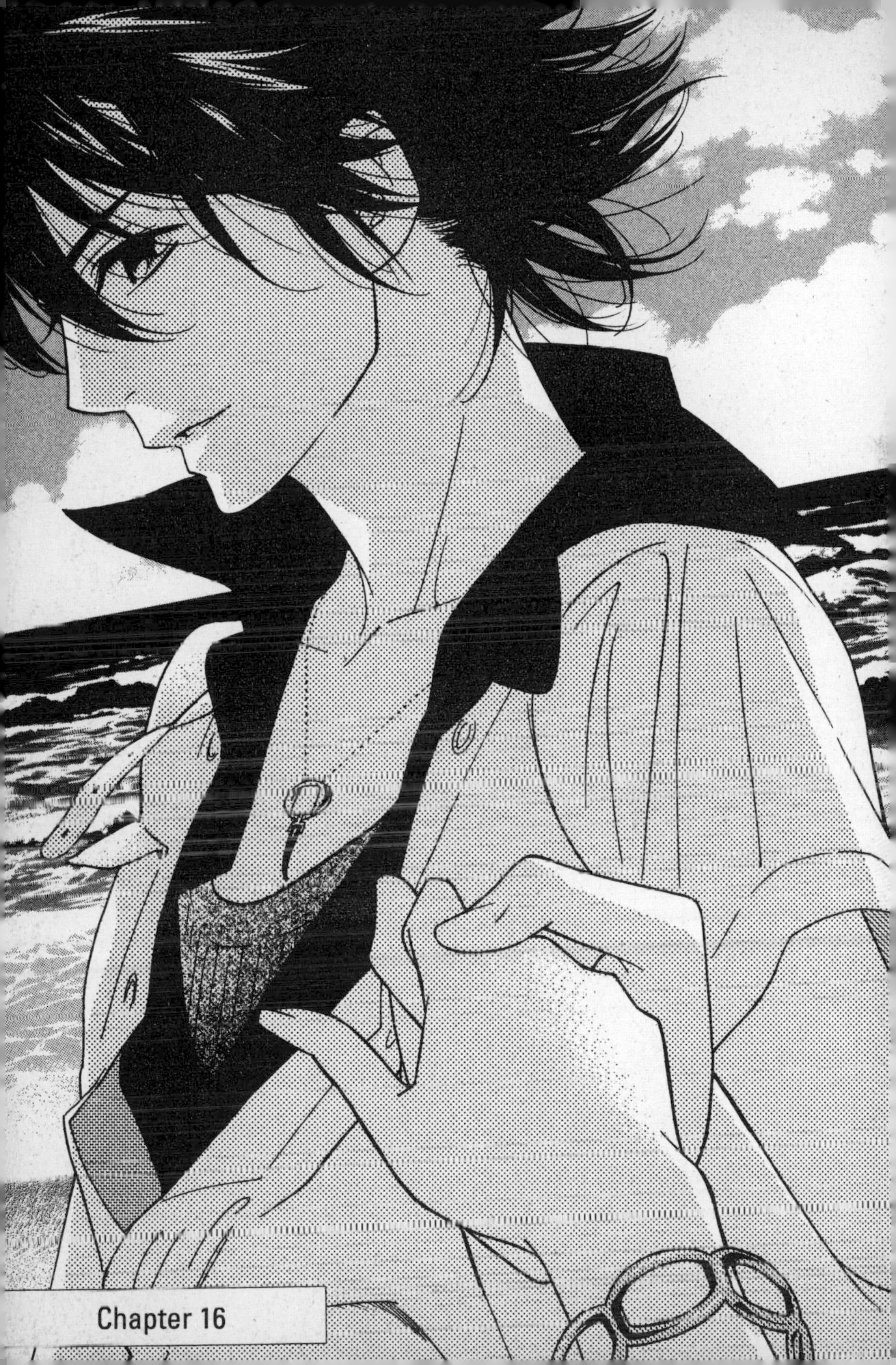

Chapter 16

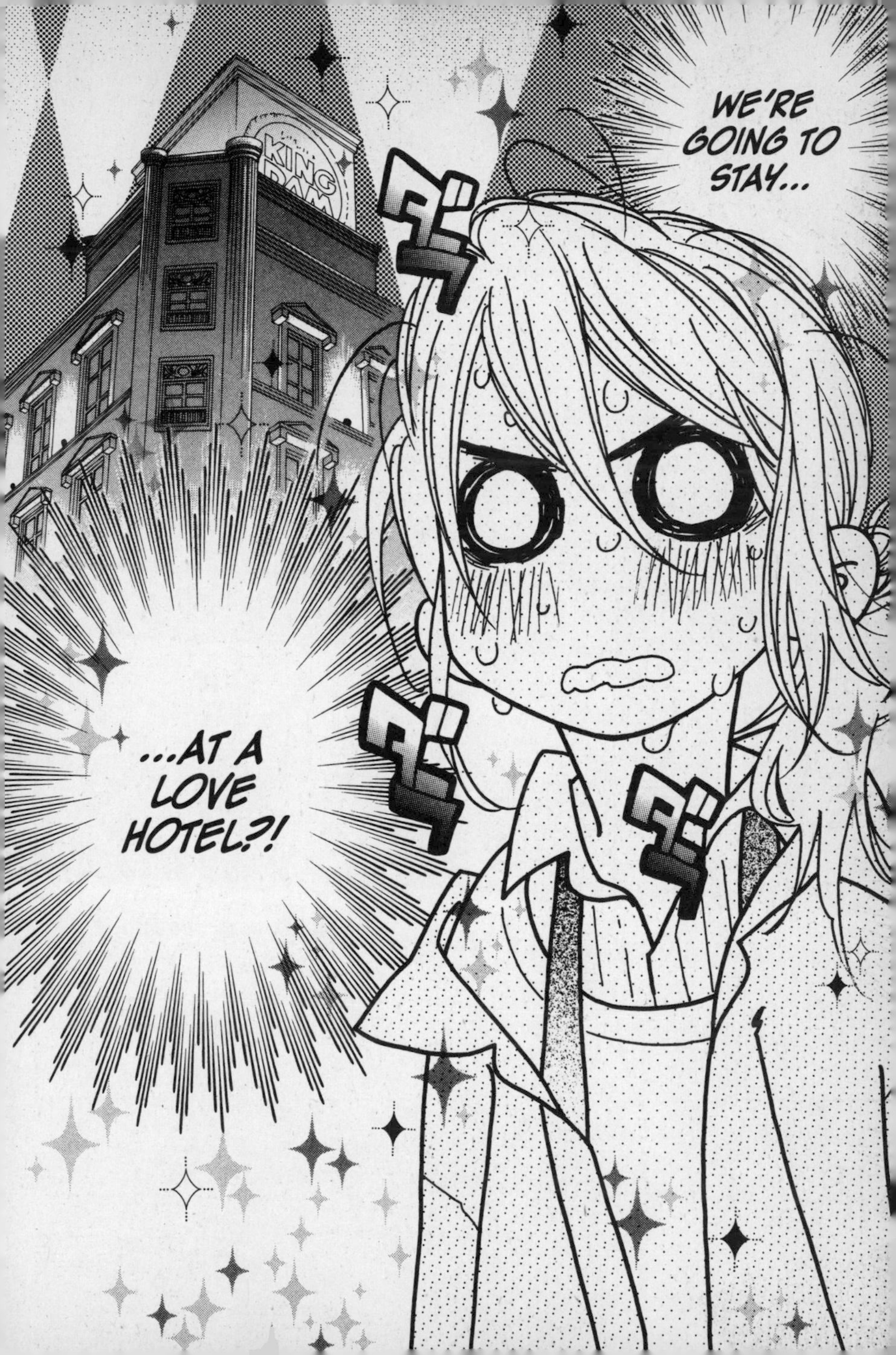
WE'RE GOING TO STAY...
...AT A LOVE HOTEL?!

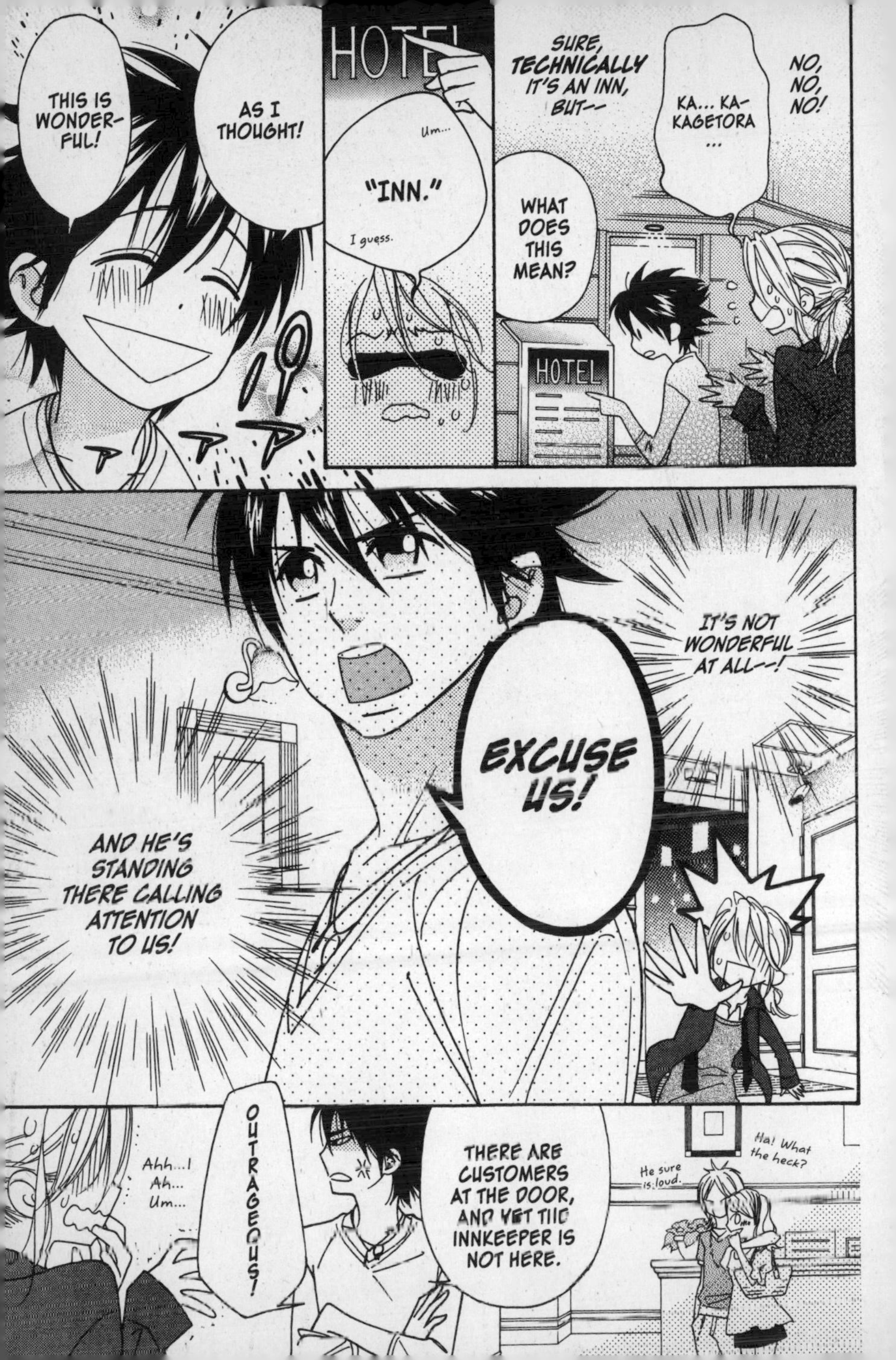
NO, NO, NO!
KA... KA-KAGETORA ...
SURE, TECHNICALLY IT'S AN INN, BUT--
WHAT DOES THIS MEAN?
Um...
"INN."
I guess.
AS I THOUGHT!
THIS IS WONDERFUL!
IT'S NOT WONDERFUL AT ALL--!
EXCUSE US!
AND HE'S STANDING THERE CALLING ATTENTION TO US!
Ha! What the heck?
He sure is loud.
THERE ARE CUSTOMERS AT THE DOOR, AND YET THE INNKEEPER IS NOT HERE.
OUTRAGEOUS!
Ahh...I
Ah...
Um...

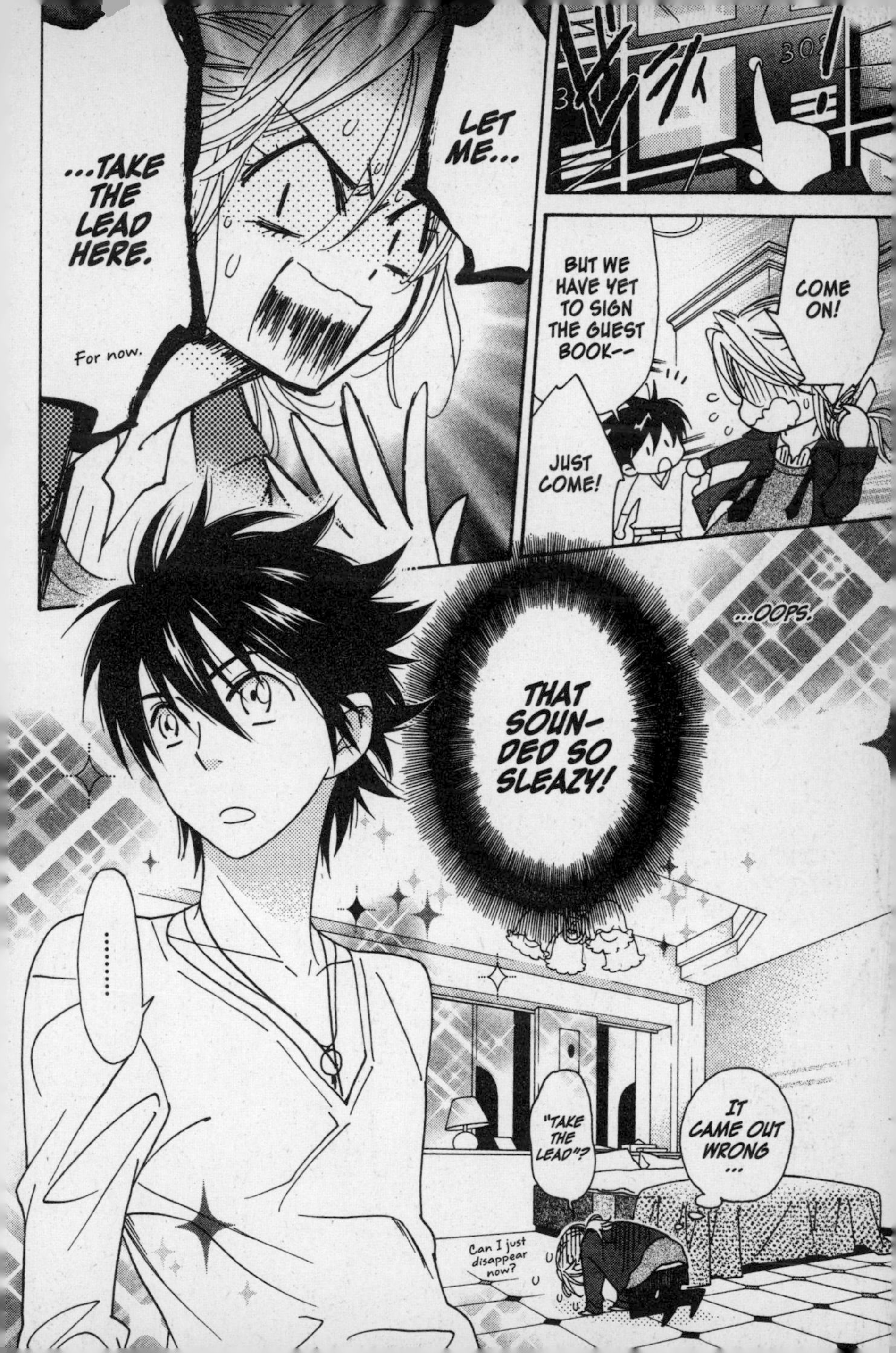
COME ON!
BUT WE HAVE YET TO SIGN THE GUEST BOOK--
JUST COME!
LET ME...
...TAKE THE LEAD HERE.
For now.
...OOPS.
THAT SOUN-DED SO SLEAZY!
......
IT CAME OUT WRONG...
"TAKE THE LEAD"?
Can I just disappear now?

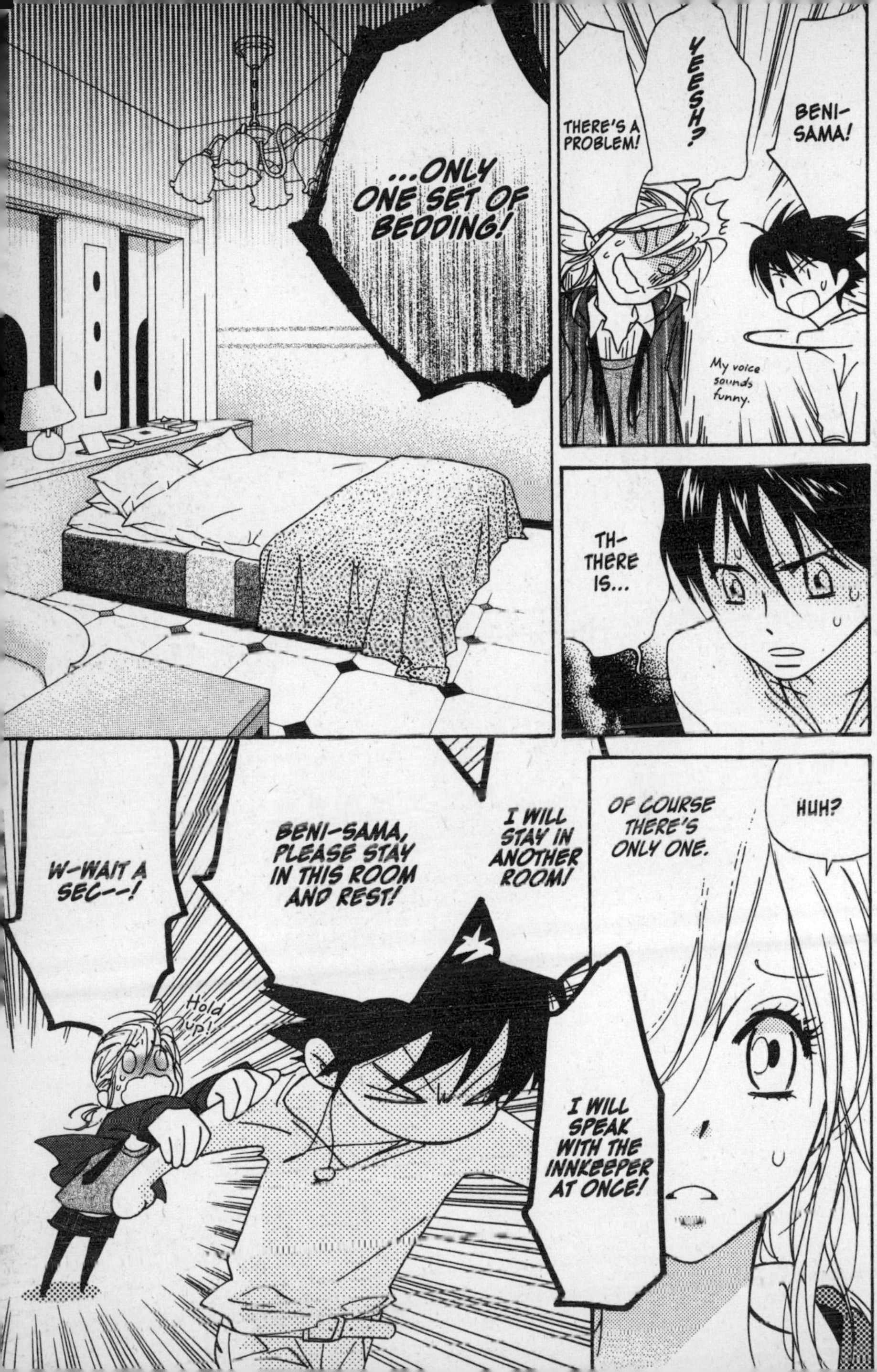
BENI-SAMA!
YEESH?
THERE'S A PROBLEM!
My voice sounds funny.
TH-THERE IS...
...ONLY ONE SET OF BEDDING!
HUH?
OF COURSE THERE'S ONLY ONE.
I WILL SPEAK WITH THE INNKEEPER AT ONCE!
I WILL STAY IN ANOTHER ROOM!
BENI-SAMA, PLEASE STAY IN THIS ROOM AND REST!
W-WAIT A SEC--!
Hold up!

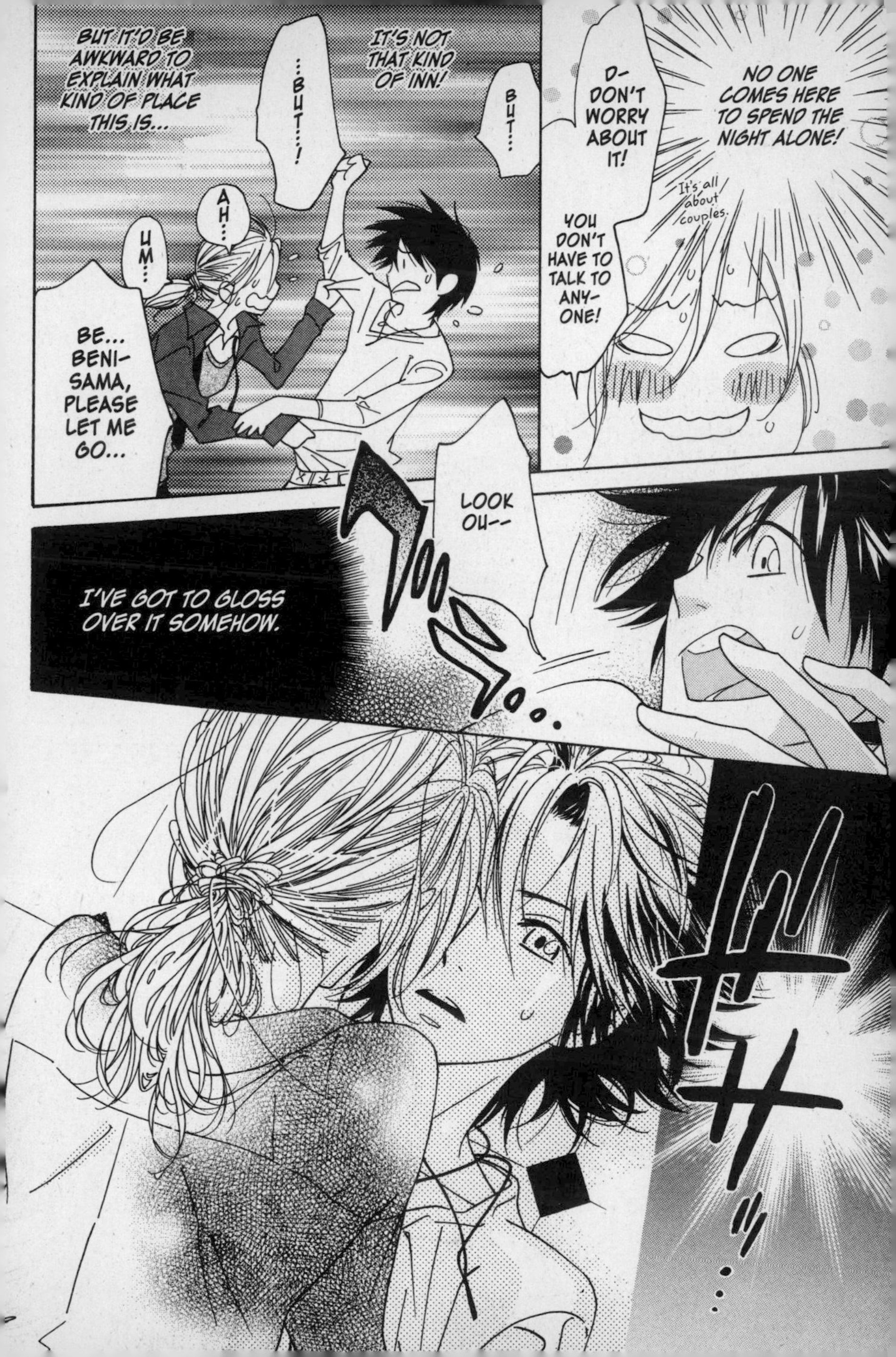
NO ONE COMES HERE TO SPEND THE NIGHT ALONE!
D-DON'T WORRY ABOUT IT!
It's all about couples.
YOU DON'T HAVE TO TALK TO ANY-ONE!
IT'S NOT THAT KIND OF INN!
BUT...
...BUT...!
BUT IT'D BE AWKWARD TO EXPLAIN WHAT KIND OF PLACE THIS IS...
AH...
UM...
BE... BENI-SAMA, PLEASE LET ME GO...
LOOK OU--
I'VE GOT TO GLOSS OVER IT SOMEHOW.

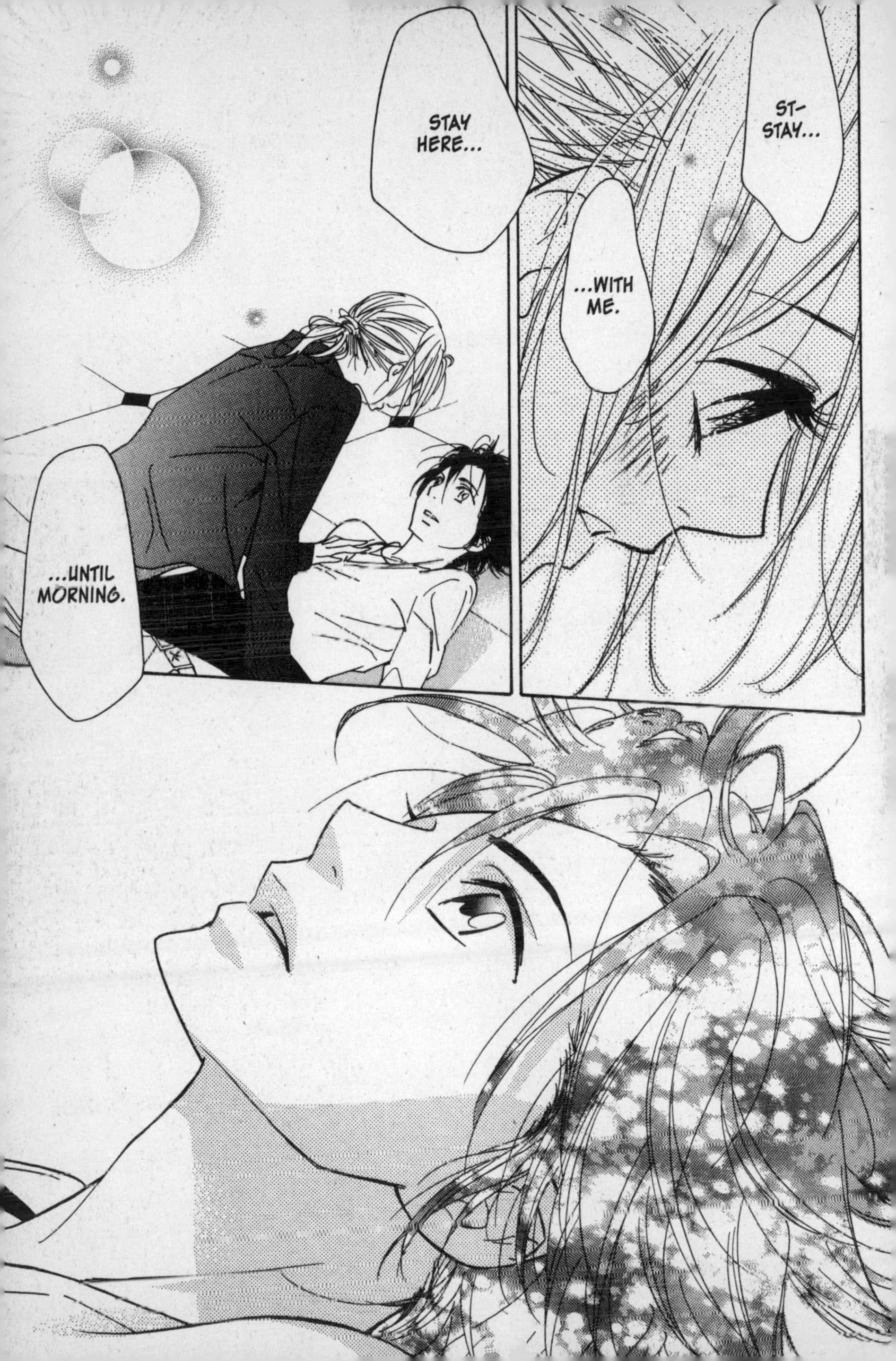
ST-STAY...
...WITH ME.
STAY HERE...
...UNTIL MORNING.

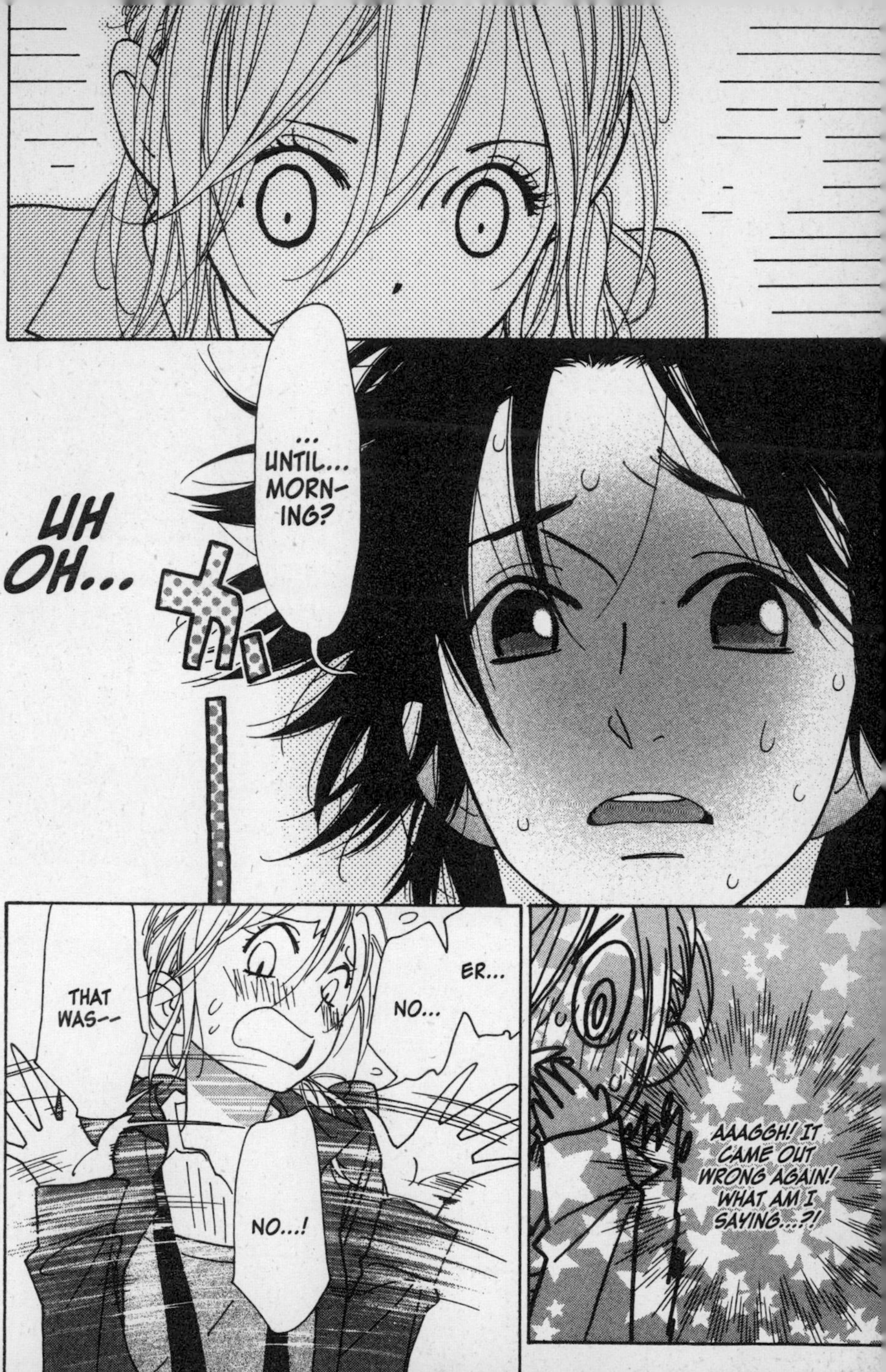

... UNTIL... MORNING?
UH OH...
AAAGGH! IT CAME OUT WRONG AGAIN! WHAT AM I SAYING...?!
ER...
NO...
THAT WAS--
NO...!

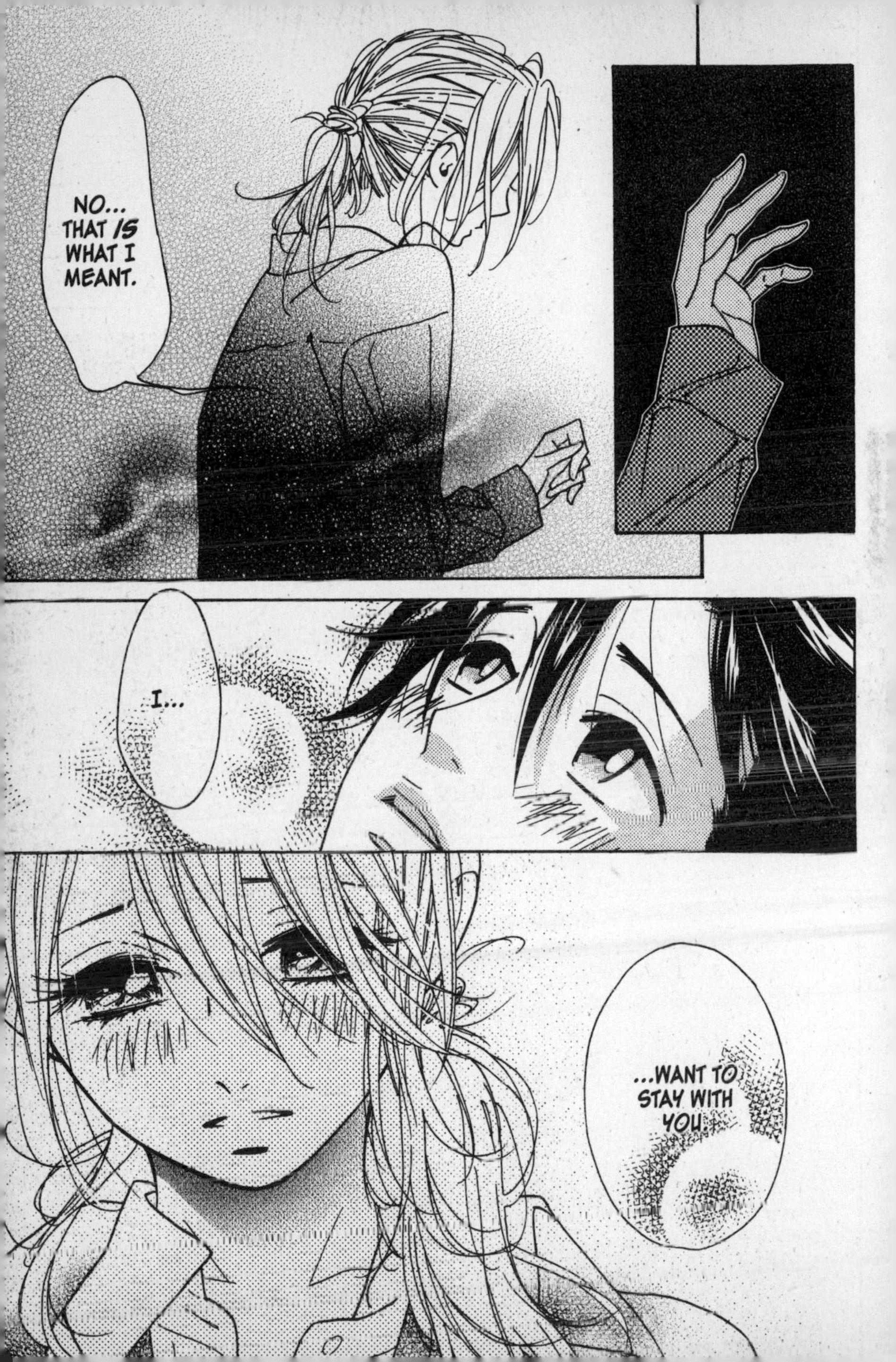
NO... THAT IS WHAT I MEANT.
I...
...WANT TO STAY WITH YOU.

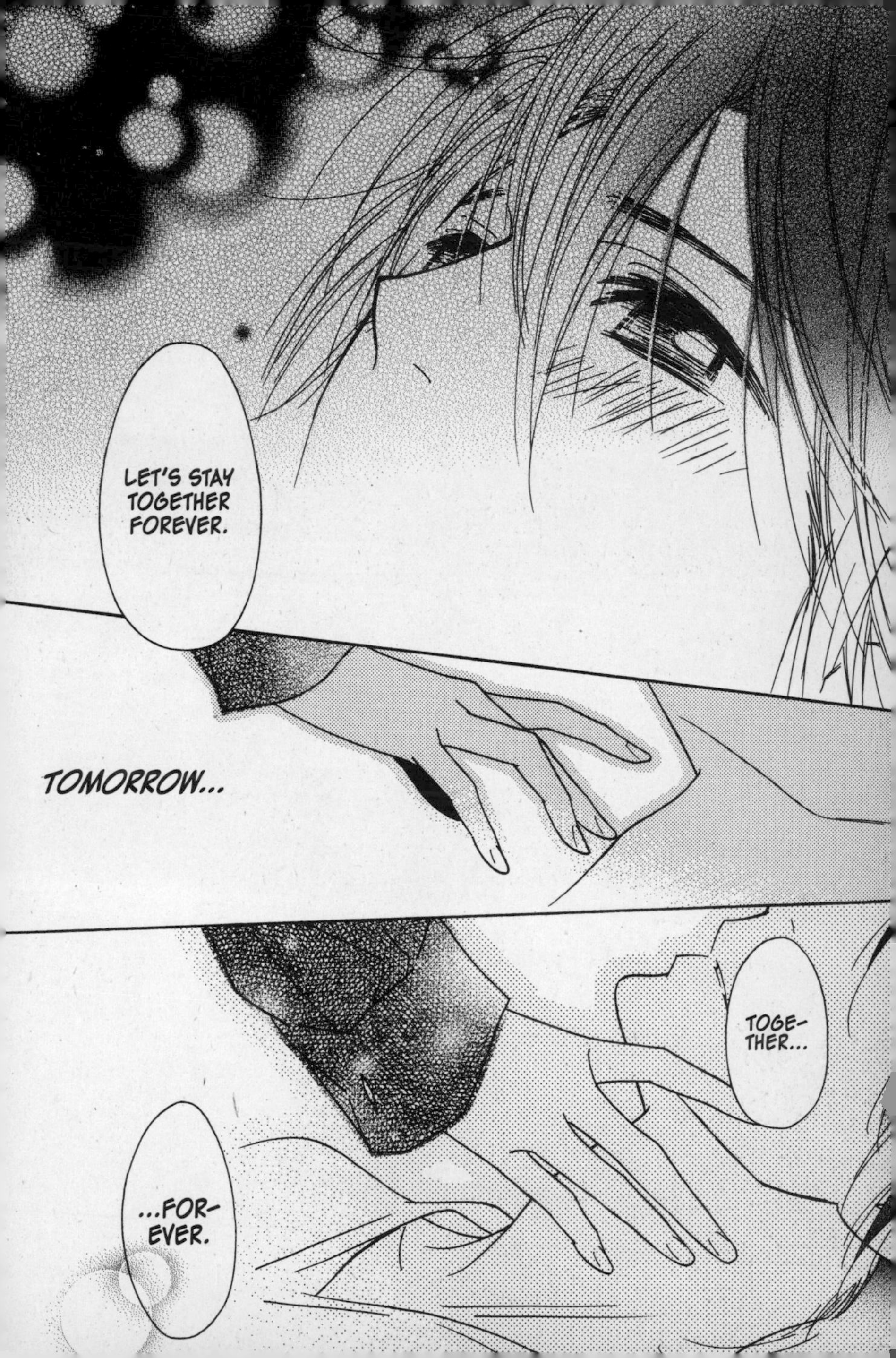
LET'S STAY TOGETHER FOREVER.
TOMORROW...
TOGE-THER...
...FOR-EVER.

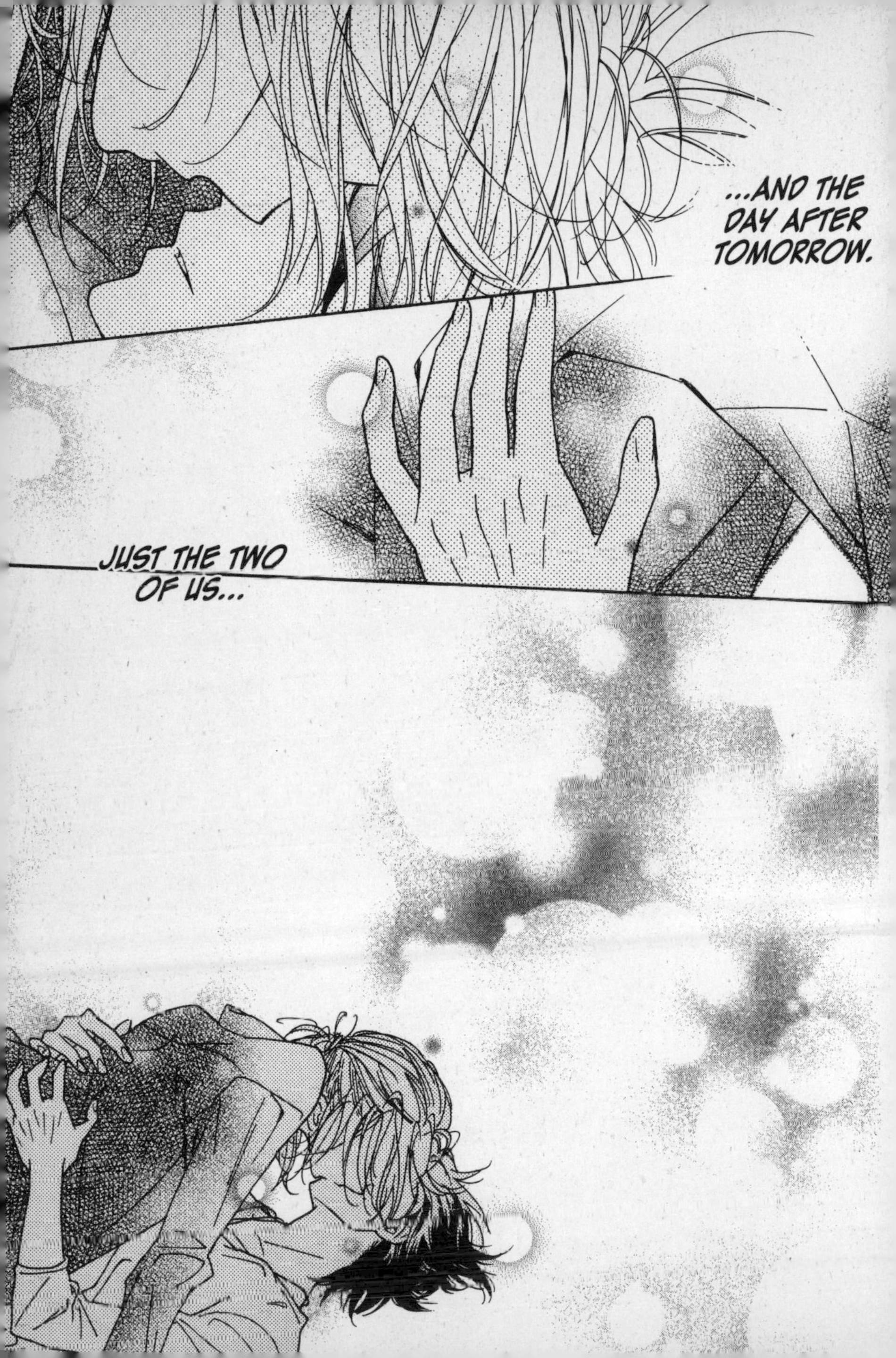
...AND THE DAY AFTER TOMORROW.
JUST THE TWO OF US...

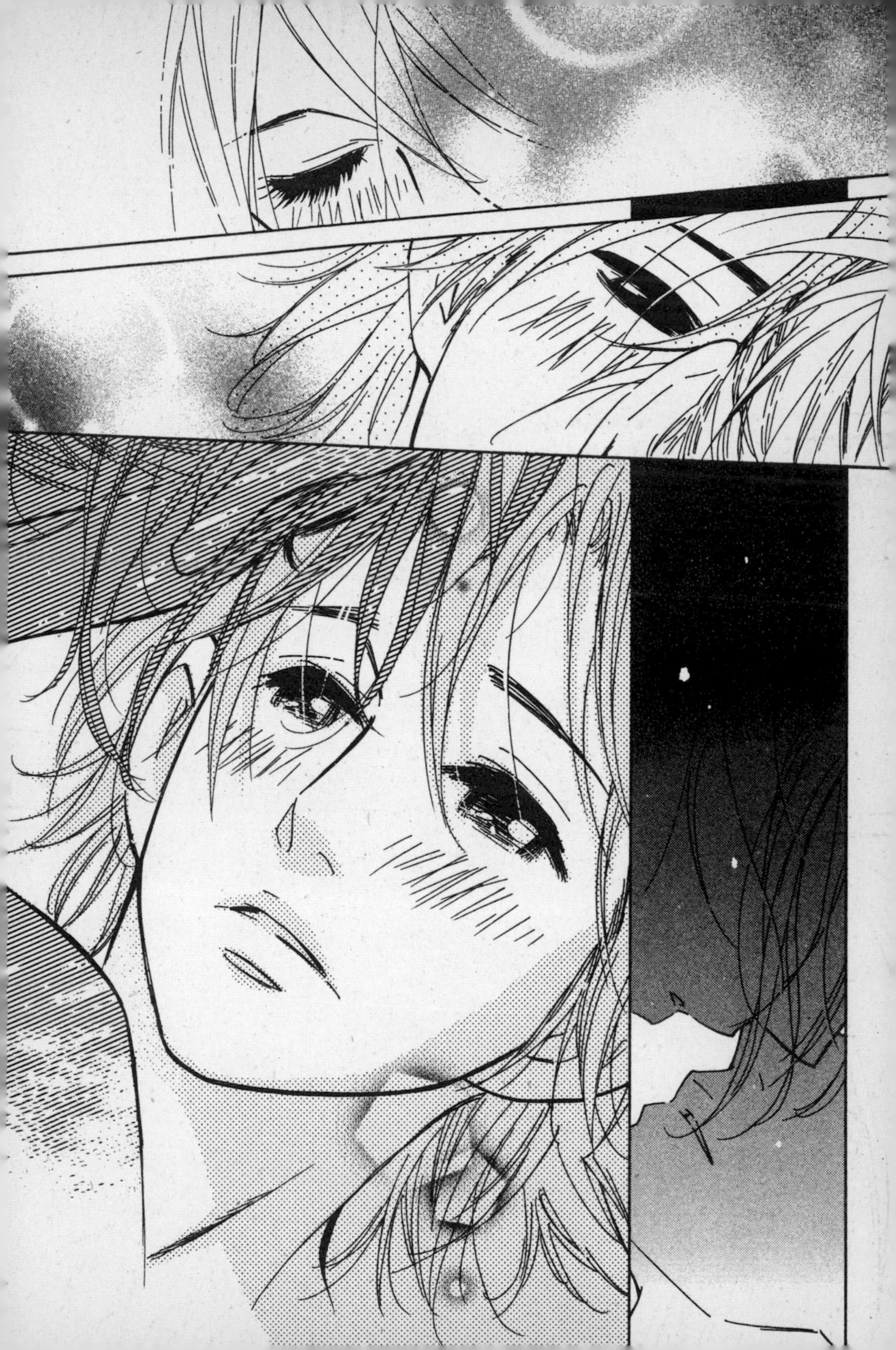

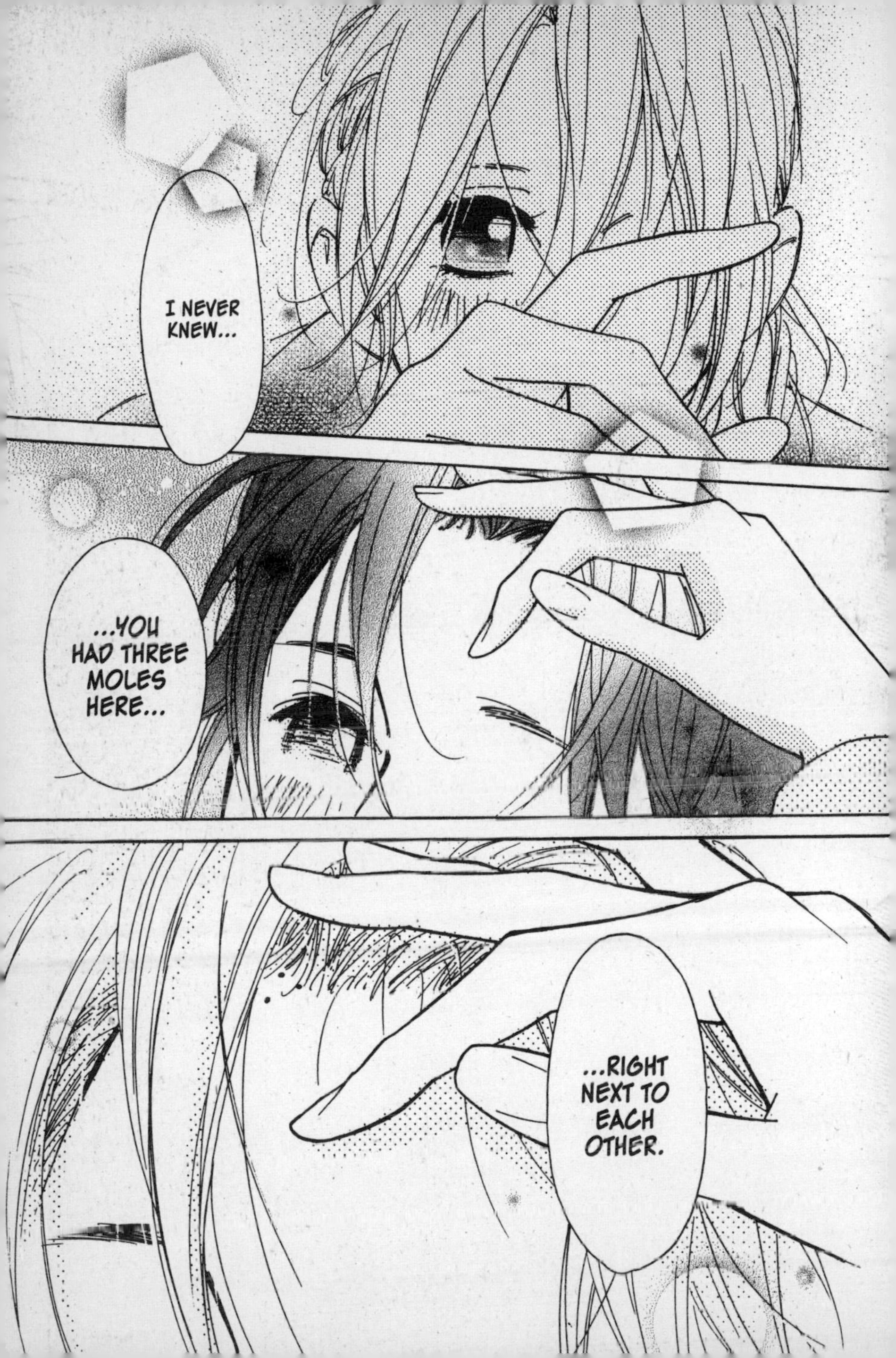
I NEVER KNEW...
...YOU HAD THREE MOLES HERE...
...RIGHT NEXT TO EACH OTHER.

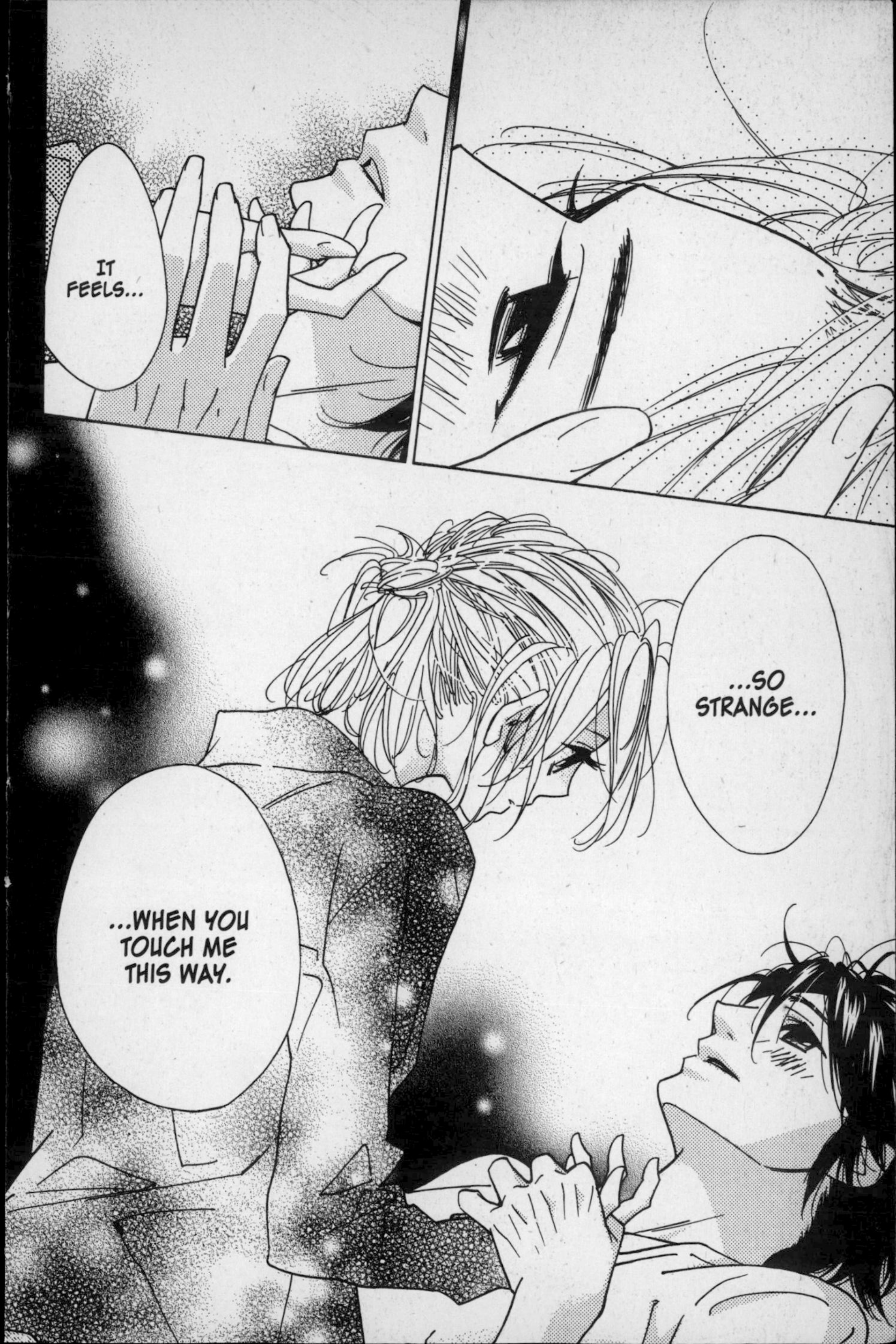
IT FEELS...
...SO STRANGE...
...WHEN YOU TOUCH ME THIS WAY.

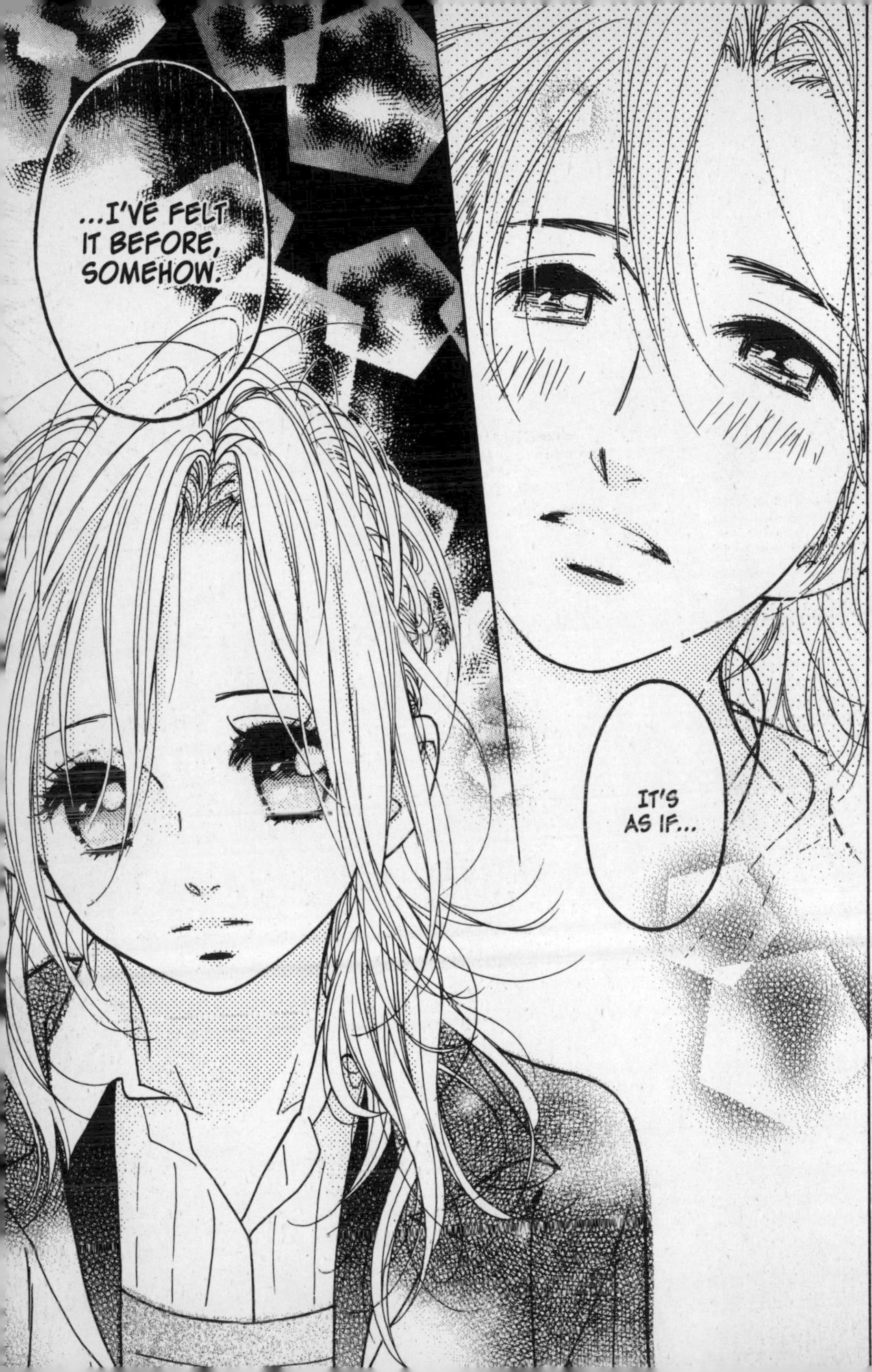
IT'S AS IF...
...I'VE FELT IT BEFORE, SOMEHOW.

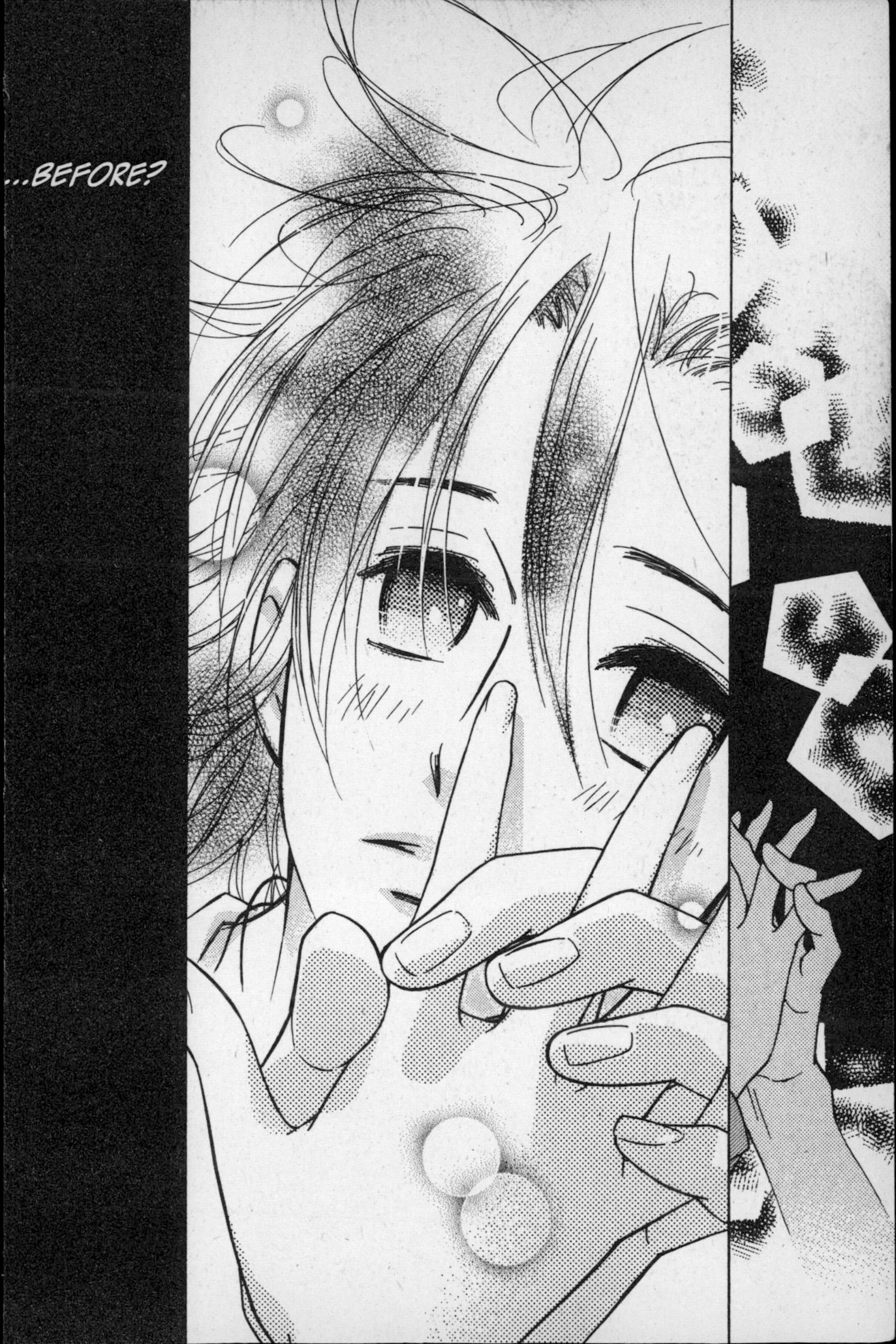
...BEFORE?

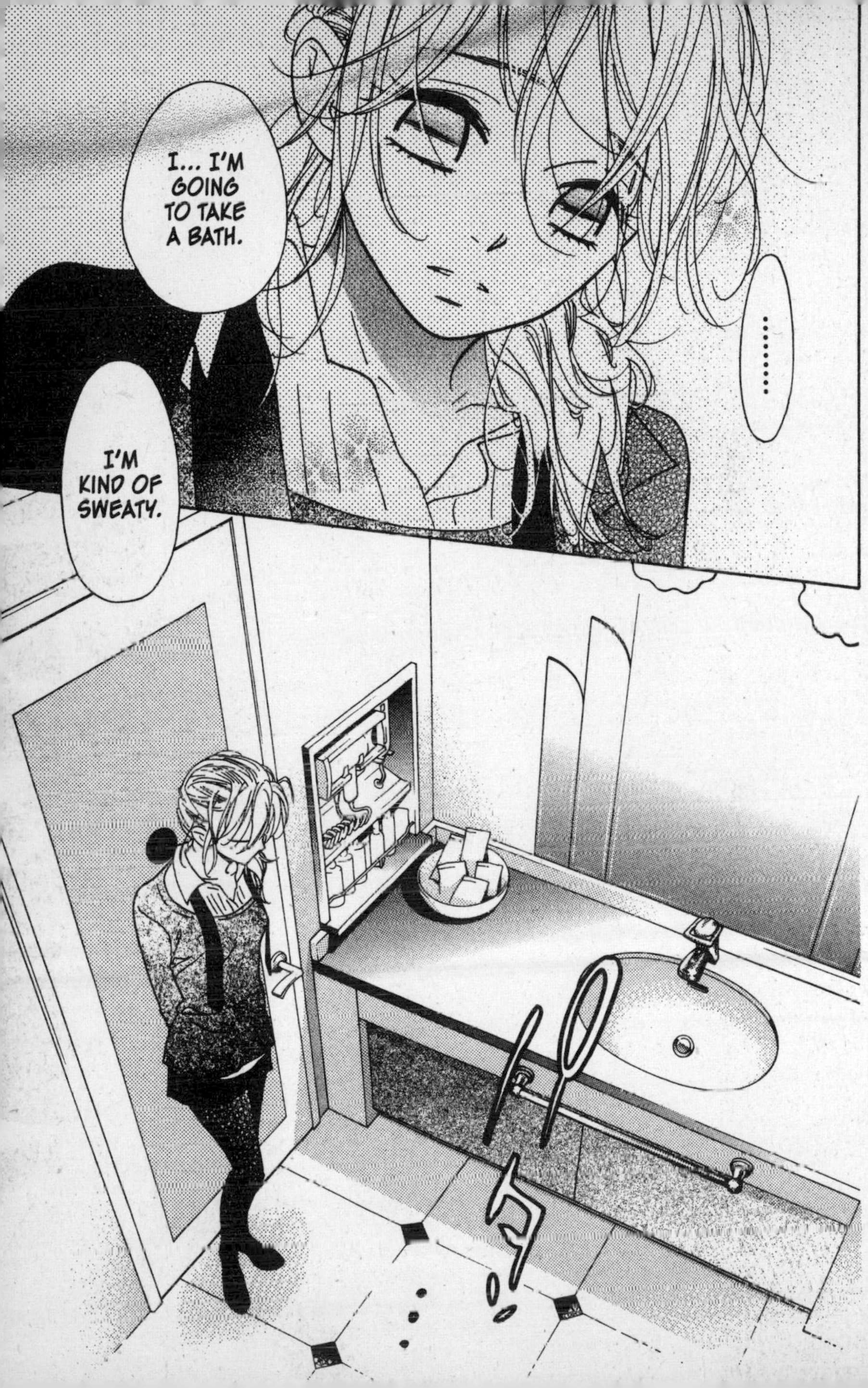
......
I... I'M GOING TO TAKE A BATH.
I'M KIND OF SWEATY.

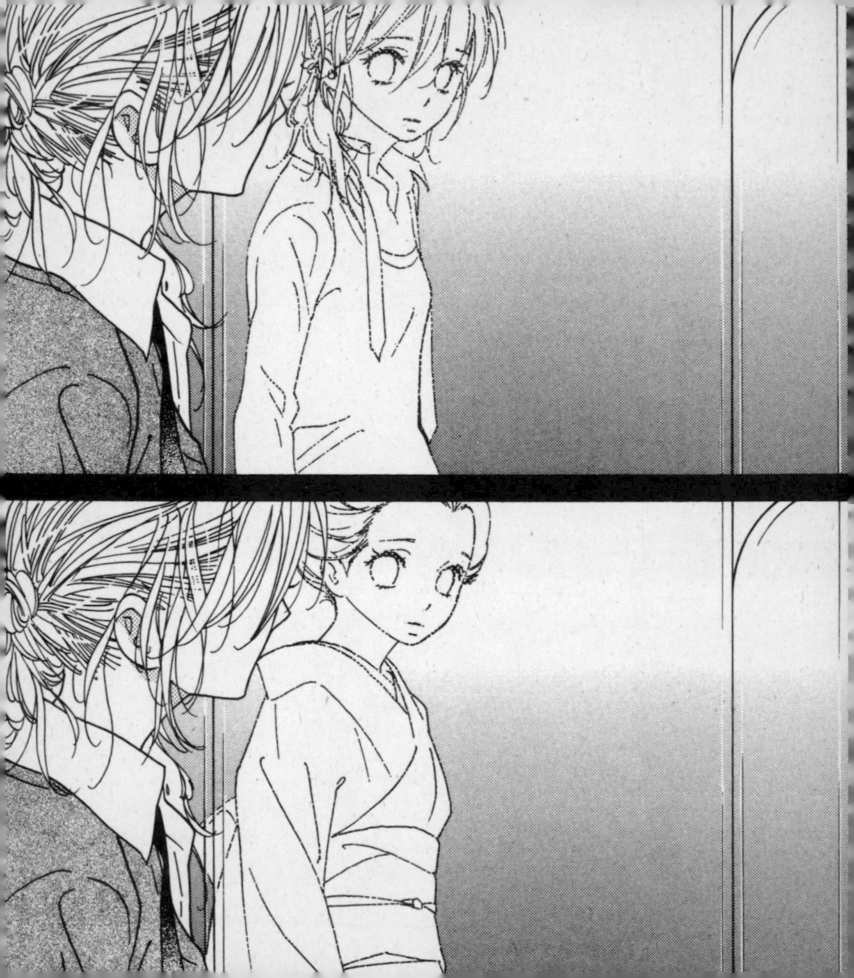

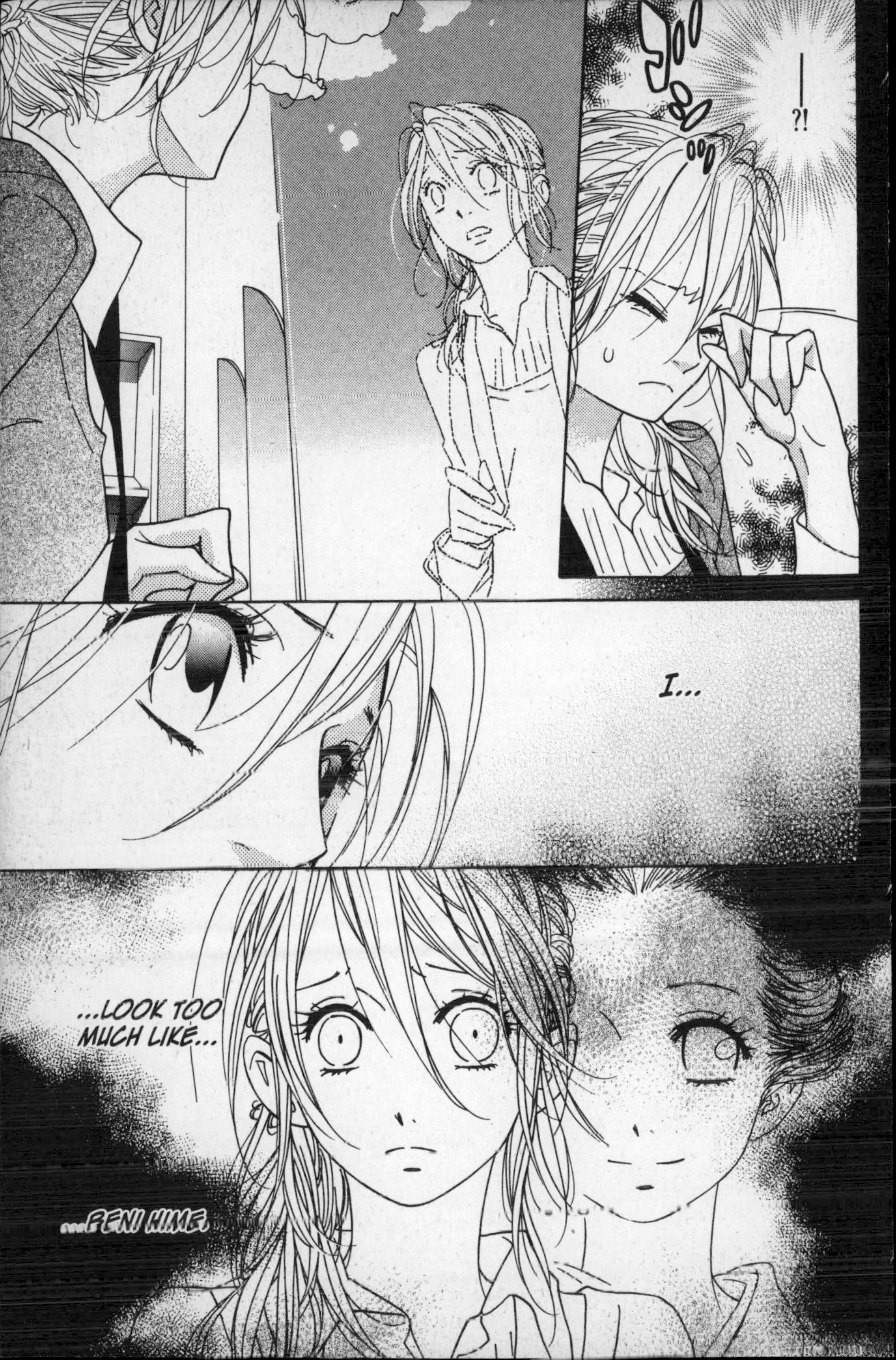
—?!
I...
...LOOK TOO MUCH LIKE...
...BENI HIME.

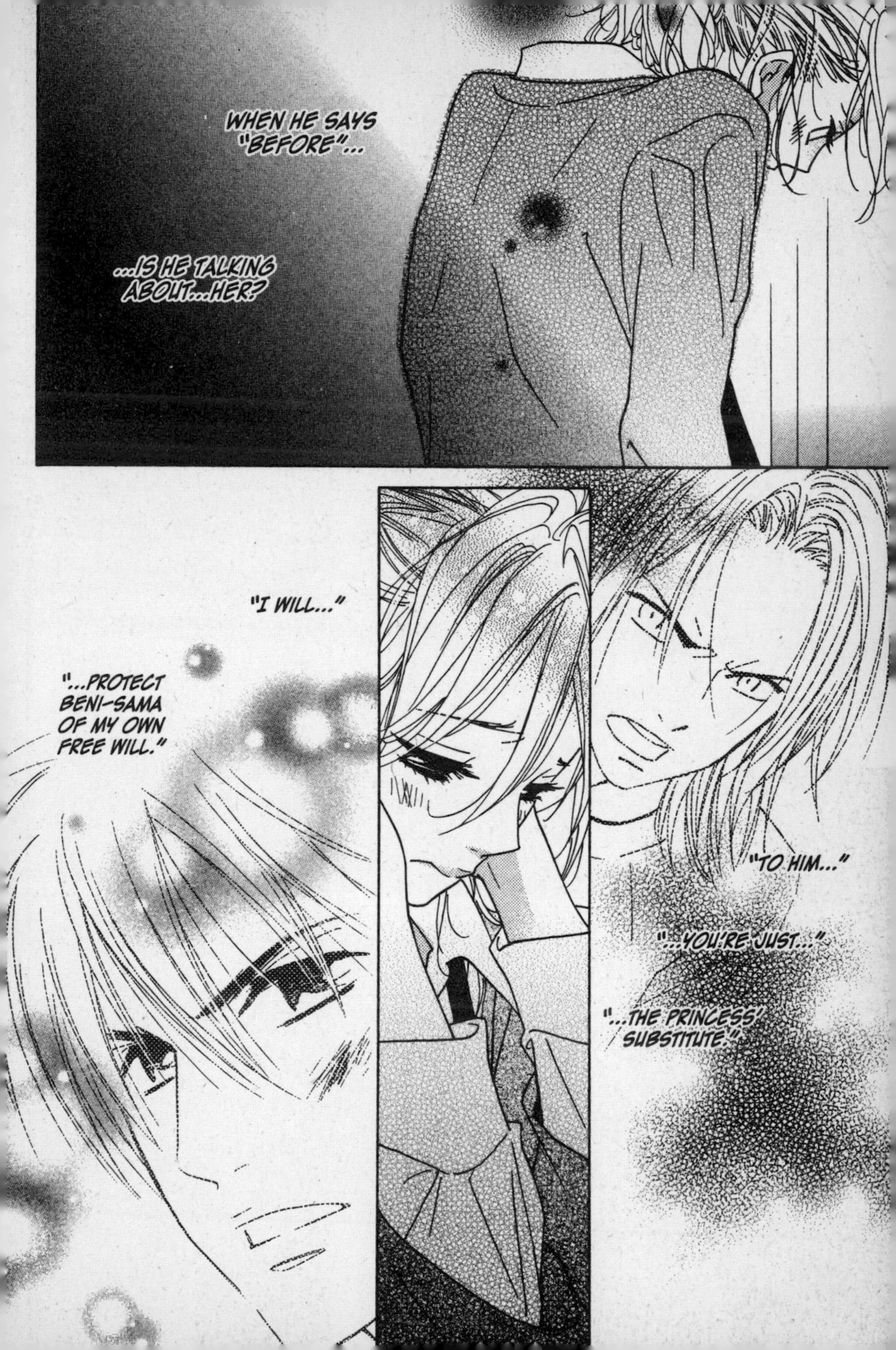

WHEN HE SAYS "BEFORE"...
...IS HE TALKING ABOUT...HER?
"TO HIM..."
"...YOU'RE JUST..."
"...THE PRINCESS' SUBSTITUTE."
"I WILL..."
"...PROTECT BENI-SAMA OF MY OWN FREE WILL."

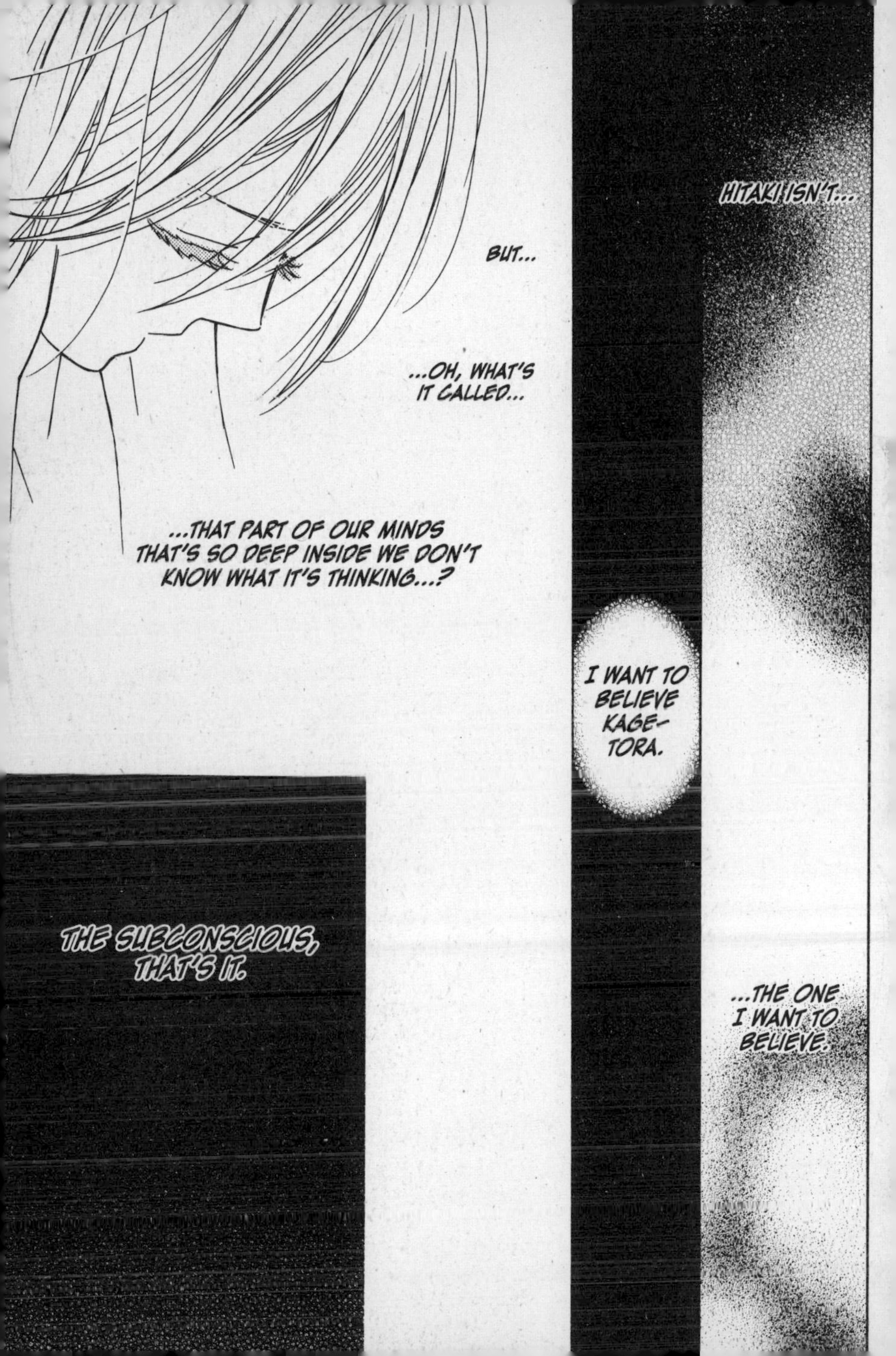
HITAKI ISN'T...
I WANT TO BELIEVE KAGE-TORA.
...THE ONE I WANT TO BELIEVE.
BUT...
...OH, WHAT'S IT CALLED...
...THAT PART OF OUR MINDS THAT'S SO DEEP INSIDE WE DON'T KNOW WHAT IT'S THINKING...?
THE SUBCONSCIOUS, THAT'S IT.

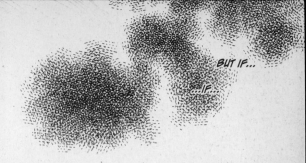

BUT IF...

...IF...

I DON'T EVEN WANT TO IMAGINE IT, BUT...

...IF KAGETORA DISAPPEARED SOMEWHERE I COULD NEVER SEE HIM AGAIN...

...AND THEN...

IF THAT EVER HAPPENED...

...THEN I'D PROBABLY...

...SOME-ONE WHO LOOKED...

...EXACTLY LIKE HIM MATERIALIZED IN FRONT OF ME...

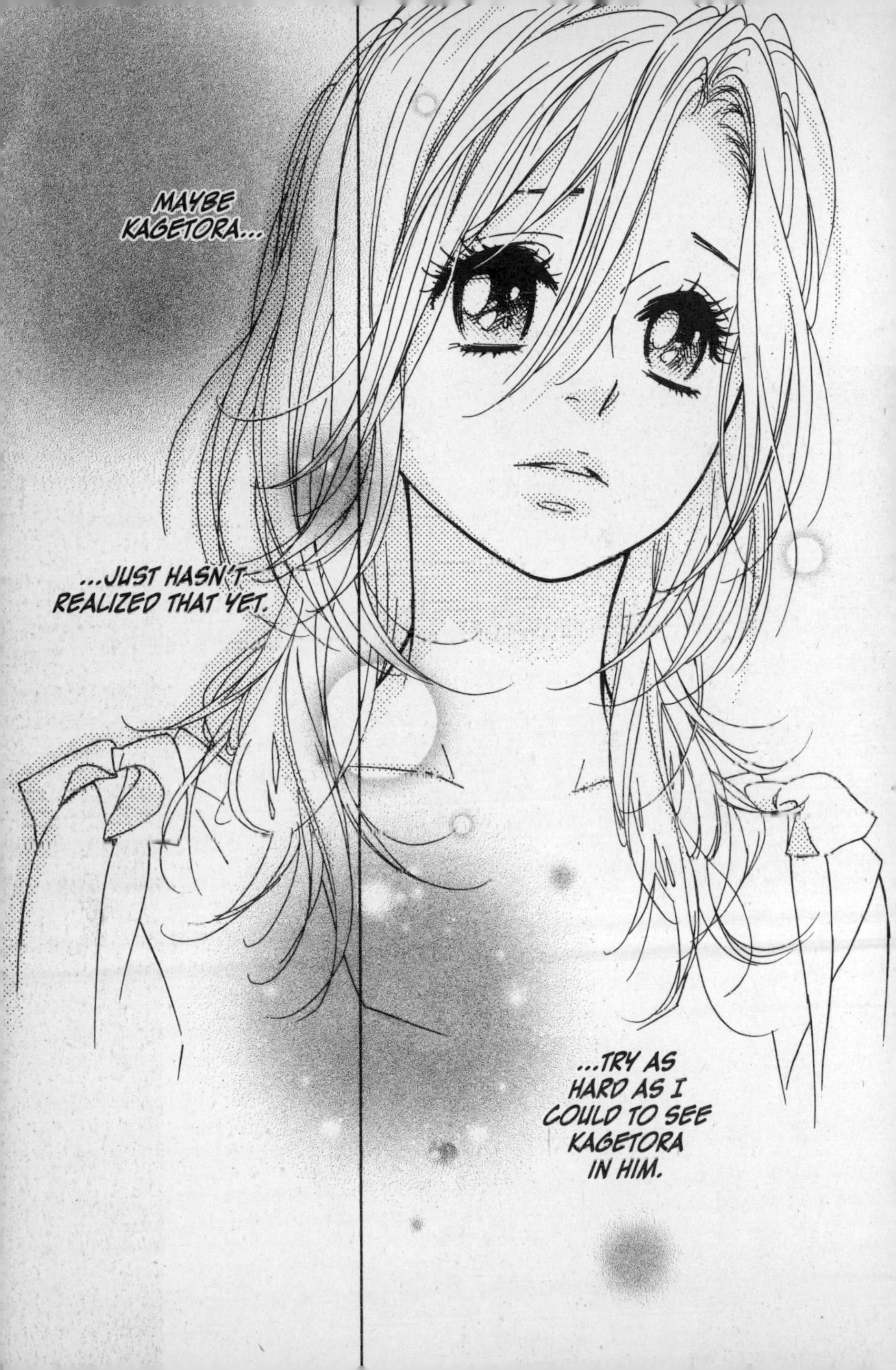
...TRY AS HARD AS I COULD TO SEE KAGETORA IN HIM.
MAYBE KAGETORA...
...JUST HASN'T REALIZED THAT YET.

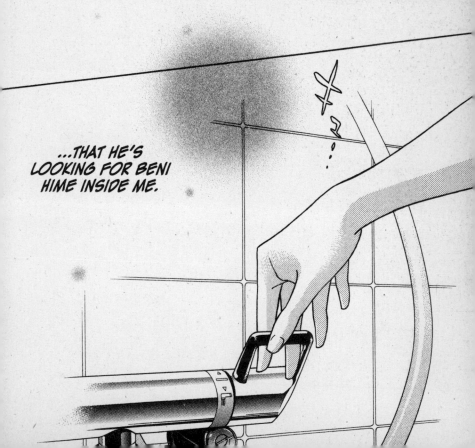

HE HASN'T
FIGURED OUT...

...ON HIS
OWN...

...THAT HE'S
LOOKING FOR BENI
HIME INSIDE ME.

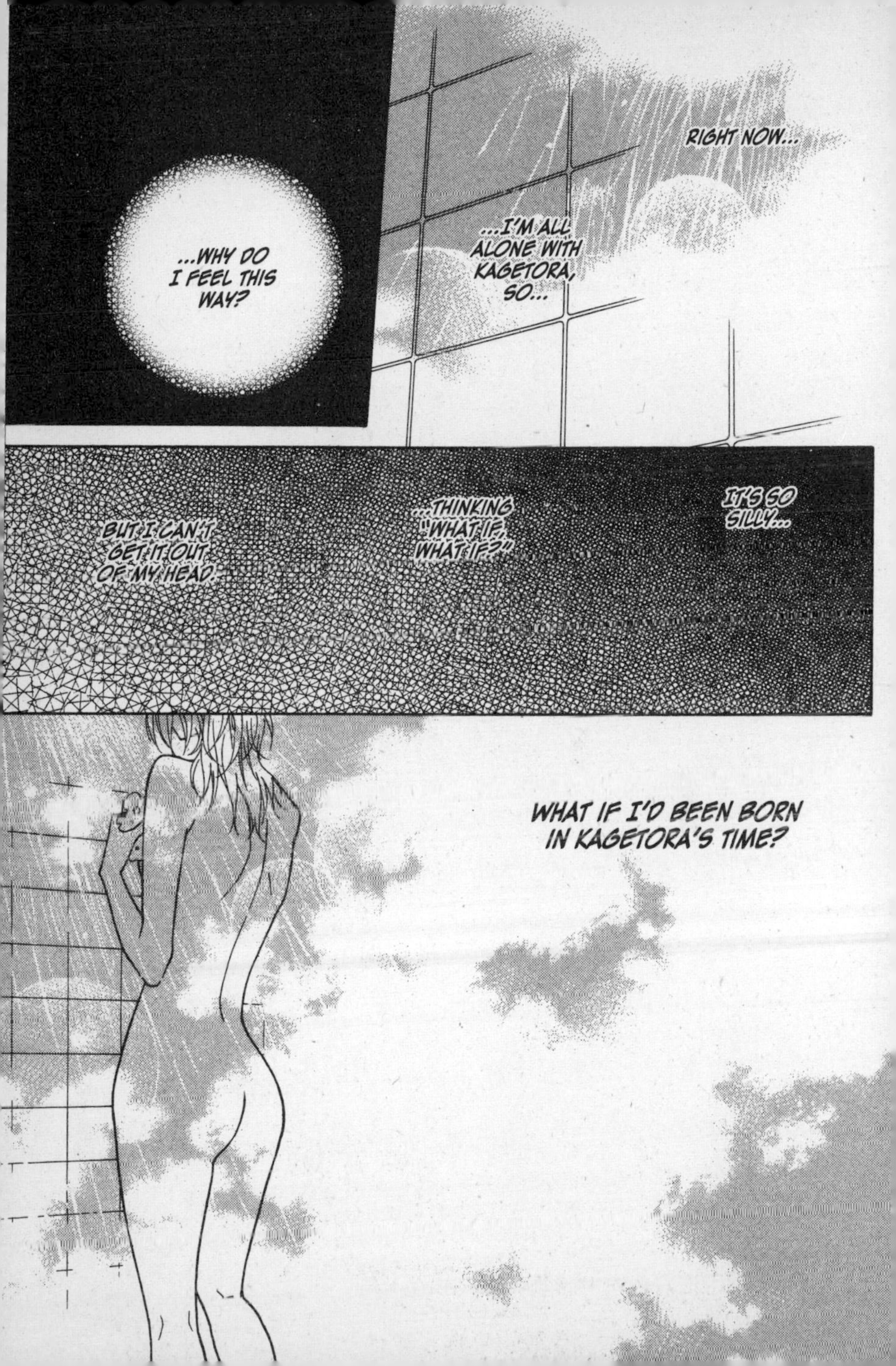
RIGHT NOW...
...I'M ALL ALONE WITH KAGETORA, SO...
...WHY DO I FEEL THIS WAY?
IT'S SO SILLY...
...THINKING "WHAT IF, WHAT IF?"
BUT I CAN'T GET IT OUT OF MY HEAD.
WHAT IF I'D BEEN BORN IN KAGETORA'S TIME?

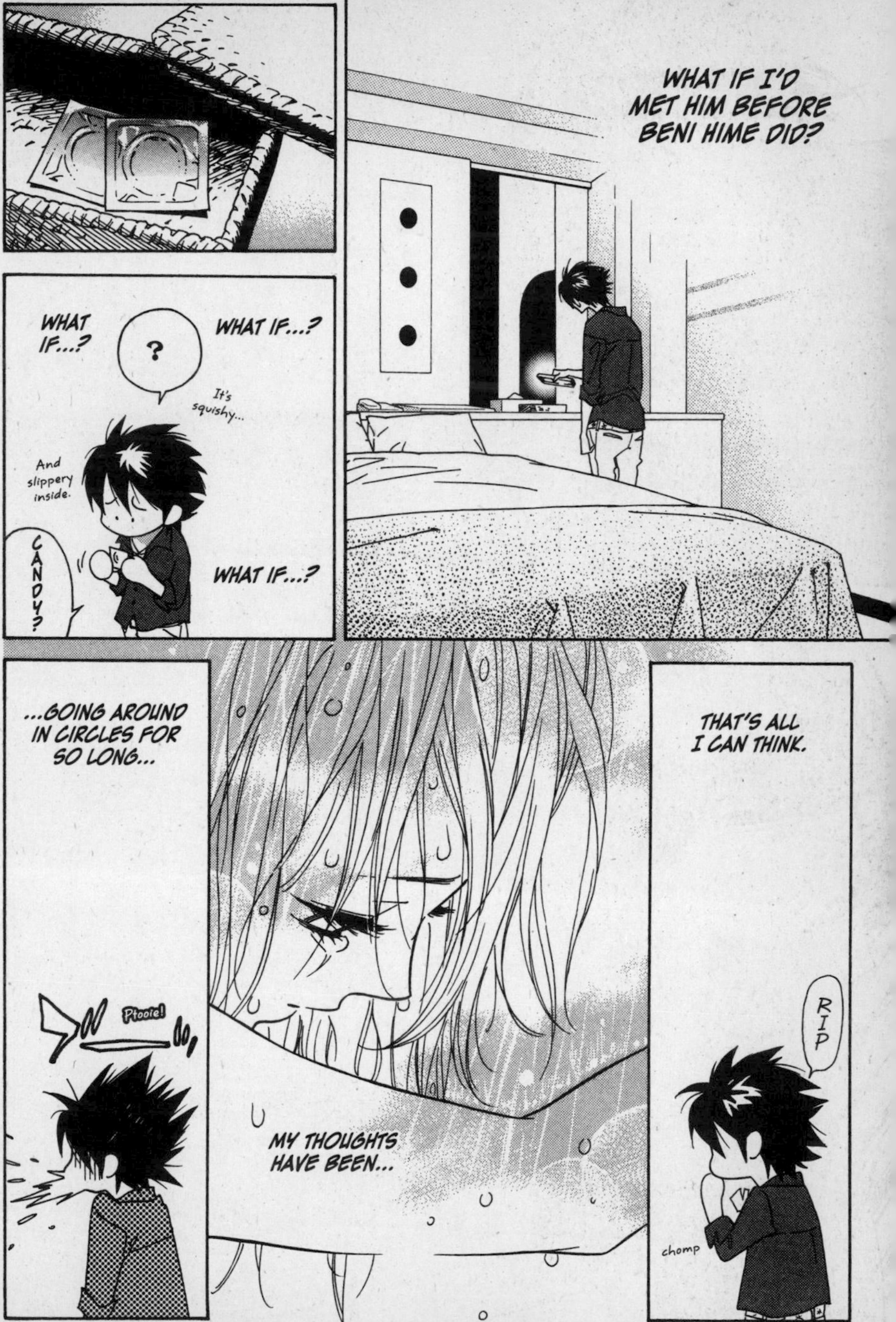

WHAT IF I'D MET HIM BEFORE BENI HIME DID?
WHAT IF...?
?
WHAT IF...?
It's squishy...
And slippery inside.
WHAT IF...?
CANDY?
THAT'S ALL I CAN THINK.
RIP
chomp
MY THOUGHTS HAVE BEEN...
...GOING AROUND IN CIRCLES FOR SO LONG...
Ptooie!

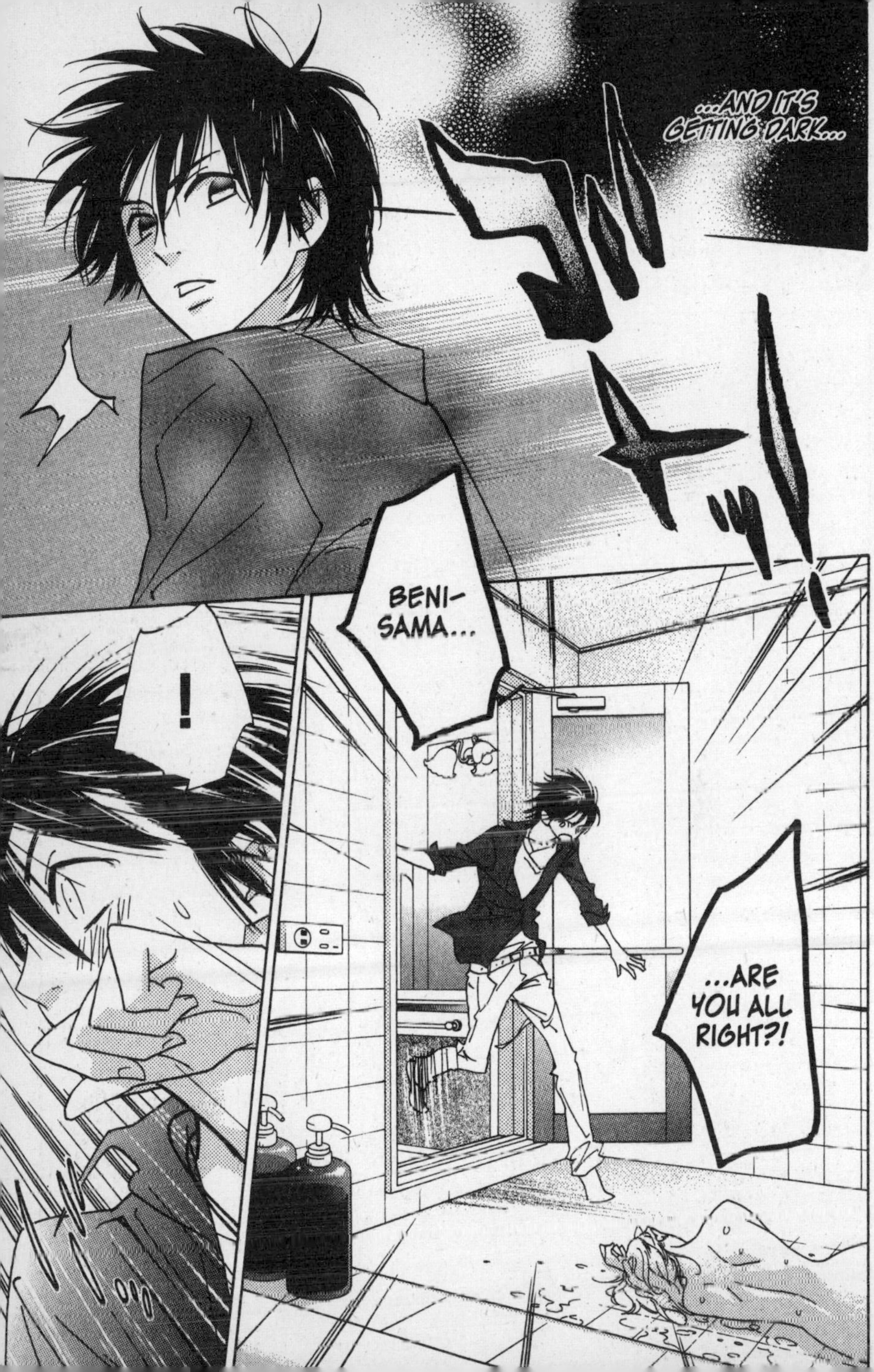
...AND IT'S GETTING DARK...
BENI-SAMA...
...ARE YOU ALL RIGHT?!
!

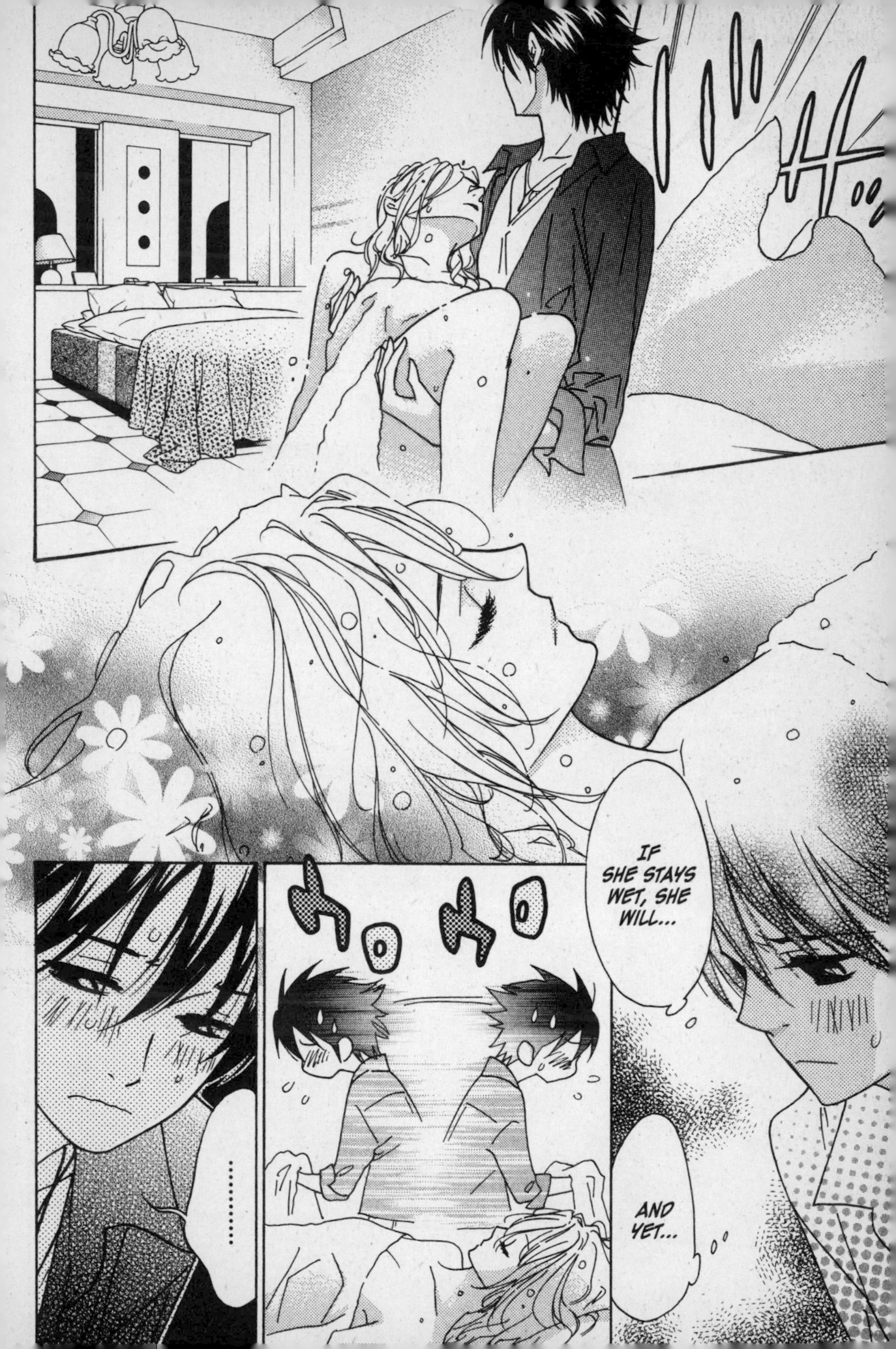

IF SHE STAYS WET, SHE WILL...
AND YET...
......

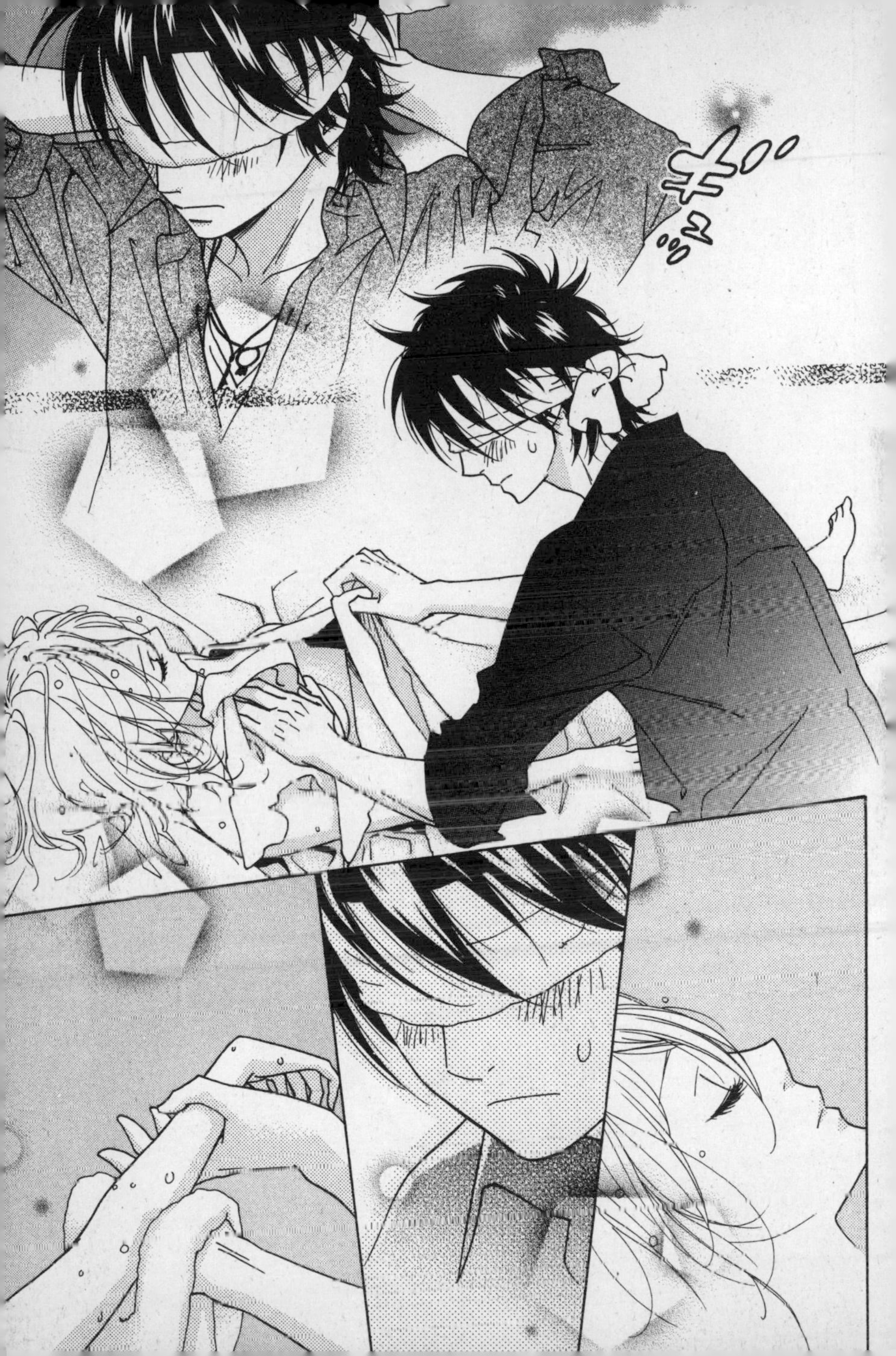
ギュ…

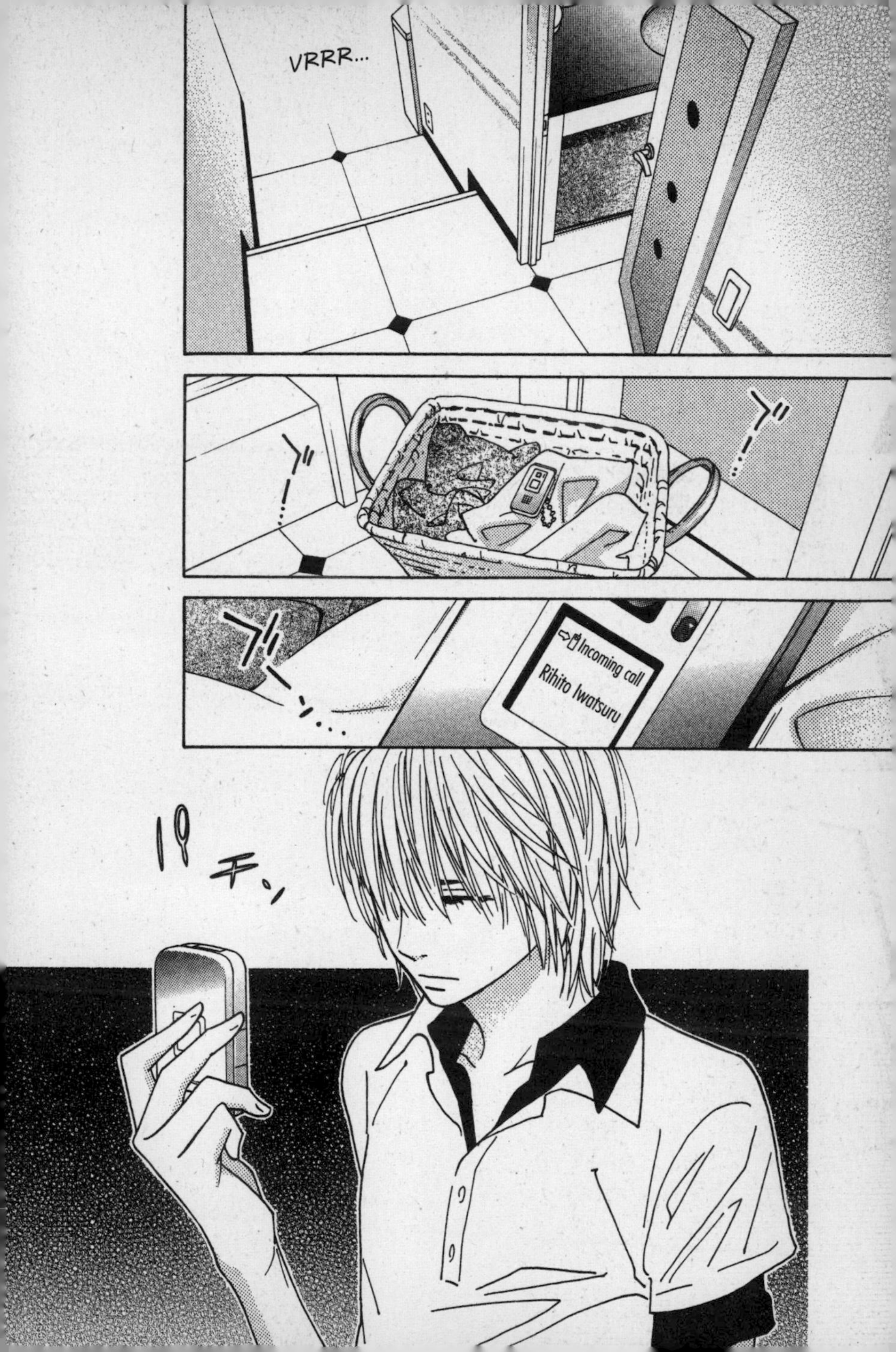
VRRR...
ヴー…
ヴー…
ヴー…
Incoming call
Rihito Iwatsuru
パチッ

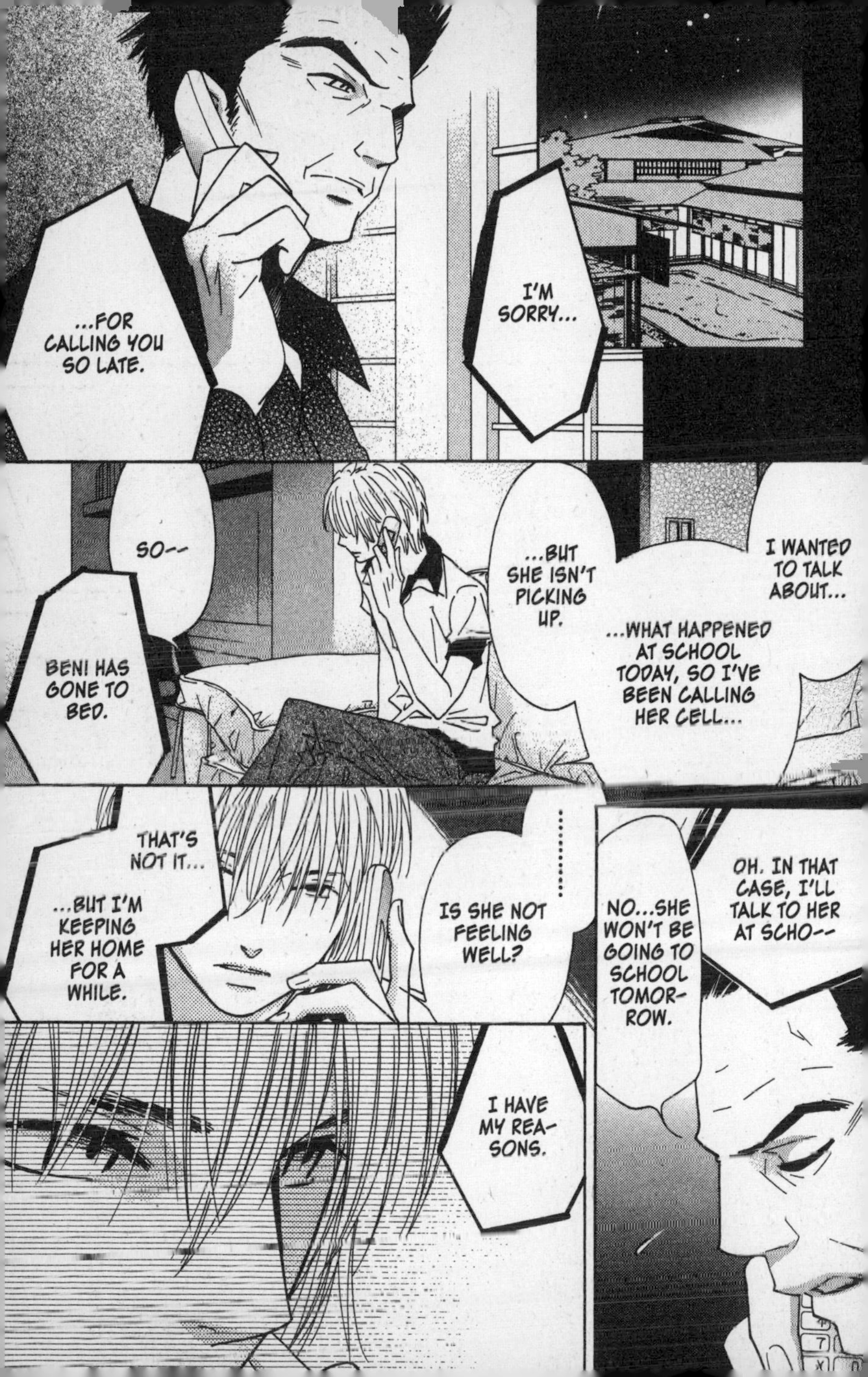
I'M SORRY...
...FOR CALLING YOU SO LATE.
I WANTED TO TALK ABOUT...
...WHAT HAPPENED AT SCHOOL TODAY, SO I'VE BEEN CALLING HER CELL...
...BUT SHE ISN'T PICKING UP.
SO--
BENI HAS GONE TO BED.
OH. IN THAT CASE, I'LL TALK TO HER AT SCHO--
NO...SHE WON'T BE GOING TO SCHOOL TOMORROW.
......
IS SHE NOT FEELING WELL?
THAT'S NOT IT...
...BUT I'M KEEPING HER HOME FOR A WHILE.
I HAVE MY REASONS.

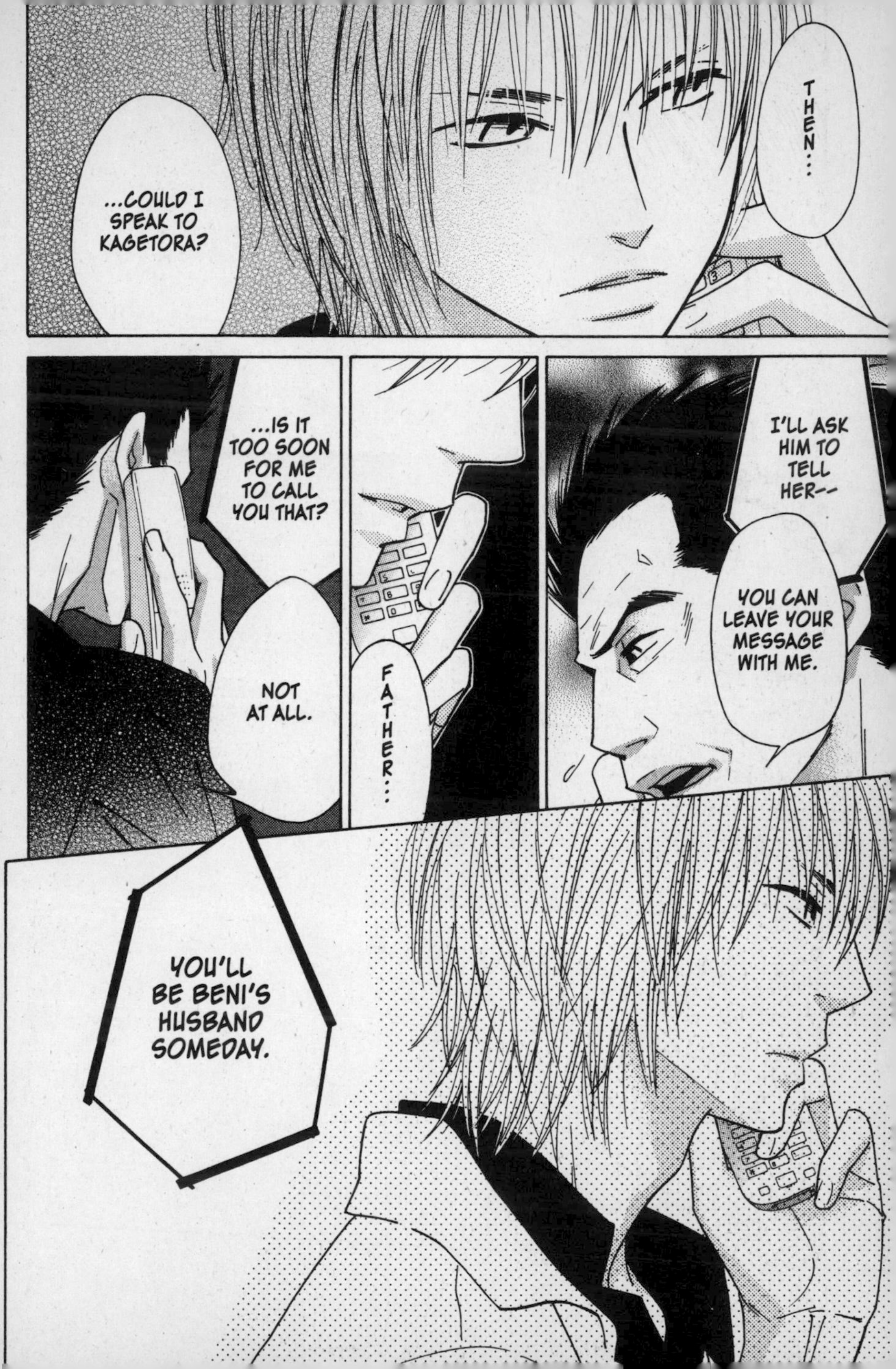
THEN...
...COULD I SPEAK TO KAGETORA?
I'LL ASK HIM TO TELL HER--
YOU CAN LEAVE YOUR MESSAGE WITH ME.
FATHER...
...IS IT TOO SOON FOR ME TO CALL YOU THAT?
NOT AT ALL.
YOU'LL BE BENI'S HUSBAND SOMEDAY.

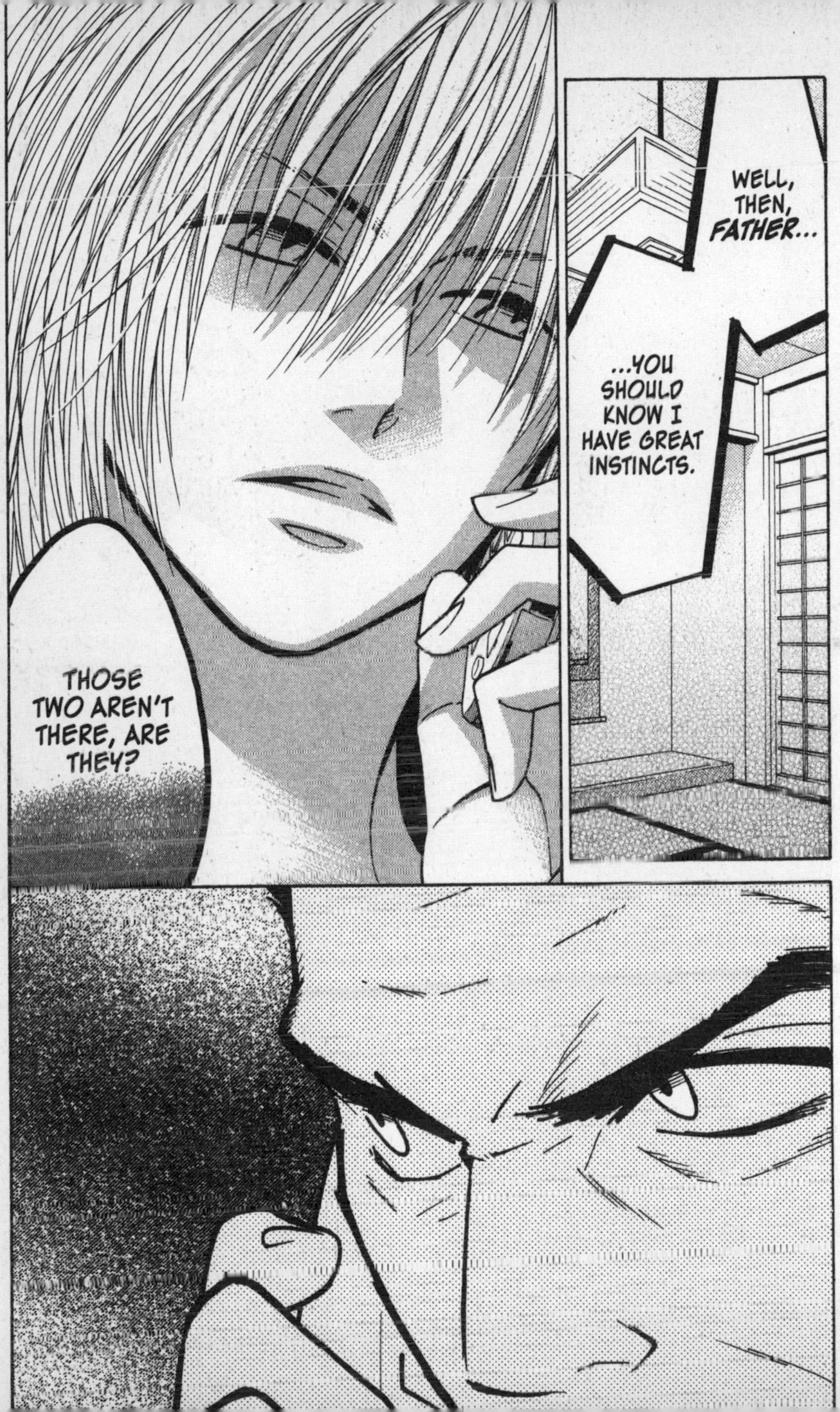
WELL, THEN, *FATHER*...
...YOU SHOULD KNOW I HAVE GREAT INSTINCTS.
THOSE TWO AREN'T THERE, ARE THEY?

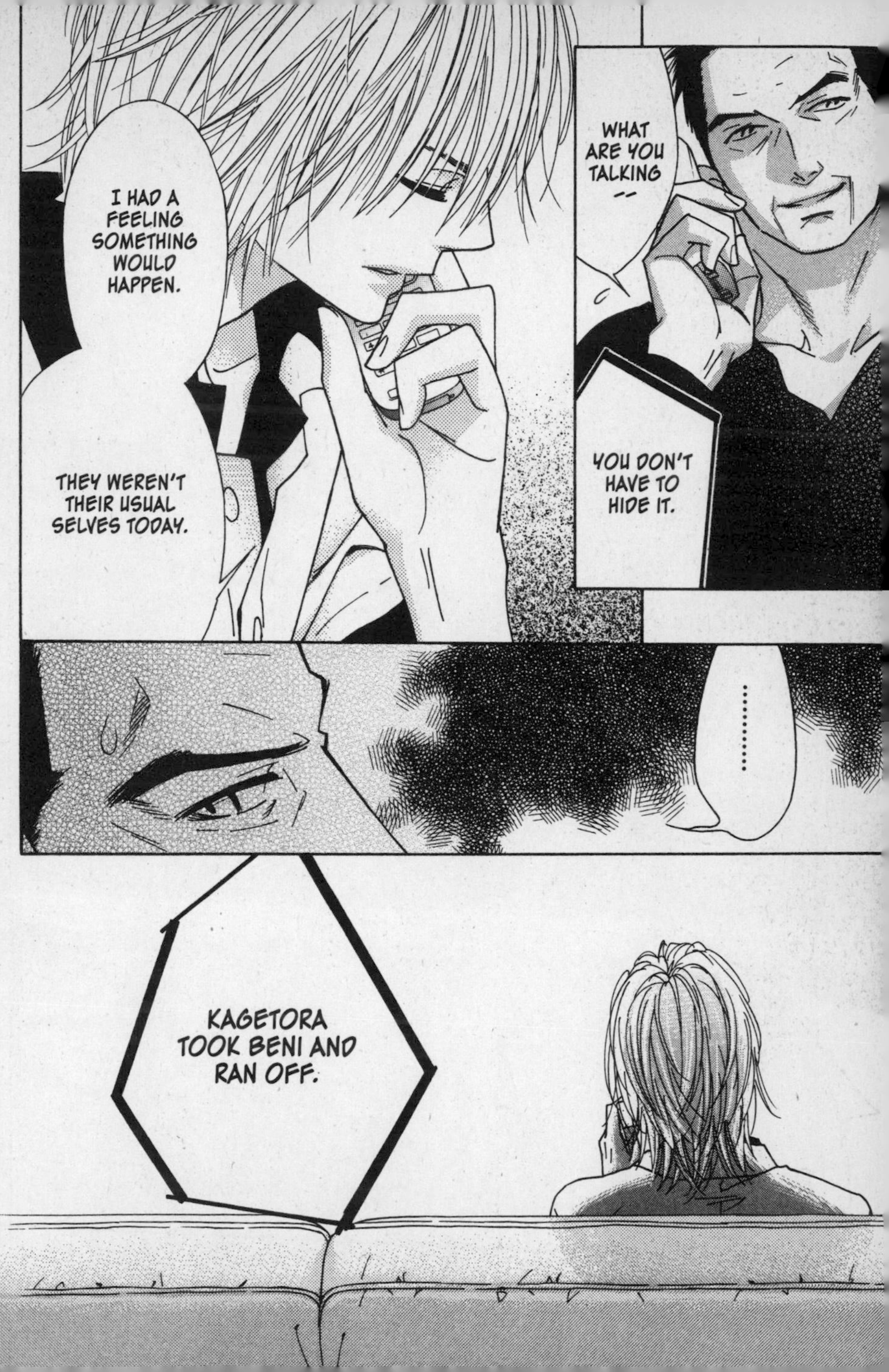
WHAT ARE YOU TALKING --
YOU DON'T HAVE TO HIDE IT.
I HAD A FEELING SOMETHING WOULD HAPPEN.
THEY WEREN'T THEIR USUAL SELVES TODAY.
....
KAGETORA TOOK BENI AND RAN OFF.

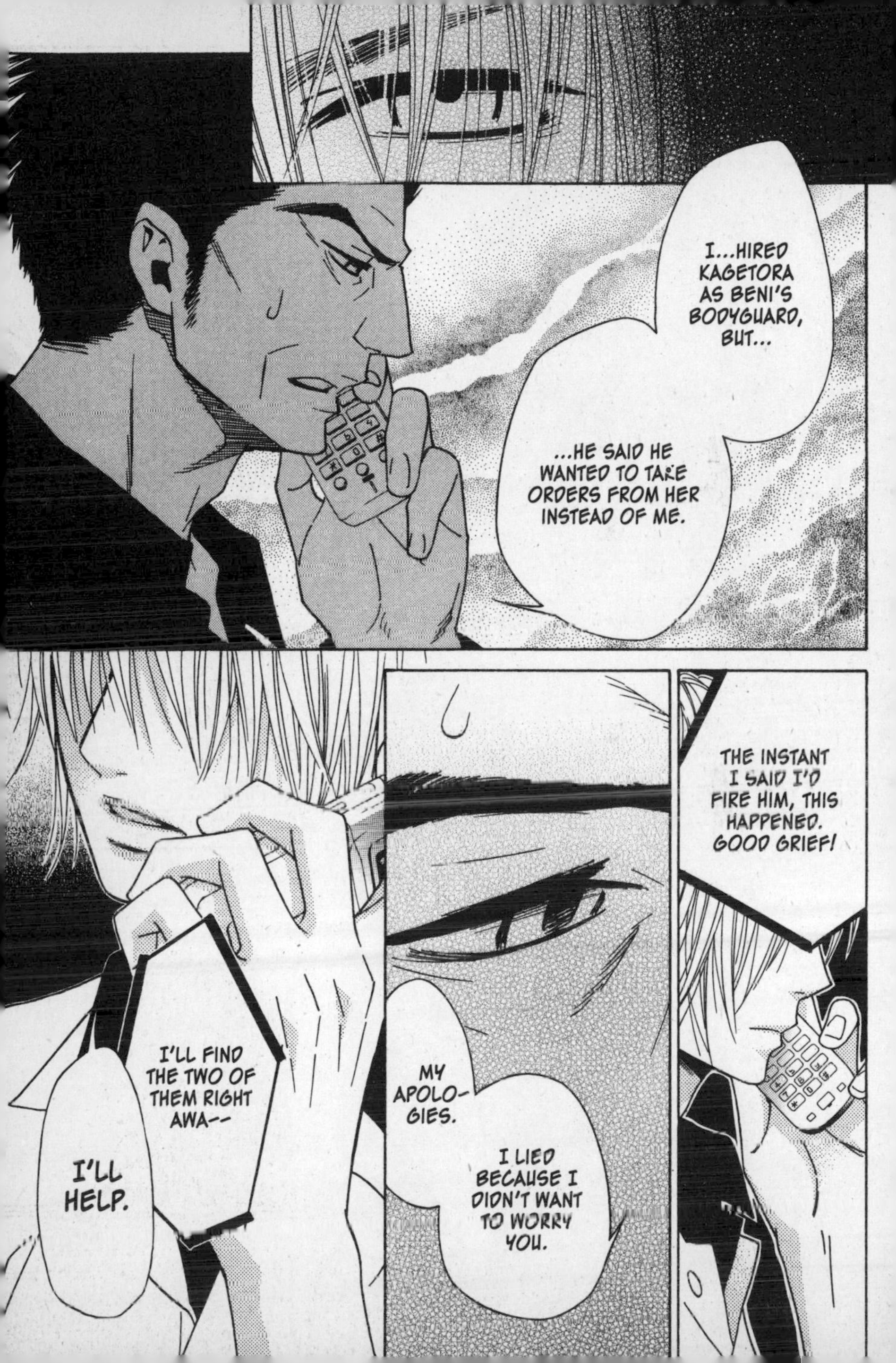

I...HIRED KAGETORA AS BENI'S BODYGUARD, BUT...
...HE SAID HE WANTED TO TAKE ORDERS FROM HER INSTEAD OF ME.
THE INSTANT I SAID I'D FIRE HIM, THIS HAPPENED. GOOD GRIEF!
MY APOLO-GIES.
I LIED BECAUSE I DIDN'T WANT TO WORRY YOU.
I'LL FIND THE TWO OF THEM RIGHT AWA--
I'LL HELP.

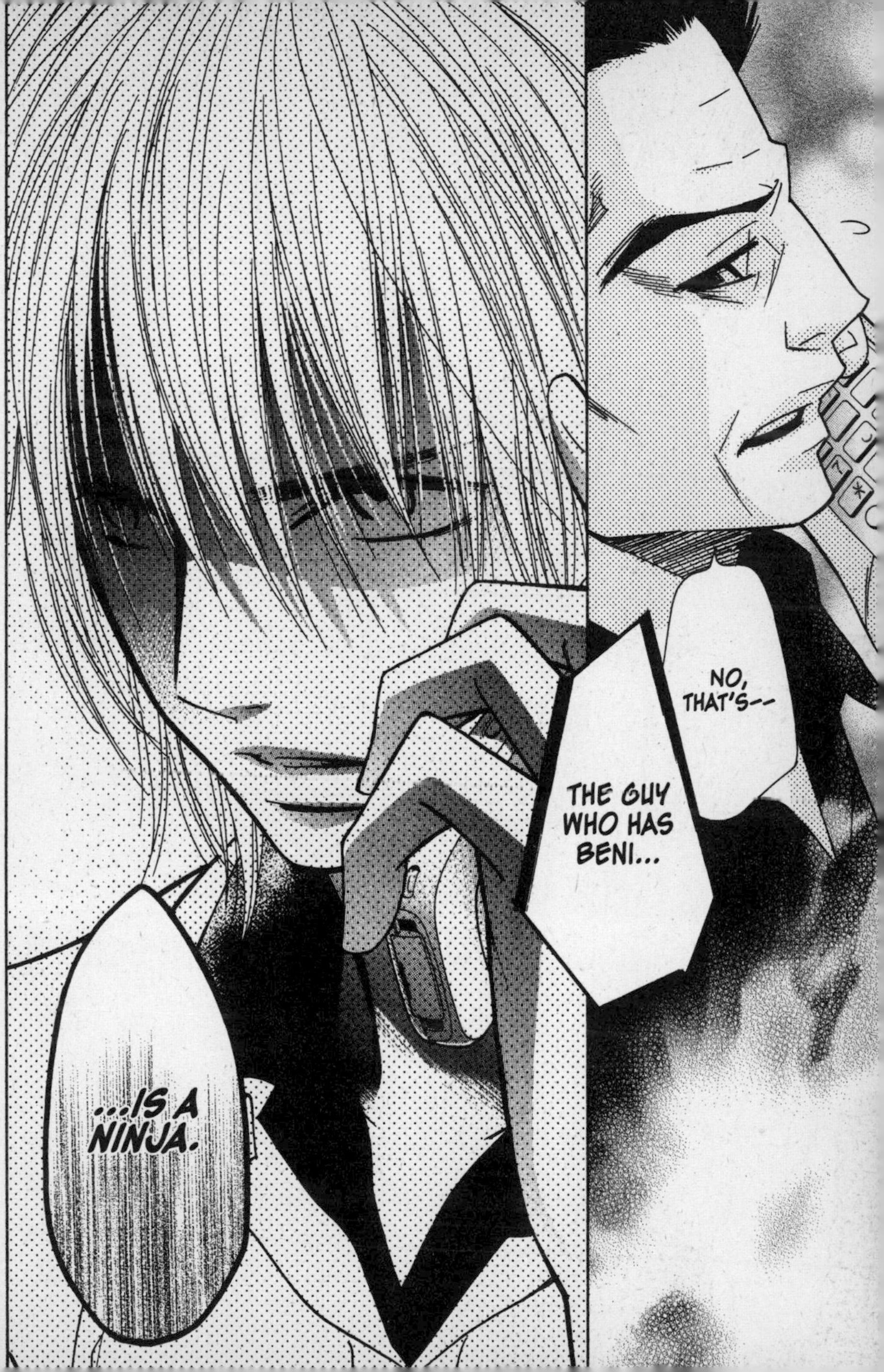
NO, THAT'S--
THE GUY WHO HAS BENI...
...IS A NINJA.

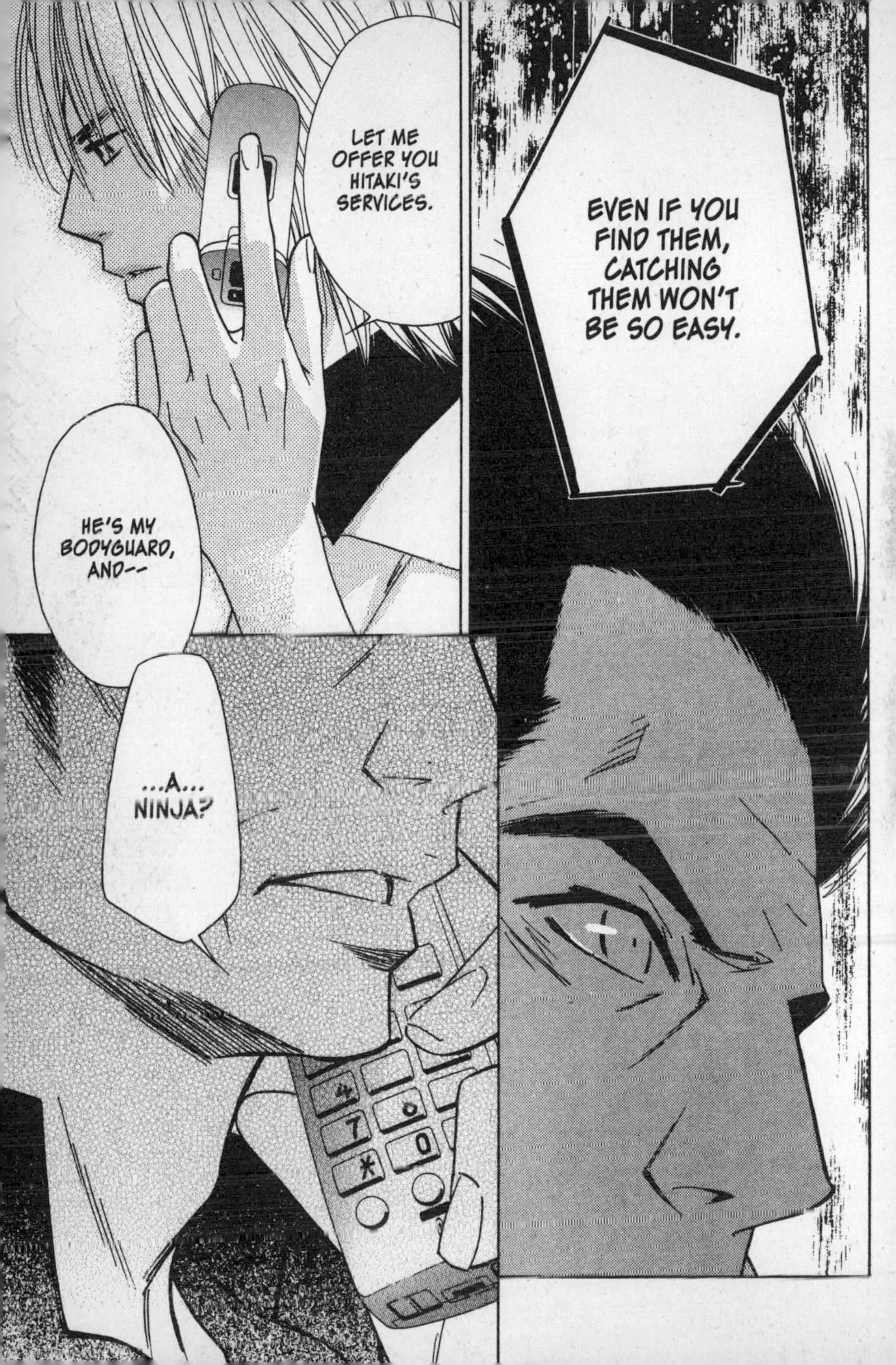
EVEN IF YOU FIND THEM, CATCHING THEM WON'T BE SO EASY.
LET ME OFFER YOU HITAKI'S SERVICES.
HE'S MY BODYGUARD, AND--
...A... NINJA?

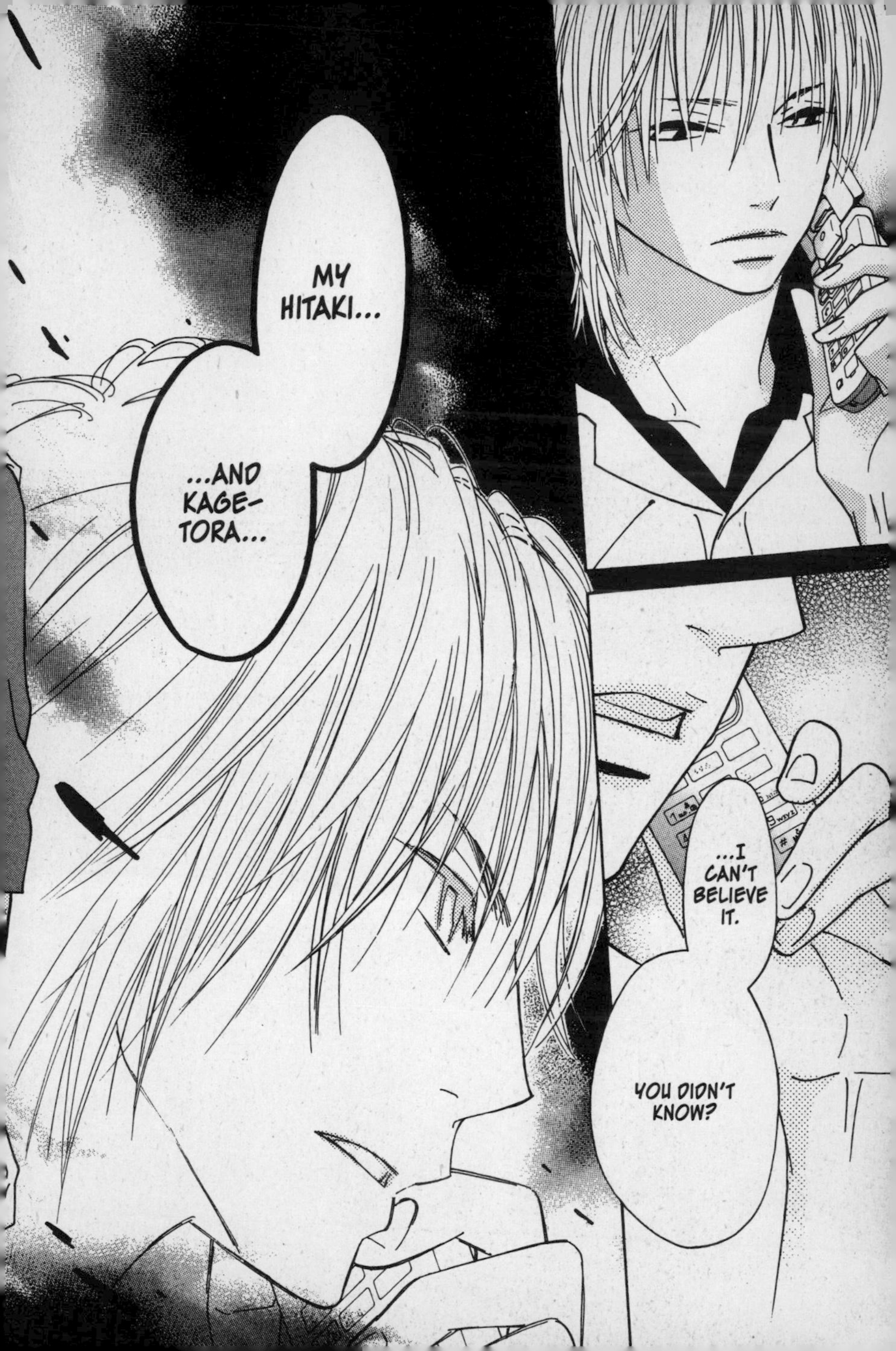
...I CAN'T BELIEVE IT.
YOU DIDN'T KNOW?
MY HITAKI...
...AND KAGE-TORA...

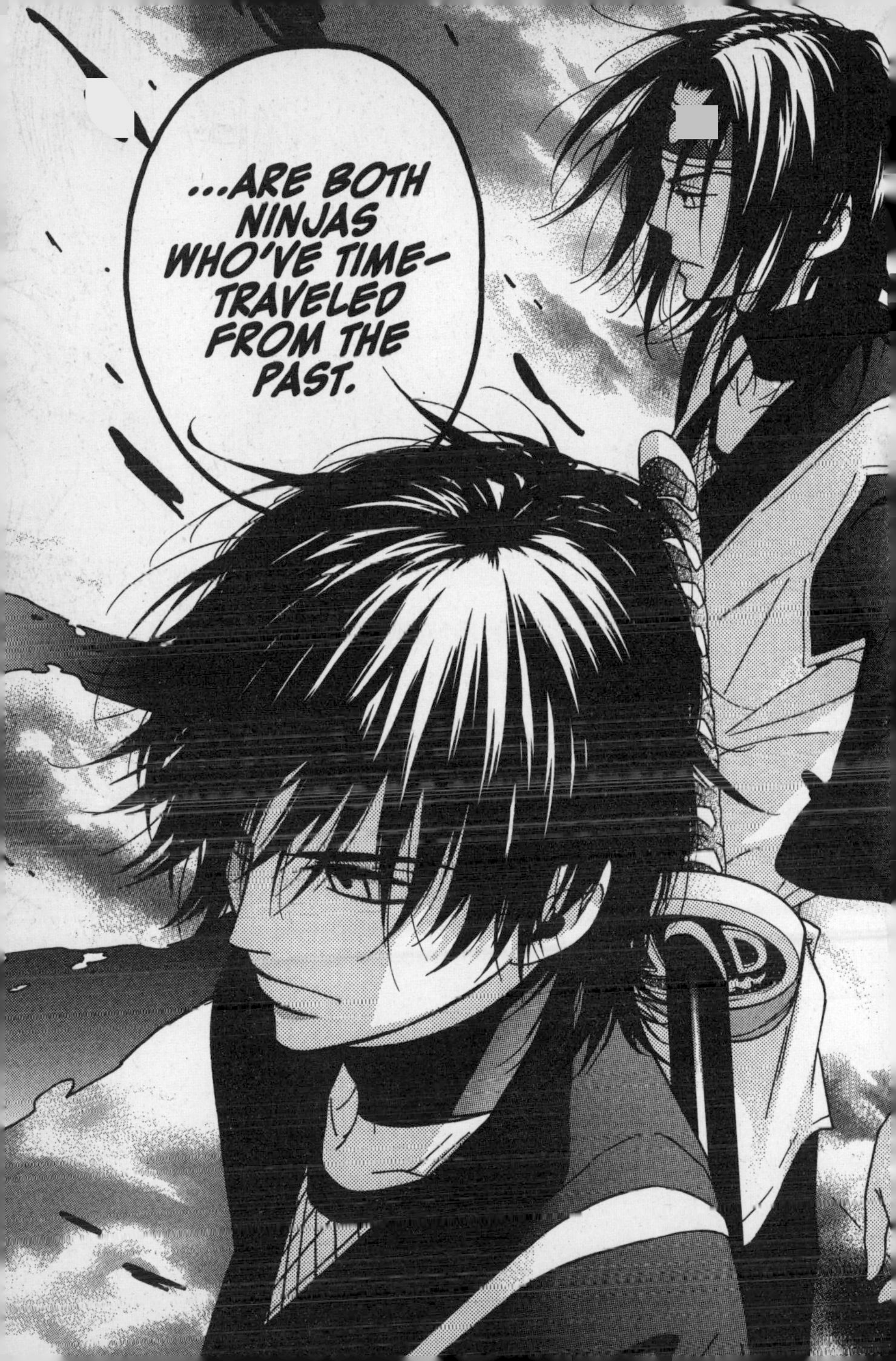
...ARE BOTH NINJAS WHO'VE TIME-TRAVELED FROM THE PAST.

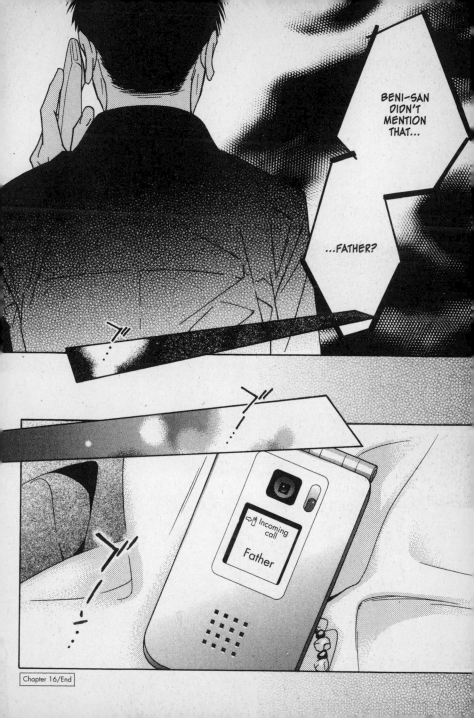

BENI-SAN DIDN'T MENTION THAT...

...FATHER?

Incoming call

Father

Chapter 16/End

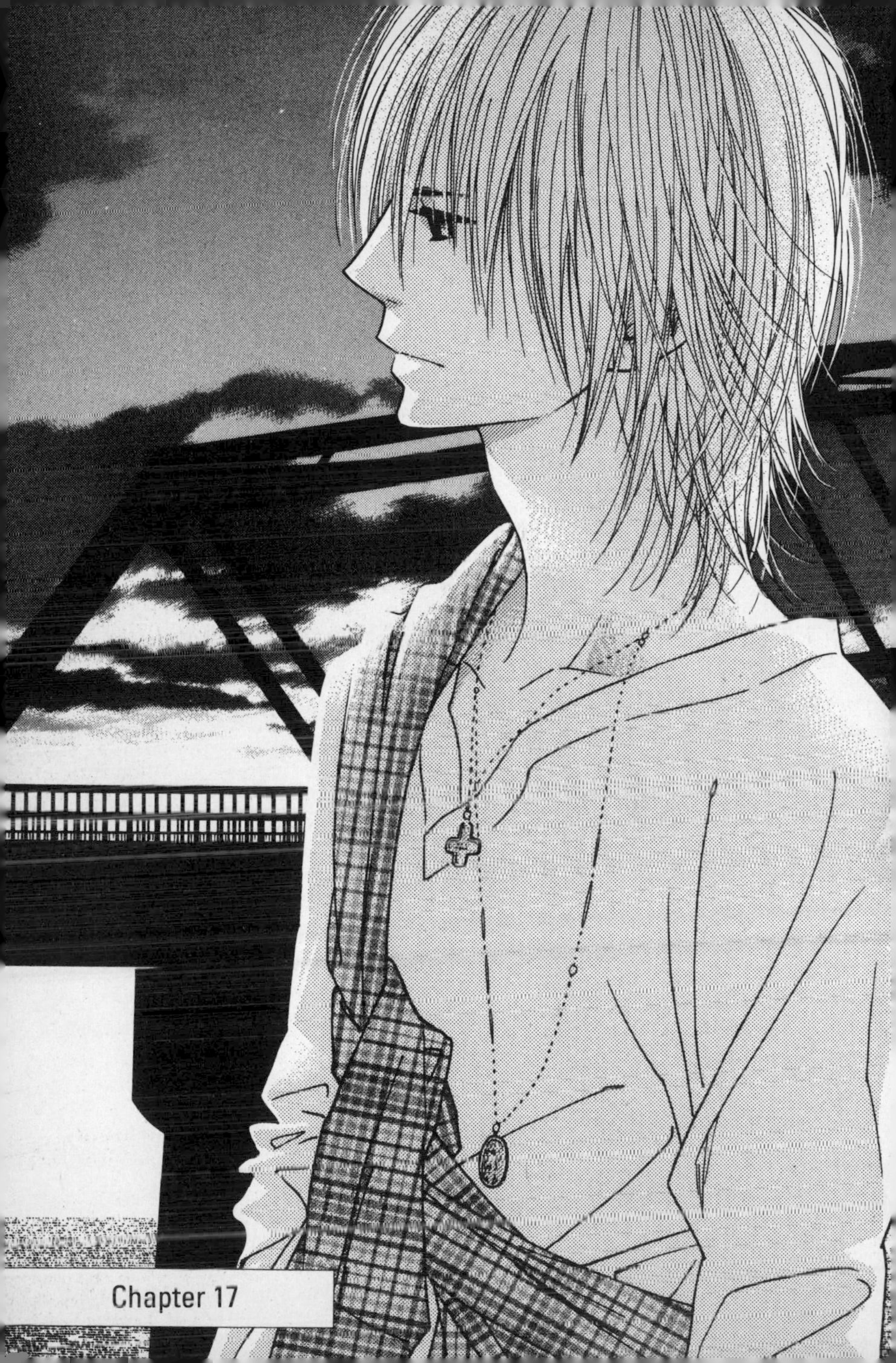

Chapter 17

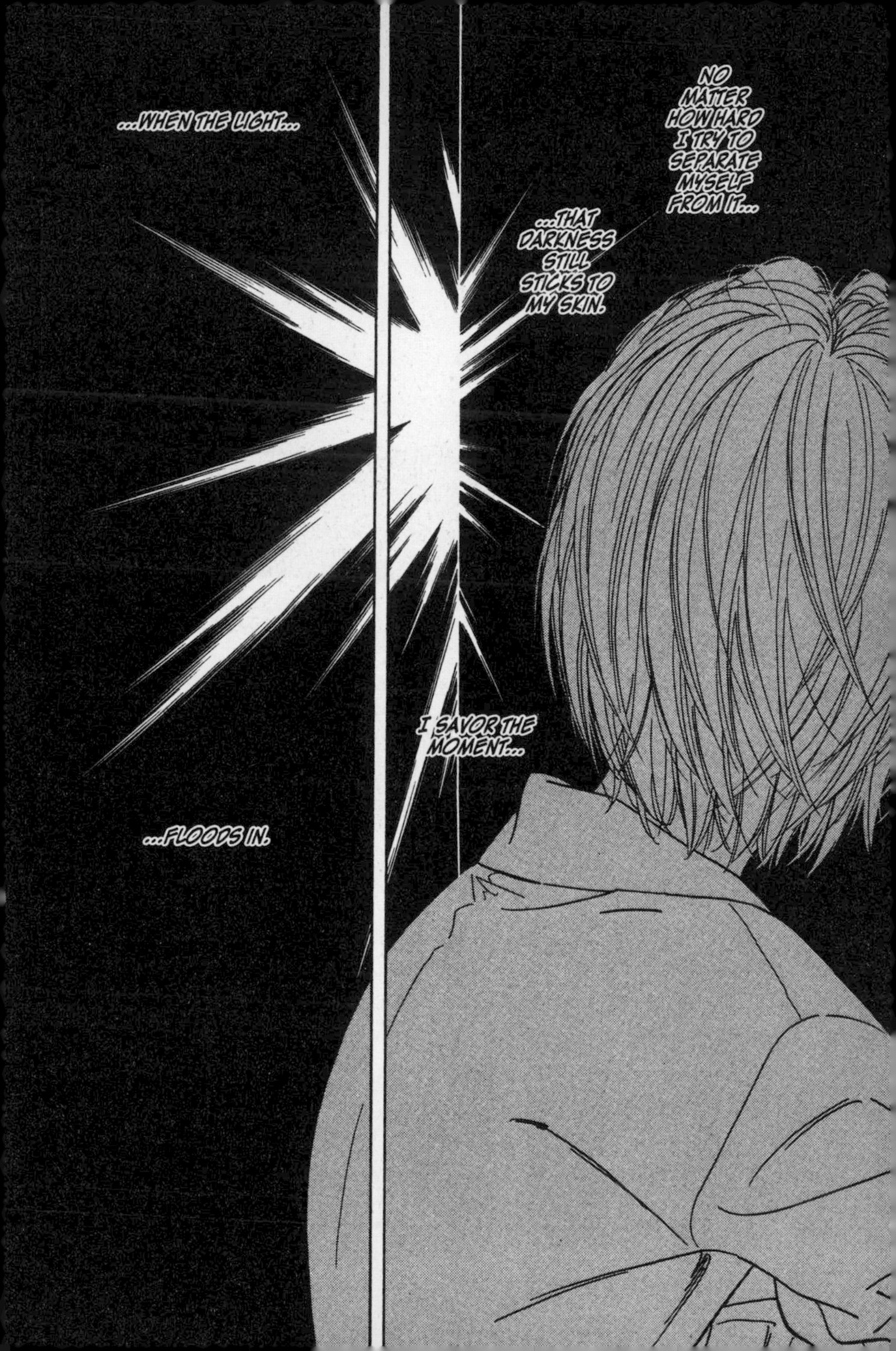
NO MATTER HOW HARD I TRY TO SEPARATE MYSELF FROM IT...
...THAT DARKNESS STILL STICKS TO MY SKIN.
I SAVOR THE MOMENT...
...WHEN THE LIGHT...
...FLOODS IN.

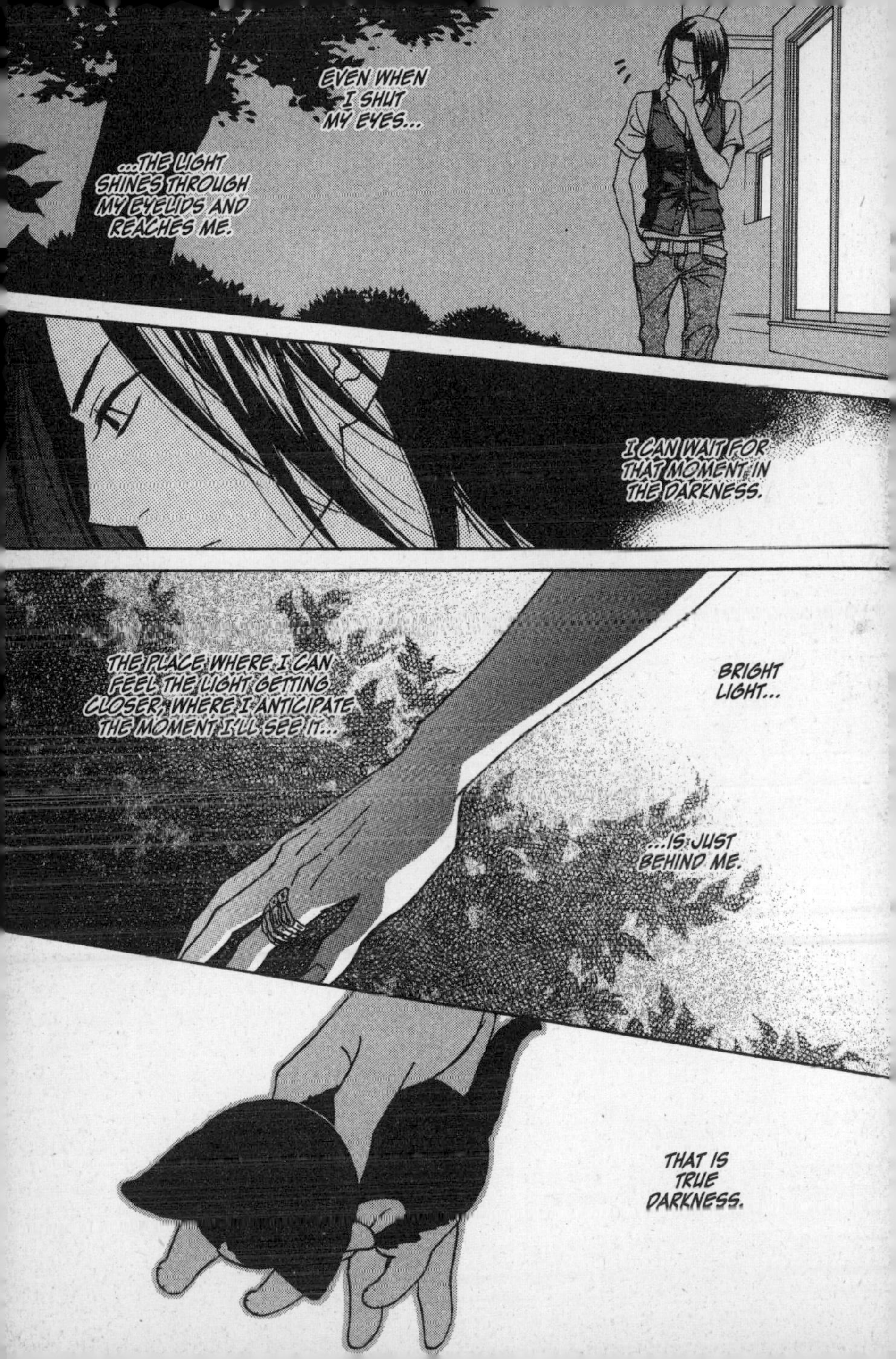
EVEN WHEN I SHUT MY EYES...
...THE LIGHT SHINES THROUGH MY EYELIDS AND REACHES ME.
I CAN WAIT FOR THAT MOMENT IN THE DARKNESS.
BRIGHT LIGHT...
...IS JUST BEHIND ME.
THE PLACE WHERE I CAN FEEL THE LIGHT GETTING CLOSER, WHERE I ANTICIPATE THE MOMENT I'LL SEE IT...
THAT IS TRUE DARKNESS.

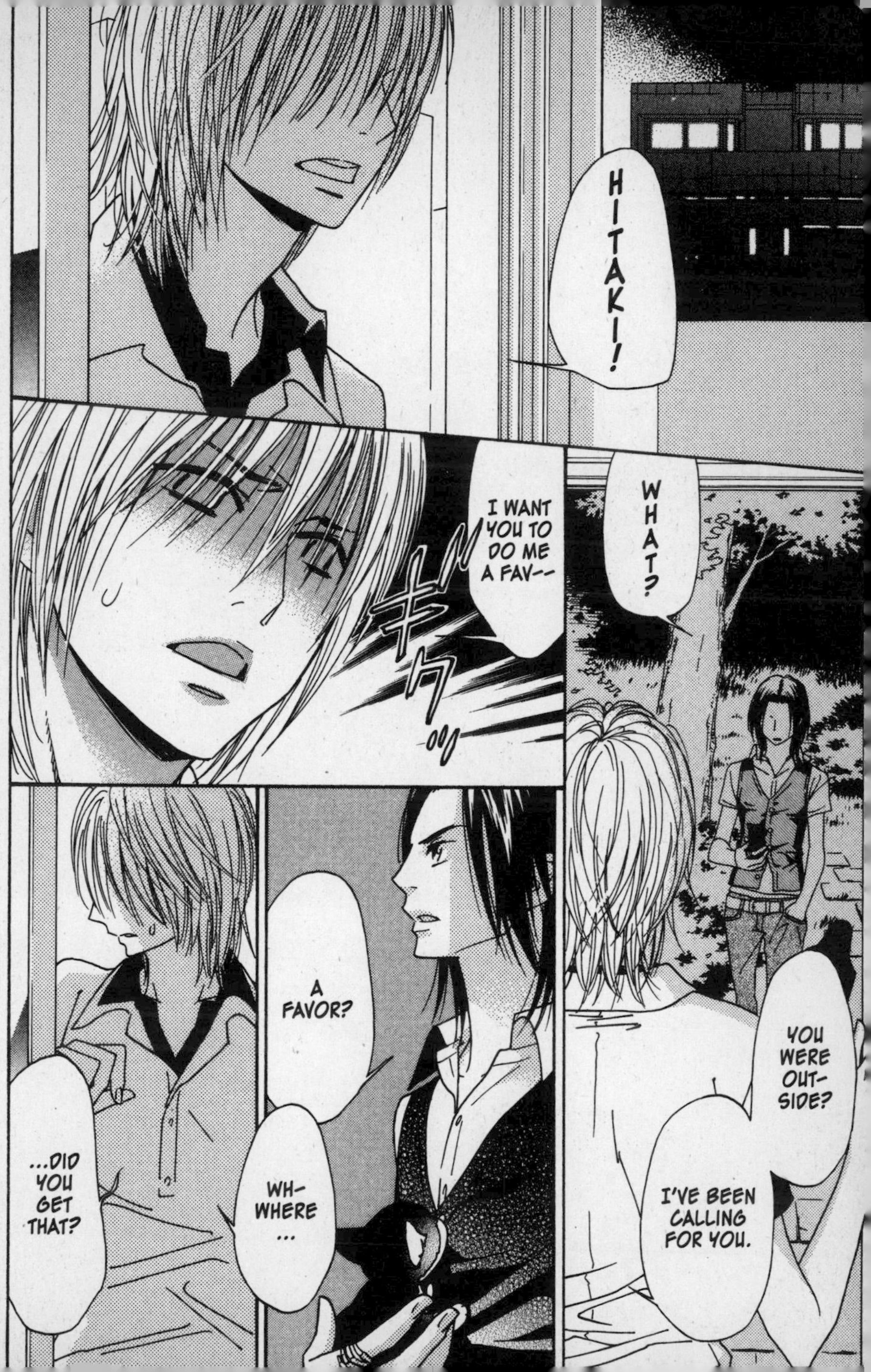
HITAKI!
WHAT?
YOU WERE OUT-SIDE?
I'VE BEEN CALLING FOR YOU.
I WANT YOU TO DO ME A FAV--
A FAVOR?
WH- WHERE ...
...DID YOU GET THAT?

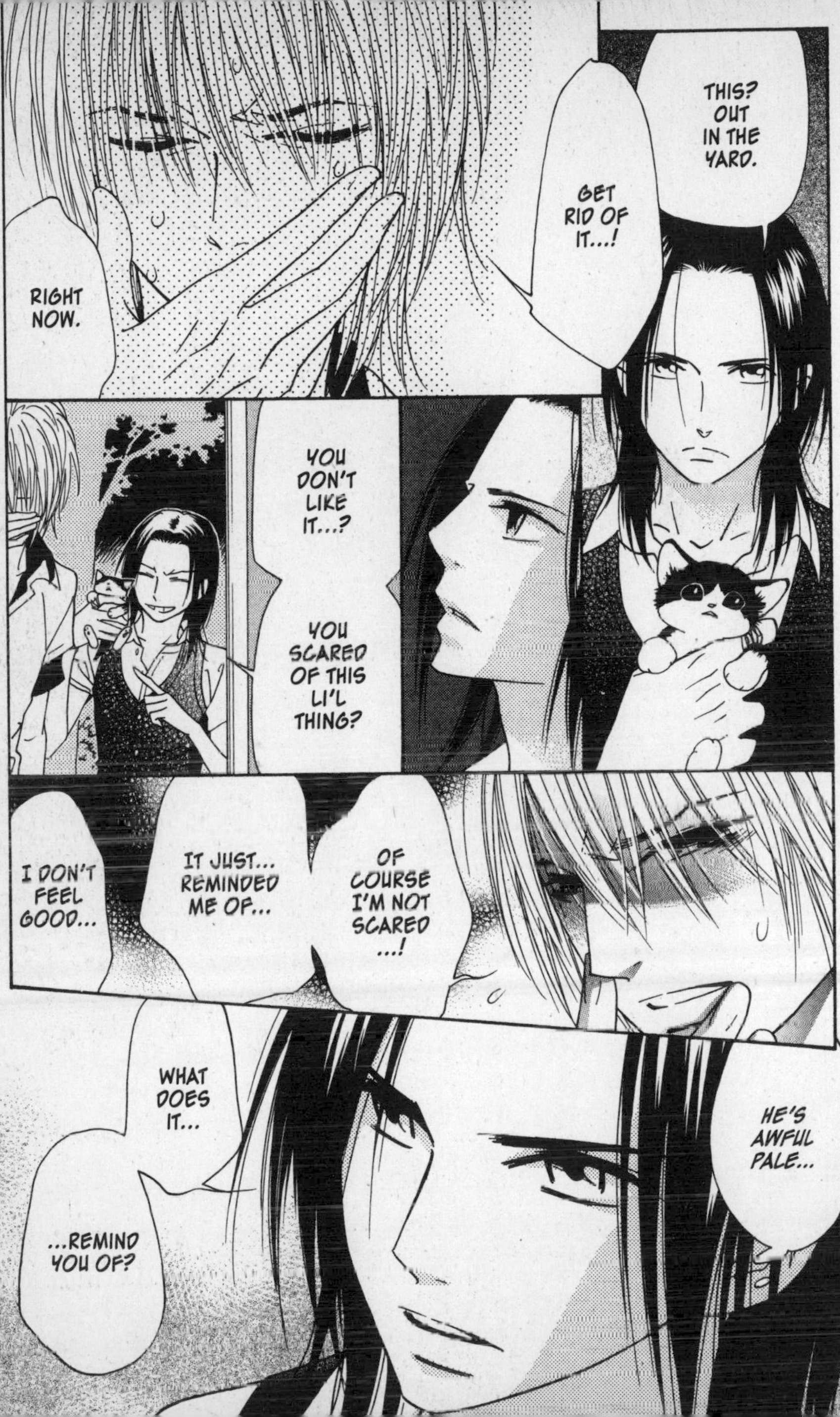
THIS? OUT IN THE YARD.
GET RID OF IT...!
RIGHT NOW.
YOU DON'T LIKE IT...?
YOU SCARED OF THIS LI'L THING?
OF COURSE I'M NOT SCARED ...!
IT JUST... REMINDED ME OF...
I DON'T FEEL GOOD...
HE'S AWFUL PALE...
WHAT DOES IT...
...REMIND YOU OF?

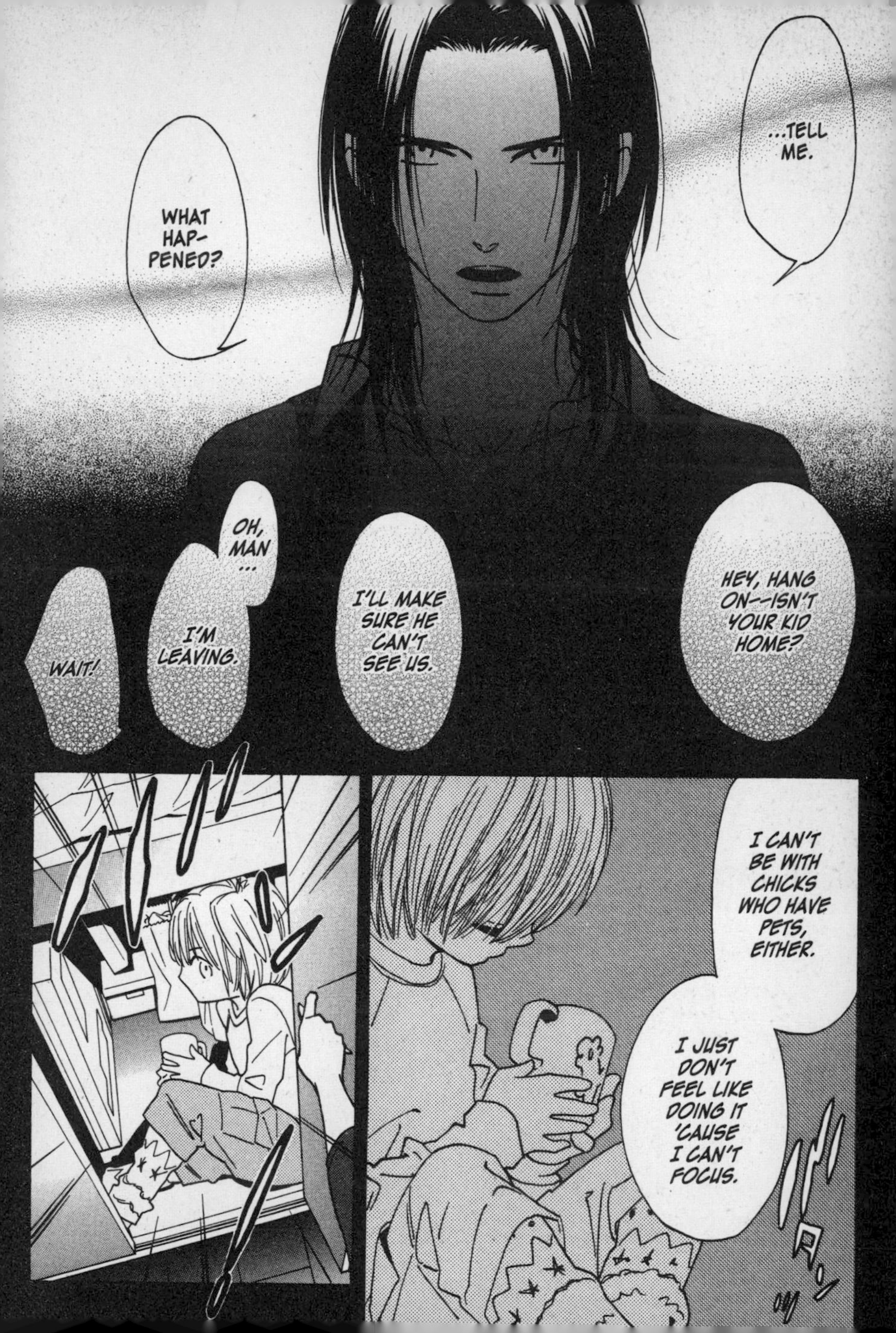
...TELL ME.
WHAT HAP-PENED?
HEY, HANG ON--ISN'T YOUR KID HOME?
I'LL MAKE SURE HE CAN'T SEE US.
OH, MAN ...
I'M LEAVING.
WAIT!
I CAN'T BE WITH CHICKS WHO HAVE PETS, EITHER.
I JUST DON'T FEEL LIKE DOING IT 'CAUSE I CAN'T FOCUS.

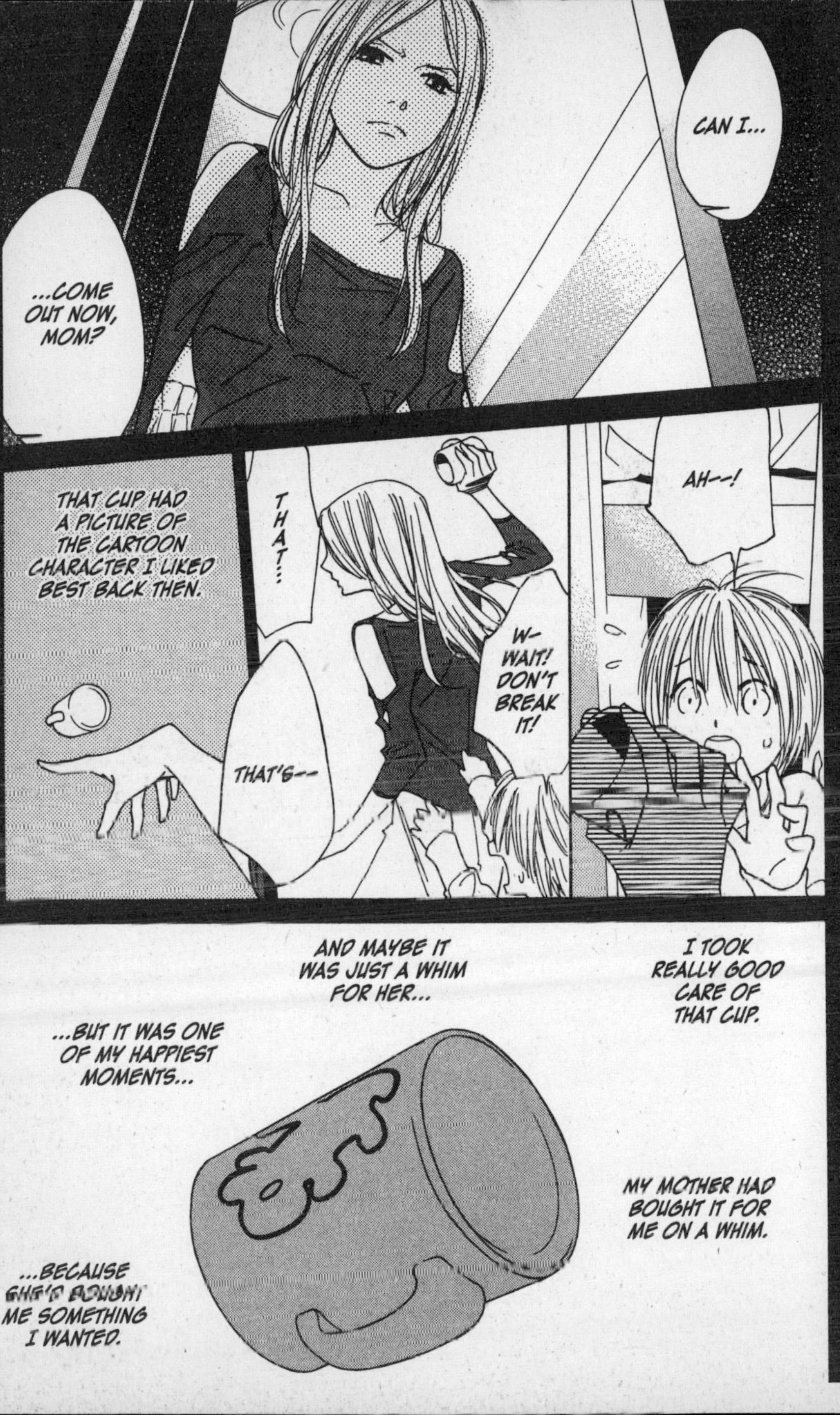
CAN I...
...COME OUT NOW, MOM?
AH--!
W-WAIT! DON'T BREAK IT!
THAT...
THAT CUP HAD A PICTURE OF THE CARTOON CHARACTER I LIKED BEST BACK THEN.
THAT'S--
I TOOK REALLY GOOD CARE OF THAT CUP.
AND MAYBE IT WAS JUST A WHIM FOR HER...
...BUT IT WAS ONE OF MY HAPPIEST MOMENTS...
MY MOTHER HAD BOUGHT IT FOR ME ON A WHIM.
...BECAUSE SHE'S BOUGHT ME SOMETHING I WANTED.

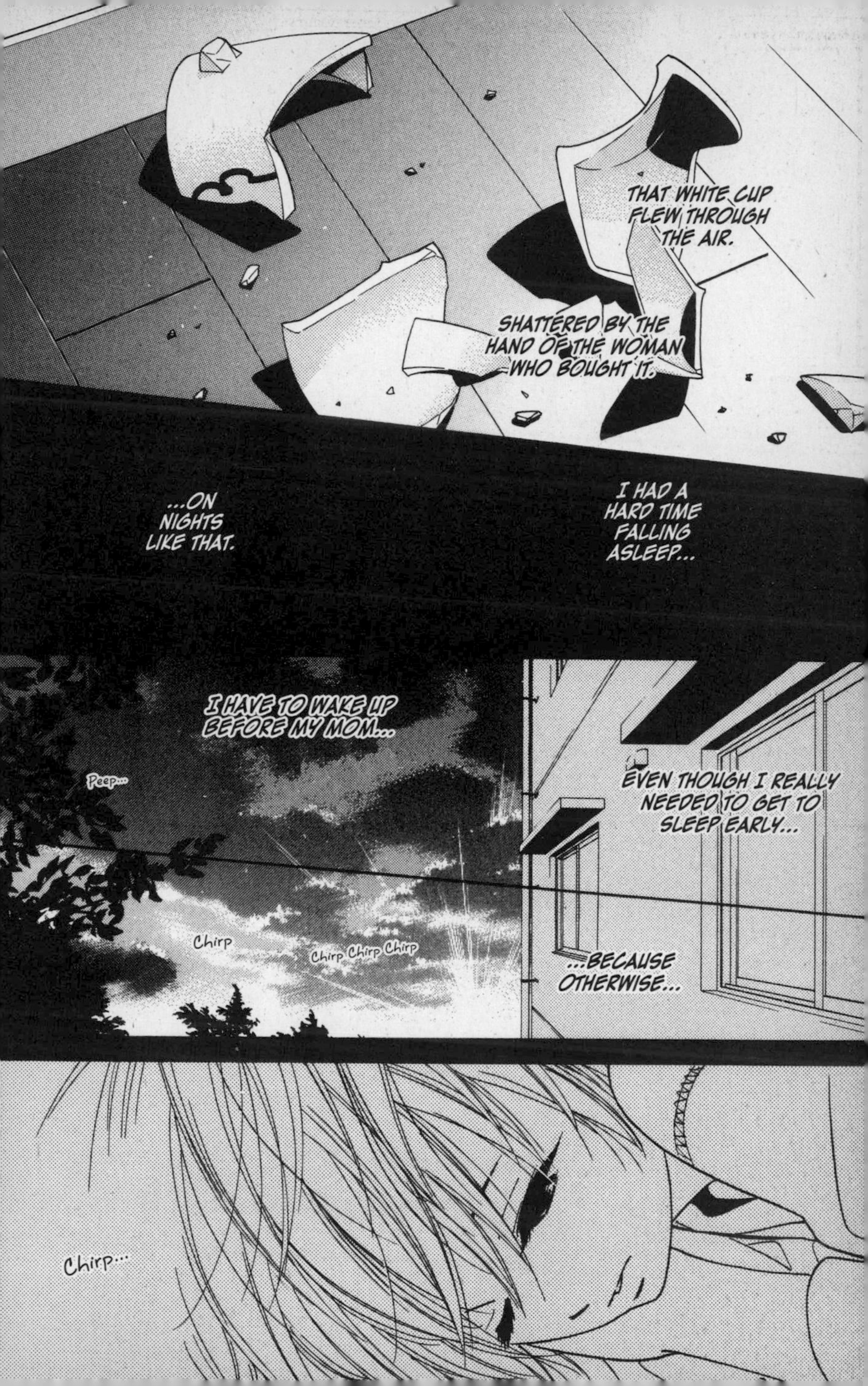
THAT WHITE CUP FLEW THROUGH THE AIR.
SHATTERED BY THE HAND OF THE WOMAN WHO BOUGHT IT.
I HAD A HARD TIME FALLING ASLEEP...
...ON NIGHTS LIKE THAT.
EVEN THOUGH I REALLY NEEDED TO GET TO SLEEP EARLY...
...BECAUSE OTHERWISE...
I HAVE TO WAKE UP BEFORE MY MOM...
Peep...
Chirp
Chirp Chirp Chirp
Chirp...

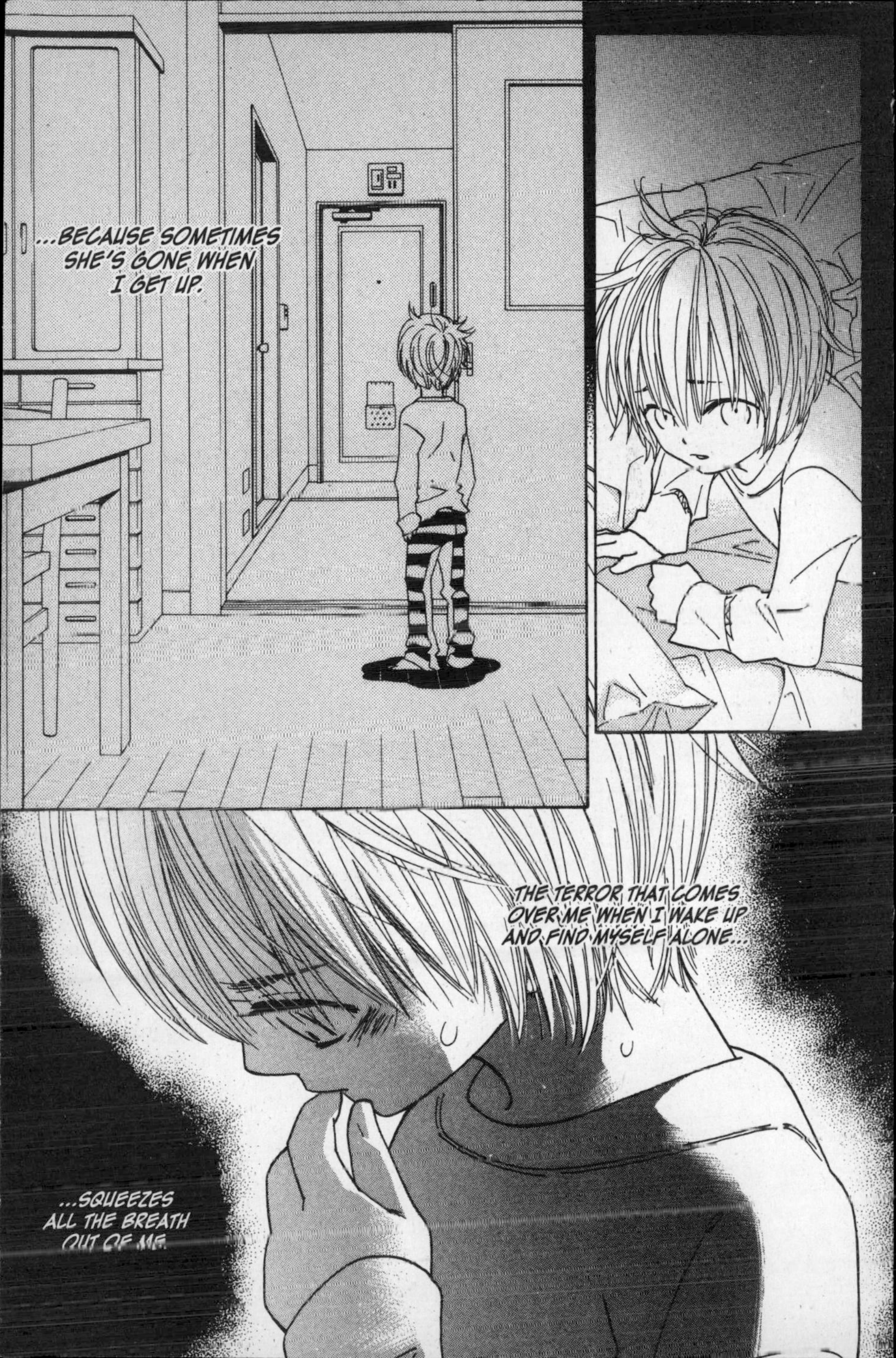
...BECAUSE SOMETIMES SHE'S GONE WHEN I GET UP.
THE TERROR THAT COMES OVER ME WHEN I WAKE UP AND FIND MYSELF ALONE...
...SQUEEZES ALL THE BREATH OUT OF ME.

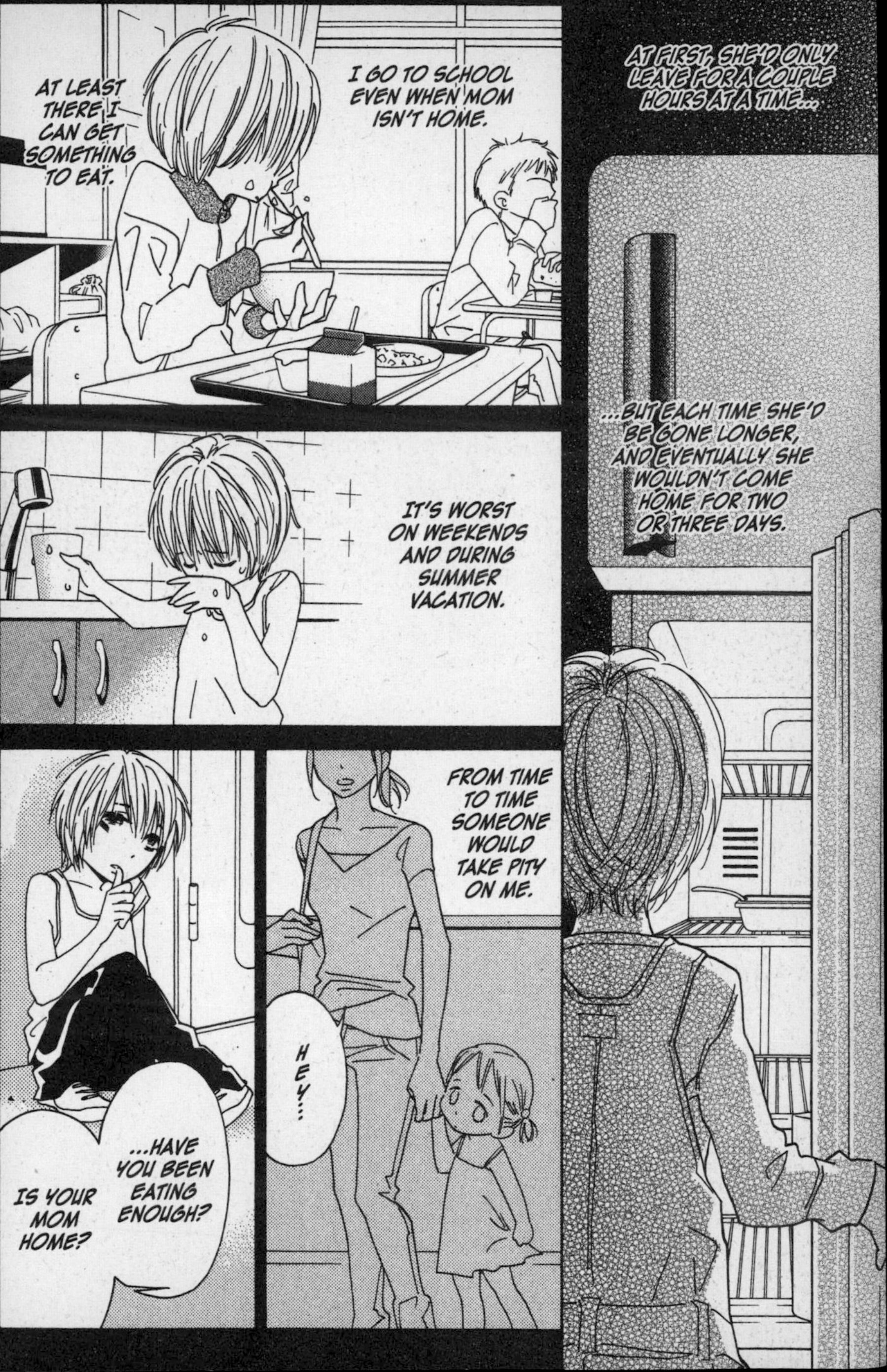
AT FIRST, SHE'D ONLY LEAVE FOR A COUPLE HOURS AT A TIME...
...BUT EACH TIME SHE'D BE GONE LONGER, AND EVENTUALLY SHE WOULDN'T COME HOME FOR TWO OR THREE DAYS.
I GO TO SCHOOL EVEN WHEN MOM ISN'T HOME.
AT LEAST THERE I CAN GET SOMETHING TO EAT.
IT'S WORST ON WEEKENDS AND DURING SUMMER VACATION.
FROM TIME TO TIME SOMEONE WOULD TAKE PITY ON ME.
HEY...
...HAVE YOU BEEN EATING ENOUGH?
IS YOUR MOM HOME?

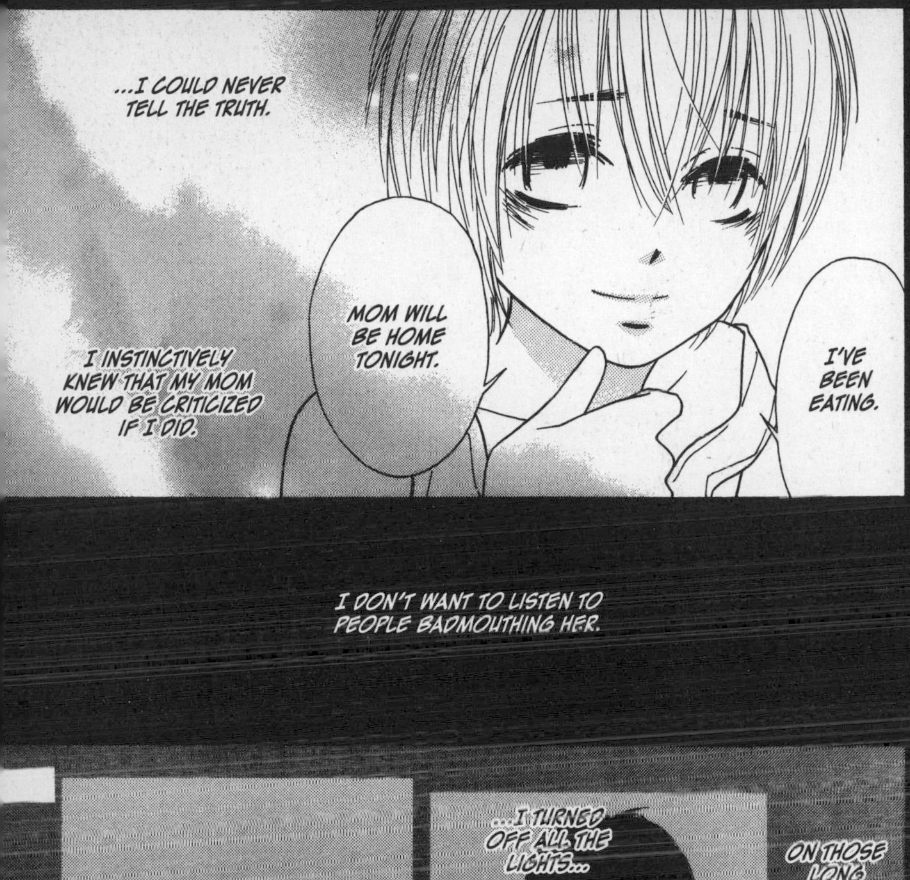

...I COULD NEVER TELL THE TRUTH.
I'VE BEEN EATING.
MOM WILL BE HOME TONIGHT.
I INSTINCTIVELY KNEW THAT MY MOM WOULD BE CRITICIZED IF I DID.
I DON'T WANT TO LISTEN TO PEOPLE BADMOUTHING HER.
ON THOSE LONG NIGHTS WHEN MY EMPTY STOMACH KEPT ME AWAKE...
...I TURNED OFF ALL THE LIGHTS...
...SO THAT EVERYTHING WAS COMPLETELY DARK...
...JUST LIKE THE INSIDE OF THAT CLOSET.

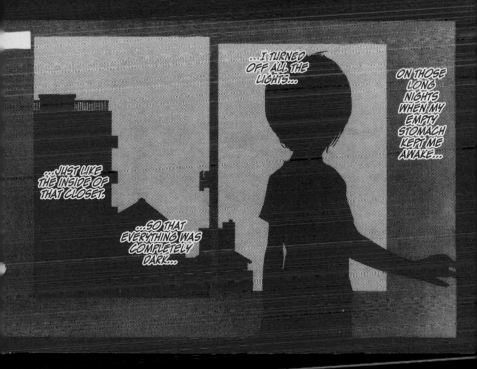

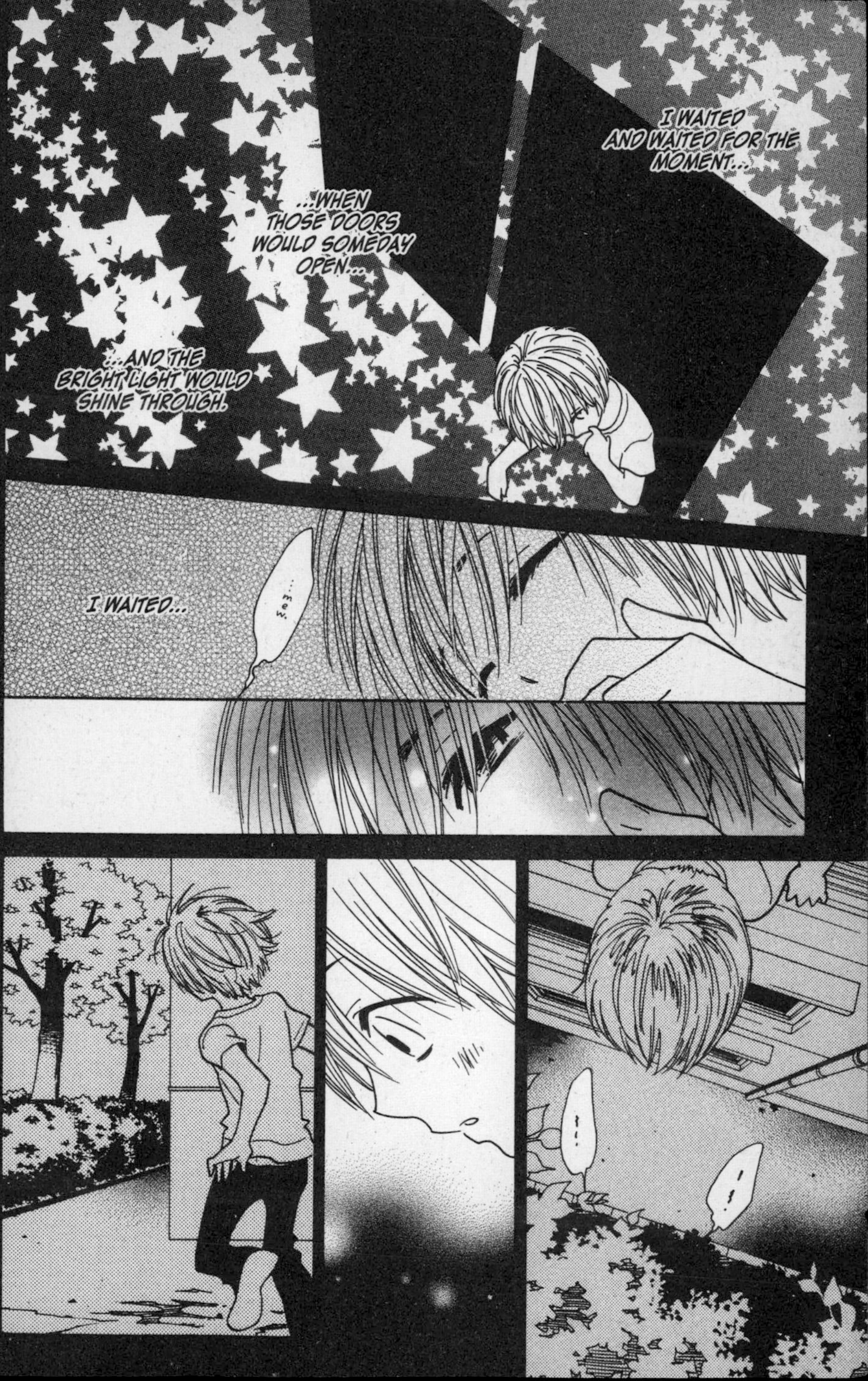
I WAITED AND WAITED FOR THE MOMENT...
...WHEN THOSE DOORS WOULD SOMEDAY OPEN...
...AND THE BRIGHT LIGHT WOULD SHINE THROUGH.
I WAITED...
...mew.
!!
!!

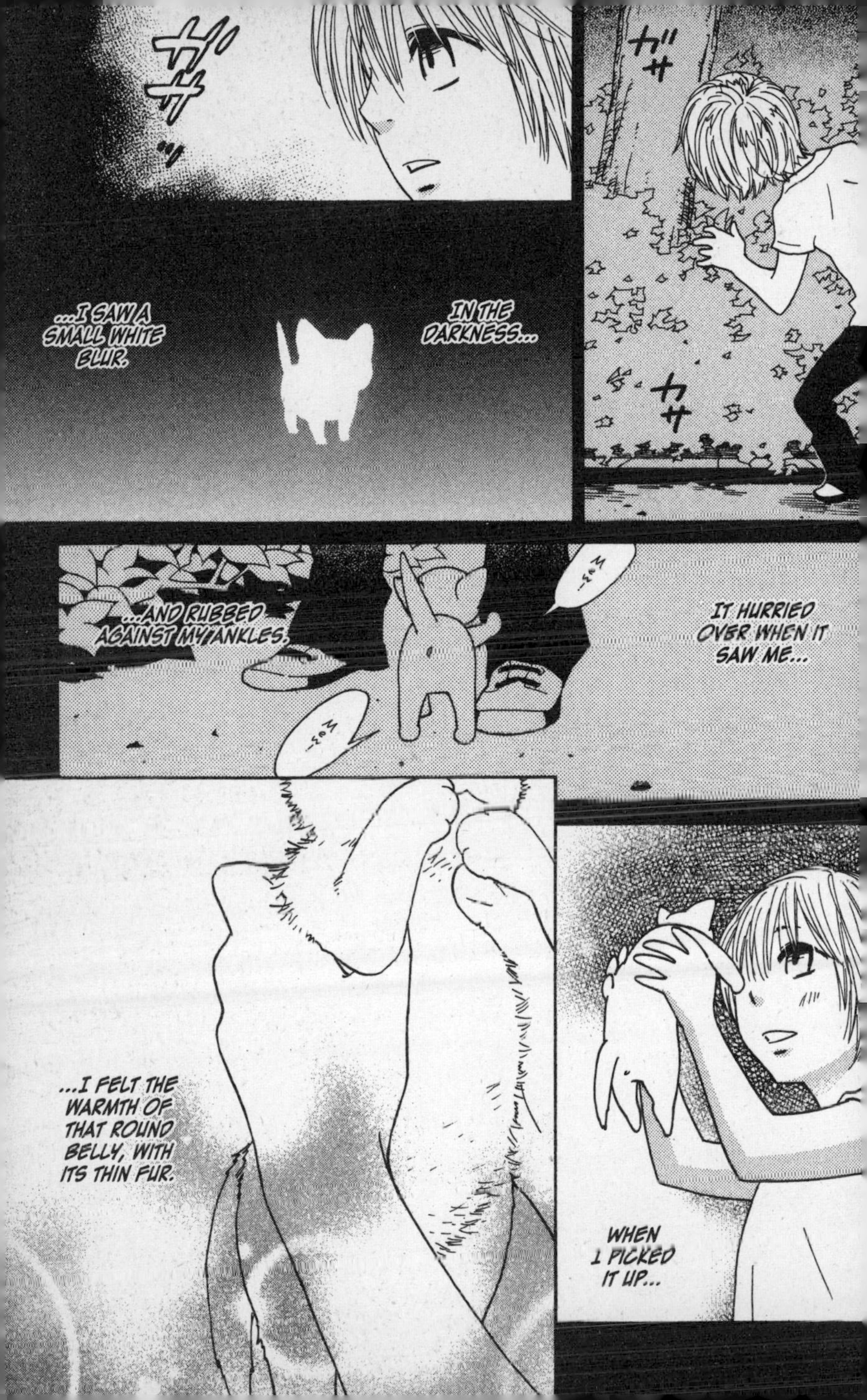
IN THE DARKNESS...
...I SAW A SMALL WHITE BLUR.
IT HURRIED OVER WHEN IT SAW ME...
Mew-
...AND RUBBED AGAINST MY ANKLES.
Mew-
WHEN I PICKED IT UP...
...I FELT THE WARMTH OF THAT ROUND BELLY, WITH ITS THIN FUR.

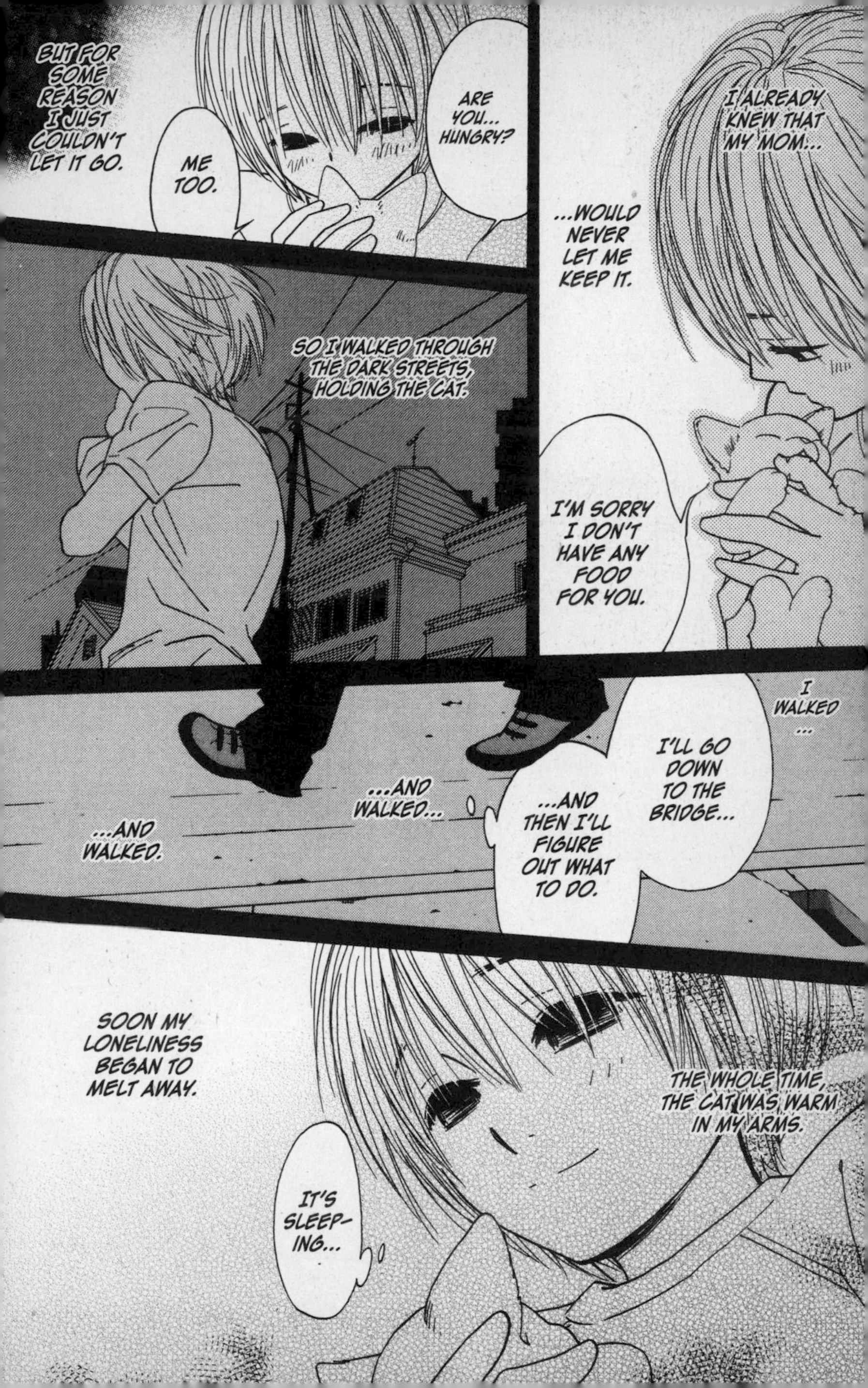
I ALREADY KNEW THAT MY MOM...
...WOULD NEVER LET ME KEEP IT.
I'M SORRY I DON'T HAVE ANY FOOD FOR YOU.
ARE YOU... HUNGRY?
ME TOO.
BUT FOR SOME REASON I JUST COULDN'T LET IT GO.
SO I WALKED THROUGH THE DARK STREETS, HOLDING THE CAT.
I WALKED...
I'LL GO DOWN TO THE BRIDGE...
...AND THEN I'LL FIGURE OUT WHAT TO DO.
...AND WALKED...
...AND WALKED.
THE WHOLE TIME, THE CAT WAS WARM IN MY ARMS.
SOON MY LONELINESS BEGAN TO MELT AWAY.
IT'S SLEEP-ING...

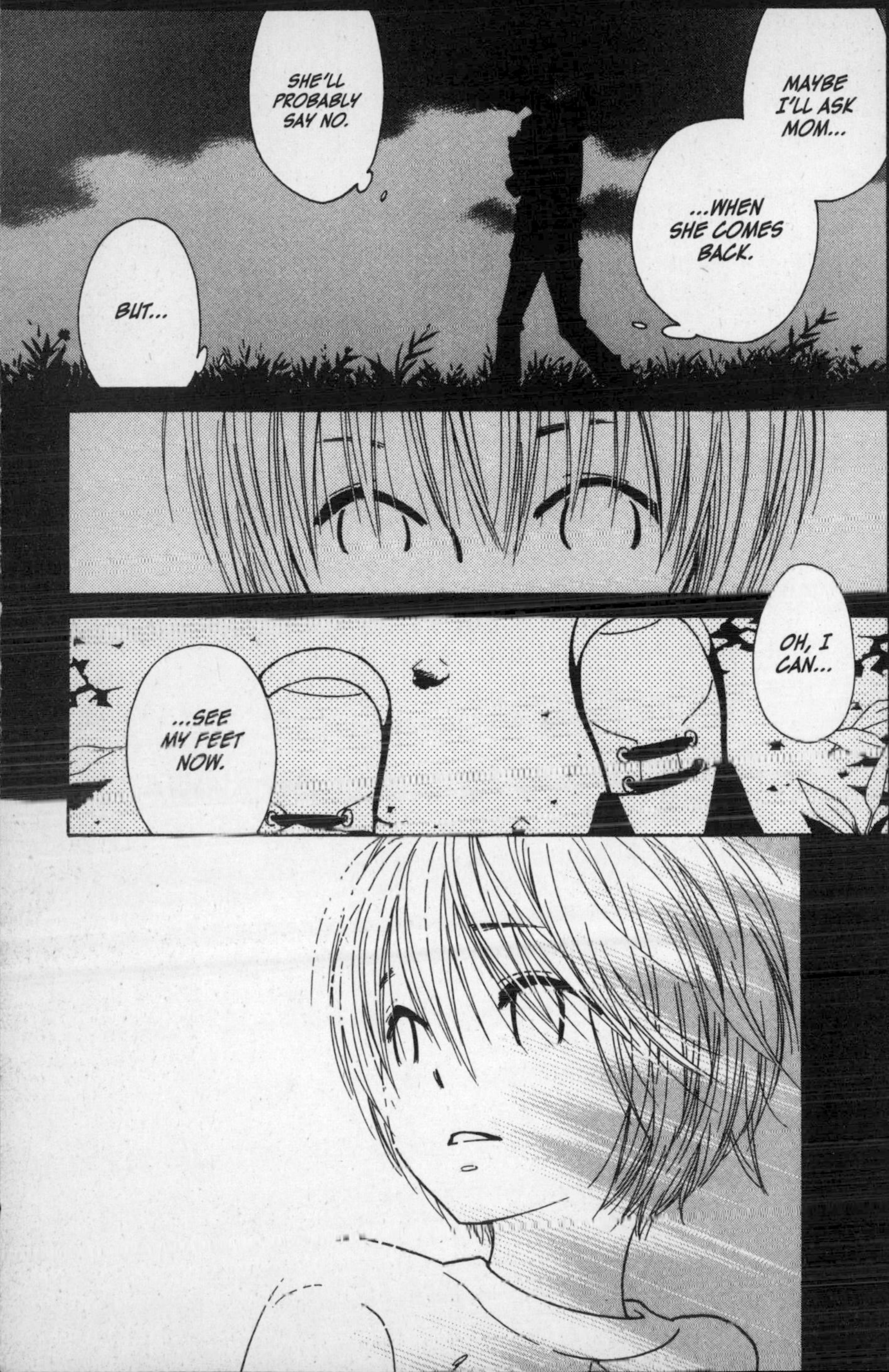
MAYBE I'LL ASK MOM...
...WHEN SHE COMES BACK.
SHE'LL PROBABLY SAY NO.
BUT...
OH, I CAN...
...SEE MY FEET NOW.

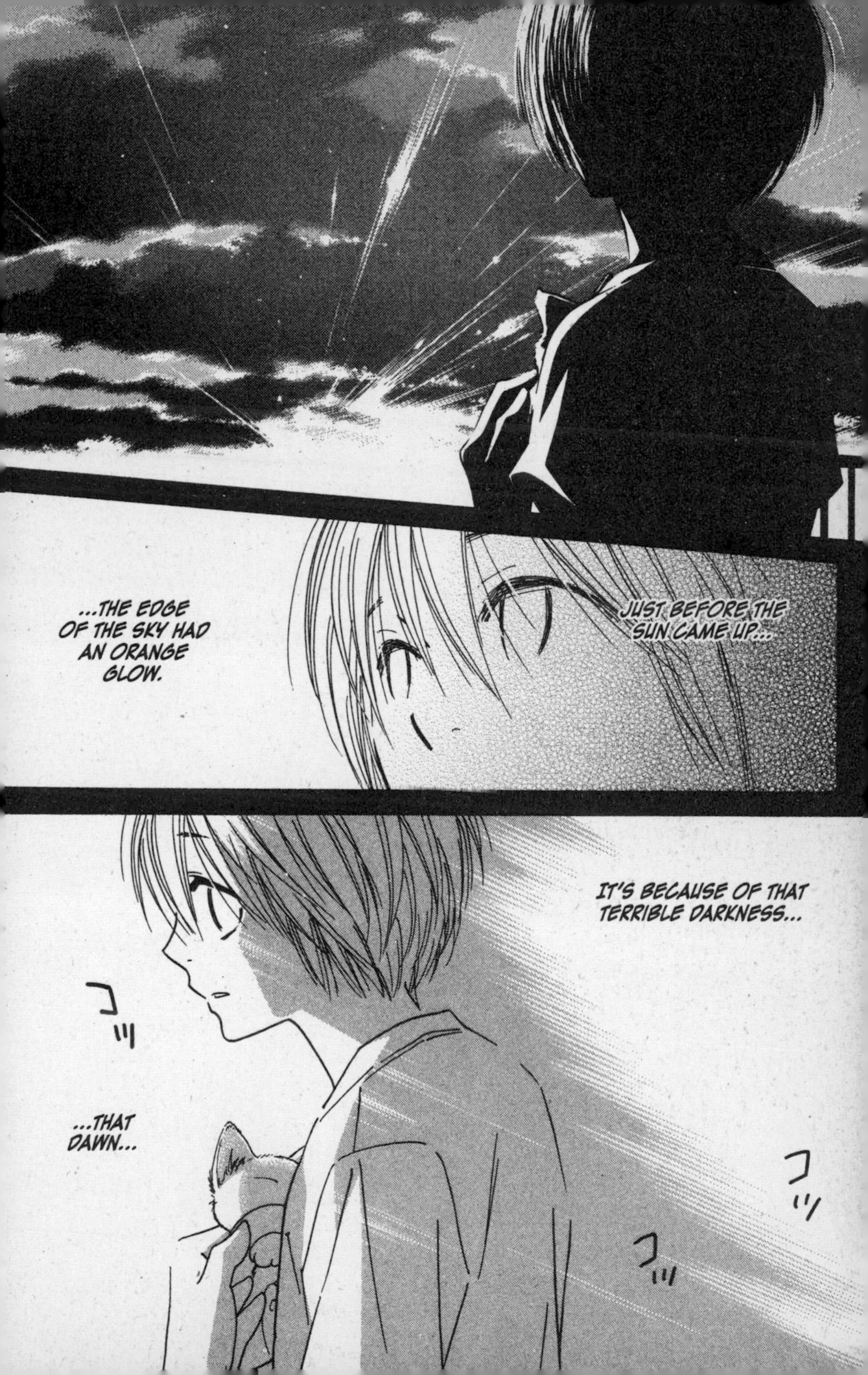
JUST BEFORE THE SUN CAME UP...
...THE EDGE OF THE SKY HAD AN ORANGE GLOW.
IT'S BECAUSE OF THAT TERRIBLE DARKNESS...
コッ
コッ
...THAT DAWN...
コッ

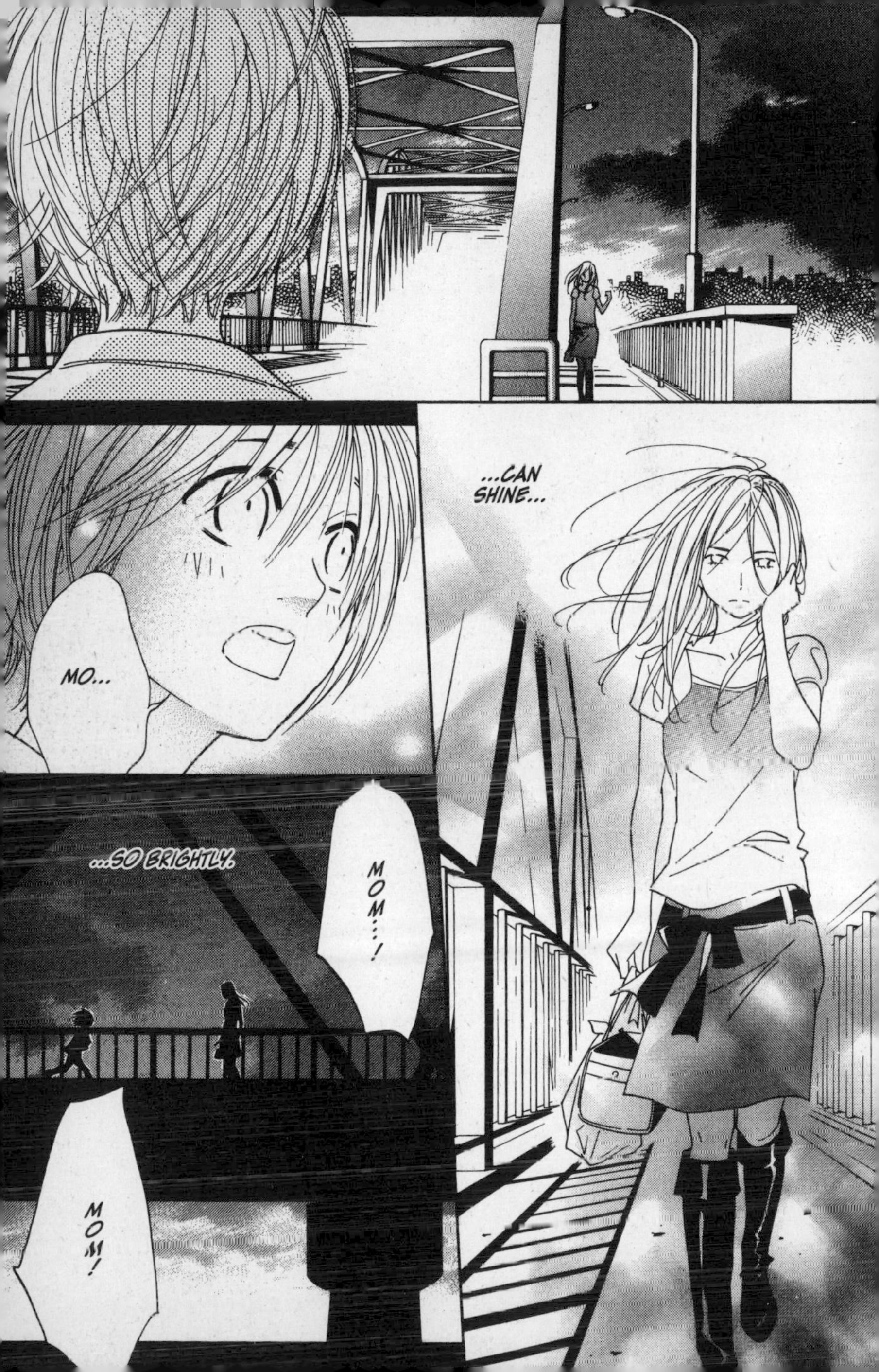
...CAN SHINE...
MO...
MOM...!
...SO BRIGHTLY.
MOM!

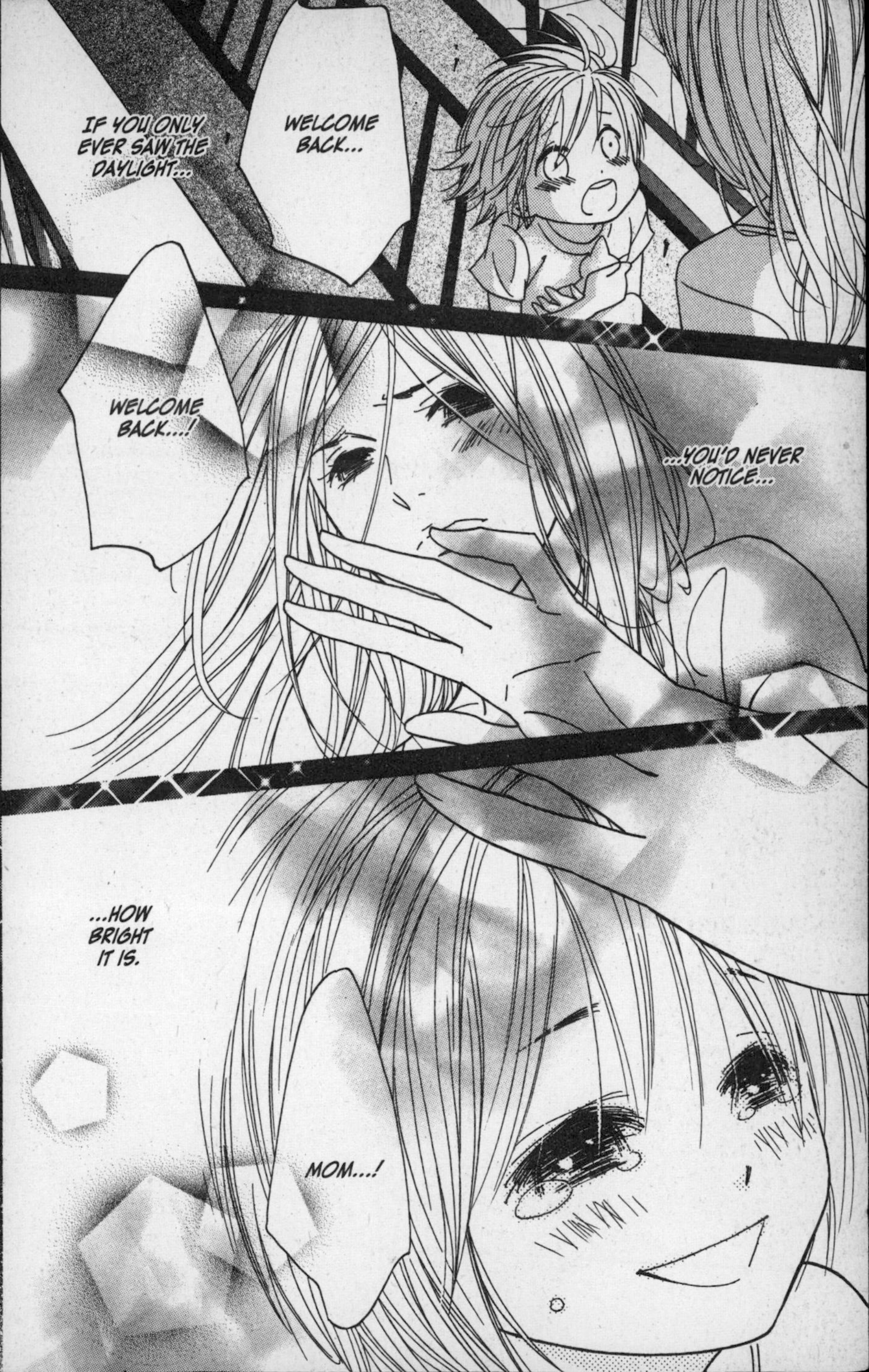
WELCOME BACK...
IF YOU ONLY EVER SAW THE DAYLIGHT...
...YOU'D NEVER NOTICE...
WELCOME BACK...!
...HOW BRIGHT IT IS.
MOM...!

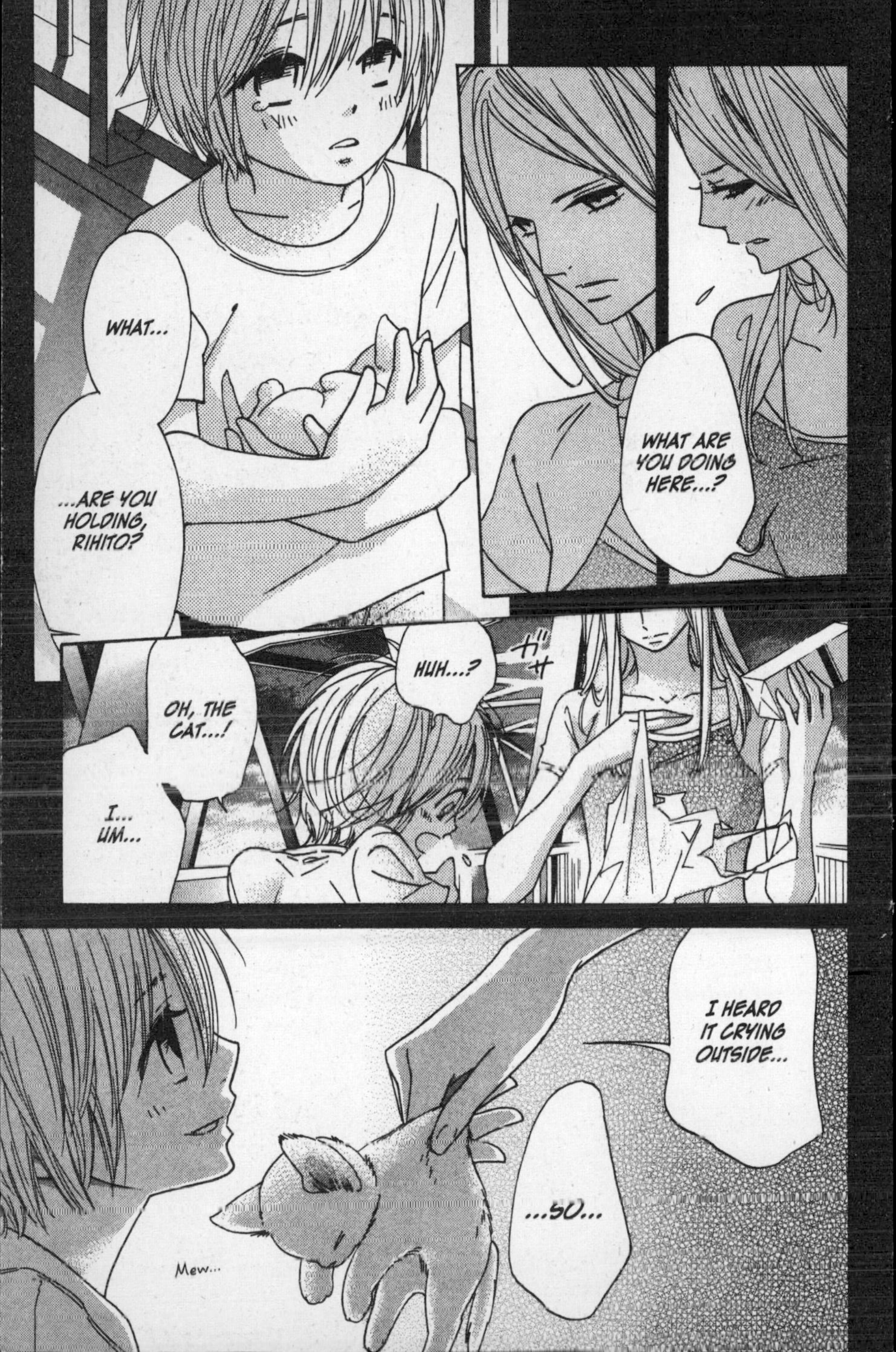
WHAT ARE YOU DOING HERE...?
WHAT...
...ARE YOU HOLDING, RIHITO?
HUH...?
ガサ
OH, THE CAT...!
I... UM...
I HEARD IT CRYING OUTSIDE...
...SO...
Mew...

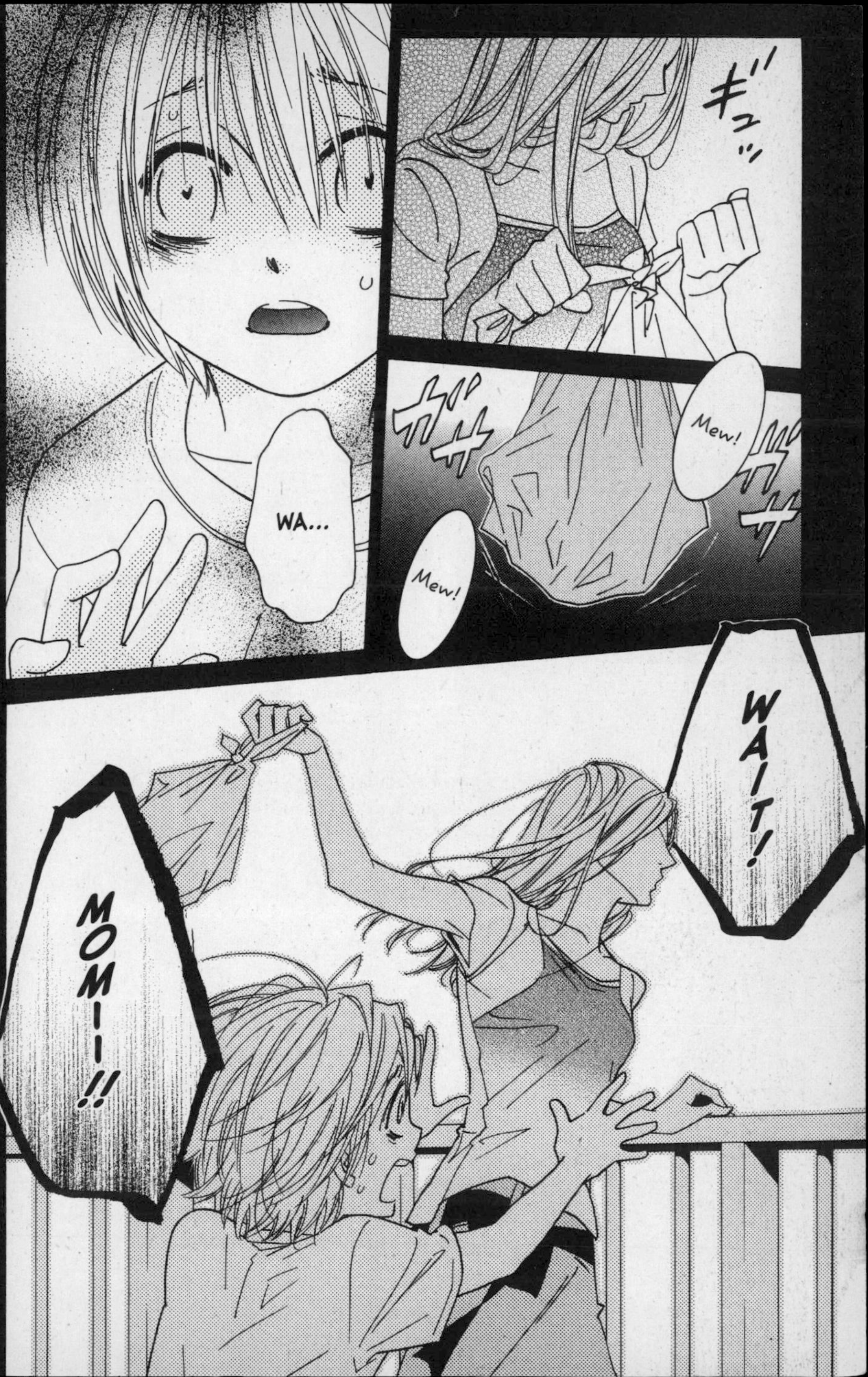
ギュッ
ガサ
Mew!
ガサ
Mew!
WA...
WAIT!
MOMI-I-I!!

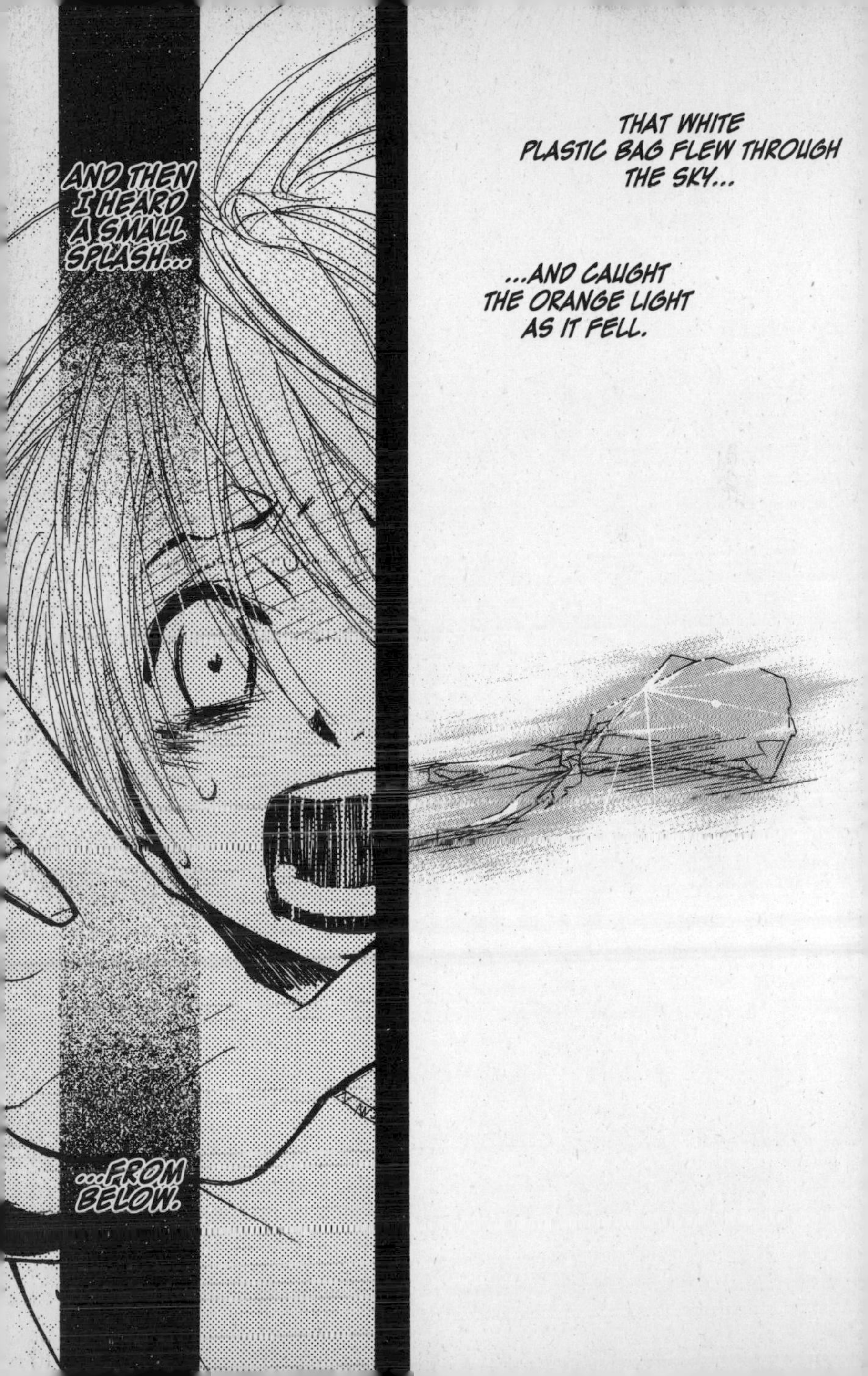
THAT WHITE PLASTIC BAG FLEW THROUGH THE SKY...
...AND CAUGHT THE ORANGE LIGHT AS IT FELL.
AND THEN I HEARD A SMALL SPLASH...
...FROM BELOW.

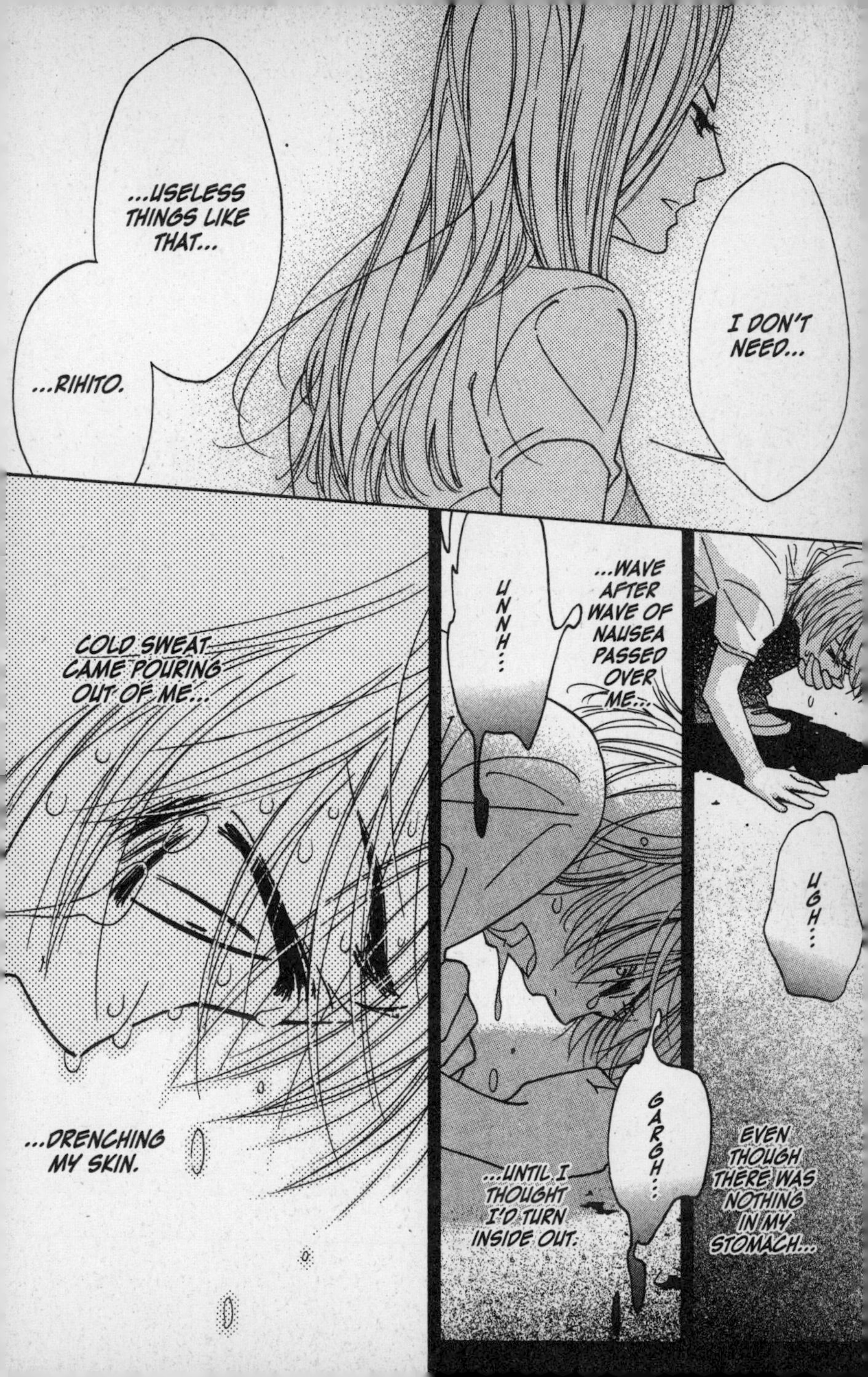
I DON'T NEED...
...USELESS THINGS LIKE THAT...
...RIHITO.
UGH...
EVEN THOUGH THERE WAS NOTHING IN MY STOMACH...
...WAVE AFTER WAVE OF NAUSEA PASSED OVER ME...
UNNH...
GARGH...
...UNTIL I THOUGHT I'D TURN INSIDE OUT.
COLD SWEAT CAME POURING OUT OF ME...
...DRENCHING MY SKIN.

THAT...

THAT'S ME.

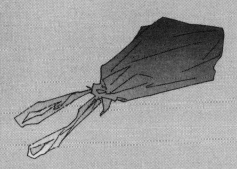

I'M THE ONE...

NO MATTER
HOW HAPPY
I FELT...

...IN THAT BAG.

...THAT MY MOM
CAME HOME
TODAY...

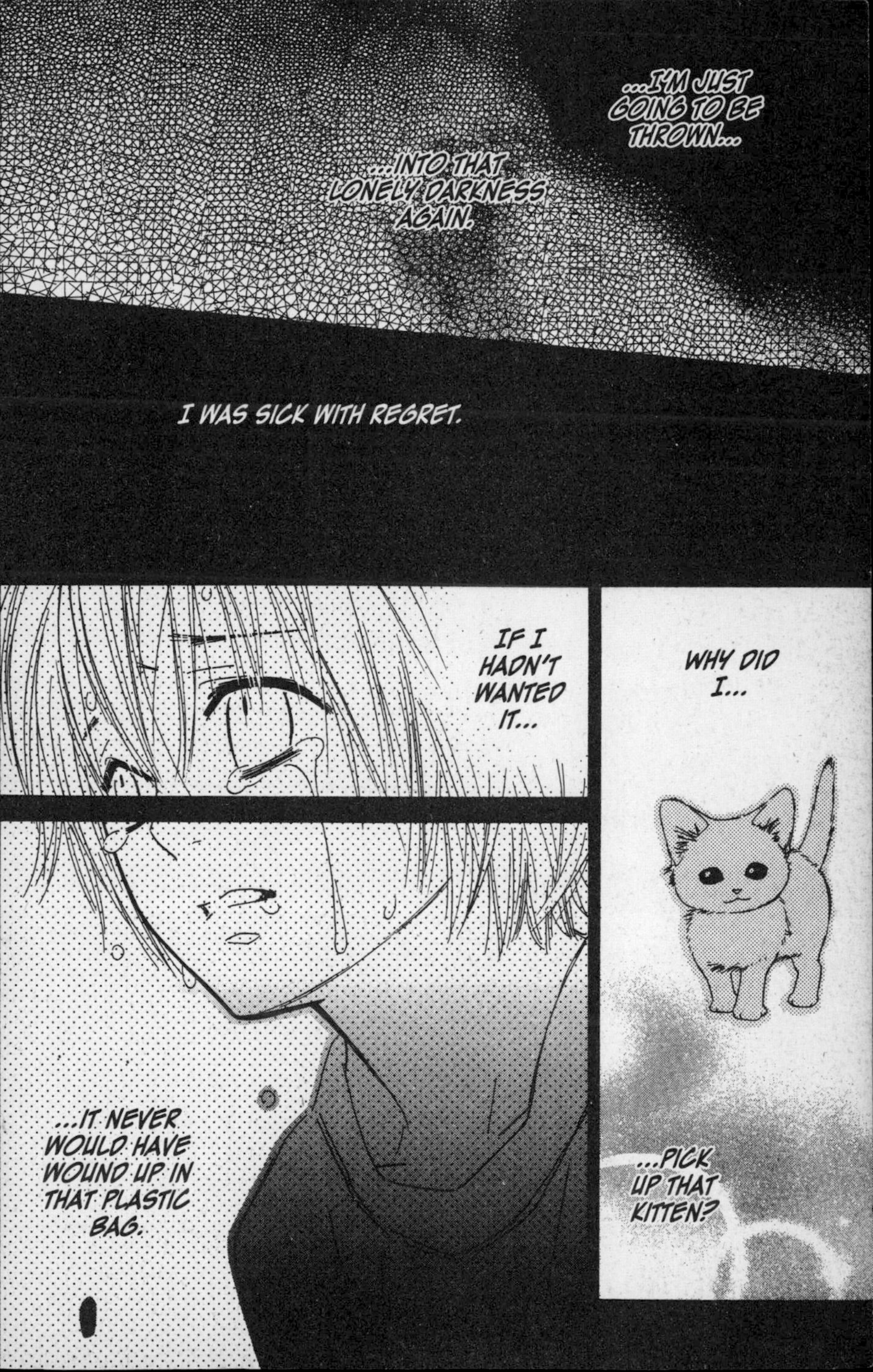
...I'M JUST GOING TO BE THROWN...
...INTO THAT LONELY DARKNESS AGAIN.
I WAS SICK WITH REGRET.
WHY DID I...
...PICK UP THAT KITTEN?
IF I HADN'T WANTED IT...
...IT NEVER WOULD HAVE WOUND UP IN THAT PLASTIC BAG.

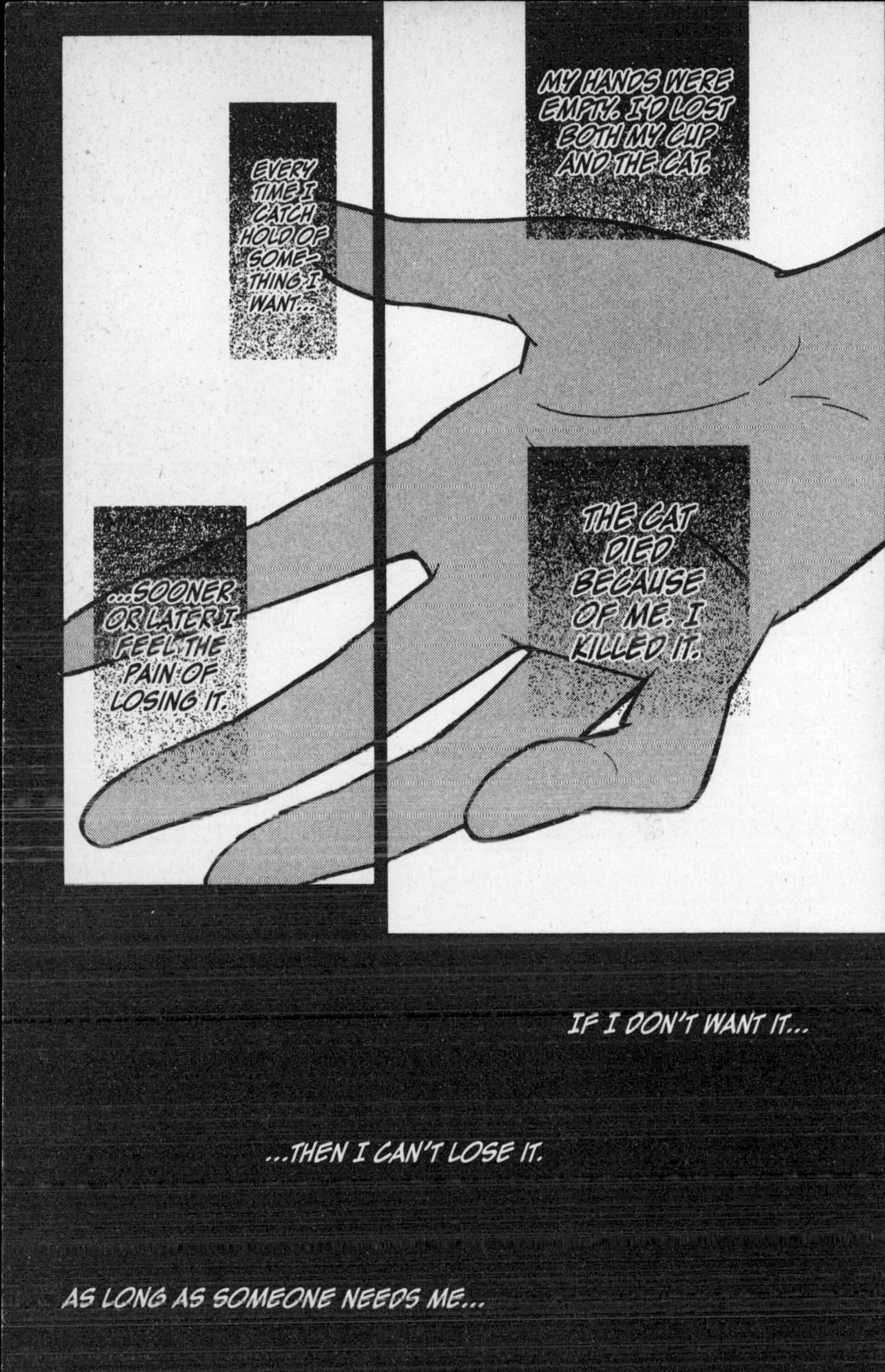
MY HANDS WERE EMPTY. I'D LOST BOTH MY CUP AND THE CAT.
THE CAT DIED BECAUSE OF ME. I KILLED IT.
EVERY TIME I CATCH HOLD OF SOME-THING I WANT...
...SOONER OR LATER I FEEL THE PAIN OF LOSING IT.
IF I DON'T WANT IT...
...THEN I CAN'T LOSE IT.
AS LONG AS SOMEONE NEEDS ME...

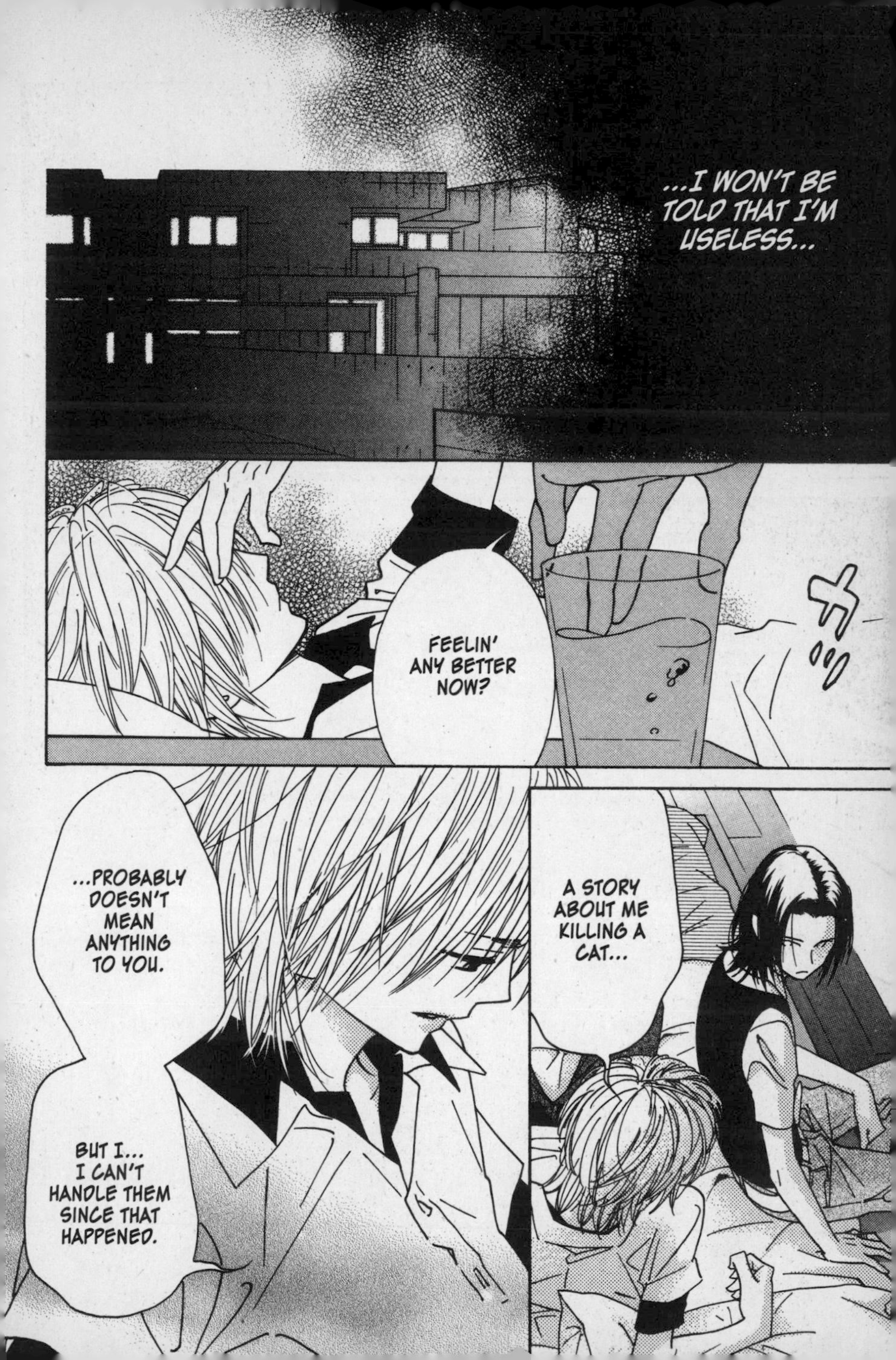
...I WON'T BE TOLD THAT I'M USELESS...
FEELIN' ANY BETTER NOW?
A STORY ABOUT ME KILLING A CAT...
...PROBABLY DOESN'T MEAN ANYTHING TO YOU.
BUT I... I CAN'T HANDLE THEM SINCE THAT HAPPENED.

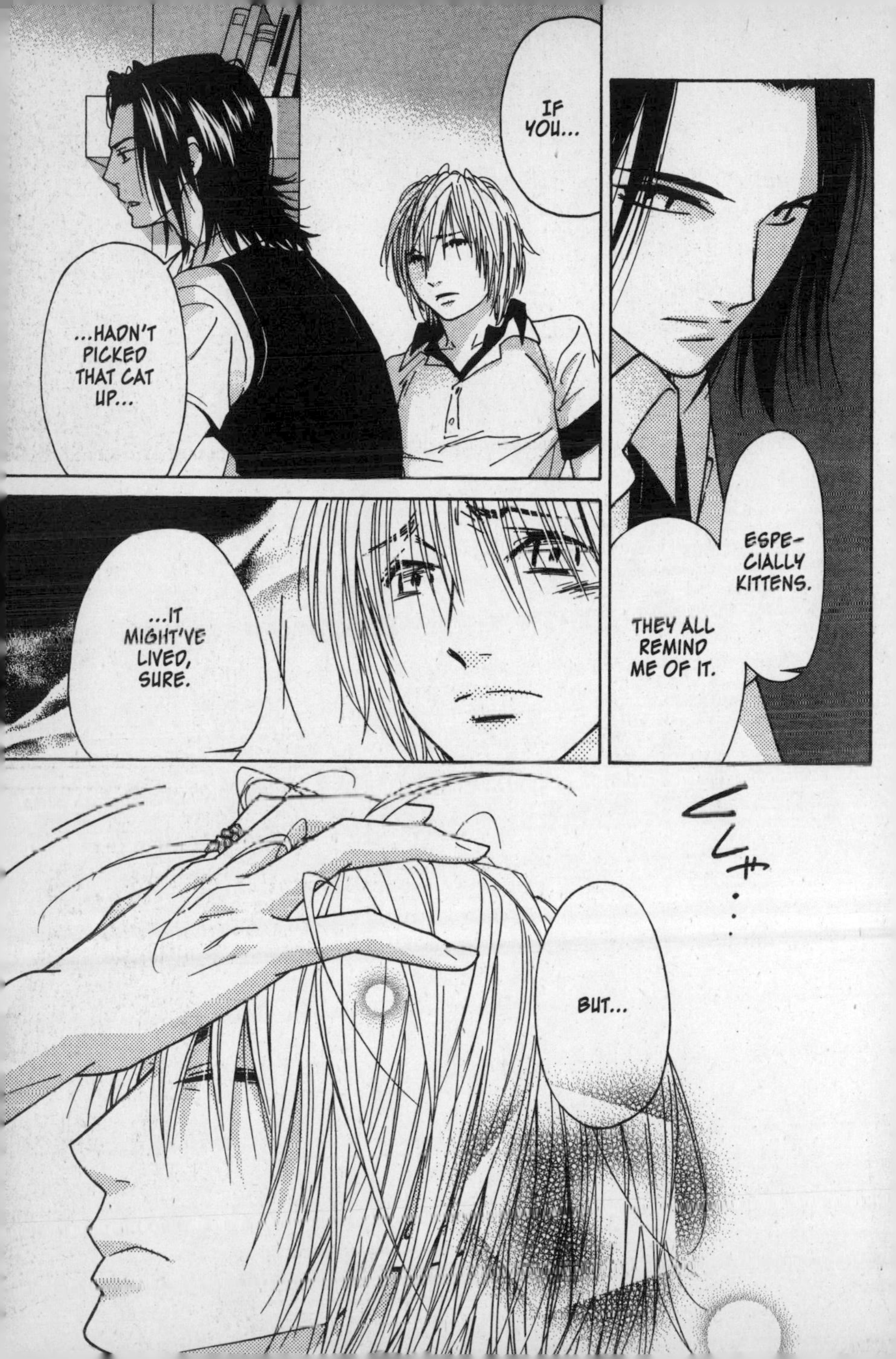
ESPE-CIALLY KITTENS.
THEY ALL REMIND ME OF IT.
IF YOU...
...HADN'T PICKED THAT CAT UP...
...IT MIGHT'VE LIVED, SURE.
くしゃ...
BUT...

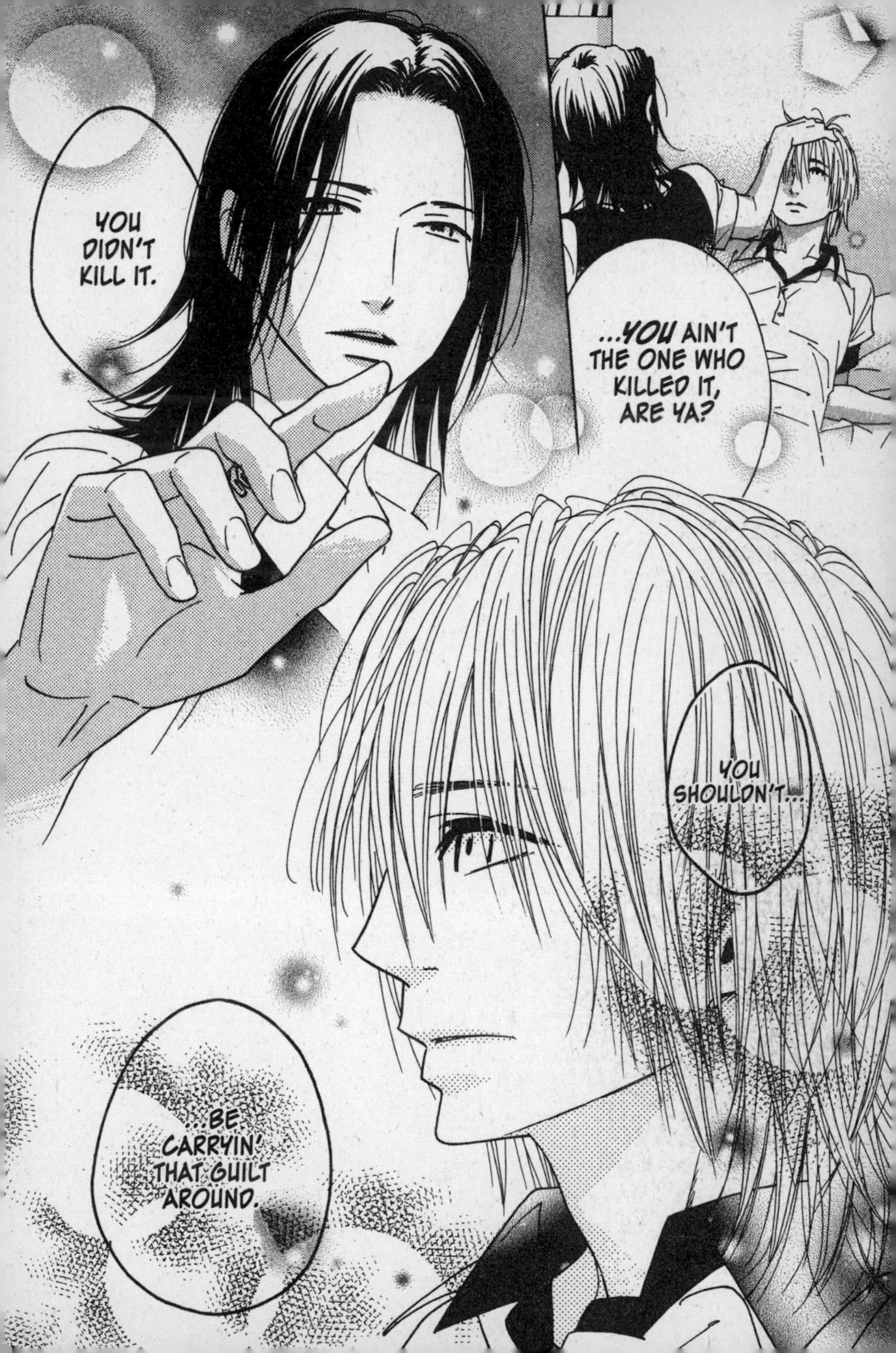
...YOU AIN'T THE ONE WHO KILLED IT, ARE YA?
YOU DIDN'T KILL IT.
YOU SHOULDN'T...
...BE CARRYIN' THAT GUILT AROUND.

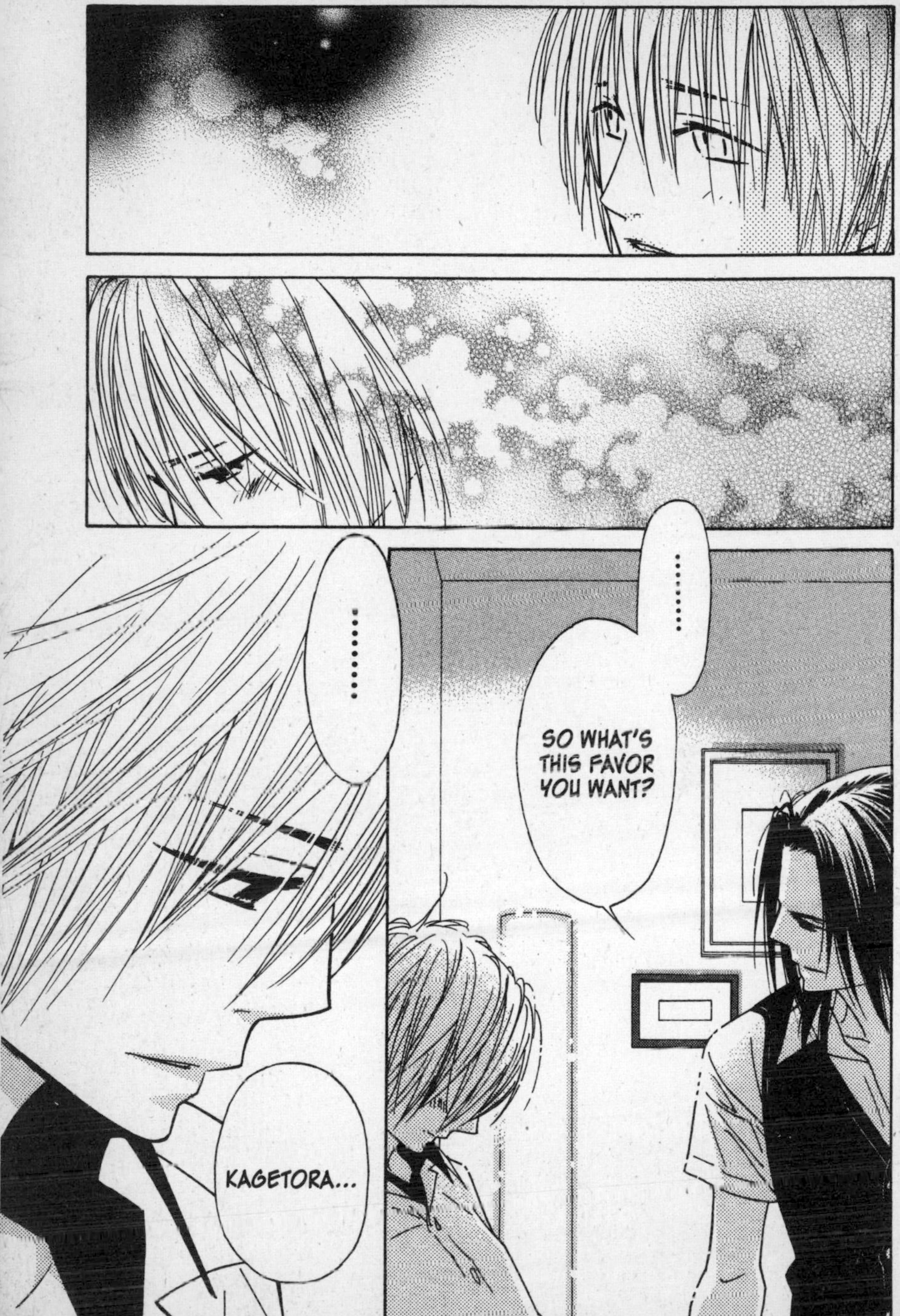
......
SO WHAT'S THIS FAVOR YOU WANT?
......
KAGETORA...

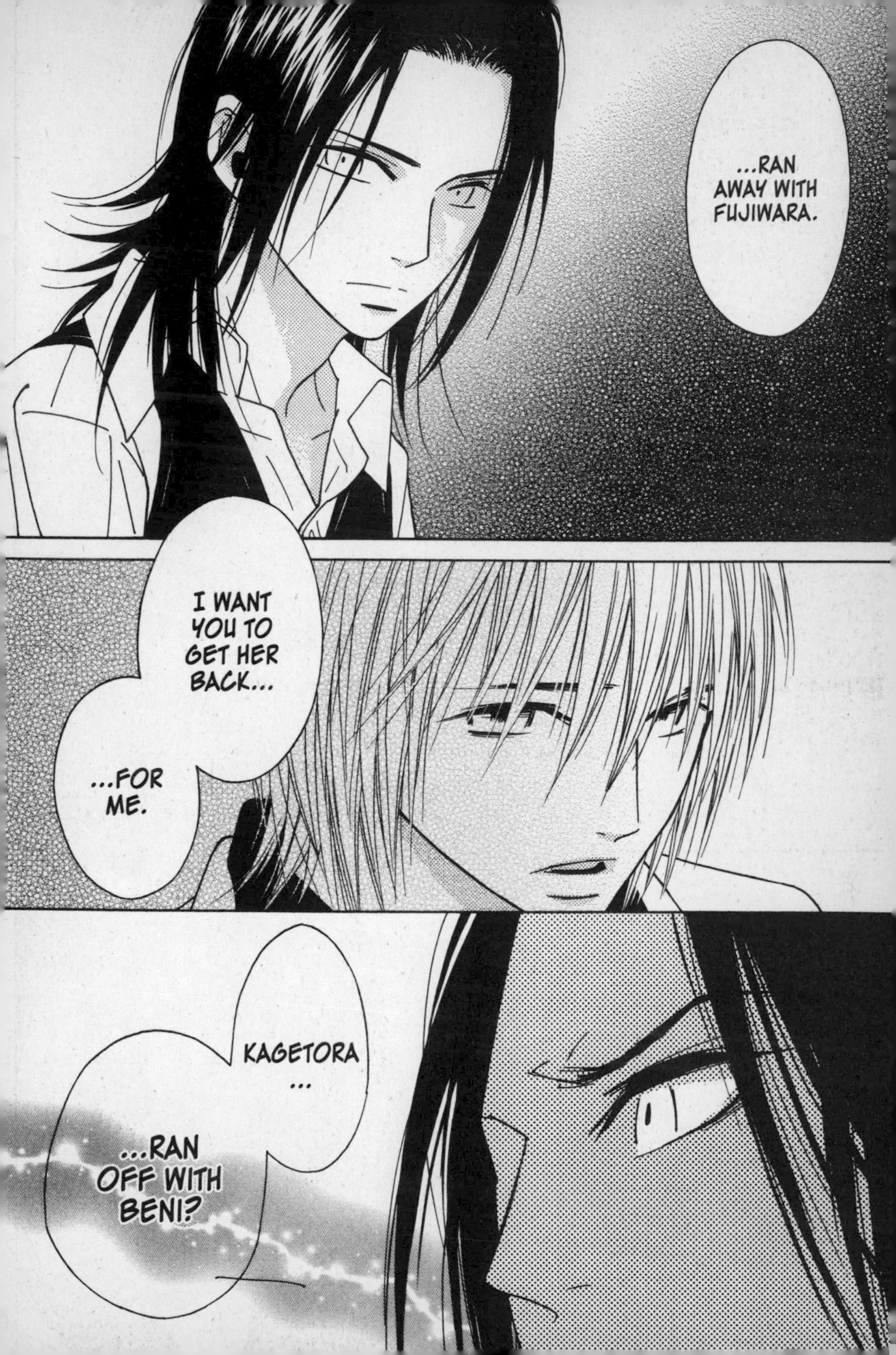
...RAN AWAY WITH FUJIWARA.
I WANT YOU TO GET HER BACK...
...FOR ME.
KAGETORA ...
...RAN OFF WITH BENI?

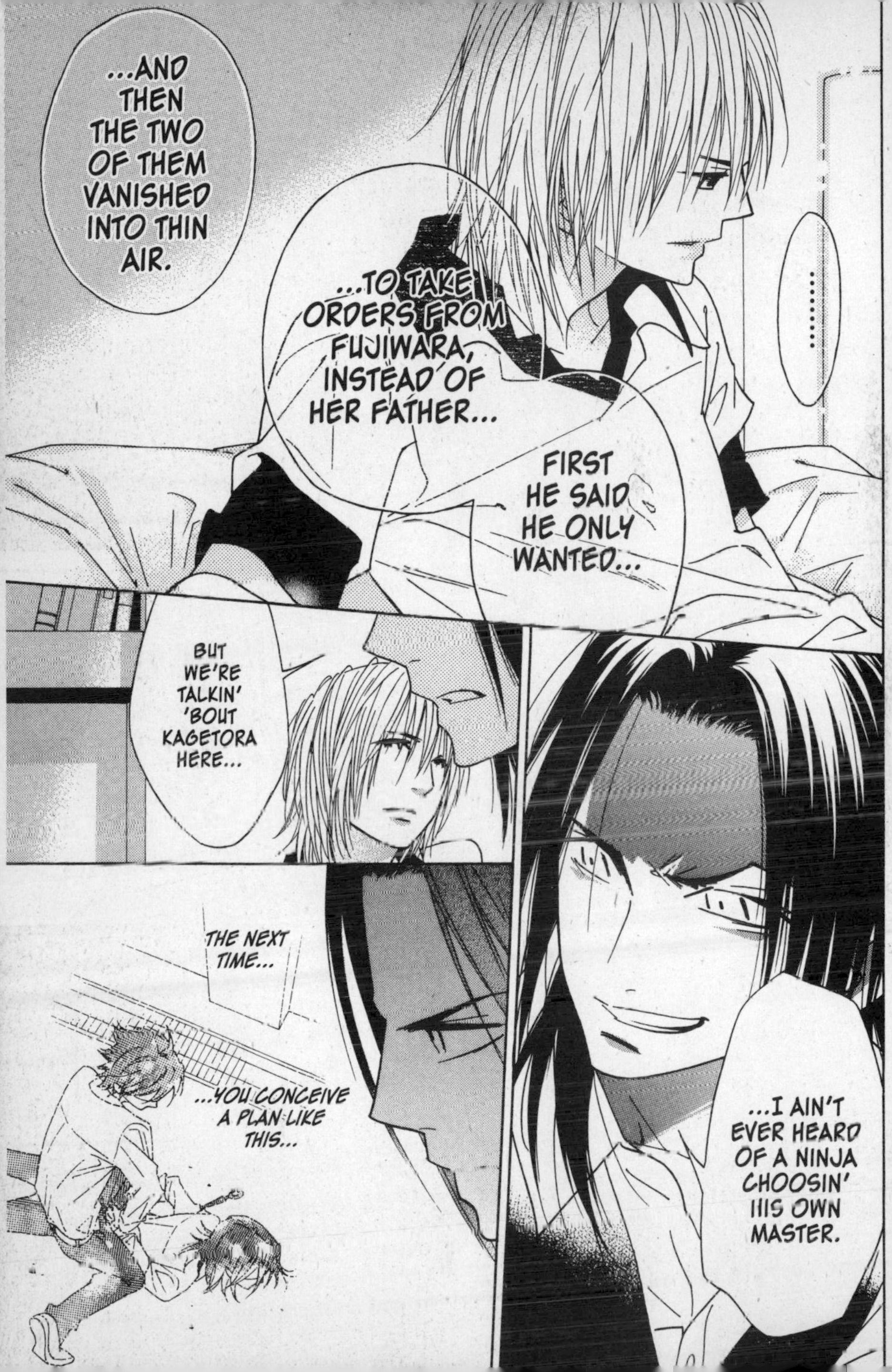
......
FIRST HE SAID HE ONLY WANTED...
...TO TAKE ORDERS FROM FUJIWARA, INSTEAD OF HER FATHER...
...AND THEN THE TWO OF THEM VANISHED INTO THIN AIR.
...I AIN'T EVER HEARD OF A NINJA CHOOSIN' HIS OWN MASTER.
BUT WE'RE TALKIN' 'BOUT KAGETORA HERE...
THE NEXT TIME...
...YOU CONCEIVE A PLAN LIKE THIS...

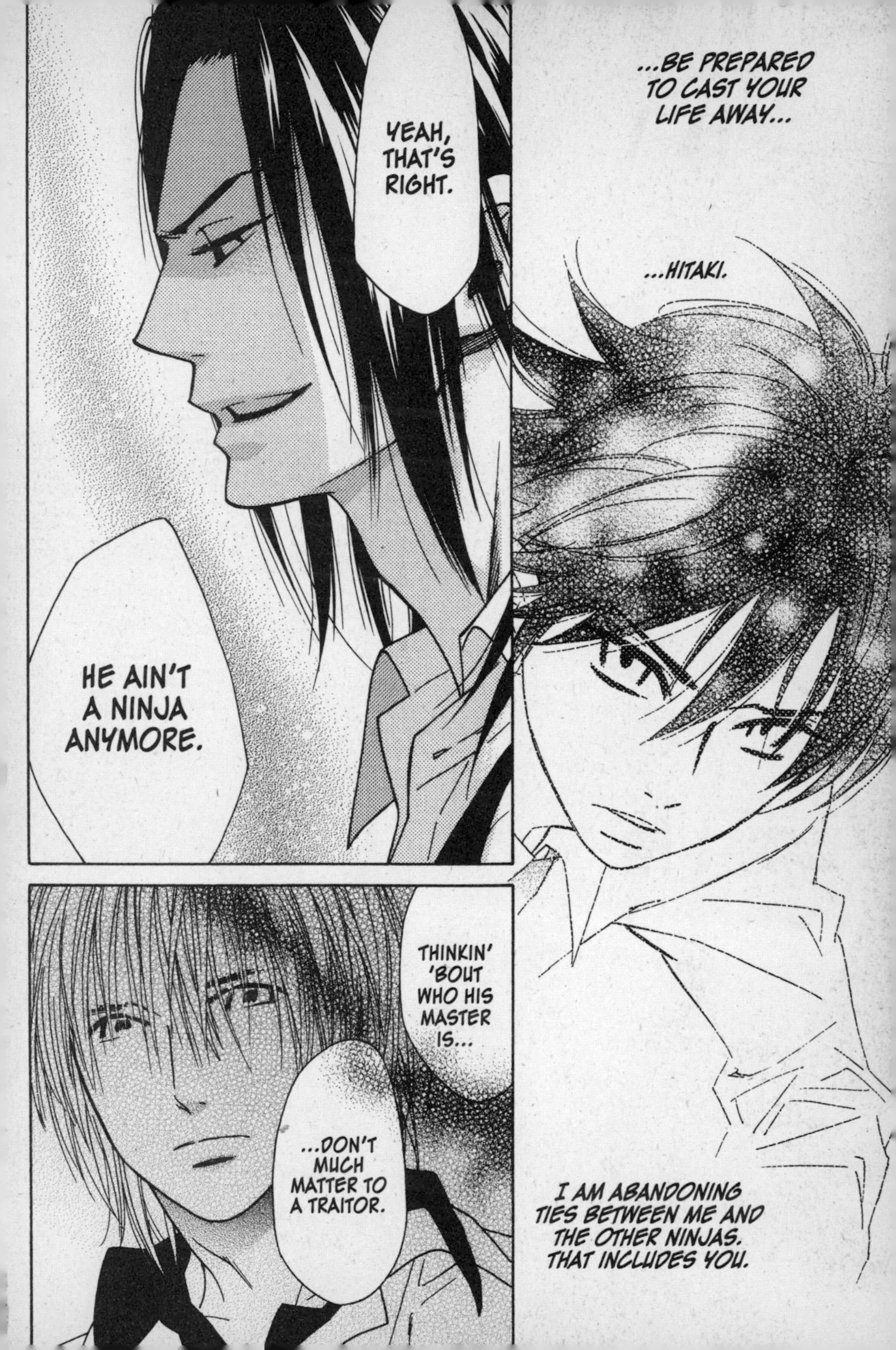
...BE PREPARED TO CAST YOUR LIFE AWAY...
...HITAKI.
I AM ABANDONING TIES BETWEEN ME AND THE OTHER NINJAS. THAT INCLUDES YOU.
YEAH, THAT'S RIGHT.
HE AIN'T A NINJA ANYMORE.
THINKIN' 'BOUT WHO HIS MASTER IS...
...DON'T MUCH MATTER TO A TRAITOR.

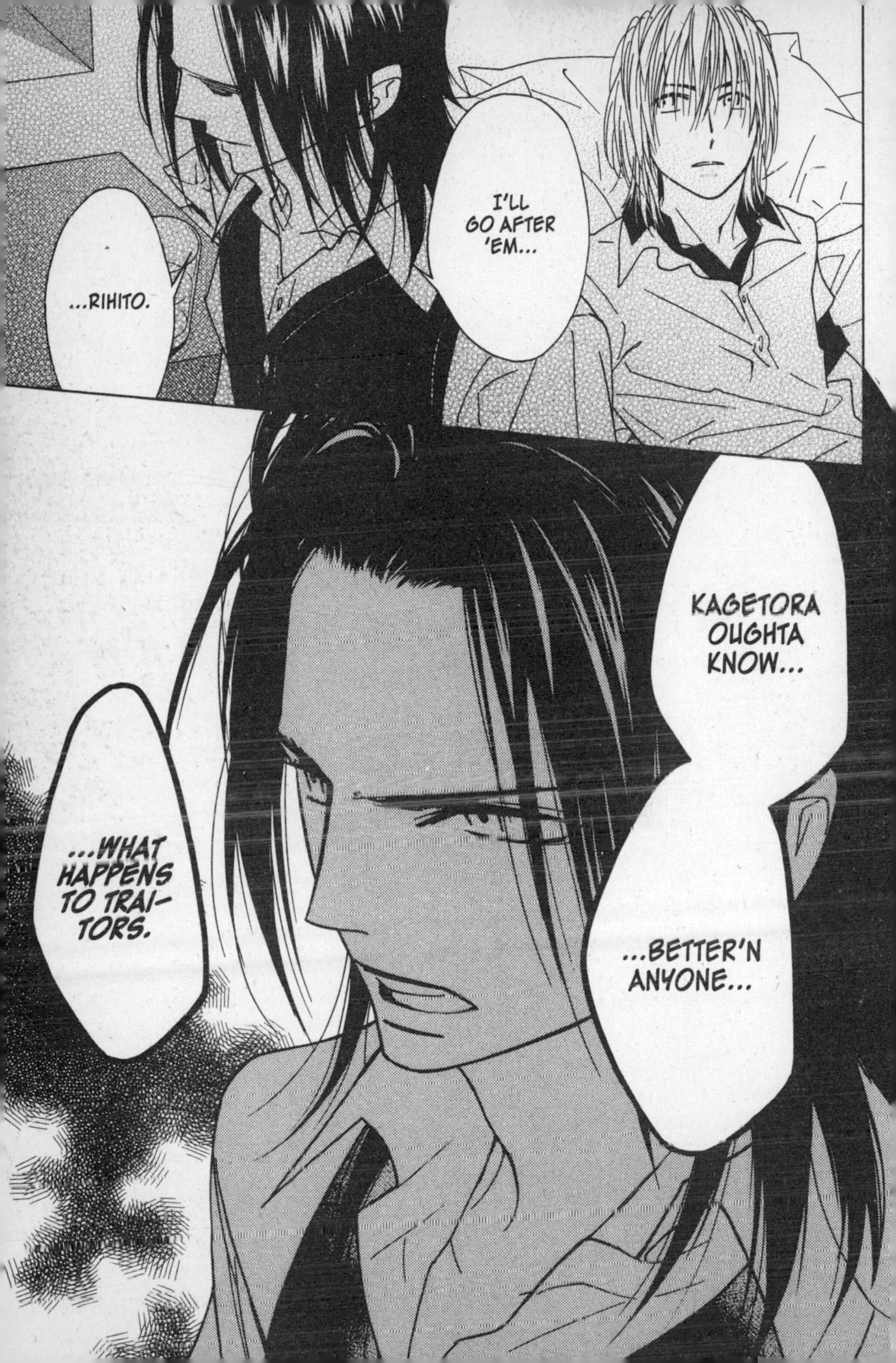
I'LL GO AFTER 'EM...
...RIHITO.
KAGETORA OUGHTA KNOW...
...BETTER'N ANYONE...
...WHAT HAPPENS TO TRAI-TORS.

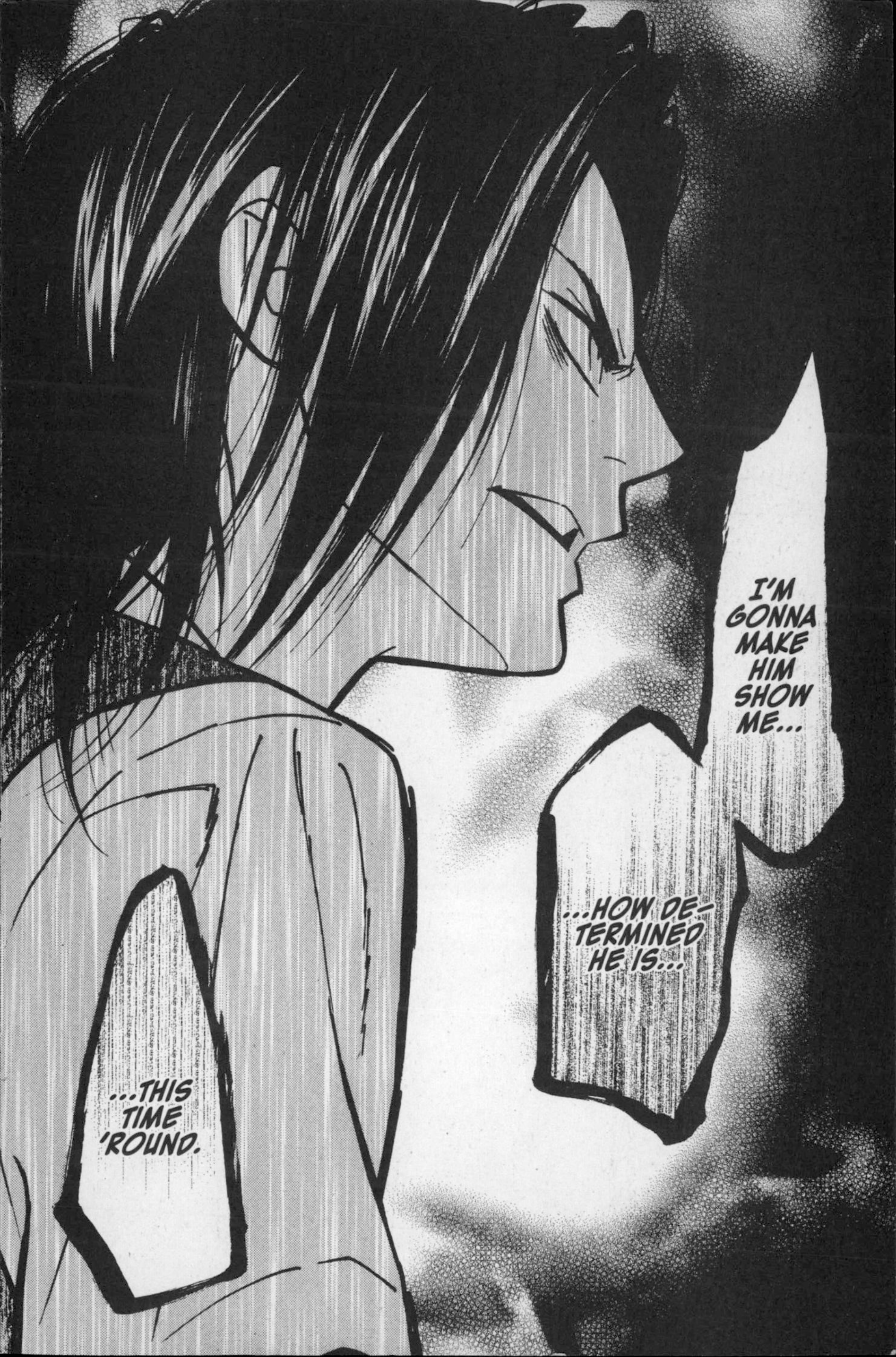
I'M GONNA MAKE HIM SHOW ME...
...HOW DE-TERMINED HE IS...
...THIS TIME 'ROUND.

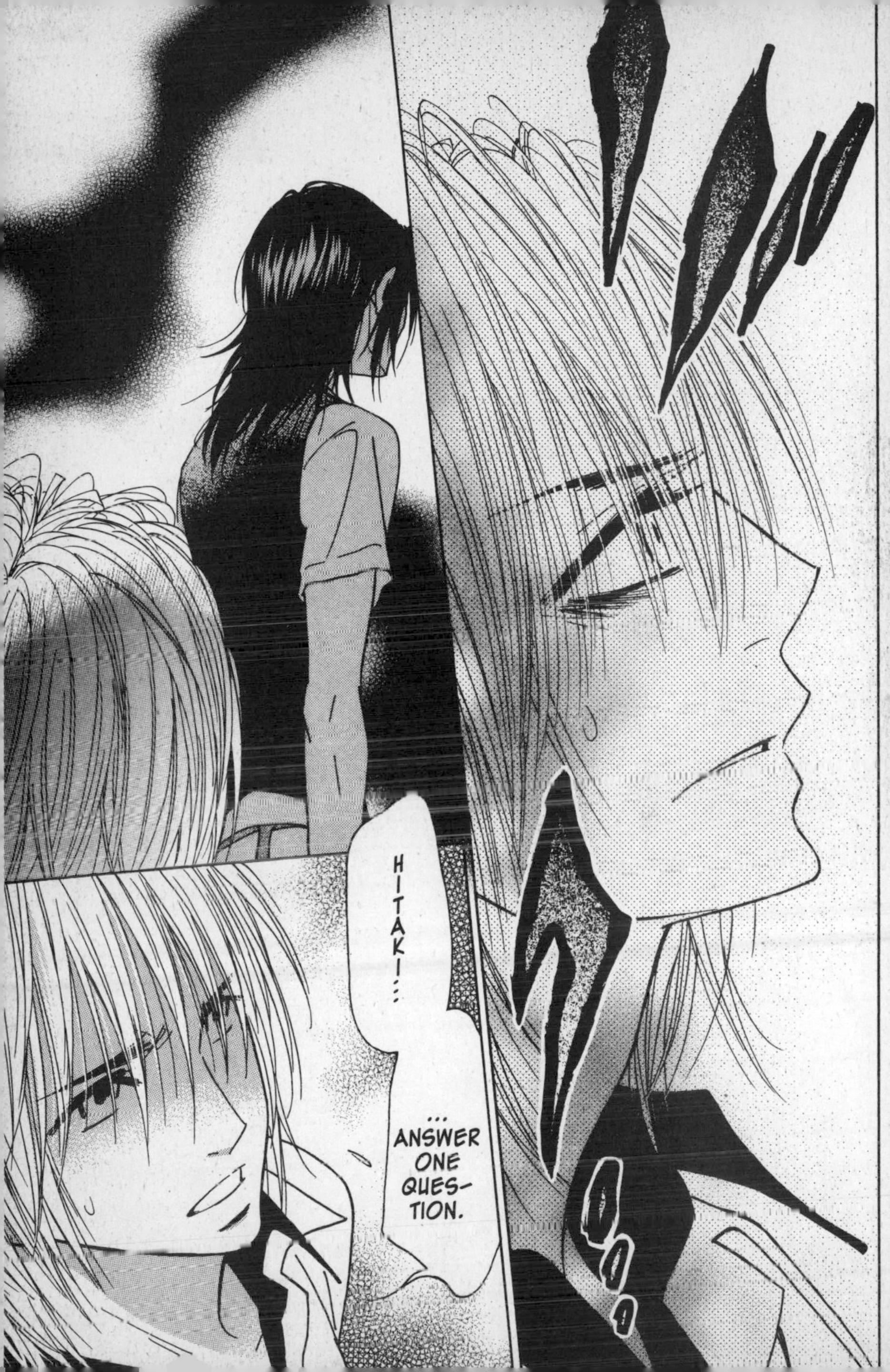
HITAKI...
...ANSWER ONE QUES-TION.

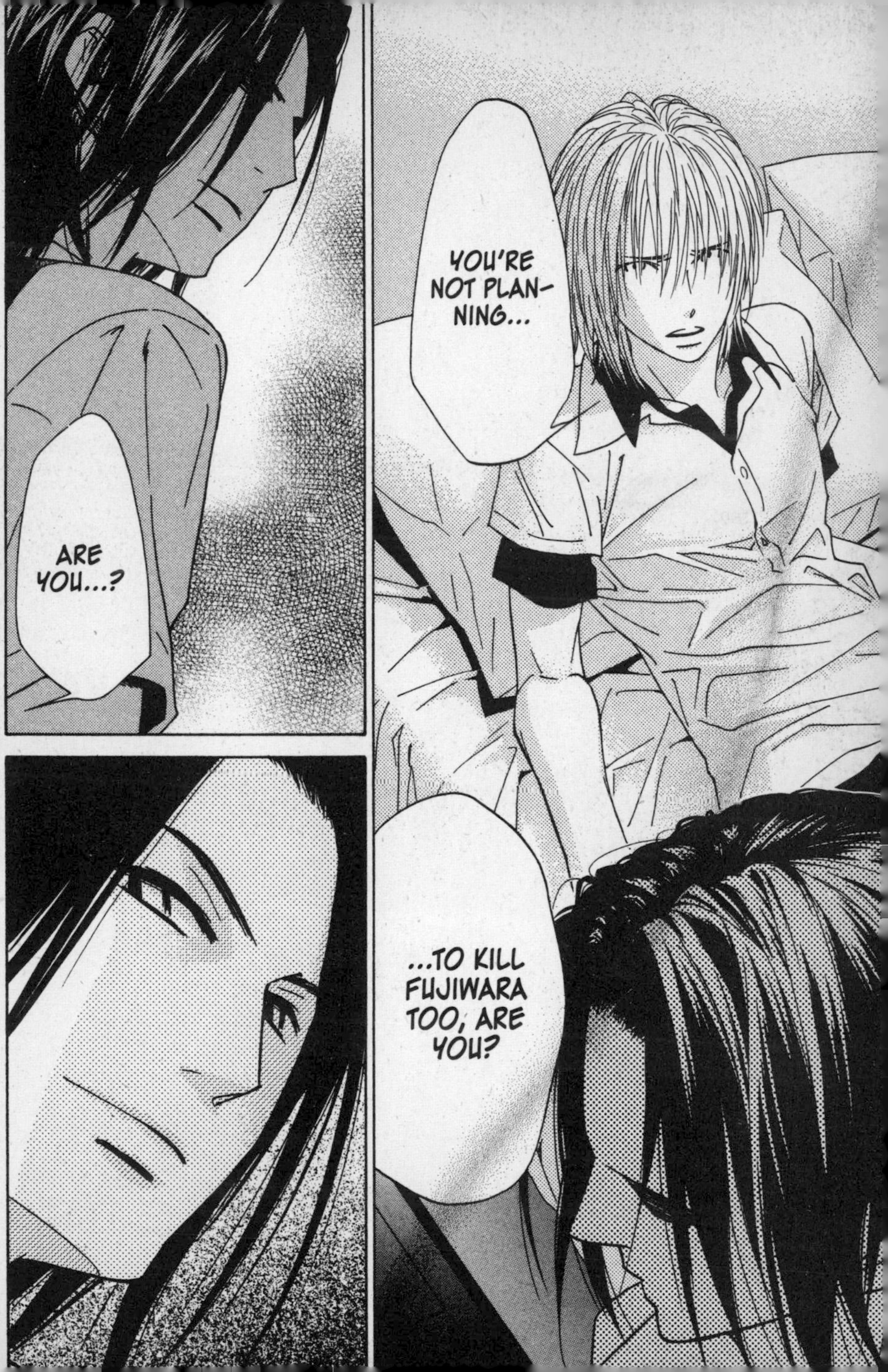
YOU'RE NOT PLAN-NING...
...TO KILL FUJIWARA TOO, ARE YOU?
ARE YOU...?

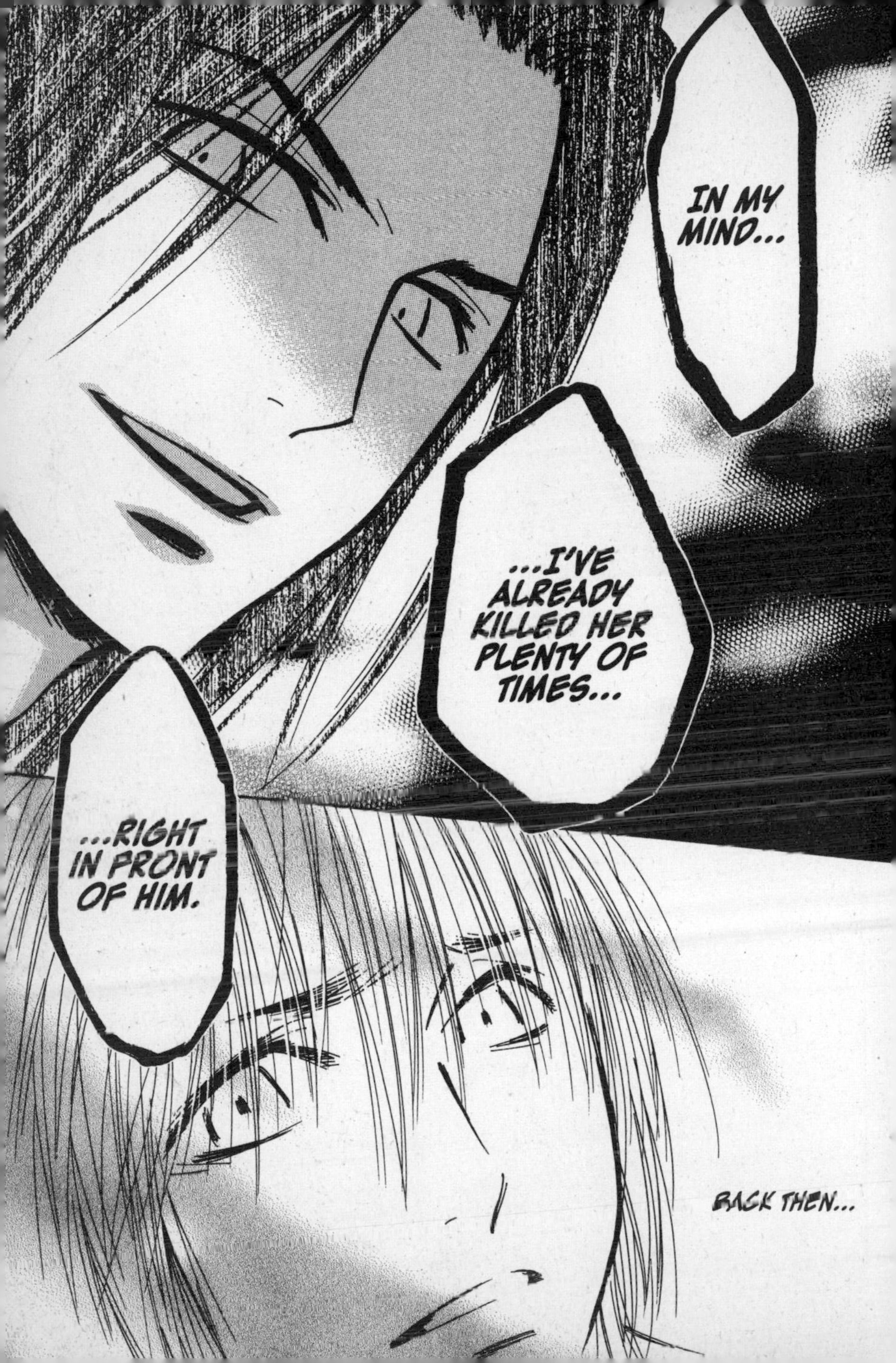
IN MY MIND...
...I'VE ALREADY KILLED HER PLENTY OF TIMES...
...RIGHT IN FRONT OF HIM.
BACK THEN...

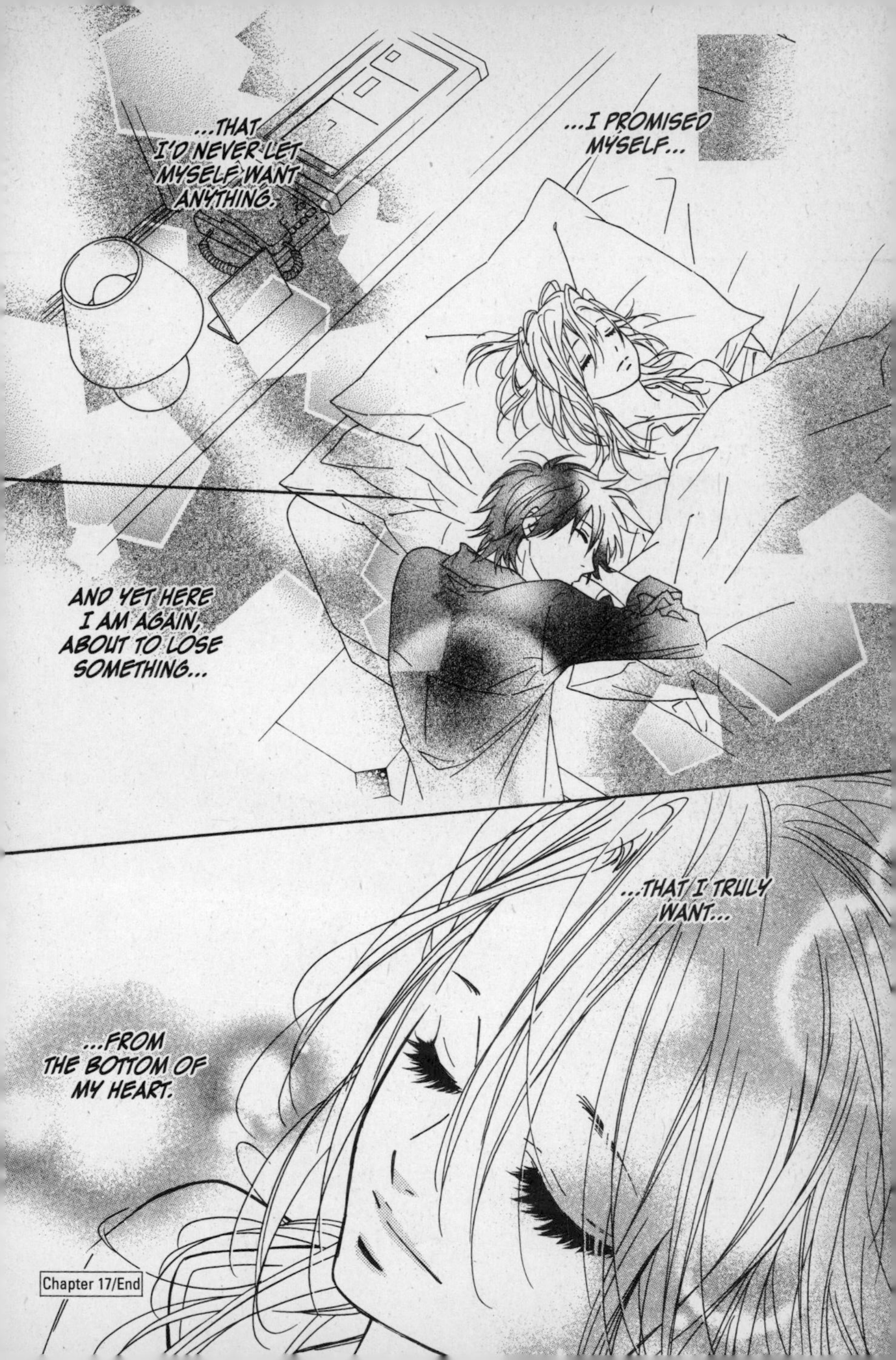

...I PROMISED MYSELF...
...THAT I'D NEVER LET MYSELF WANT ANYTHING.
AND YET HERE I AM AGAIN, ABOUT TO LOSE SOMETHING...
...THAT I TRULY WANT...
...FROM THE BOTTOM OF MY HEART.
Chapter 17/End

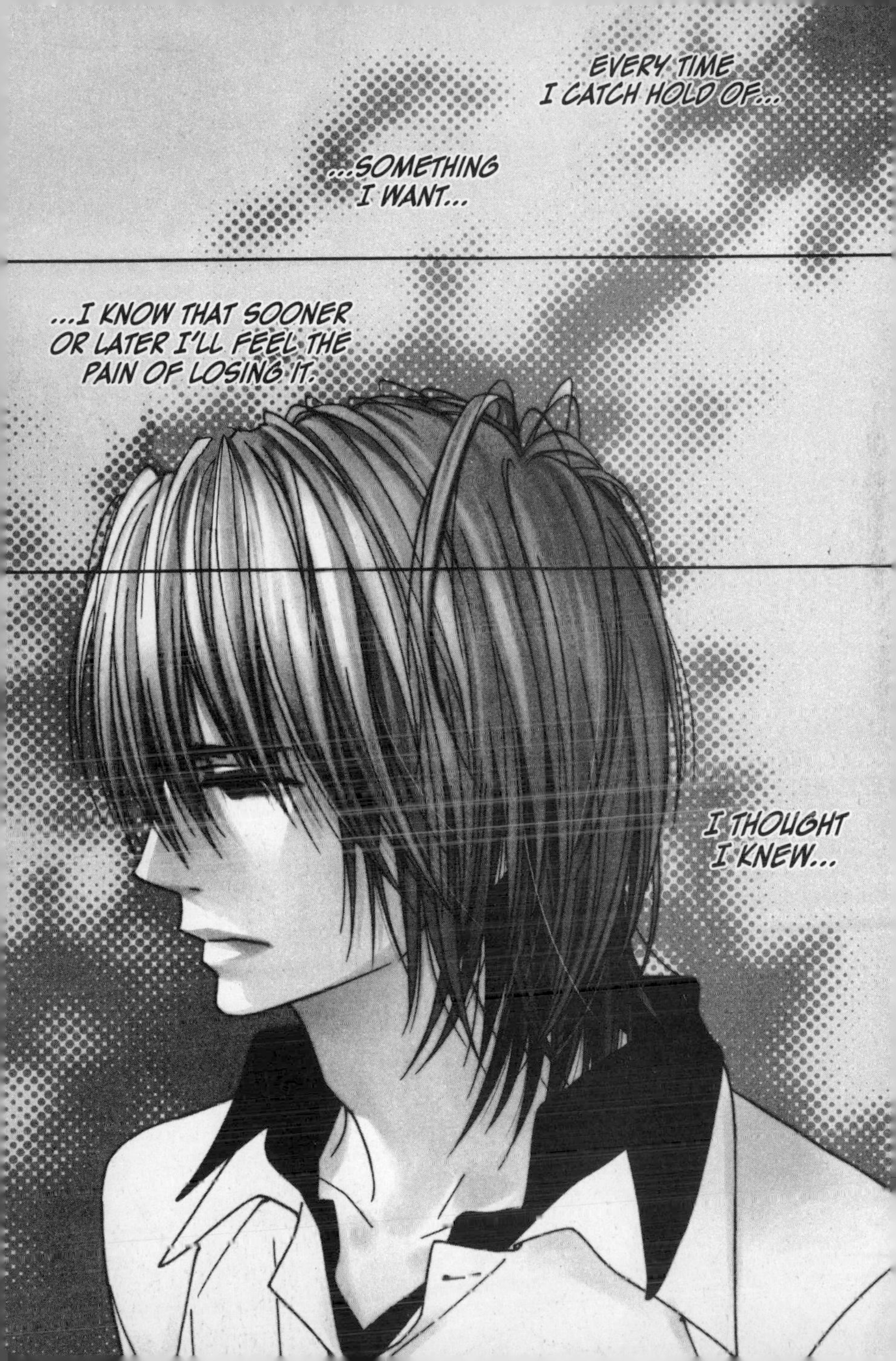
EVERY TIME I CATCH HOLD OF...
...SOMETHING I WANT...
...I KNOW THAT SOONER OR LATER I'LL FEEL THE PAIN OF LOSING IT.
I THOUGHT I KNEW...

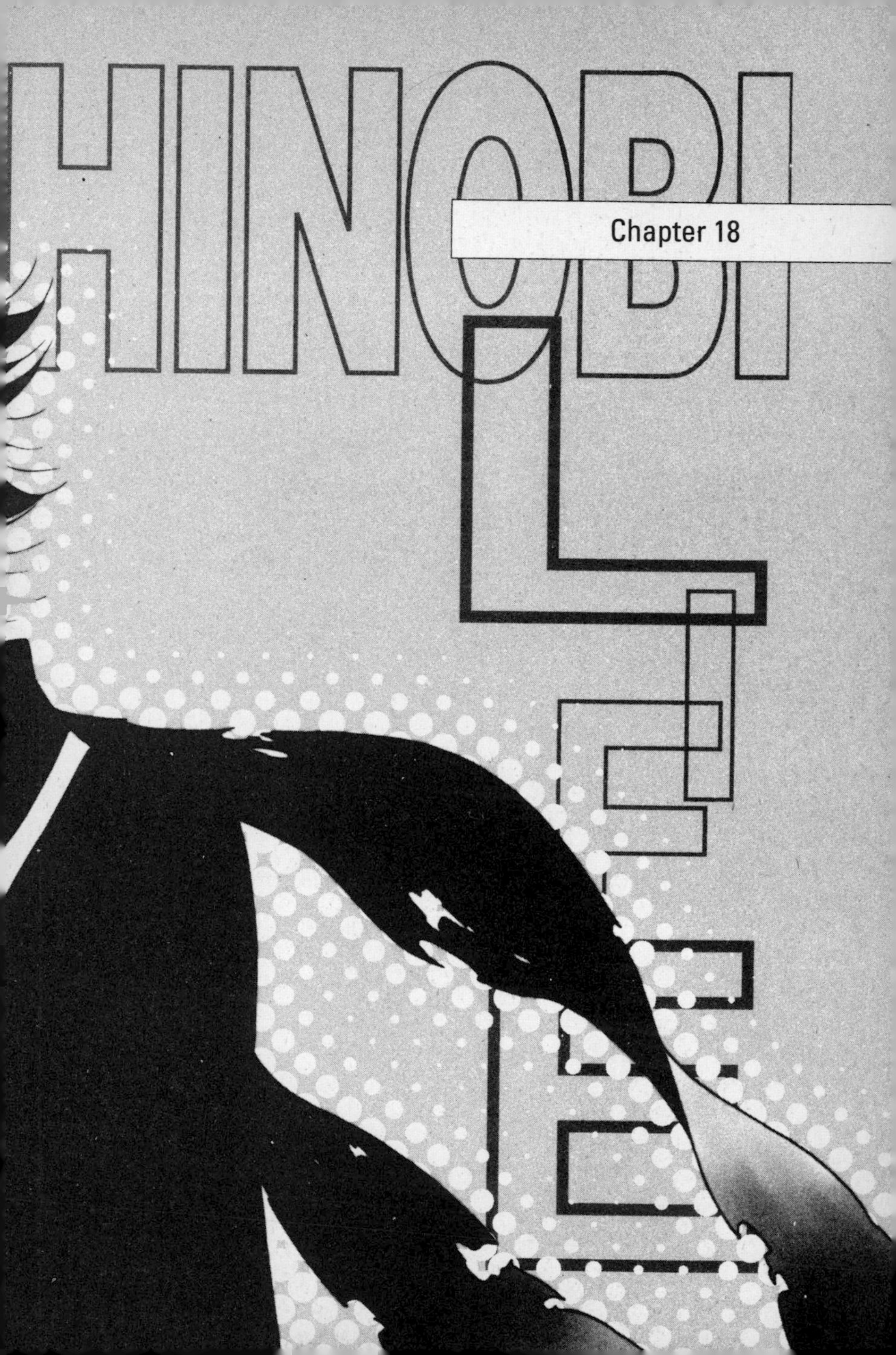
HINOBI
Chapter 18

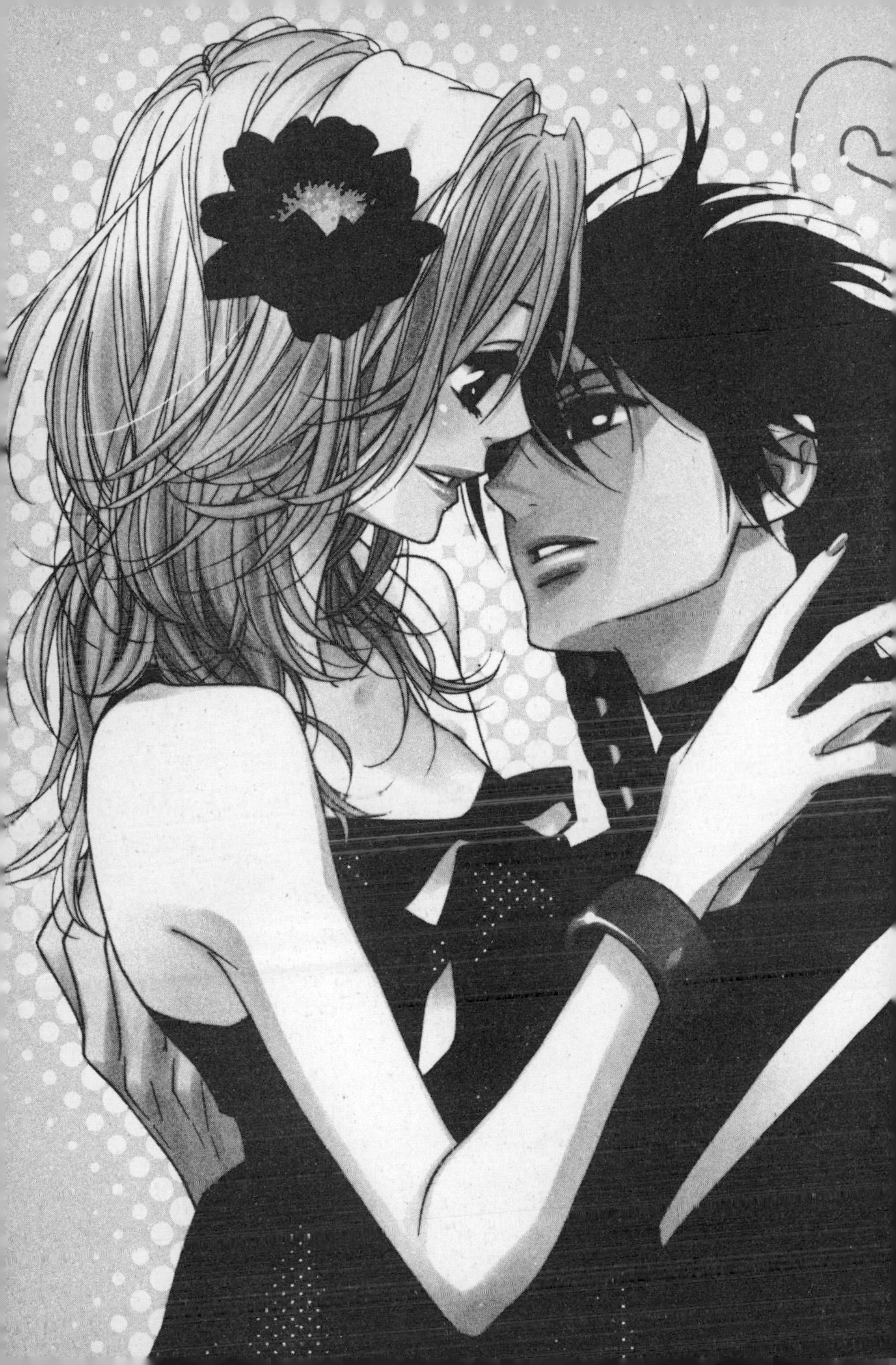

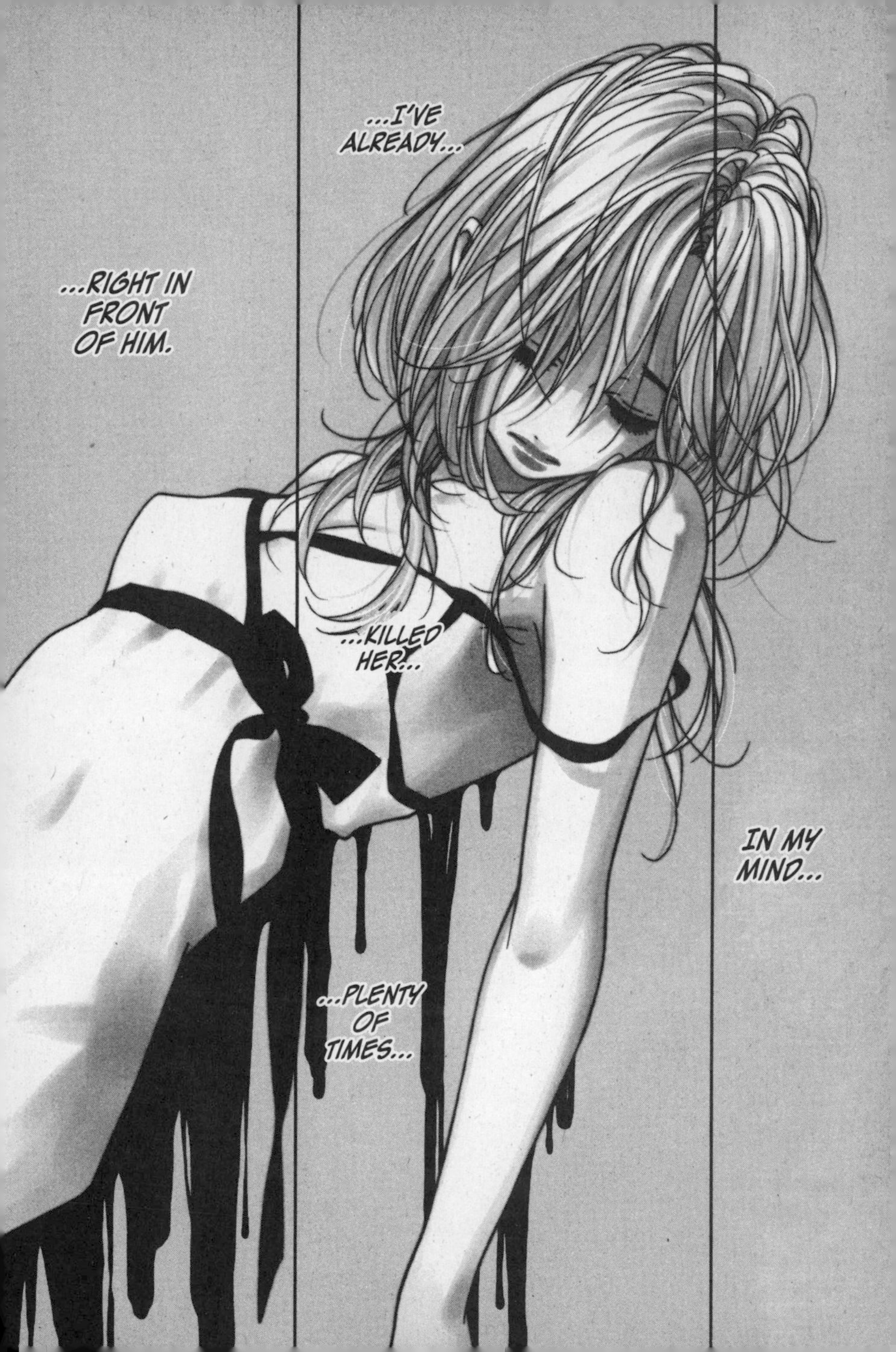
IN MY MIND...
...I'VE ALREADY...
...KILLED HER...
...PLENTY OF TIMES...
...RIGHT IN FRONT OF HIM.

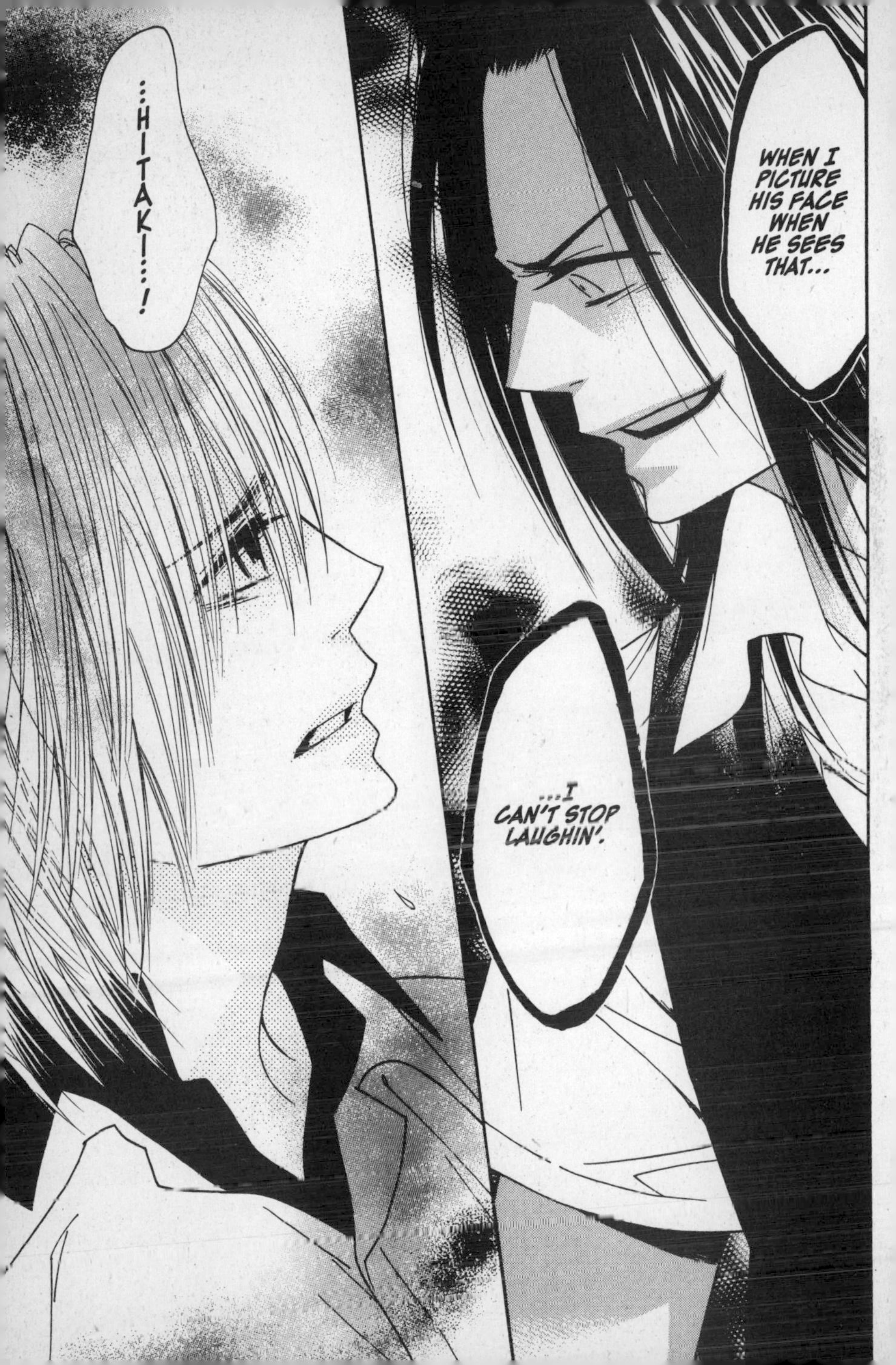
WHEN I PICTURE HIS FACE WHEN HE SEES THAT...
...I CAN'T STOP LAUGHIN'.
...HITAKI...!

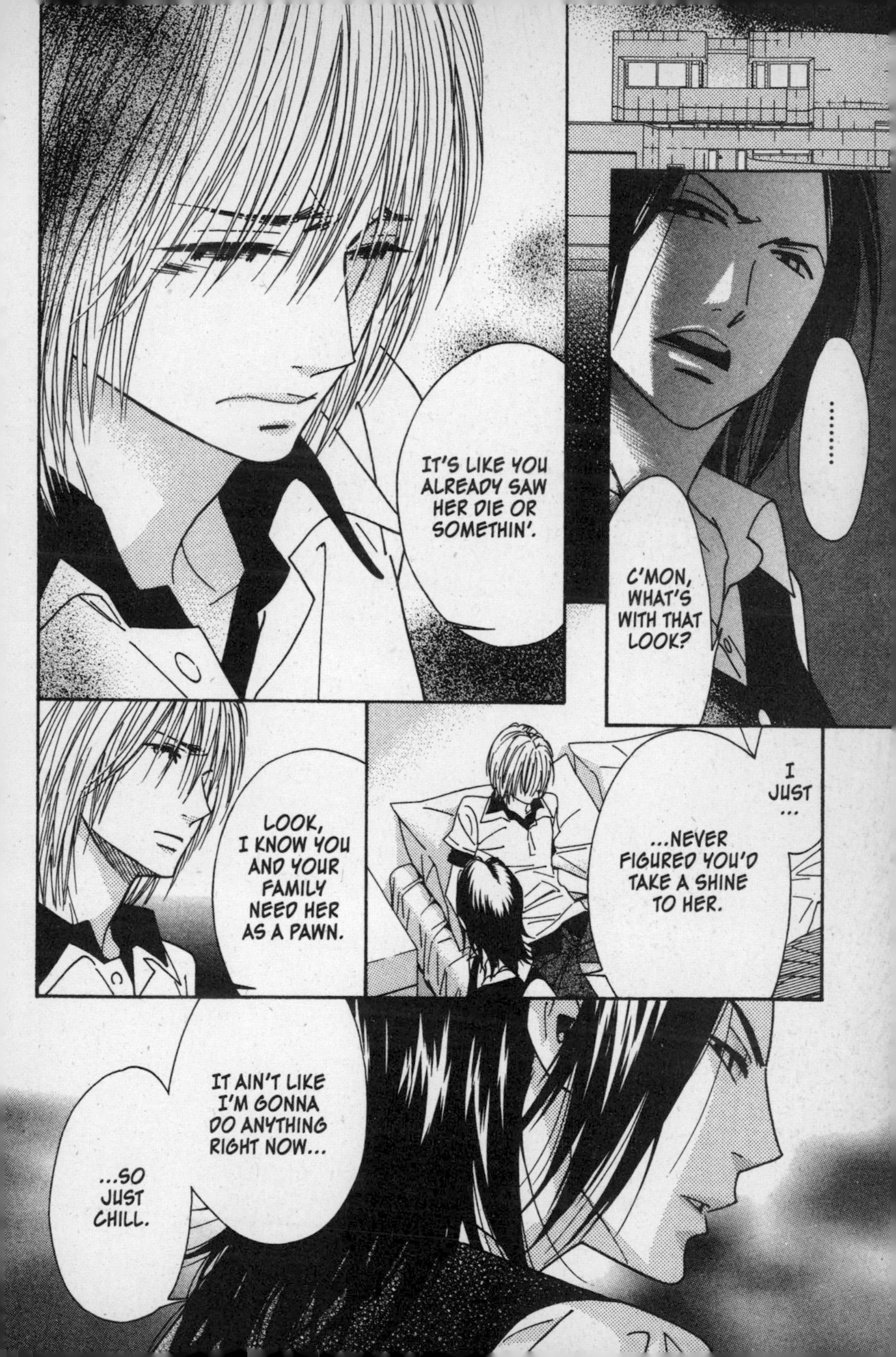

......
C'MON, WHAT'S WITH THAT LOOK?
IT'S LIKE YOU ALREADY SAW HER DIE OR SOMETHIN'.
I JUST ...
...NEVER FIGURED YOU'D TAKE A SHINE TO HER.
LOOK, I KNOW YOU AND YOUR FAMILY NEED HER AS A PAWN.
IT AIN'T LIKE I'M GONNA DO ANYTHING RIGHT NOW...
...SO JUST CHILL.

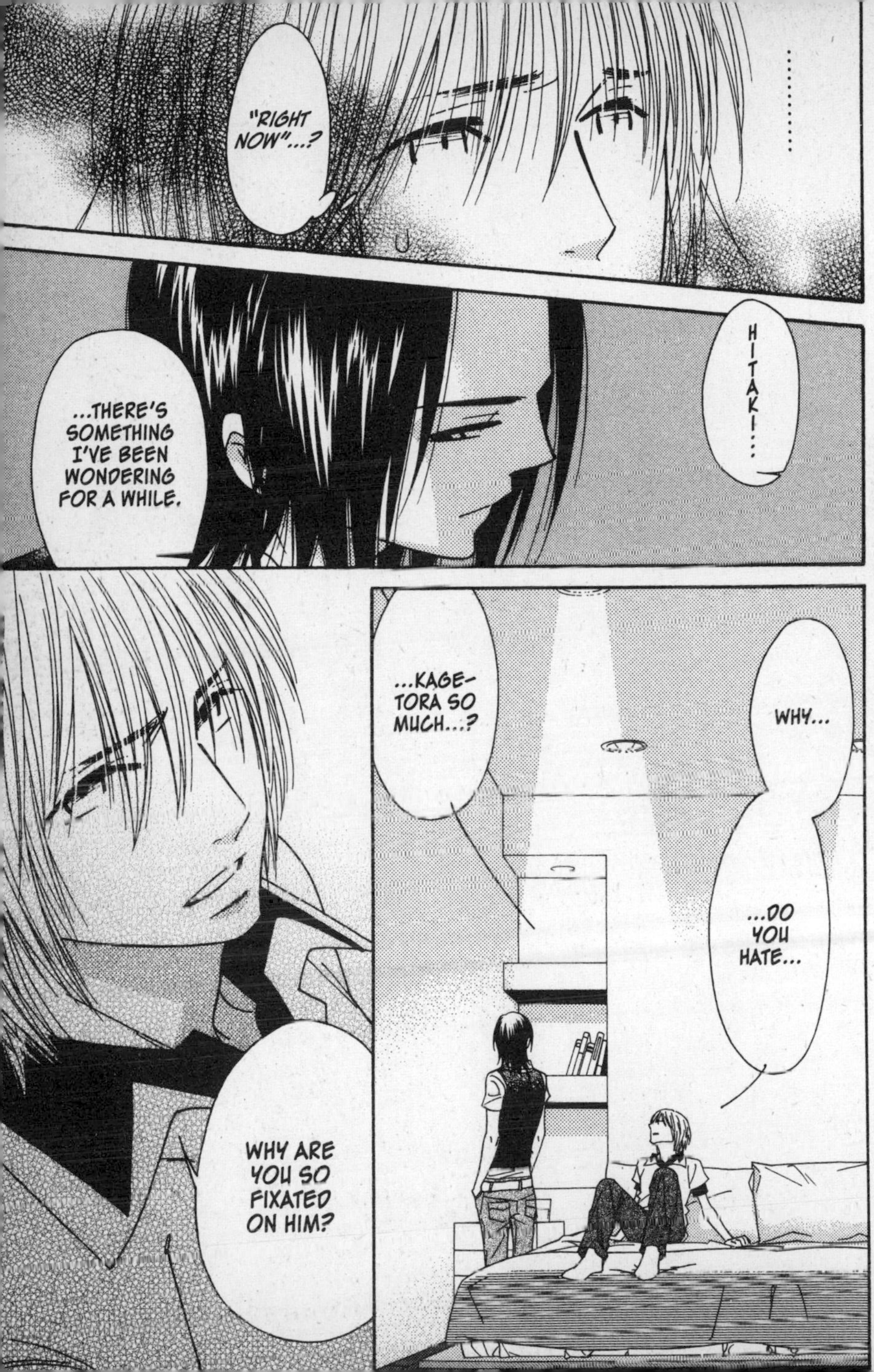
......
"RIGHT NOW"...?
HITAKI...
...THERE'S SOMETHING I'VE BEEN WONDERING FOR A WHILE.
WHY...
...DO YOU HATE...
...KAGE-TORA SO MUCH...?
WHY ARE YOU SO FIXATED ON HIM?

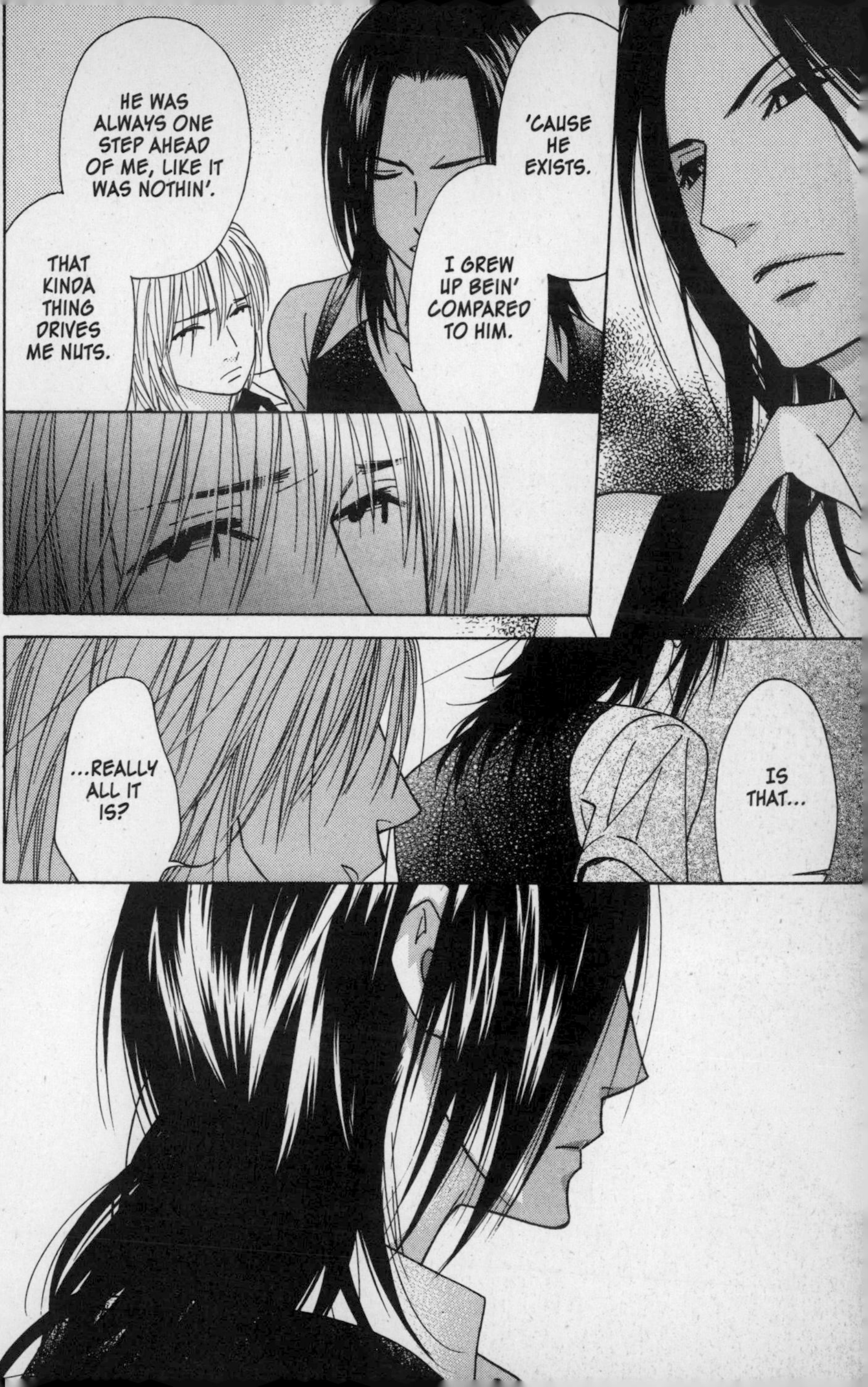
'CAUSE HE EXISTS.
I GREW UP BEIN' COMPARED TO HIM.
HE WAS ALWAYS ONE STEP AHEAD OF ME, LIKE IT WAS NOTHIN'.
THAT KINDA THING DRIVES ME NUTS.
IS THAT...
...REALLY ALL IT IS?

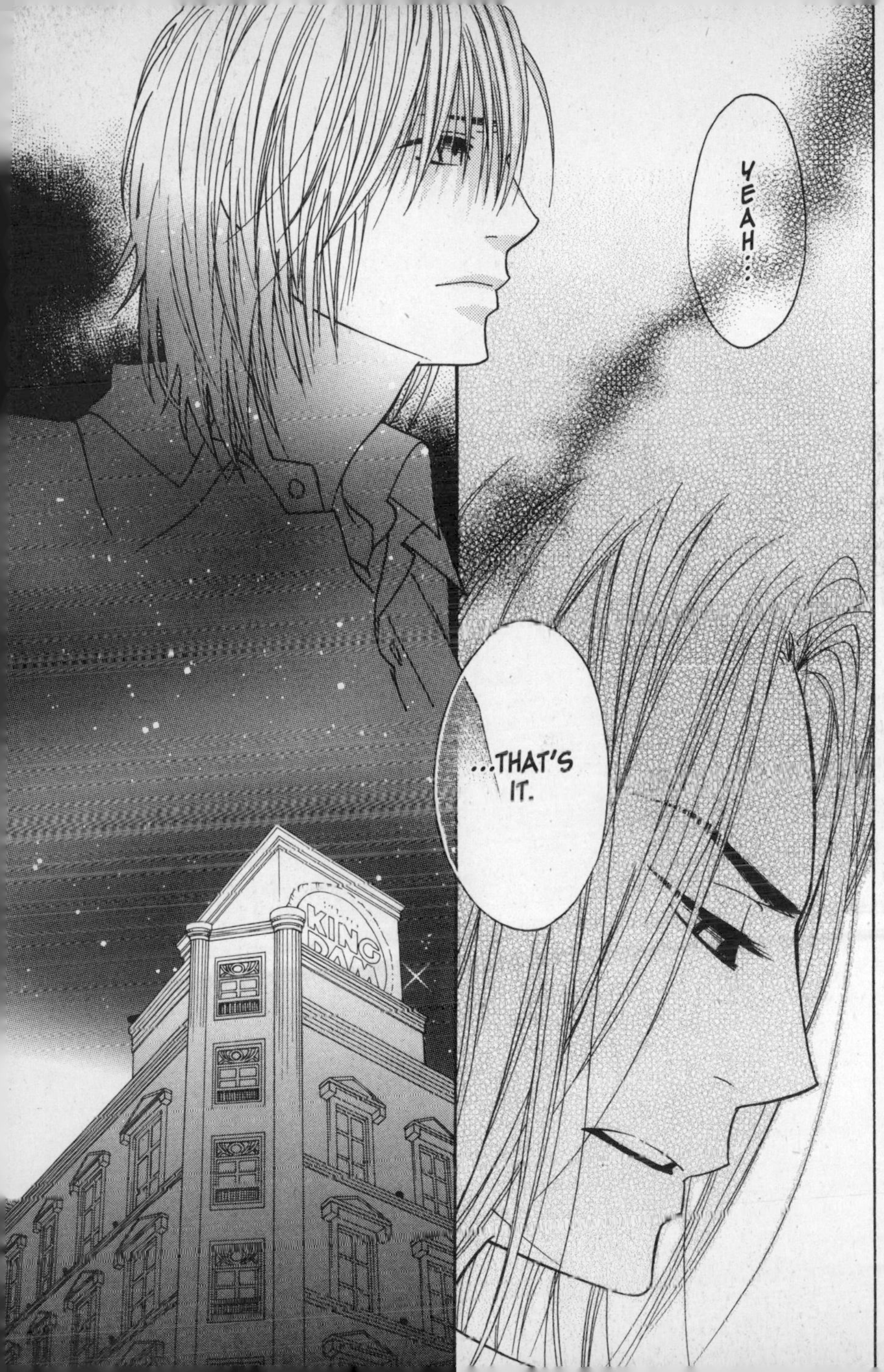
YEAH...
...THAT'S IT.

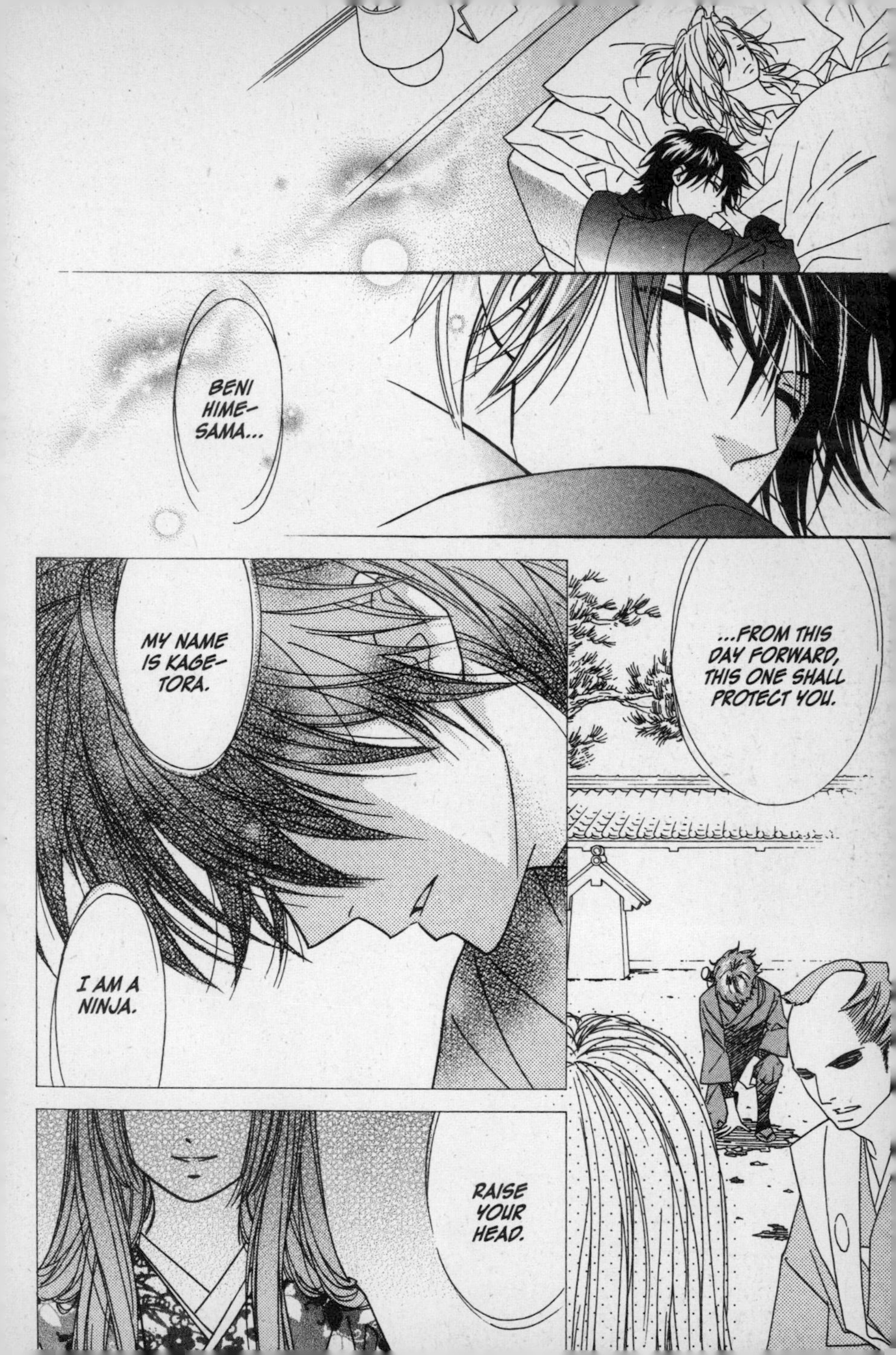
BENI HIME-SAMA...
...FROM THIS DAY FORWARD, THIS ONE SHALL PROTECT YOU.
MY NAME IS KAGE-TORA.
I AM A NINJA.
RAISE YOUR HEAD.

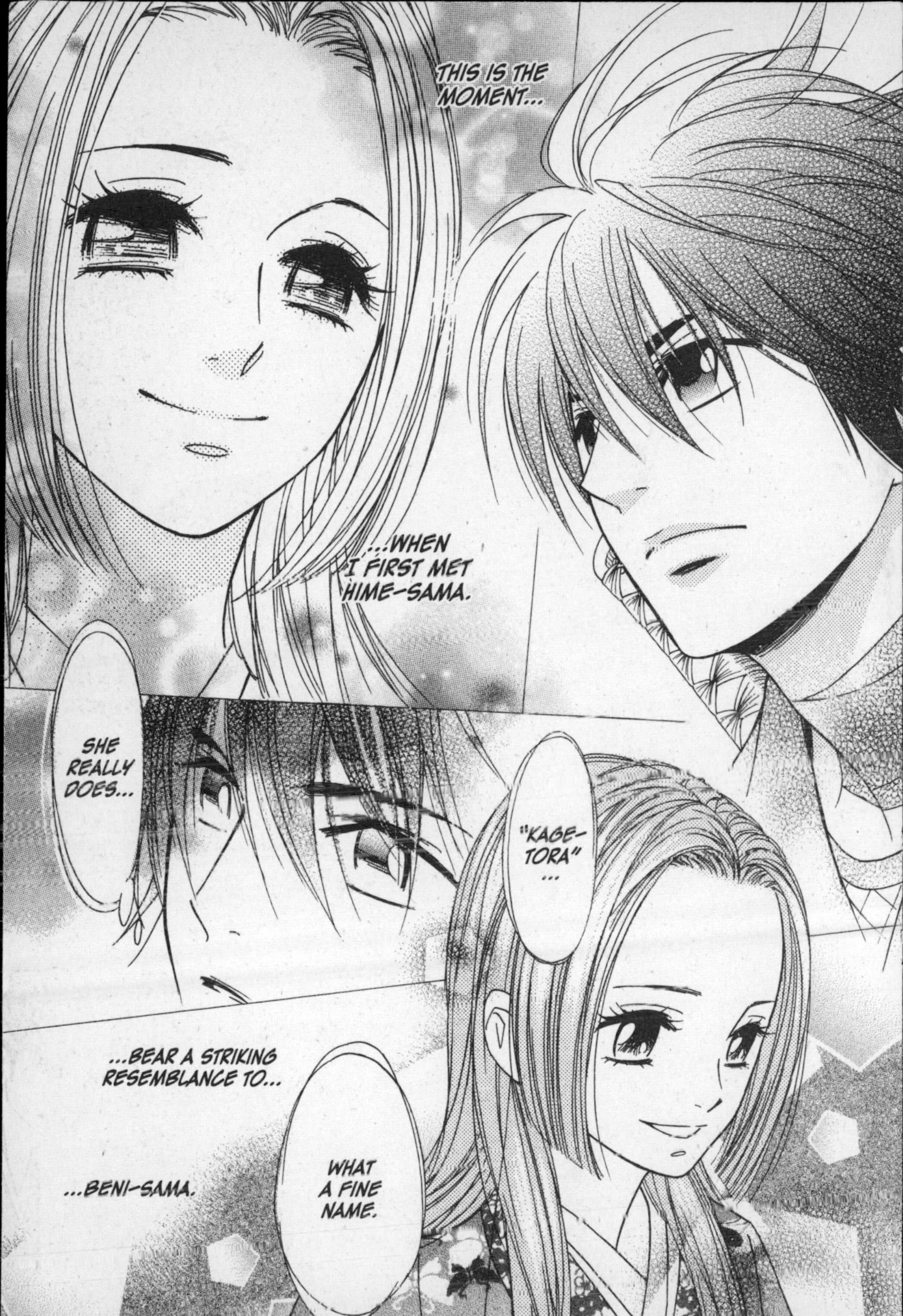
THIS IS THE MOMENT...
...WHEN I FIRST MET HIME-SAMA.
"KAGE-TORA"...
SHE REALLY DOES...
WHAT A FINE NAME.
...BEAR A STRIKING RESEMBLANCE TO...
...BENI-SAMA.

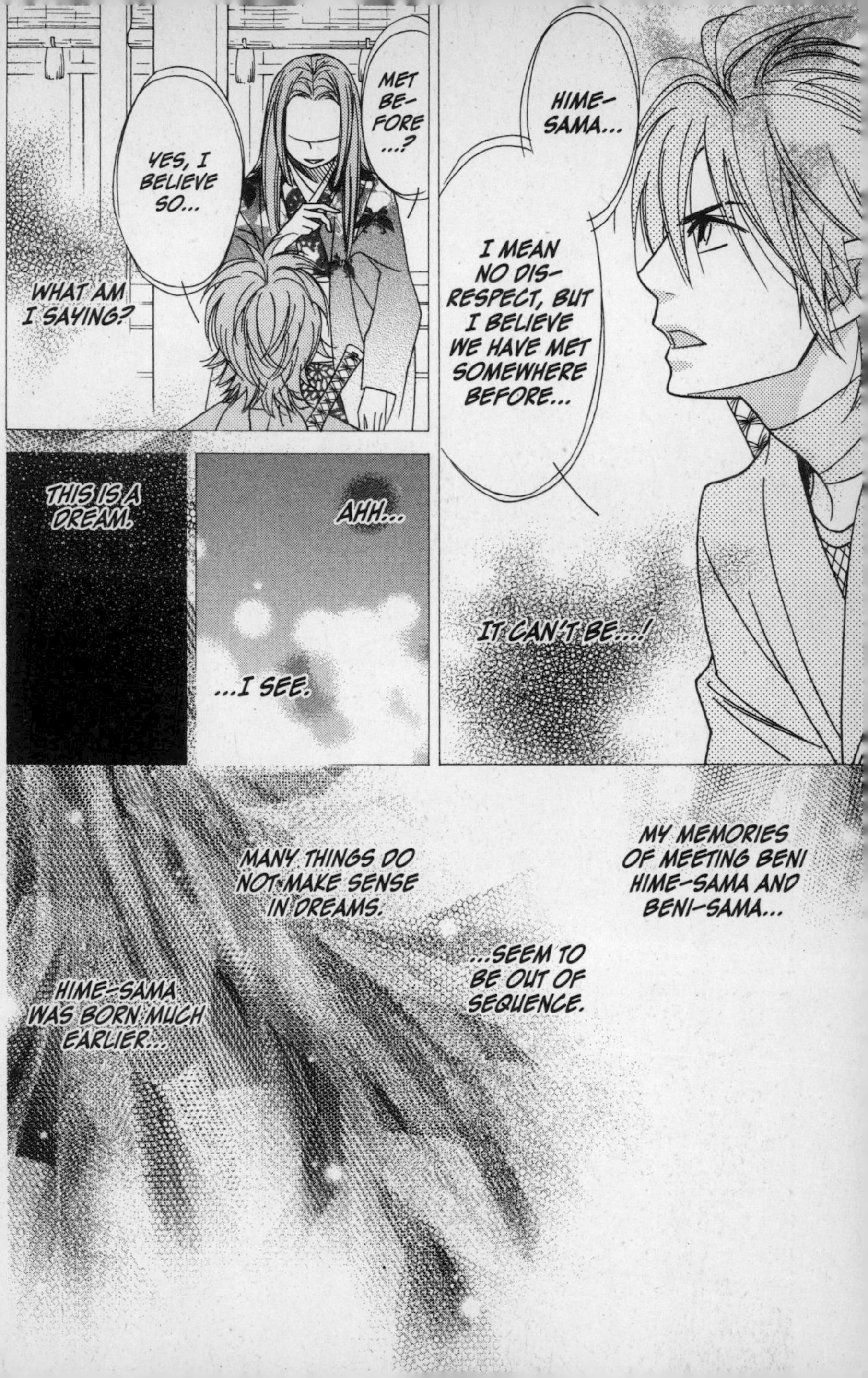
HIME-SAMA...
I MEAN NO DISRESPECT, BUT I BELIEVE WE HAVE MET SOMEWHERE BEFORE...
IT CAN'T BE...!
MET BEFORE...?
YES, I BELIEVE SO...
WHAT AM I SAYING?
AHH...
...I SEE.
THIS IS A DREAM.
MY MEMORIES OF MEETING BENI HIME-SAMA AND BENI-SAMA...
...SEEM TO BE OUT OF SEQUENCE.
MANY THINGS DO NOT MAKE SENSE IN DREAMS.
HIME-SAMA WAS BORN MUCH EARLIER...

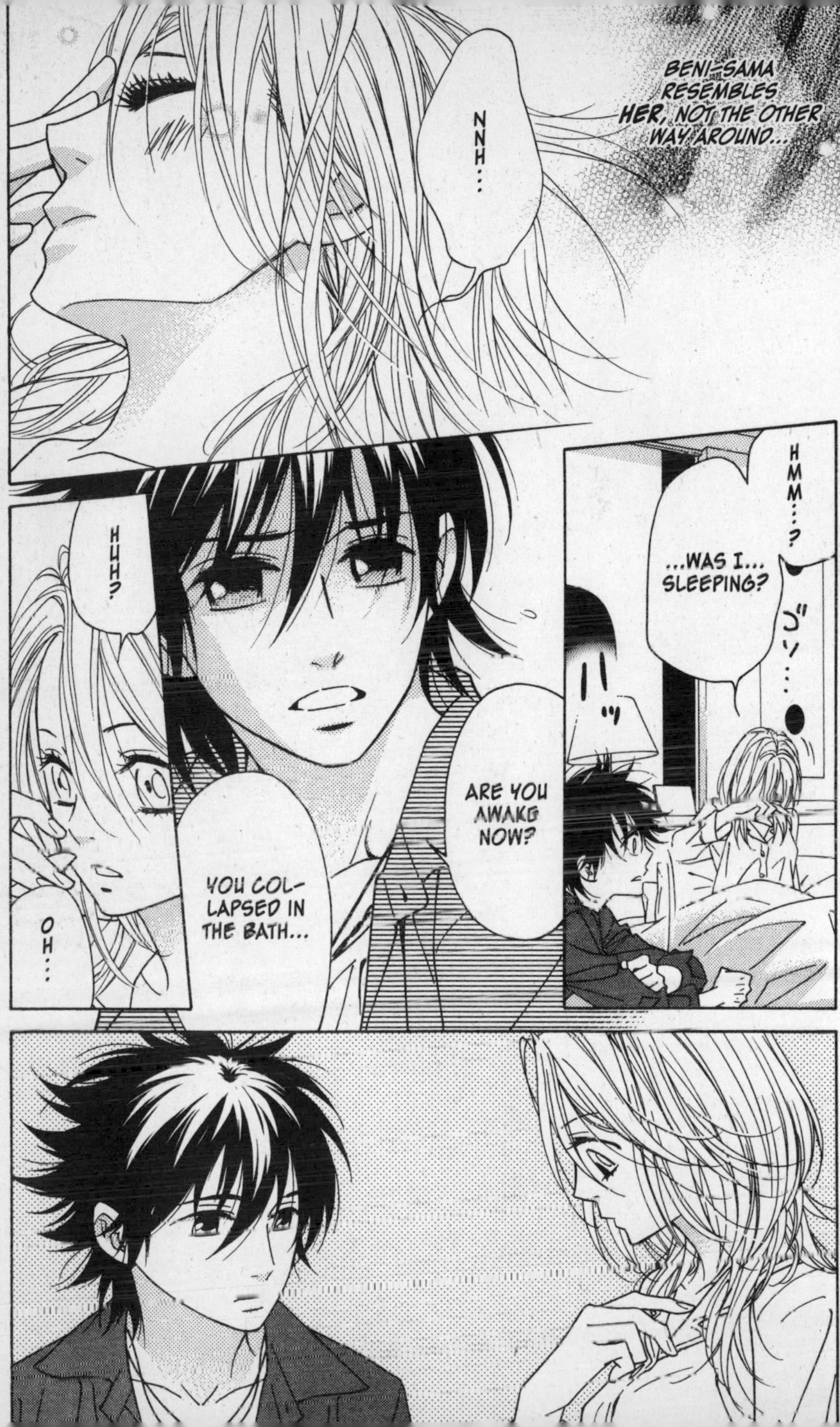

BENI-SAMA RESEMBLES HER, NOT THE OTHER WAY AROUND...
NNH...
HMM...?
...WAS I... SLEEPING?
ゴソ…
ARE YOU AWAKE NOW?
HUH?
YOU COL-LAPSED IN THE BATH...
OH...

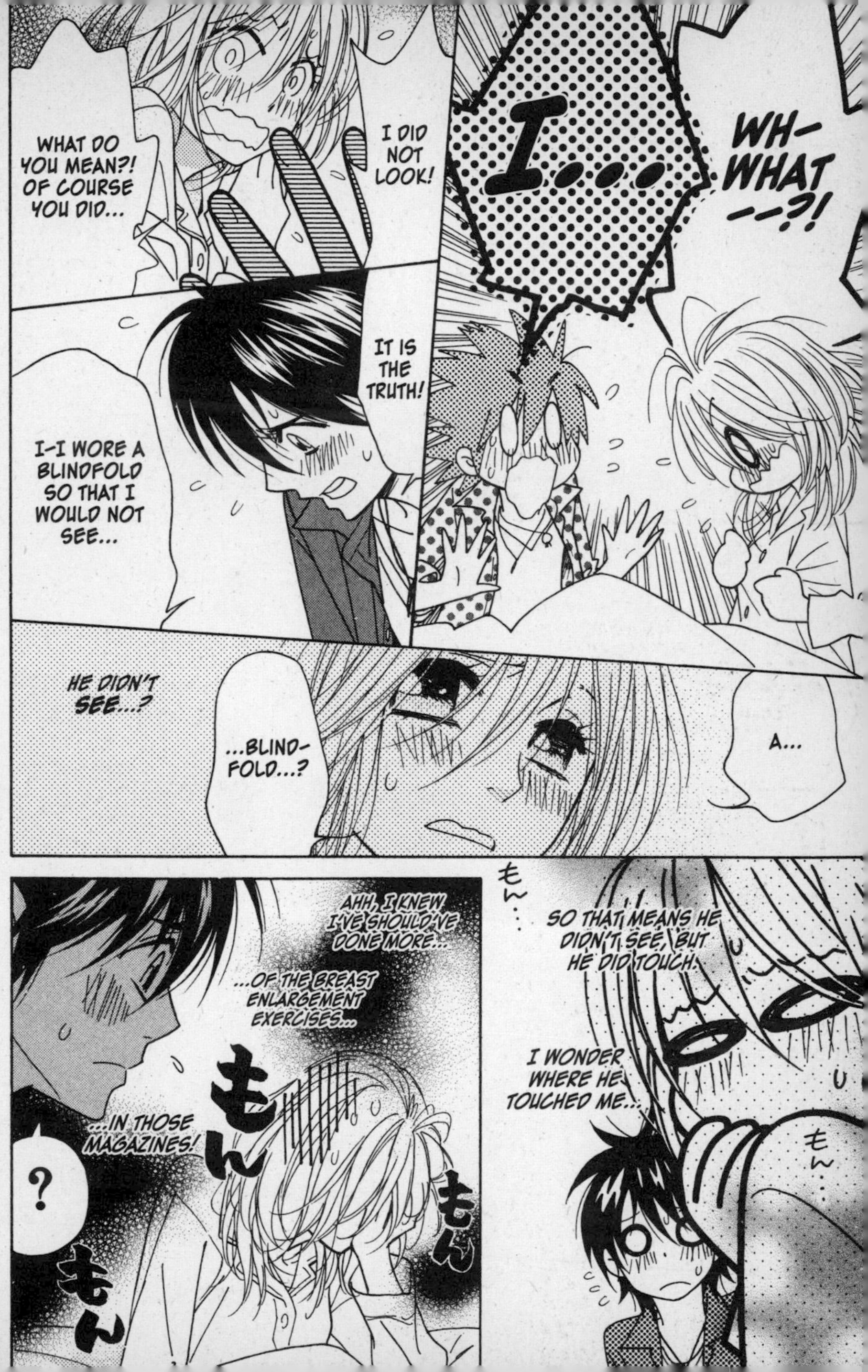
WH-WHAT--?!
I...
I DID NOT LOOK!
WHAT DO YOU MEAN?! OF COURSE YOU DID...
IT IS THE TRUTH!
I-I WORE A BLINDFOLD SO THAT I WOULD NOT SEE...
A...
...BLIND-FOLD...?
HE DIDN'T SEE...?
もん...
SO THAT MEANS HE DIDN'T SEE, BUT HE DID TOUCH.
I WONDER WHERE HE TOUCHED ME...
もん...
AHH, I KNEW I'VE SHOULD'VE DONE MORE...
...OF THE BREAST ENLARGEMENT EXERCISES...
もん
...IN THOSE MAGAZINES!
もん
?
もん

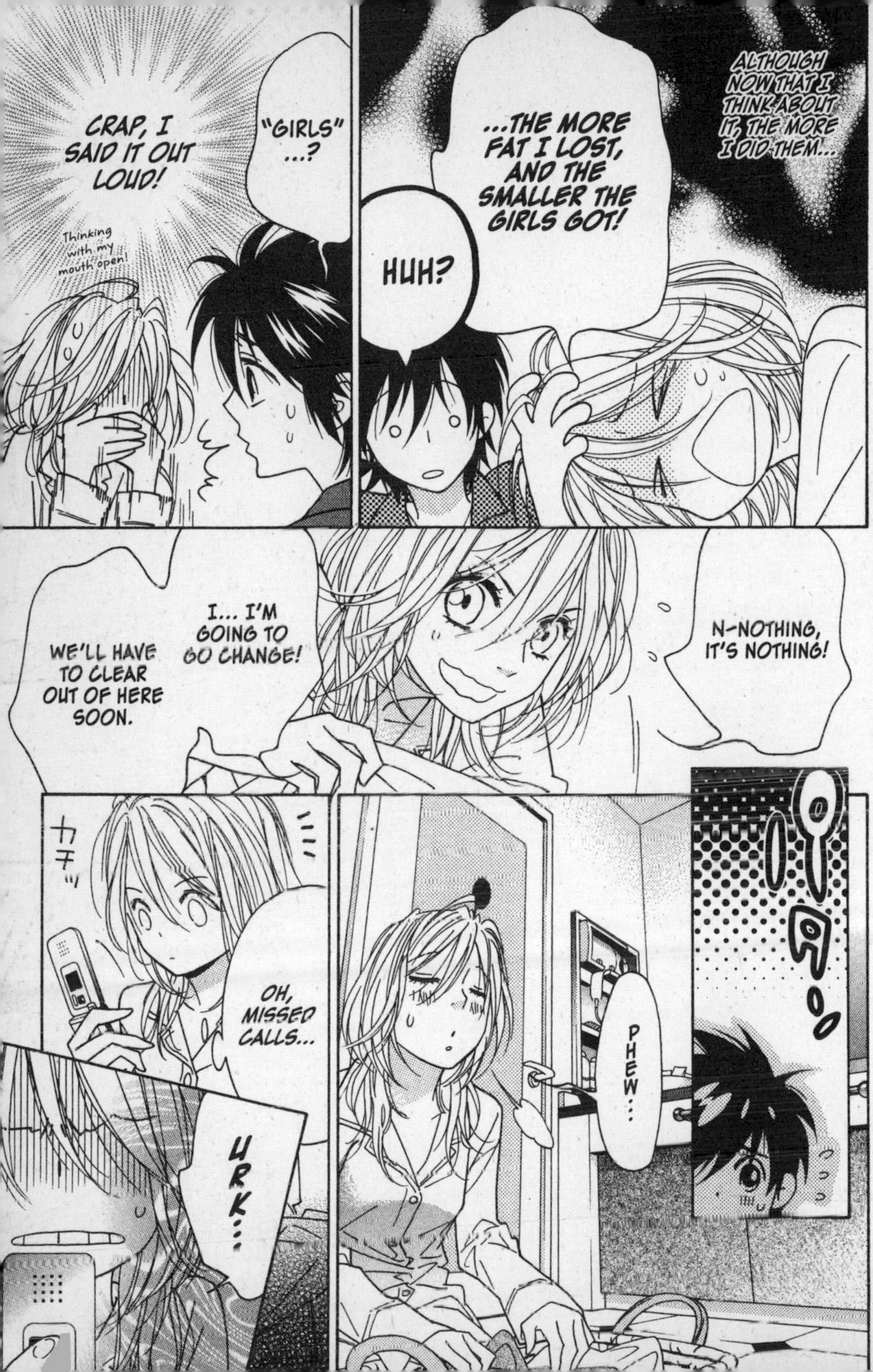
ALTHOUGH NOW THAT I THINK ABOUT IT, THE MORE I DID THEM...
...THE MORE FAT I LOST, AND THE SMALLER THE GIRLS GOT!
HUH?
"GIRLS" ...?
CRAP, I SAID IT OUT LOUD!
Thinking with my mouth open!
N-NOTHING, IT'S NOTHING!
I... I'M GOING TO GO CHANGE!
WE'LL HAVE TO CLEAR OUT OF HERE SOON.
PHEW...
カチッ
OH, MISSED CALLS...
URK...

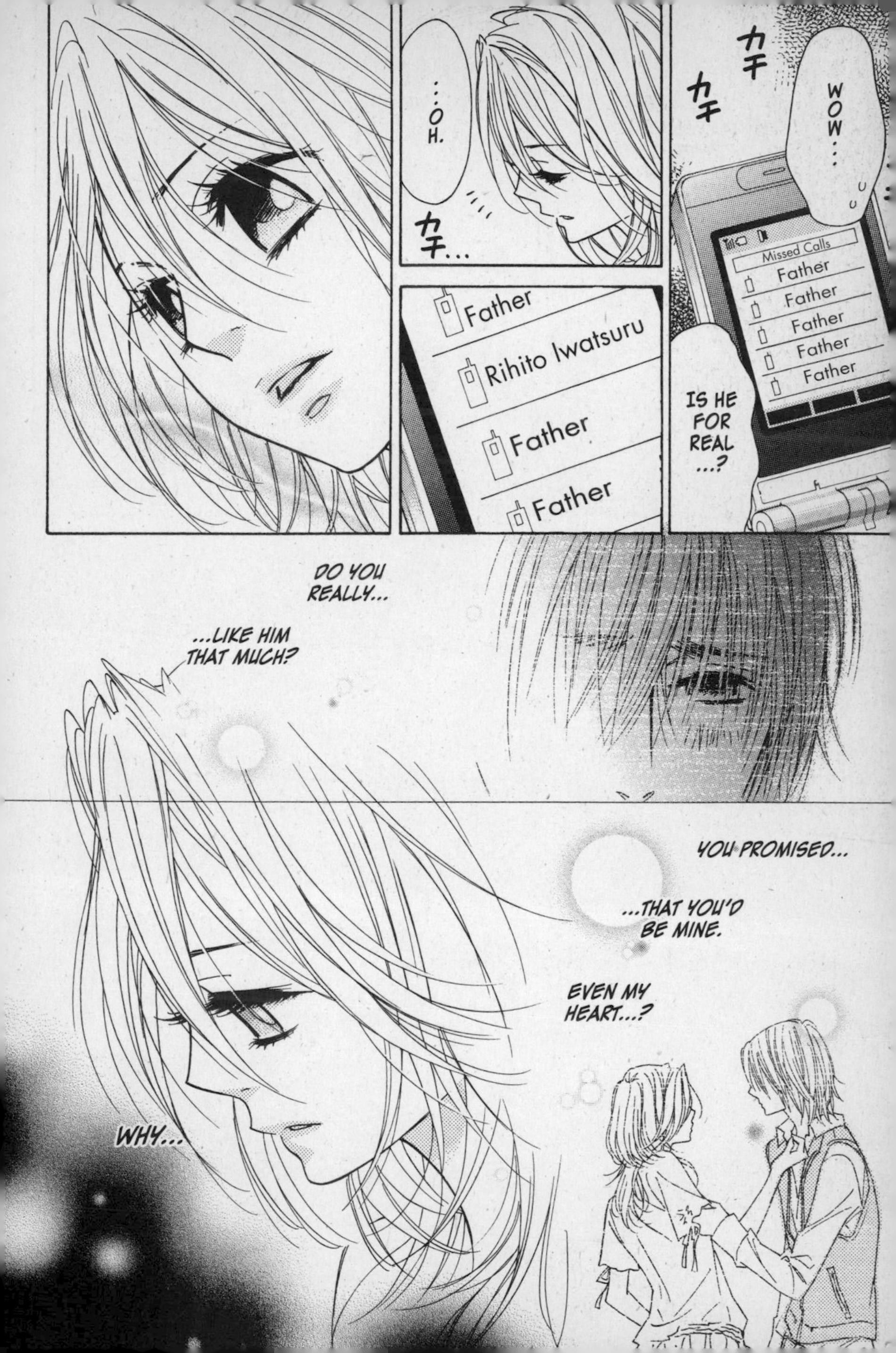

カチ
カチ
WOW...
Missed Calls
Father
Father
Father
Father
Father
IS HE FOR REAL ...?
...OH.
カチ...
Father
Rihito Iwatsuru
Father
Father
DO YOU REALLY...
...LIKE HIM THAT MUCH?
YOU PROMISED...
...THAT YOU'D BE MINE.
EVEN MY HEART...?
WHY...

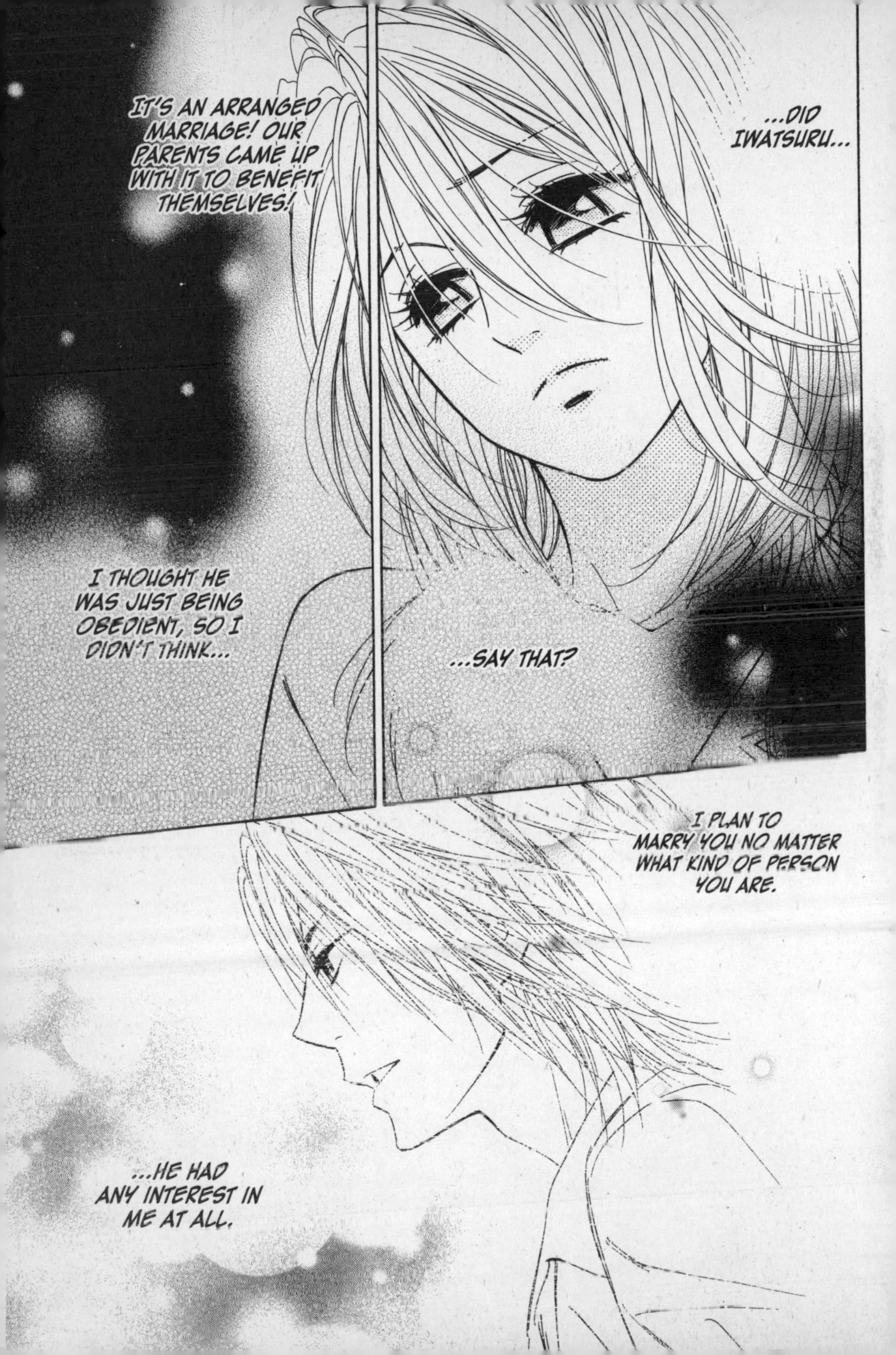
...DID IWATSURU...
...SAY THAT?
IT'S AN ARRANGED MARRIAGE! OUR PARENTS CAME UP WITH IT TO BENEFIT THEMSELVES!
I THOUGHT HE WAS JUST BEING OBEDIENT, SO I DIDN'T THINK...
I PLAN TO MARRY YOU NO MATTER WHAT KIND OF PERSON YOU ARE.
...HE HAD ANY INTEREST IN ME AT ALL.

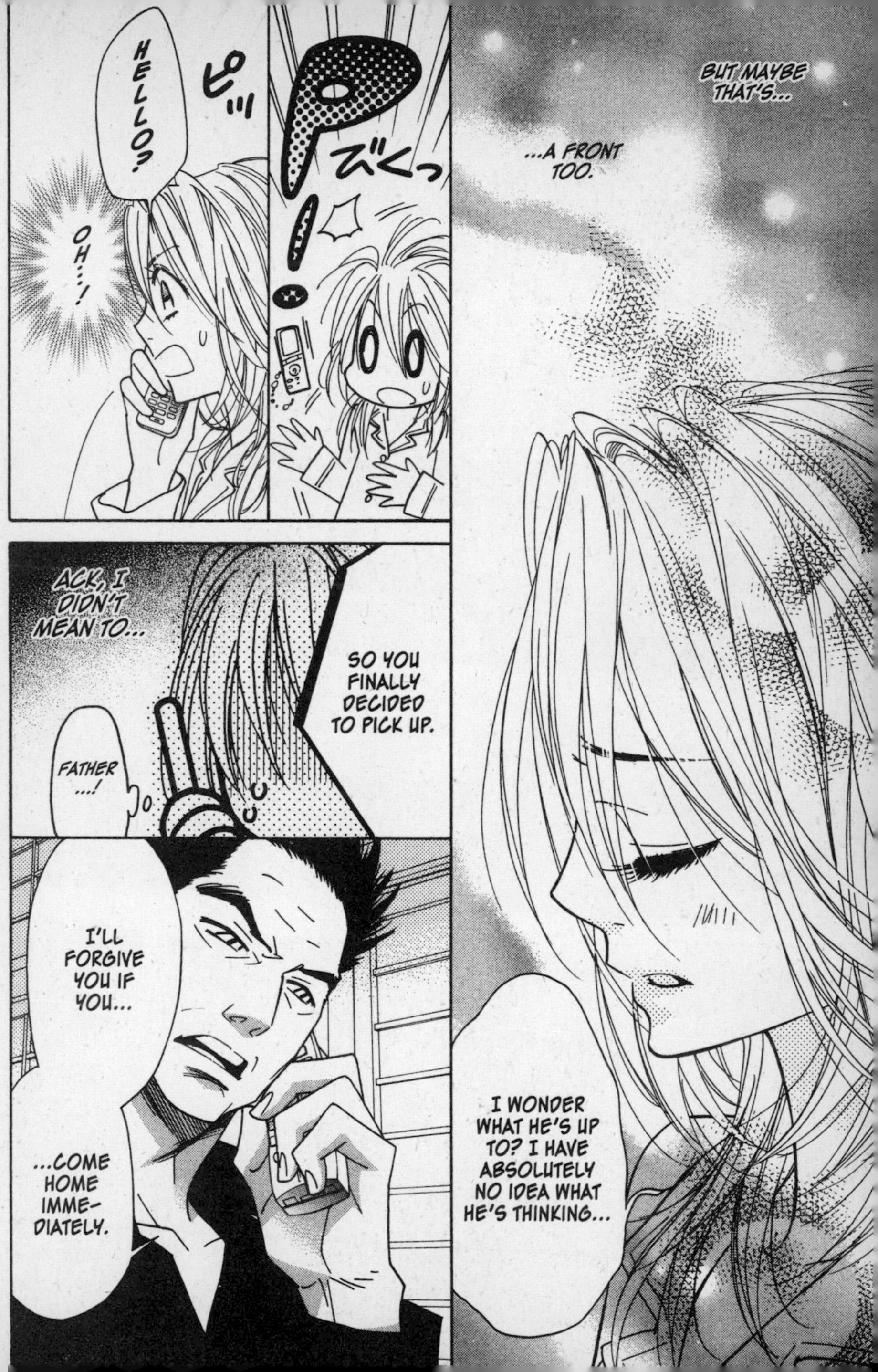
BUT MAYBE THAT'S...
...A FRONT TOO.
I WONDER WHAT HE'S UP TO? I HAVE ABSOLUTELY NO IDEA WHAT HE'S THINKING...
P
びくっ
!
ピッ
HELLO?
OH...!
SO YOU FINALLY DECIDED TO PICK UP.
ACK, I DIDN'T MEAN TO...
FATHER...!
I'LL FORGIVE YOU IF YOU...
...COME HOME IMME-DIATELY.

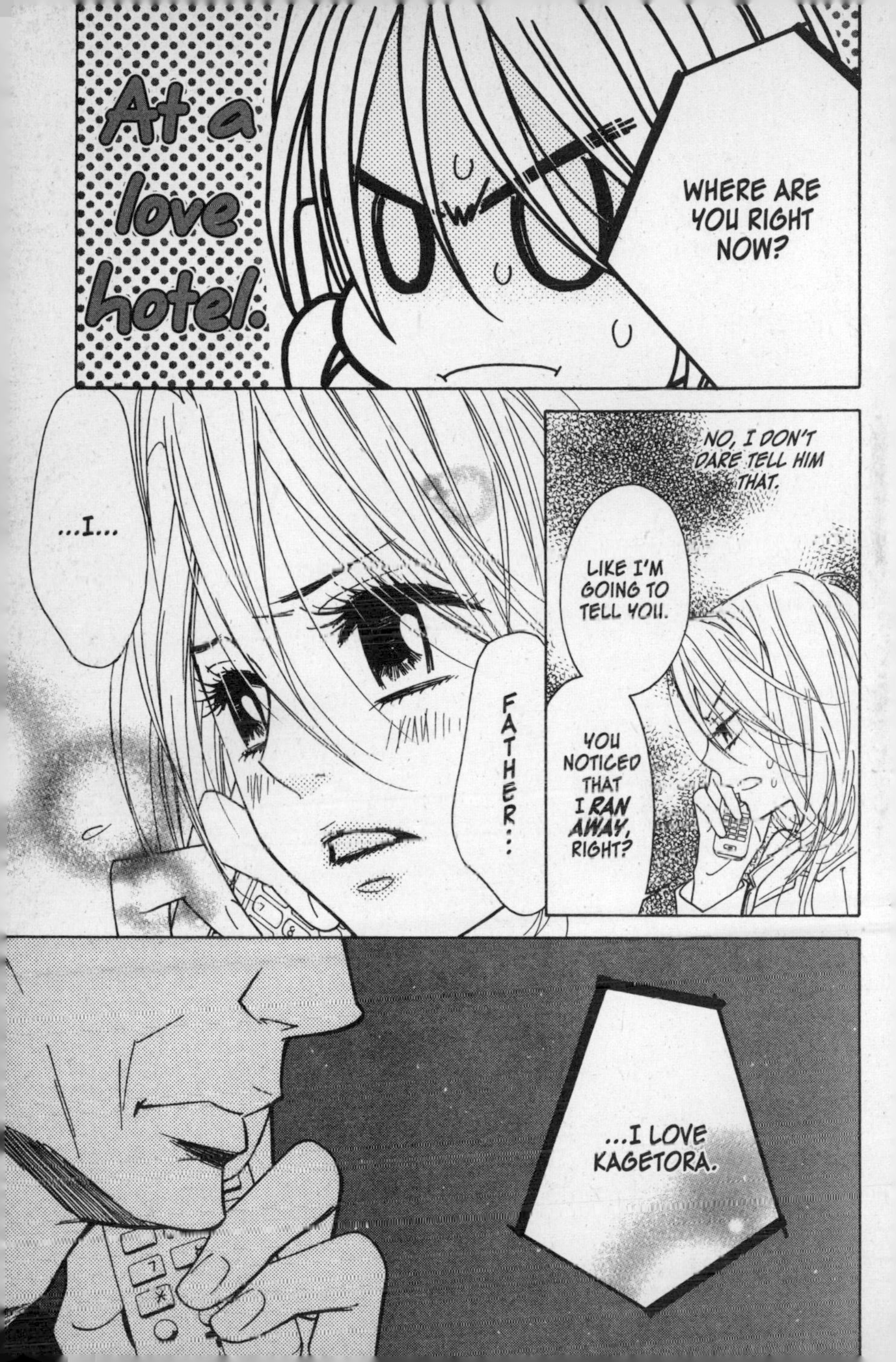
WHERE ARE YOU RIGHT NOW?
At a love hotel.
NO, I DON'T DARE TELL HIM THAT.
LIKE I'M GOING TO TELL YOU.
YOU NOTICED THAT I RAN AWAY, RIGHT?
FATHER...
...I...
...I LOVE KAGETORA.

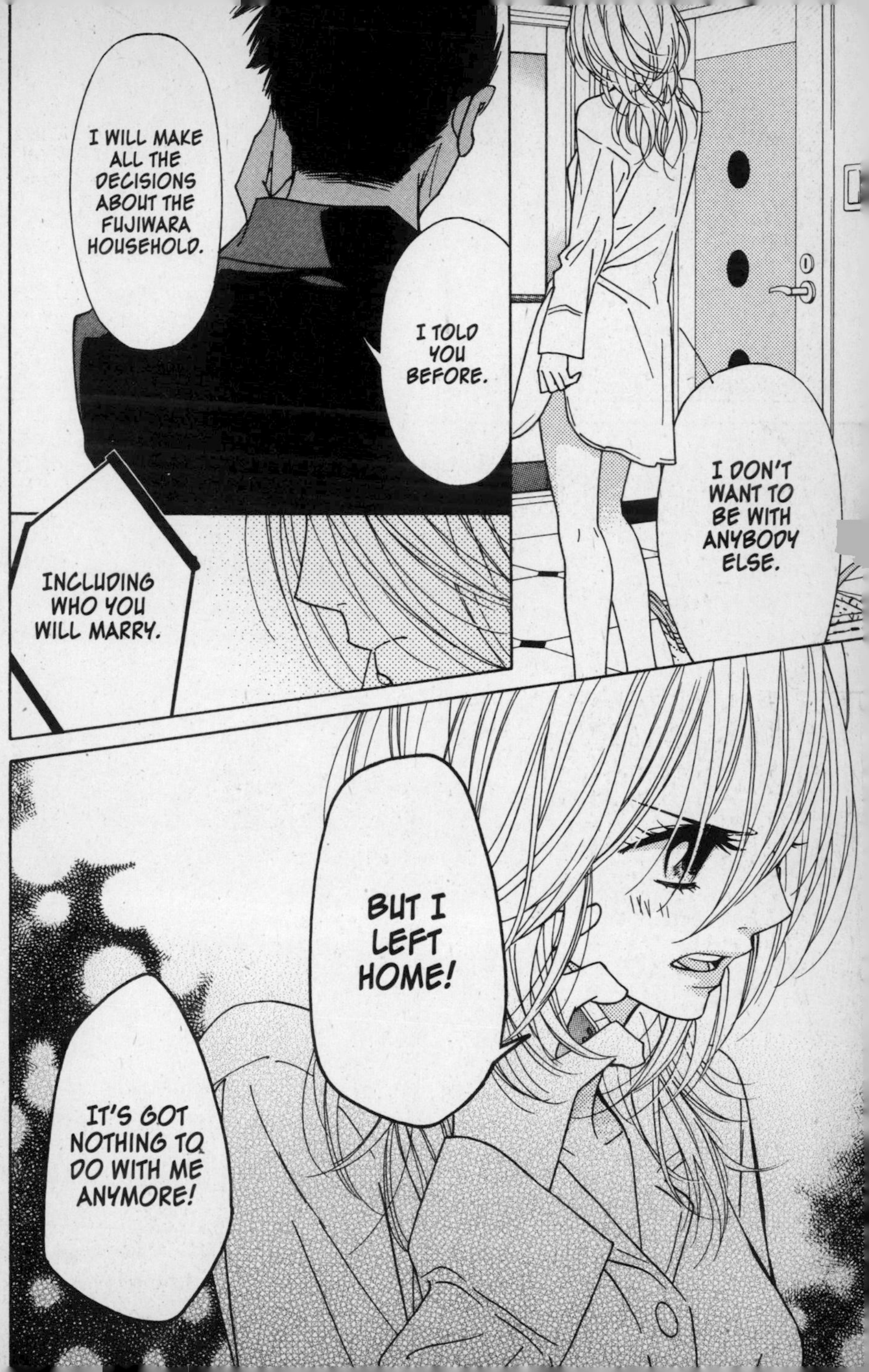
I DON'T WANT TO BE WITH ANYBODY ELSE.
I TOLD YOU BEFORE.
I WILL MAKE ALL THE DECISIONS ABOUT THE FUJIWARA HOUSEHOLD.
INCLUDING WHO YOU WILL MARRY.
BUT I LEFT HOME!
IT'S GOT NOTHING TO DO WITH ME ANYMORE!

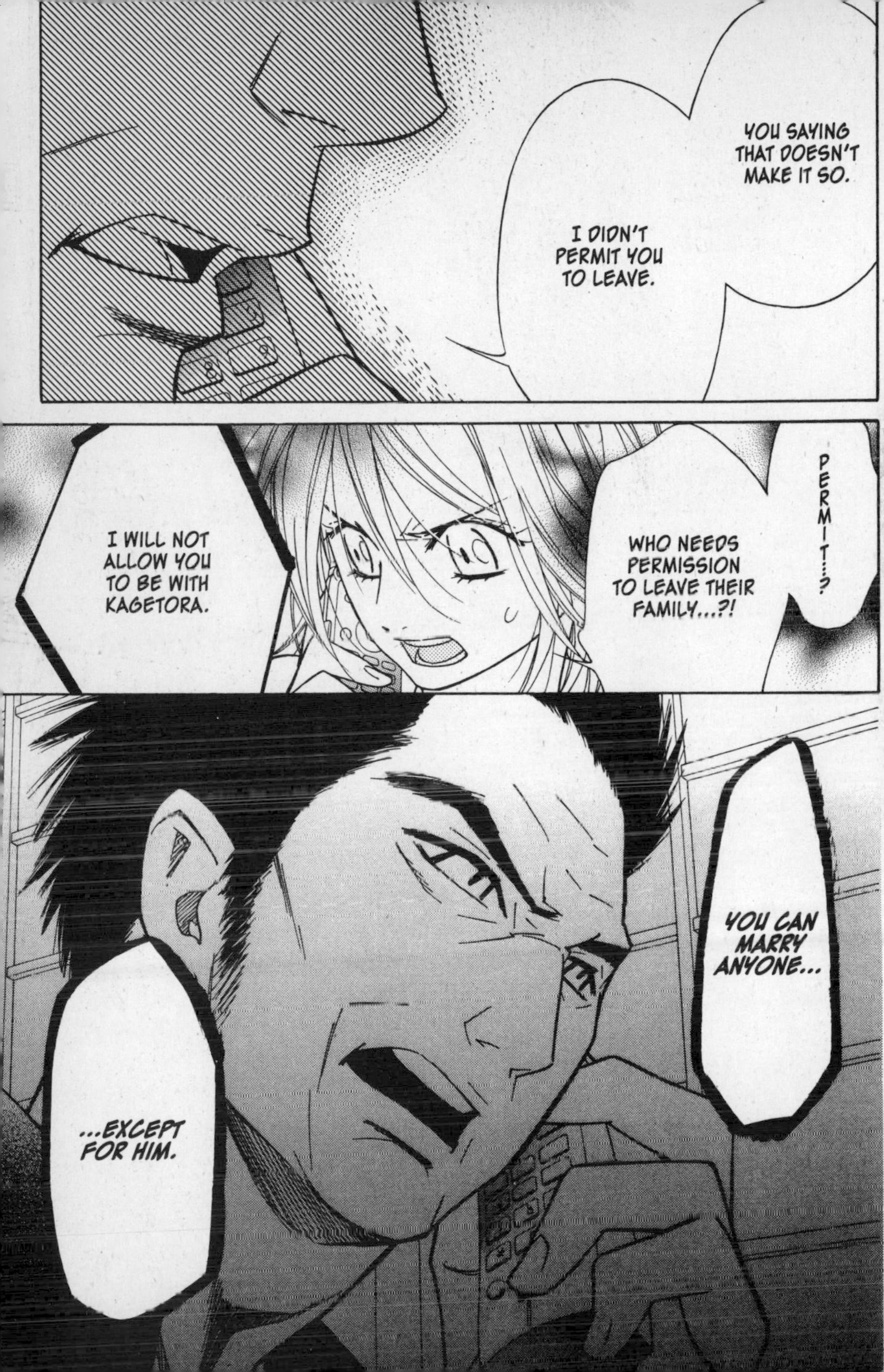
YOU SAYING THAT DOESN'T MAKE IT SO.
I DIDN'T PERMIT YOU TO LEAVE.
PERMIT...?
WHO NEEDS PERMISSION TO LEAVE THEIR FAMILY...?!
I WILL NOT ALLOW YOU TO BE WITH KAGETORA.
YOU CAN MARRY ANYONE...
...EXCEPT FOR HIM.

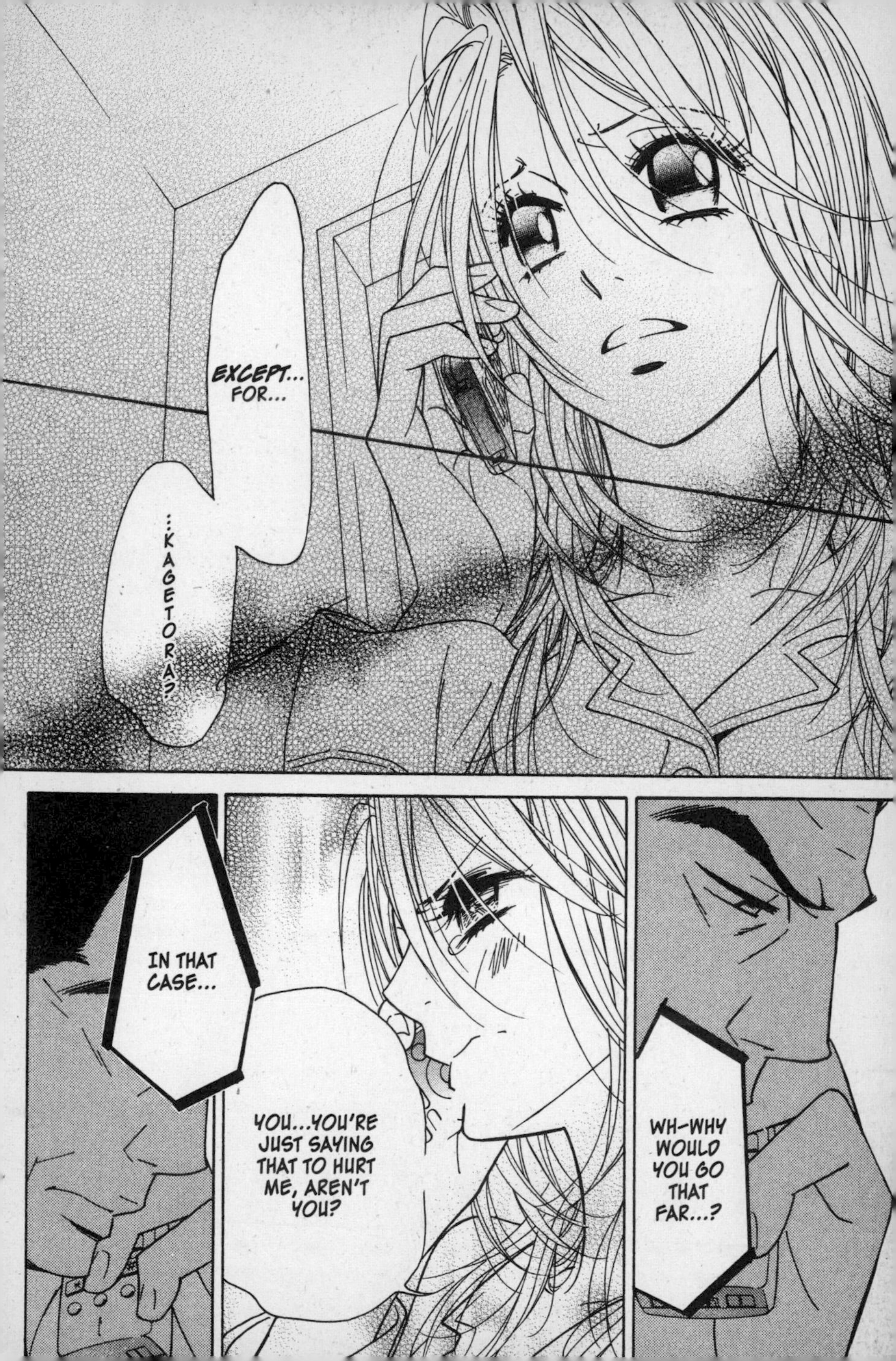
EXCEPT... FOR...
...KAGETORA?
WH-WHY WOULD YOU GO THAT FAR...?
YOU...YOU'RE JUST SAYING THAT TO HURT ME, AREN'T YOU?
IN THAT CASE...

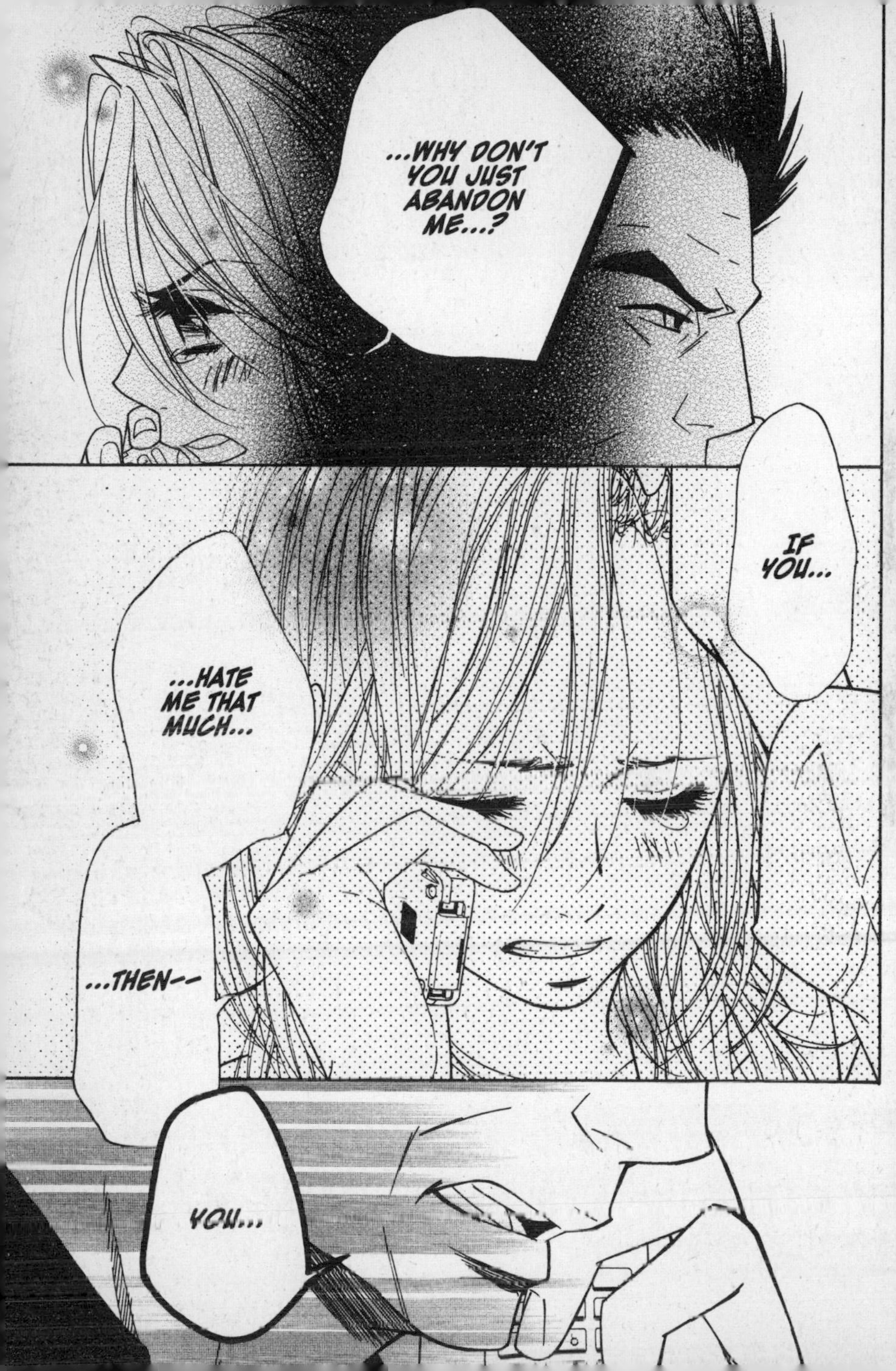
...WHY DON'T YOU JUST ABANDON ME...?
IF YOU...
...HATE ME THAT MUCH...
...THEN--
YOU...

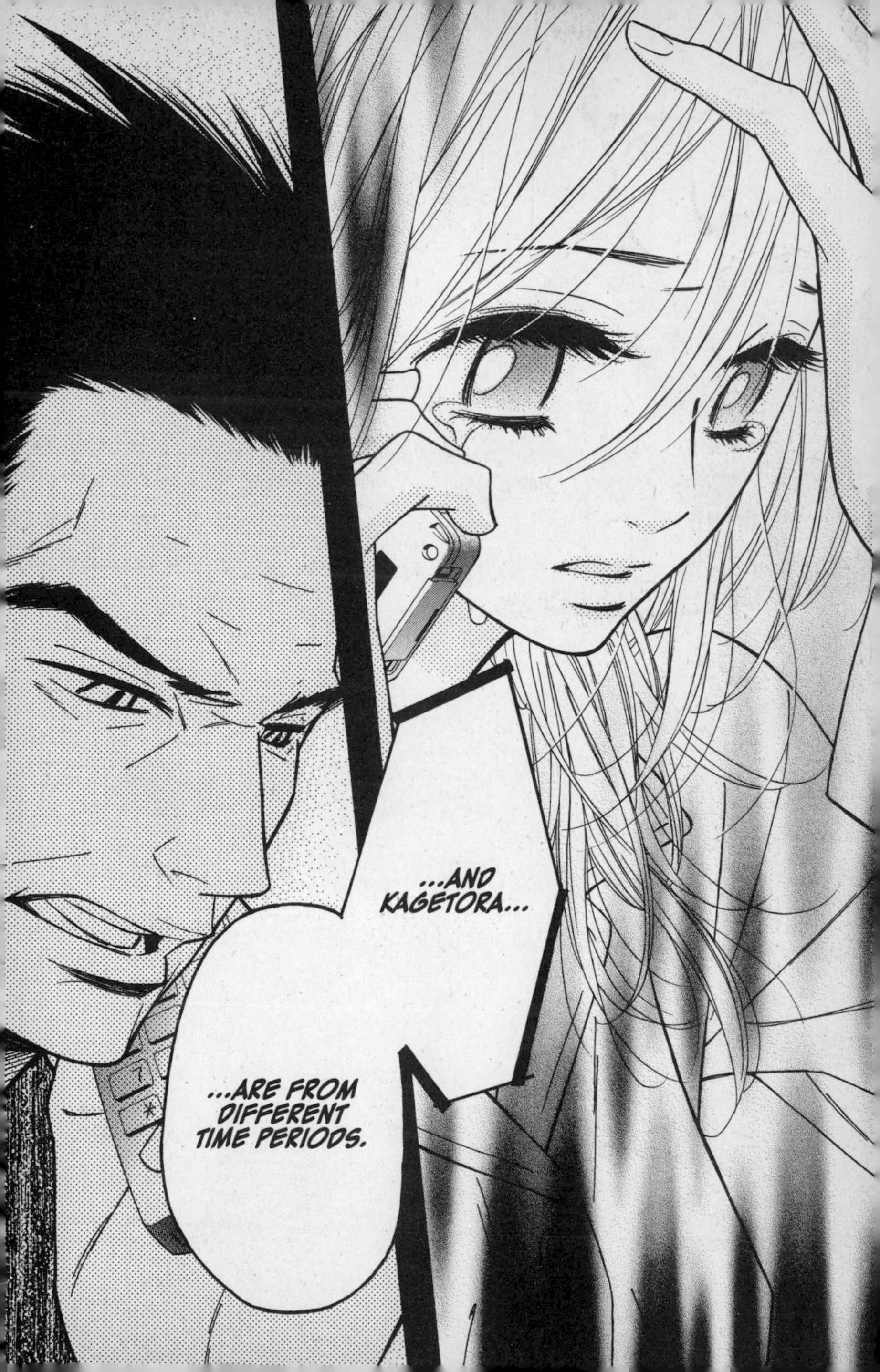
...AND KAGETORA...
...ARE FROM DIFFERENT TIME PERIODS.

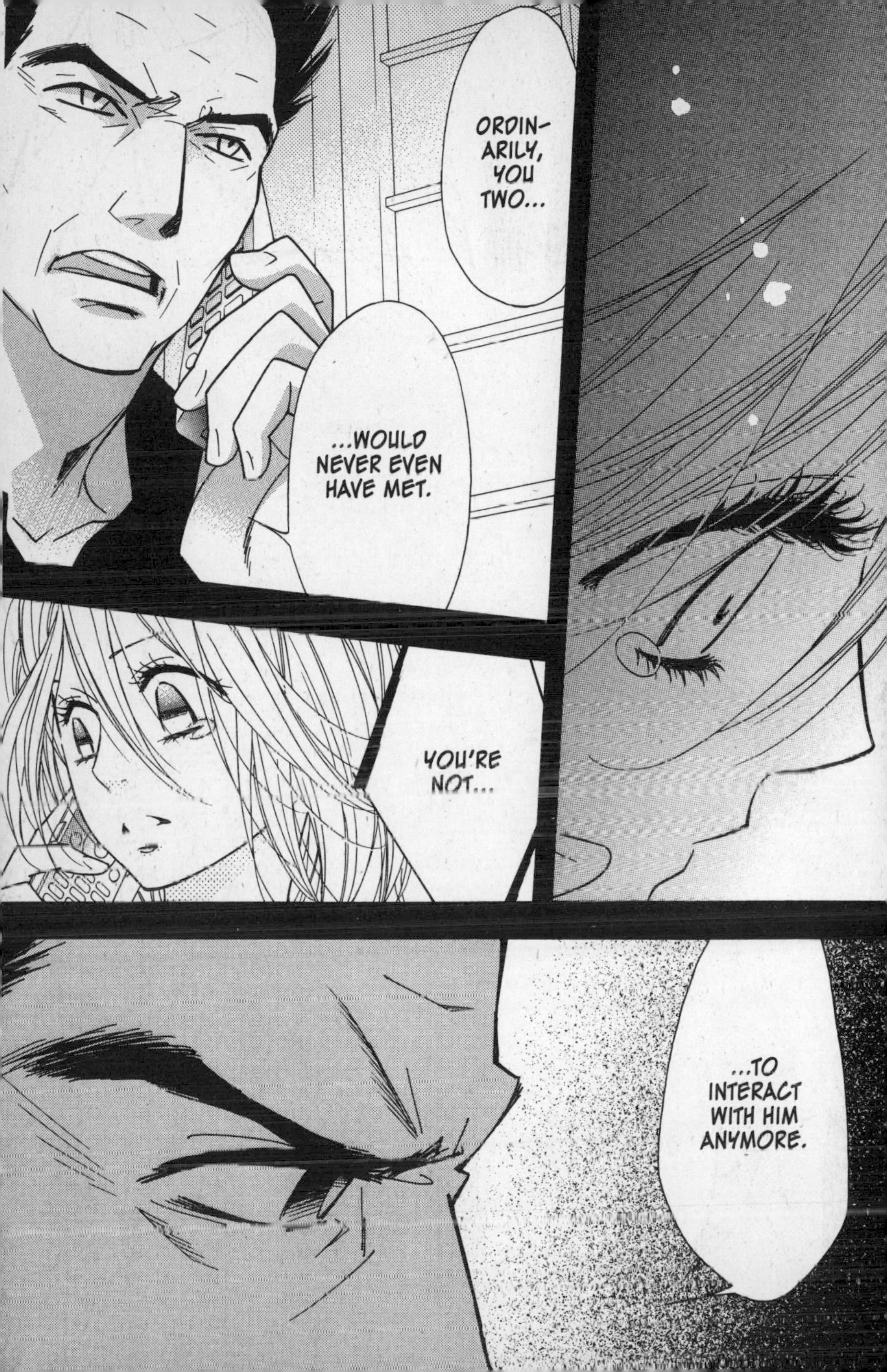
ORDIN-ARILY, YOU TWO...
...WOULD NEVER EVEN HAVE MET.
YOU'RE NOT...
...TO INTERACT WITH HIM ANYMORE.

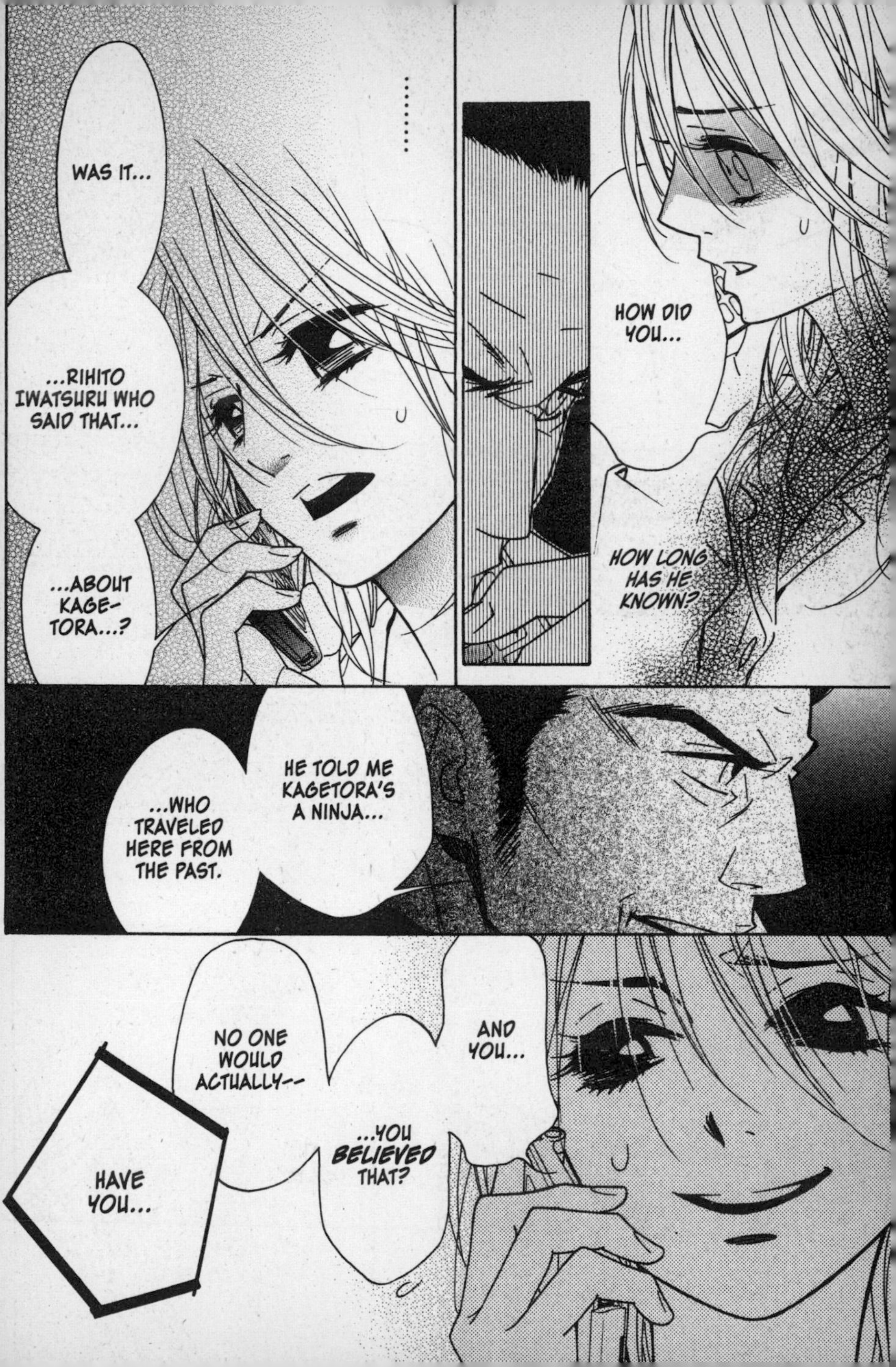
HOW DID YOU...
HOW LONG HAS HE KNOWN?
......
WAS IT...
...RIHITO IWATSURU WHO SAID THAT...
...ABOUT KAGETORA...?
HE TOLD ME KAGETORA'S A NINJA...
...WHO TRAVELED HERE FROM THE PAST.
AND YOU...
...YOU **BELIEVED** THAT?
NO ONE WOULD ACTUALLY--
HAVE YOU...

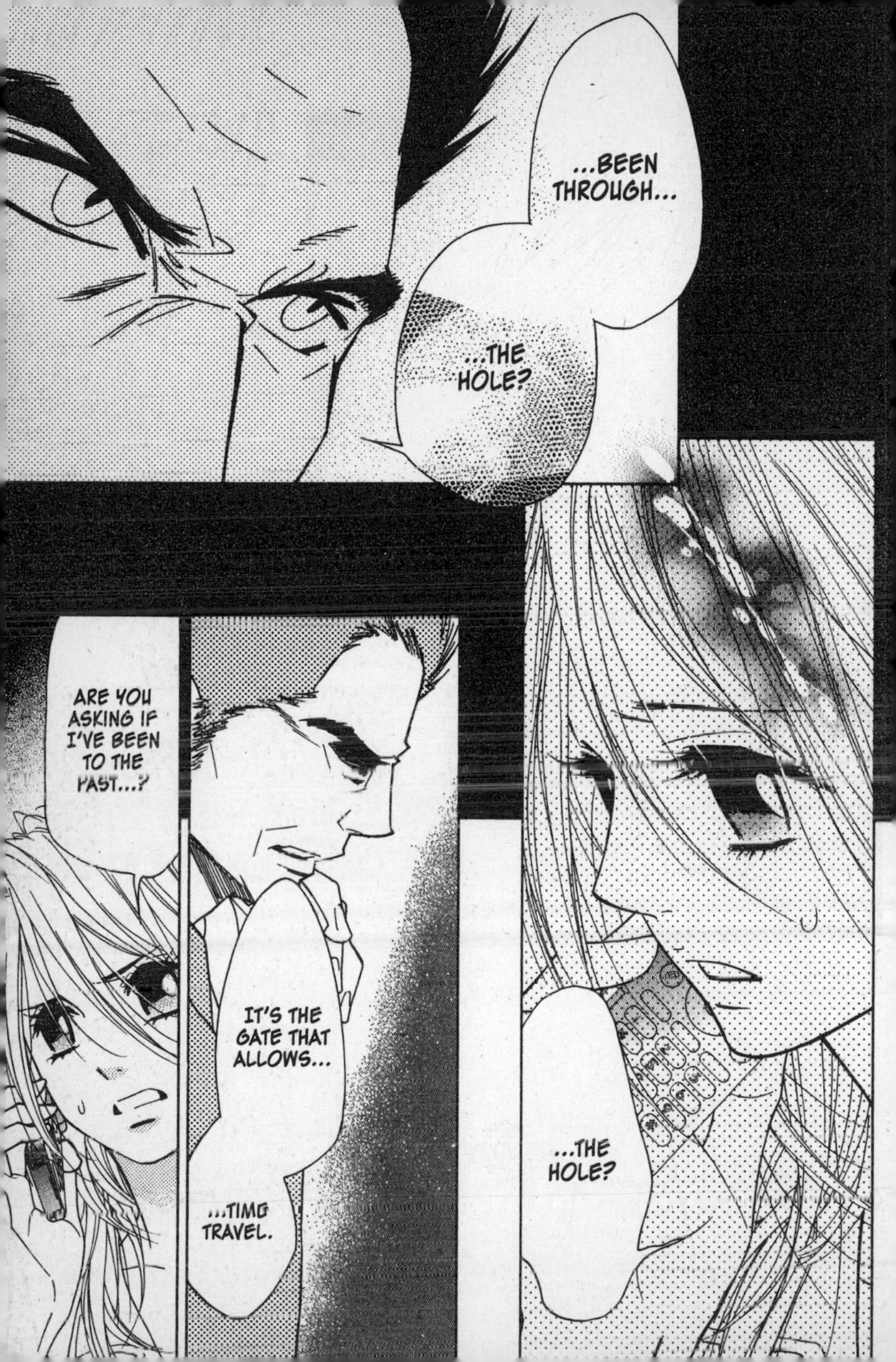
...BEEN THROUGH...
...THE HOLE?
...THE HOLE?
IT'S THE GATE THAT ALLOWS...
...TIME TRAVEL.
ARE YOU ASKING IF I'VE BEEN TO THE PAST...?

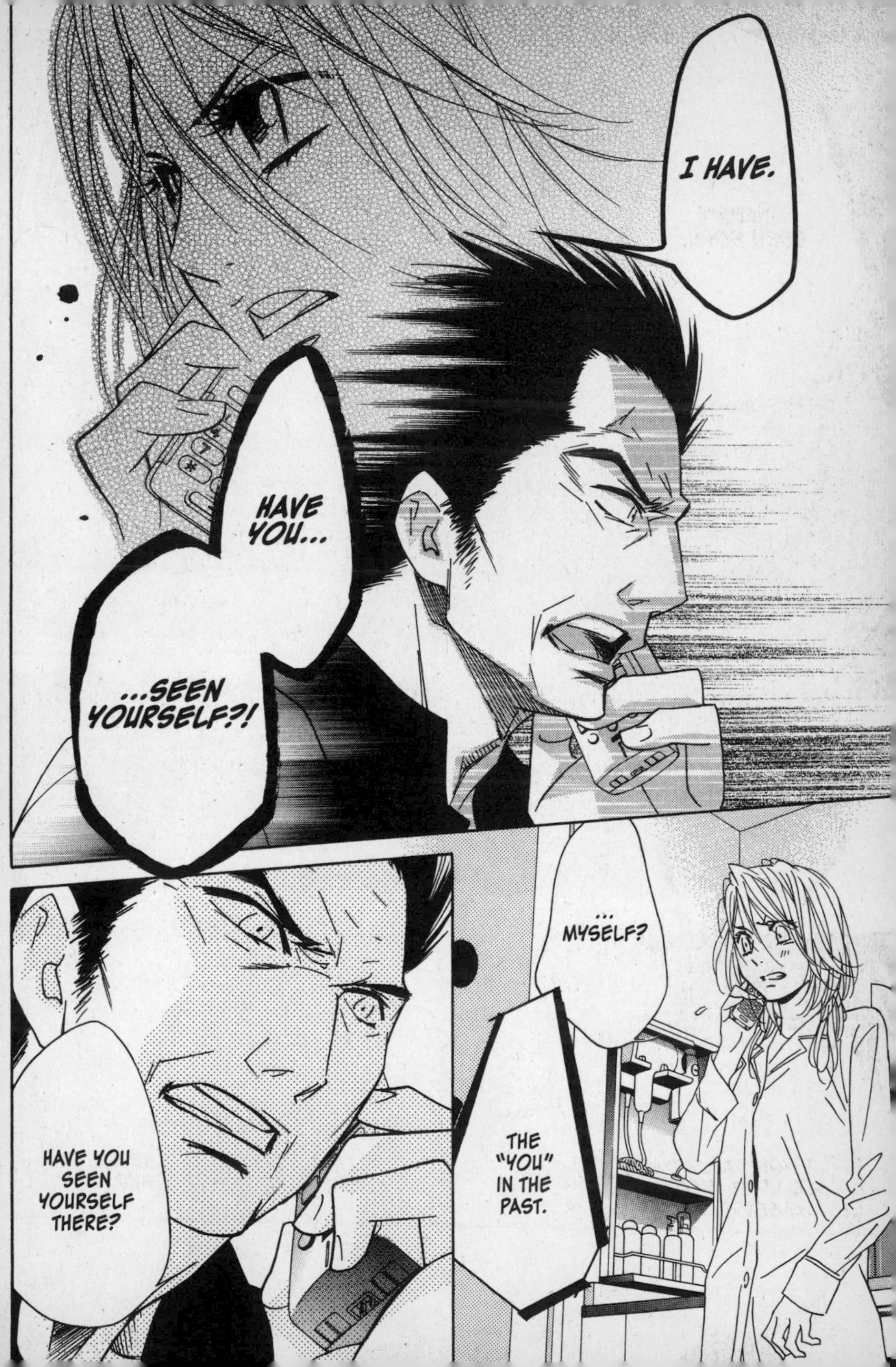
I HAVE.
HAVE YOU...
...SEEN YOURSELF?!
...MYSELF?
THE "YOU" IN THE PAST.
HAVE YOU SEEN YOURSELF THERE?

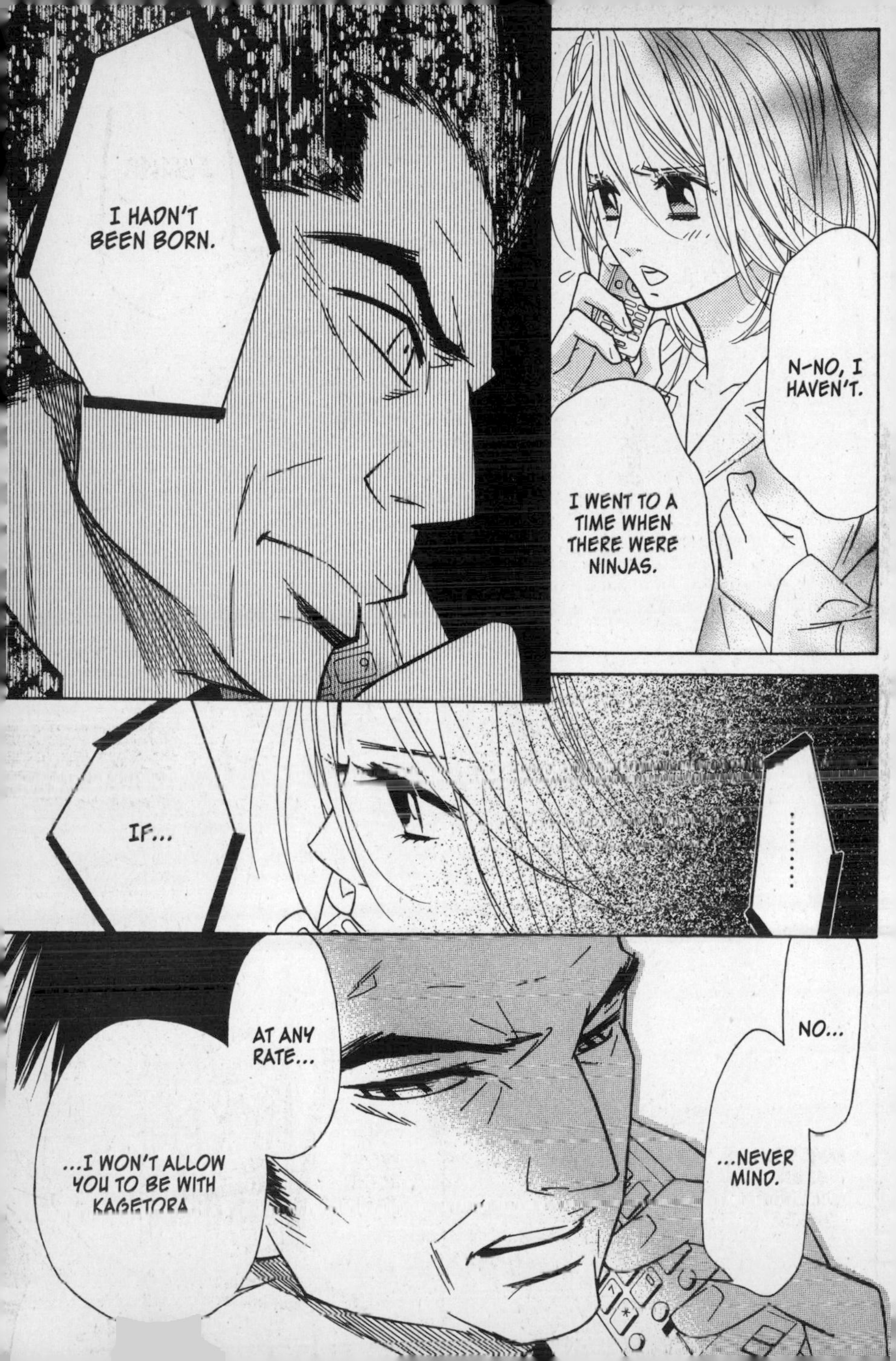
N-NO, I HAVEN'T.
I WENT TO A TIME WHEN THERE WERE NINJAS.
I HADN'T BEEN BORN.
......
IF...
NO...
...NEVER MIND.
AT ANY RATE...
...I WON'T ALLOW YOU TO BE WITH KAGETORA

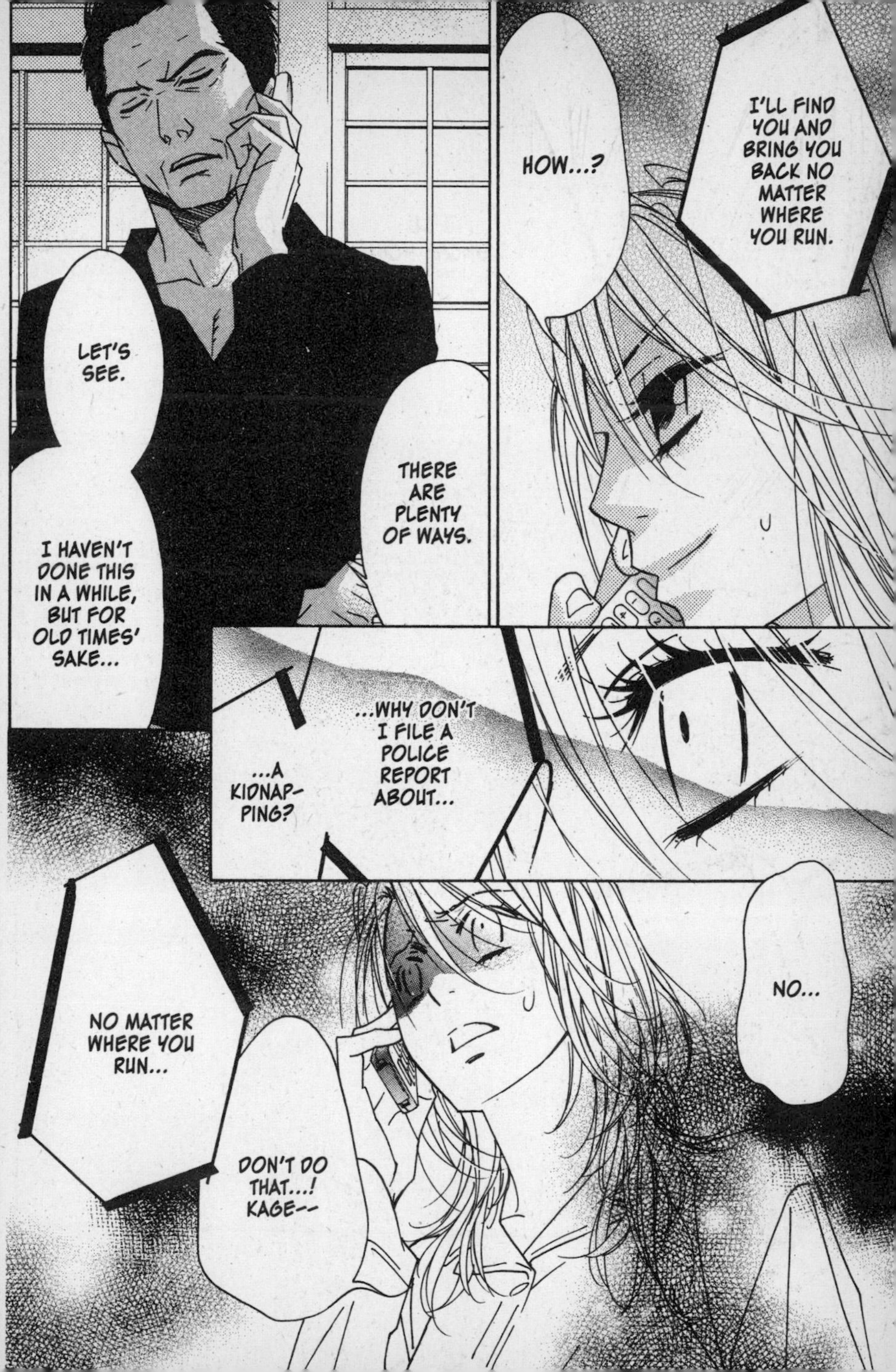
I'LL FIND YOU AND BRING YOU BACK NO MATTER WHERE YOU RUN.
HOW...?
LET'S SEE.
THERE ARE PLENTY OF WAYS.
I HAVEN'T DONE THIS IN A WHILE, BUT FOR OLD TIMES' SAKE...
...WHY DON'T I FILE A POLICE REPORT ABOUT...
...A KIDNAP-PING?
NO...
NO MATTER WHERE YOU RUN...
DON'T DO THAT...! KAGE--

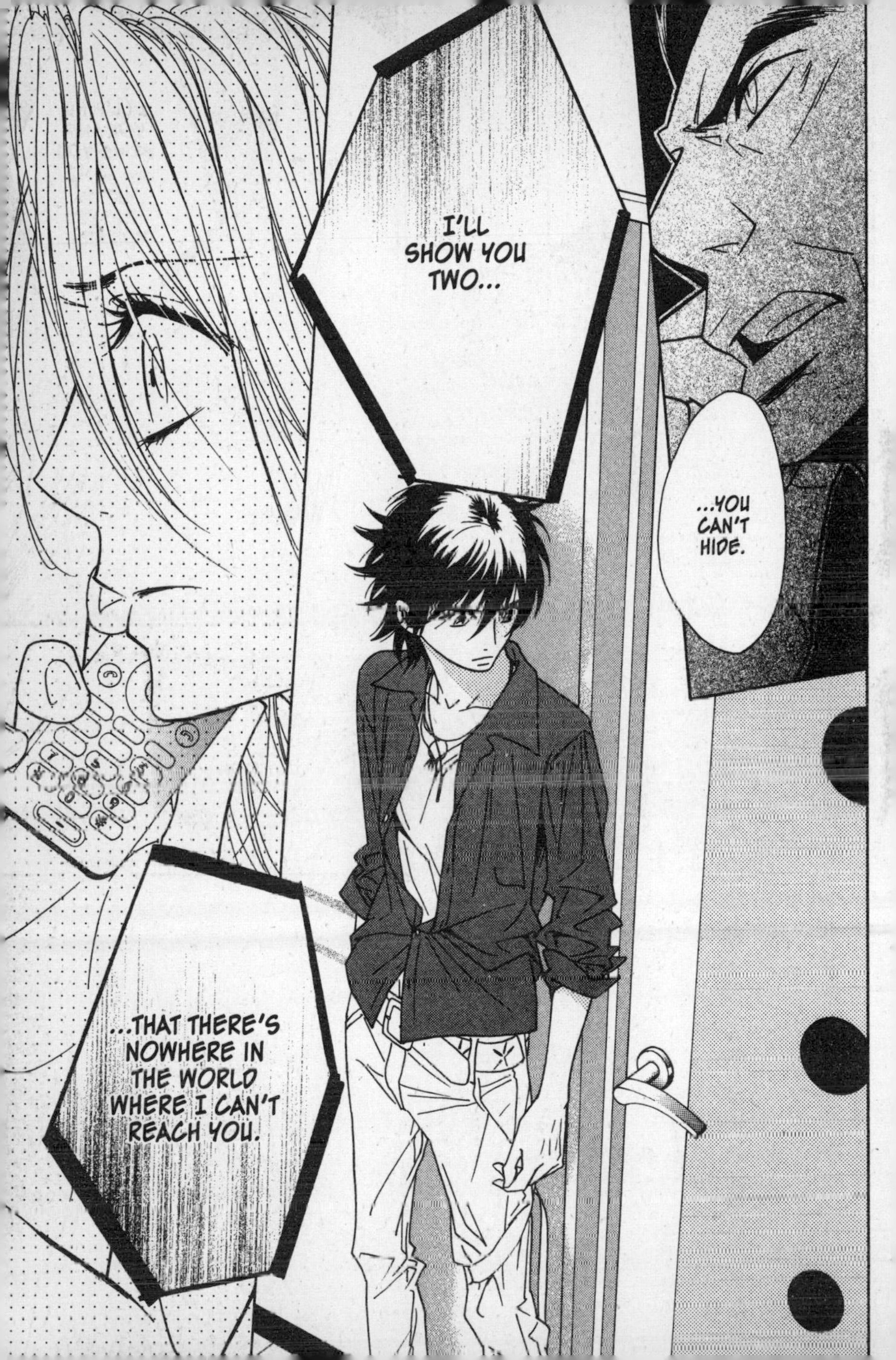
...YOU CAN'T HIDE.
I'LL SHOW YOU TWO...
...THAT THERE'S NOWHERE IN THE WORLD WHERE I CAN'T REACH YOU.

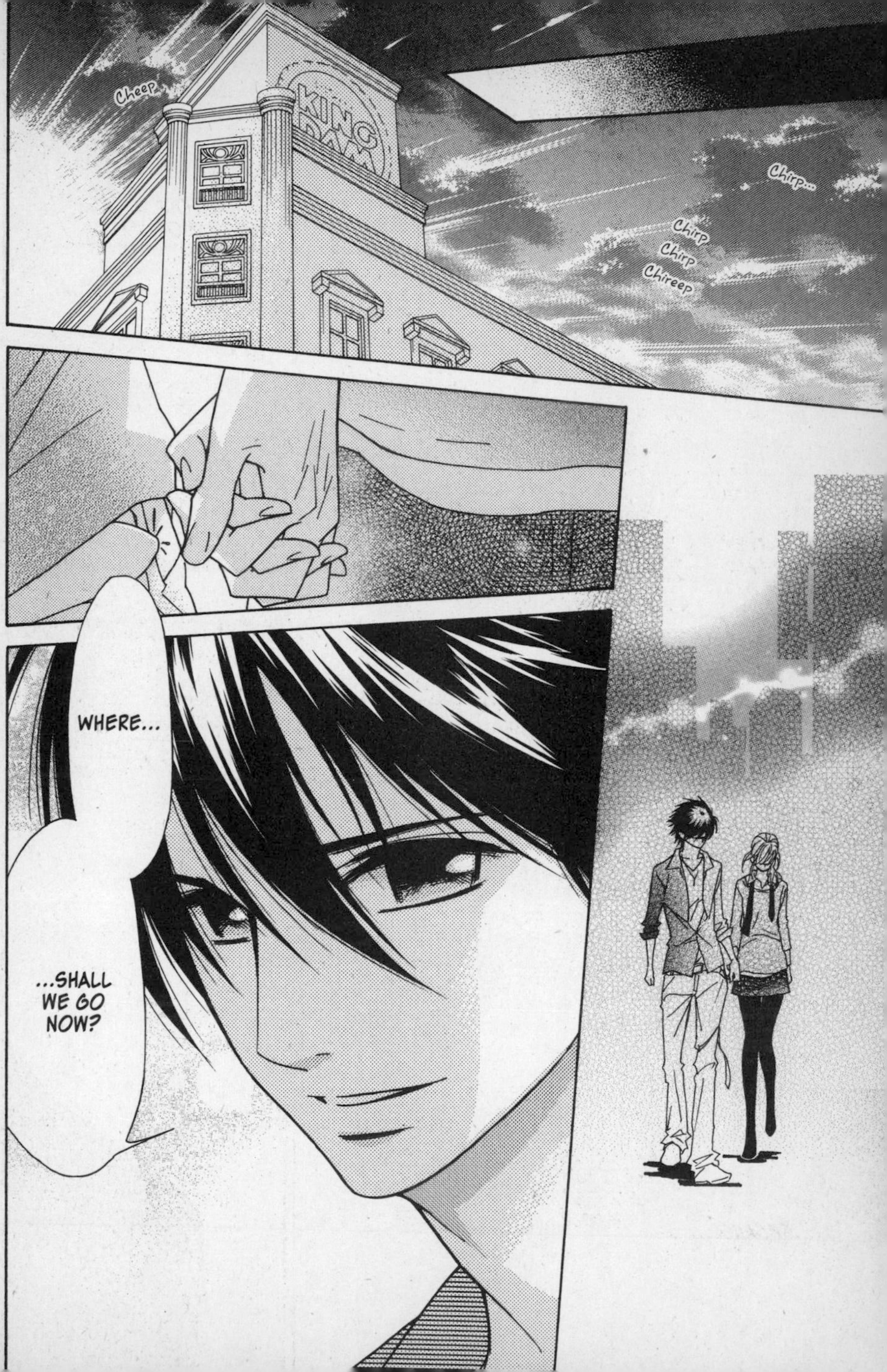

Chirp...
Chirp
Chirp
Chireep
Cheep
WHERE...
...SHALL WE GO NOW?

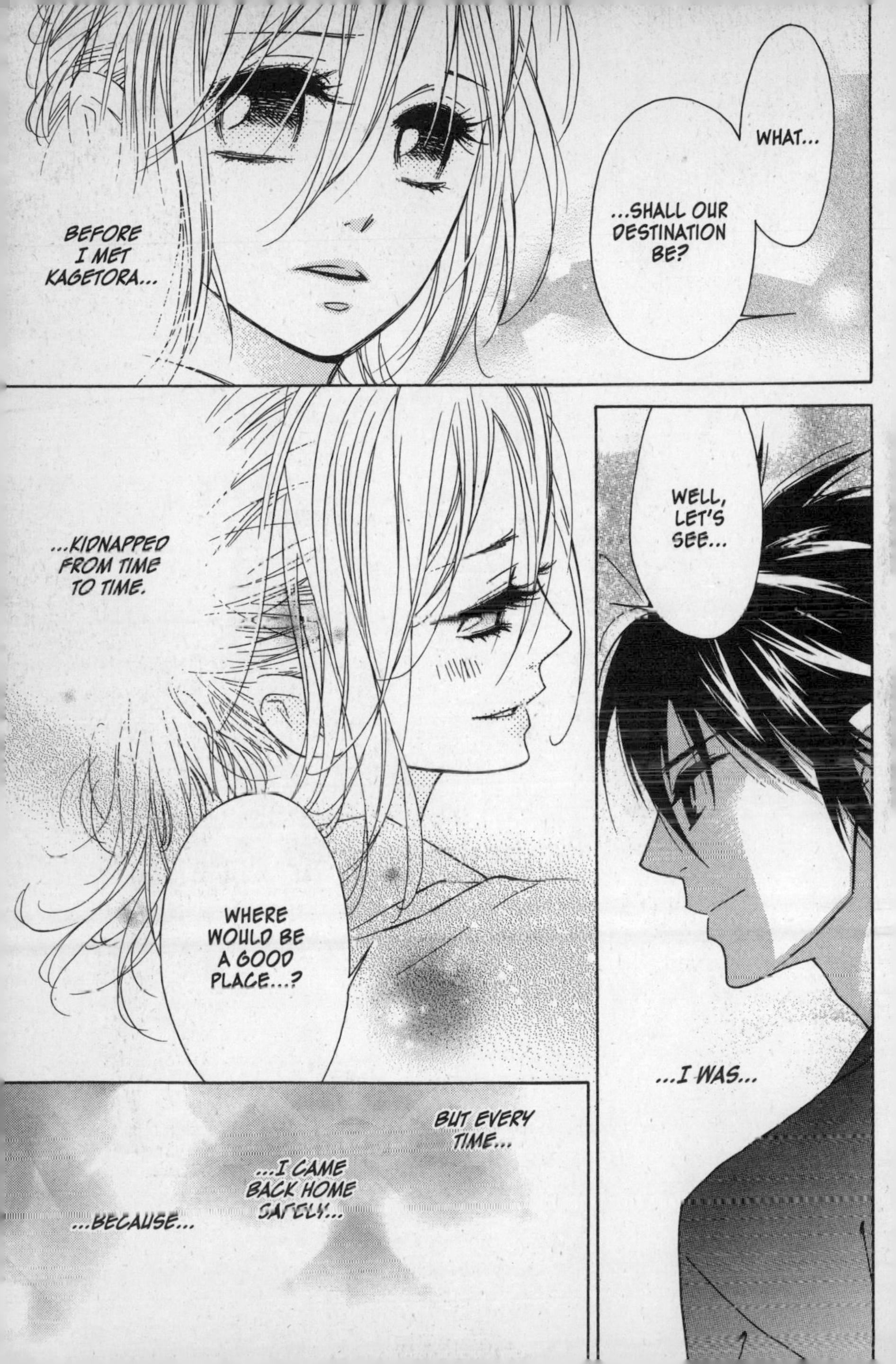
WHAT...
...SHALL OUR DESTINATION BE?
BEFORE I MET KAGETORA...
WELL, LET'S SEE...
...I WAS...
...KIDNAPPED FROM TIME TO TIME.
WHERE WOULD BE A GOOD PLACE...?
BUT EVERY TIME...
...I CAME BACK HOME SAFELY...
...BECAUSE...

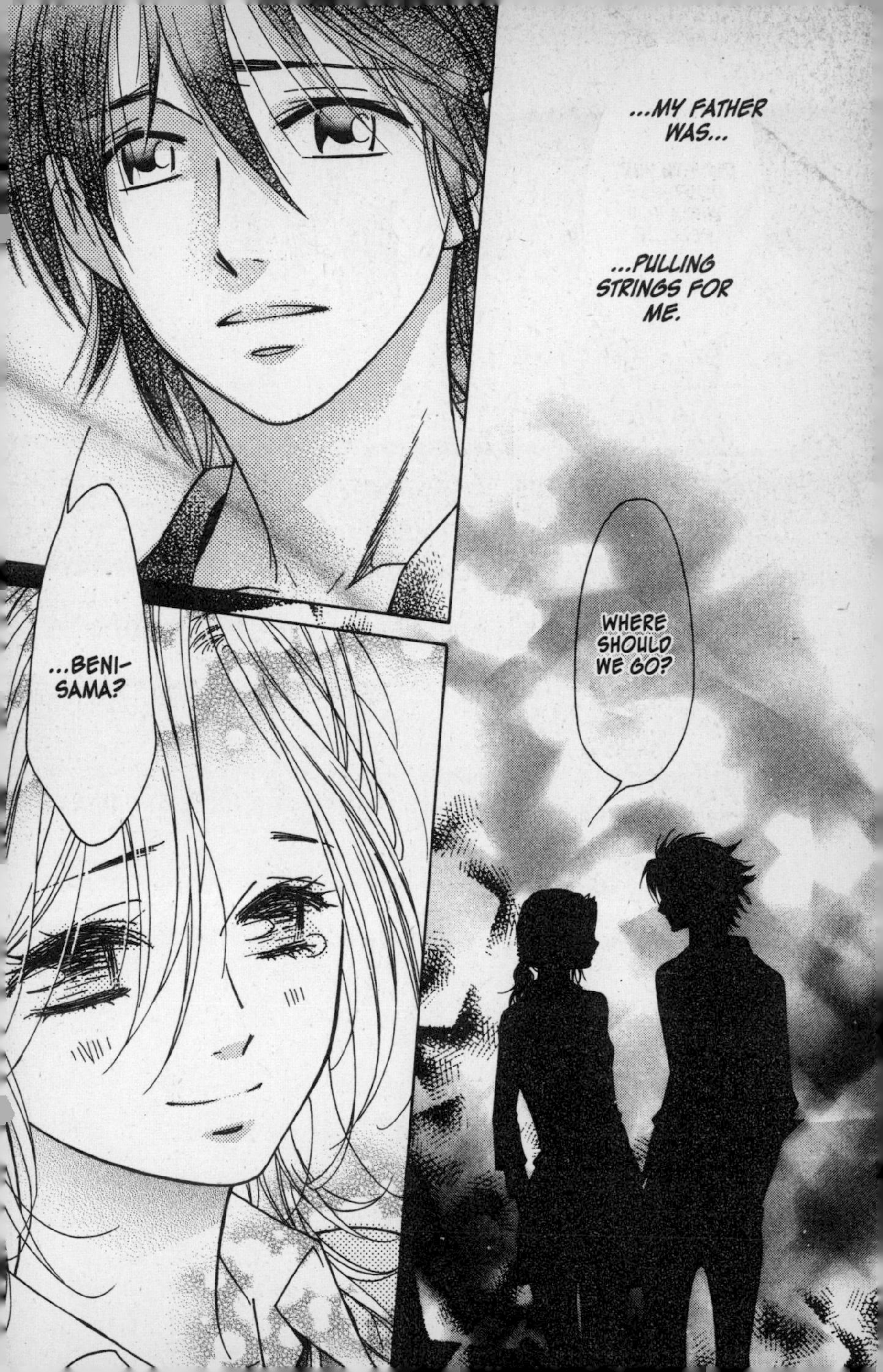
...MY FATHER WAS...
...PULLING STRINGS FOR ME.
WHERE SHOULD WE GO?
...BENI-SAMA?

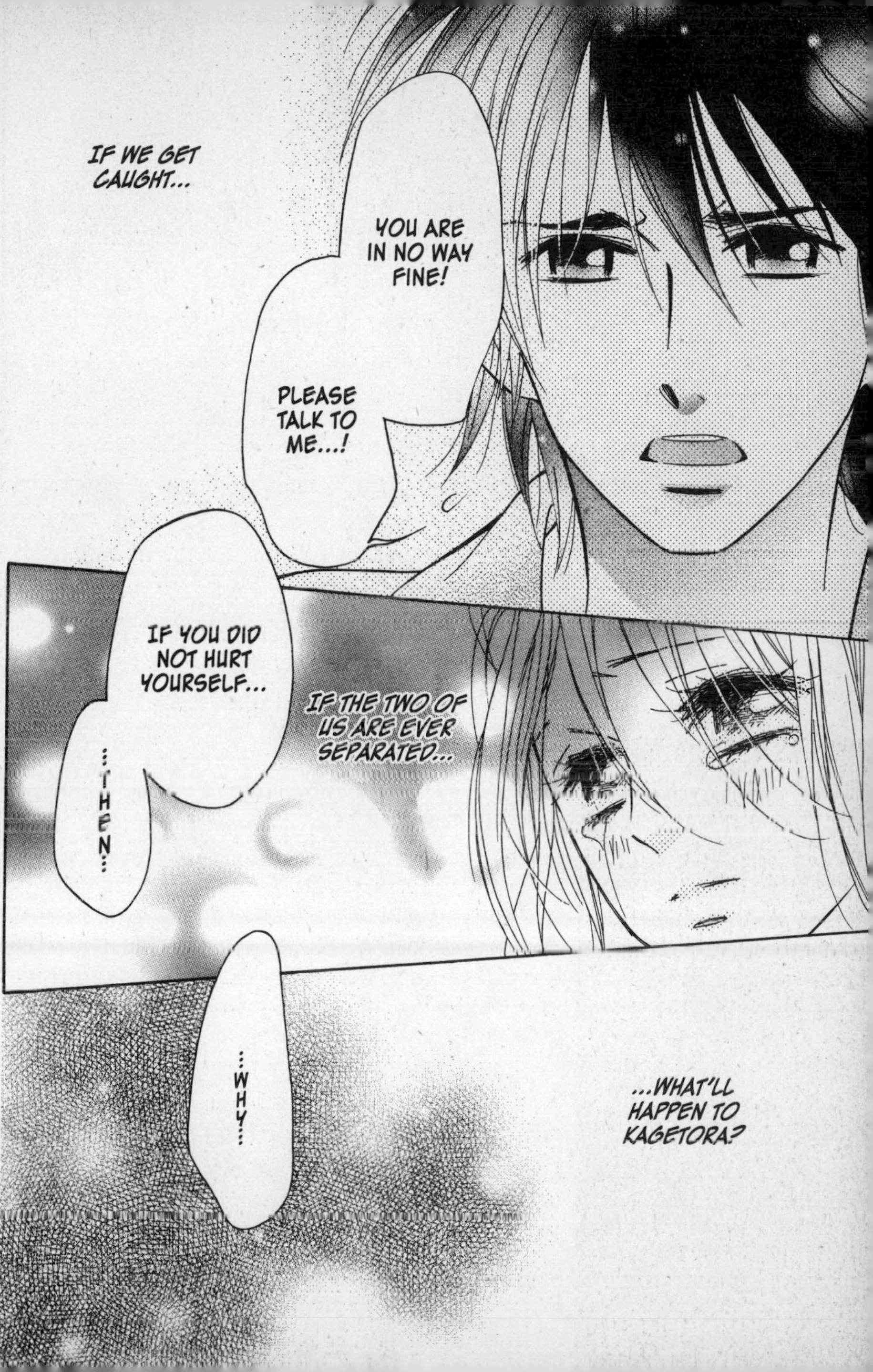
YOU ARE IN NO WAY FINE!
PLEASE TALK TO ME...!
IF WE GET CAUGHT...
IF YOU DID NOT HURT YOURSELF...
...THEN...
IF THE TWO OF US ARE EVER SEPARATED...
...WHY...
...WHAT'LL HAPPEN TO KAGETORA?

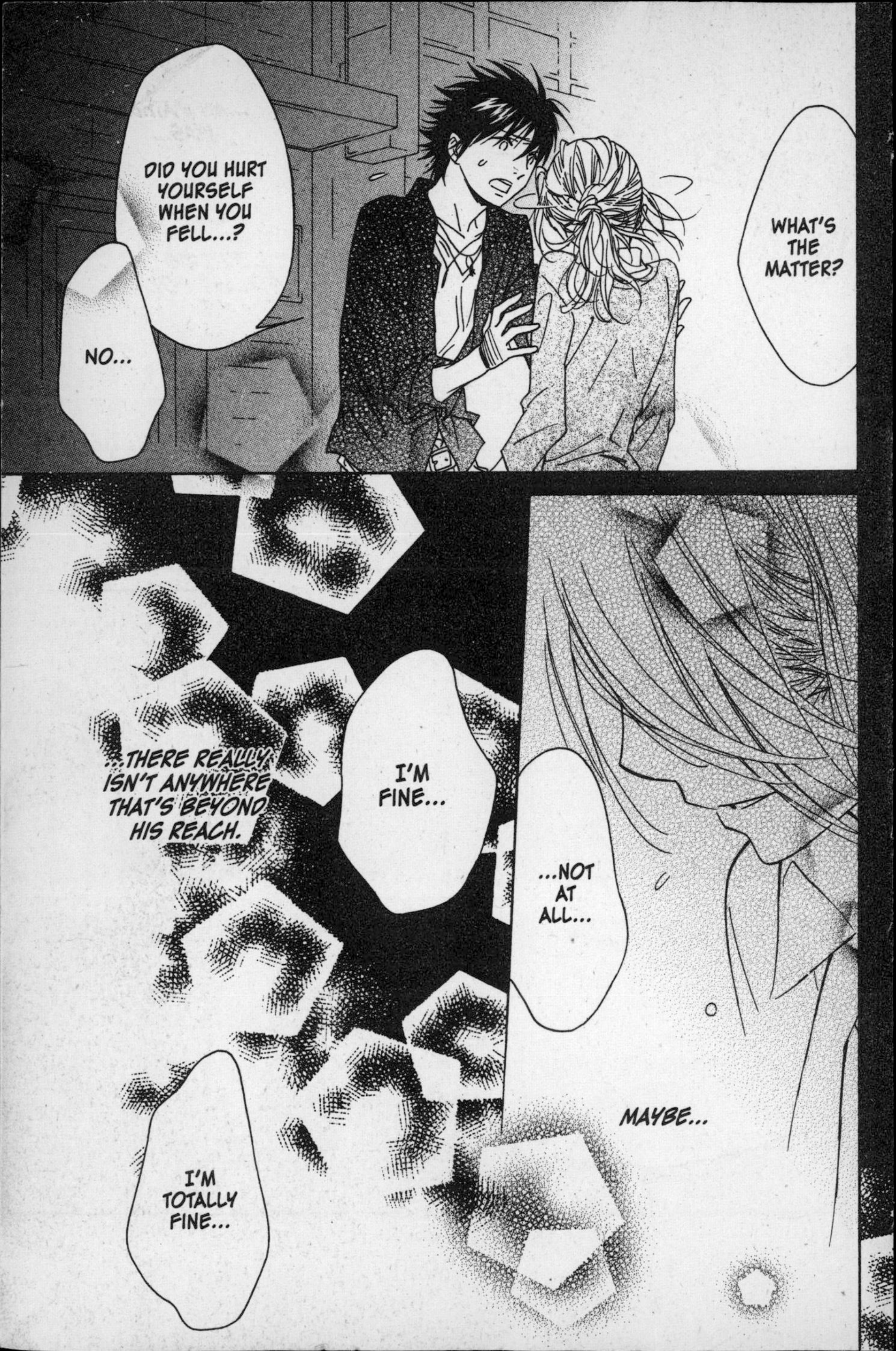
WHAT'S THE MATTER?
DID YOU HURT YOURSELF WHEN YOU FELL...?
NO...
...NOT AT ALL...
MAYBE...
I'M FINE...
...THERE REALLY ISN'T ANYWHERE THAT'S BEYOND HIS REACH.
I'M TOTALLY FINE...

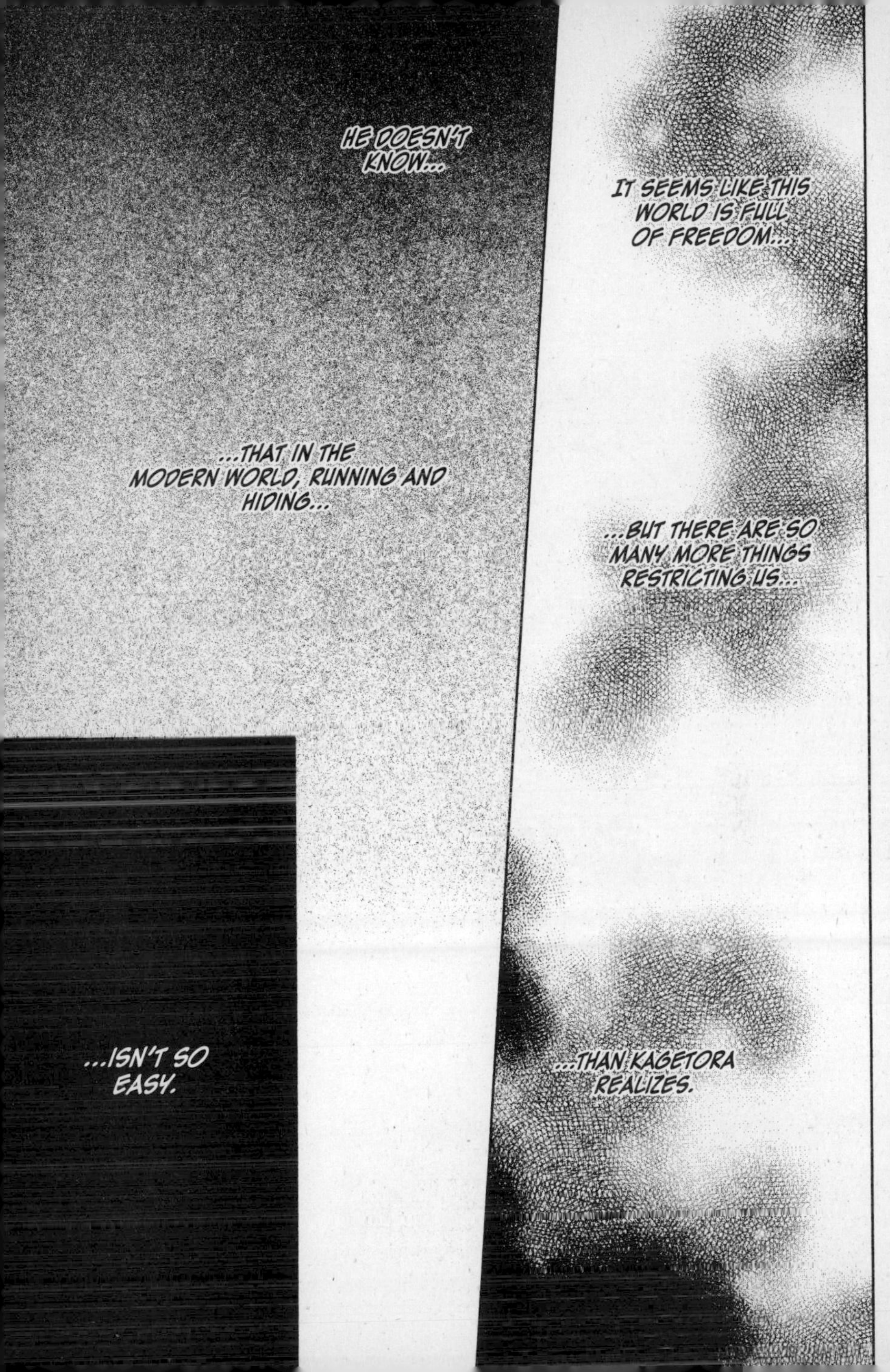
IT SEEMS LIKE THIS WORLD IS FULL OF FREEDOM...
...BUT THERE ARE SO MANY MORE THINGS RESTRICTING US...
...THAN KAGETORA REALIZES.
HE DOESN'T KNOW...
...THAT IN THE MODERN WORLD, RUNNING AND HIDING...
...ISN'T SO EASY.

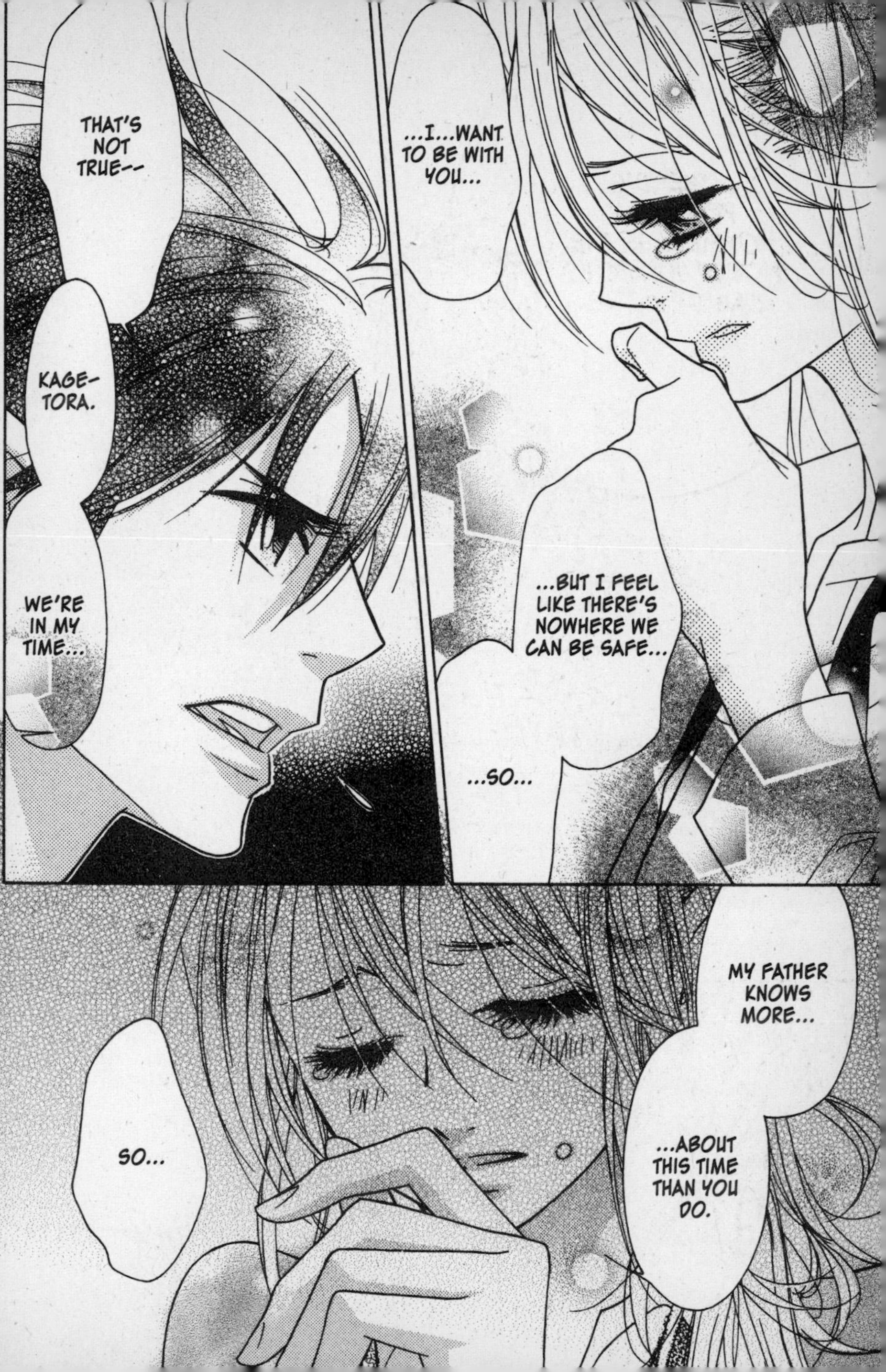
...I...WANT TO BE WITH YOU...
...BUT I FEEL LIKE THERE'S NOWHERE WE CAN BE SAFE...
...SO...
THAT'S NOT TRUE--
KAGE-TORA.
WE'RE IN MY TIME...
MY FATHER KNOWS MORE...
...ABOUT THIS TIME THAN YOU DO.
SO...

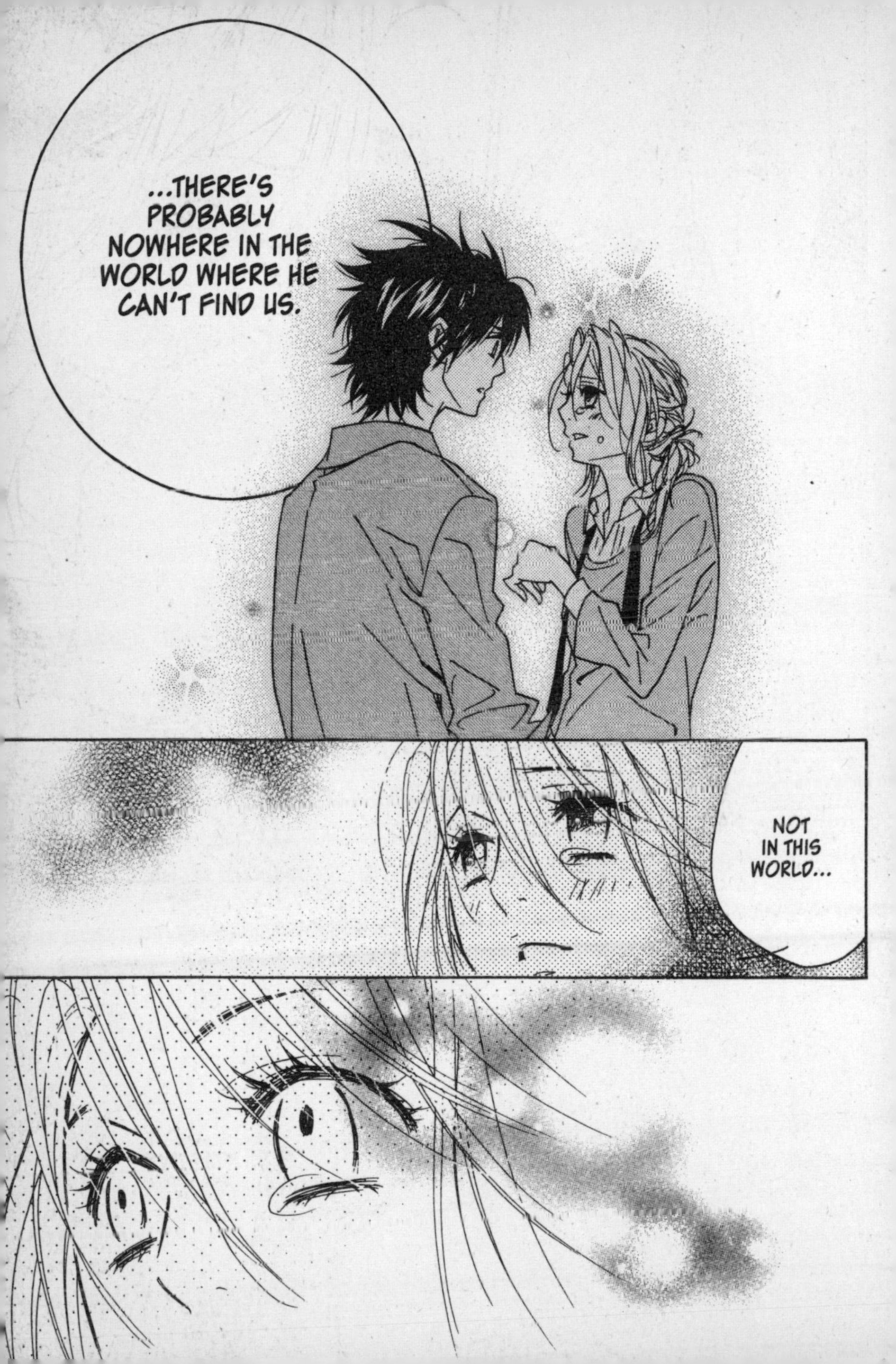
...THERE'S PROBABLY NOWHERE IN THE WORLD WHERE HE CAN'T FIND US.
NOT IN THIS WORLD...

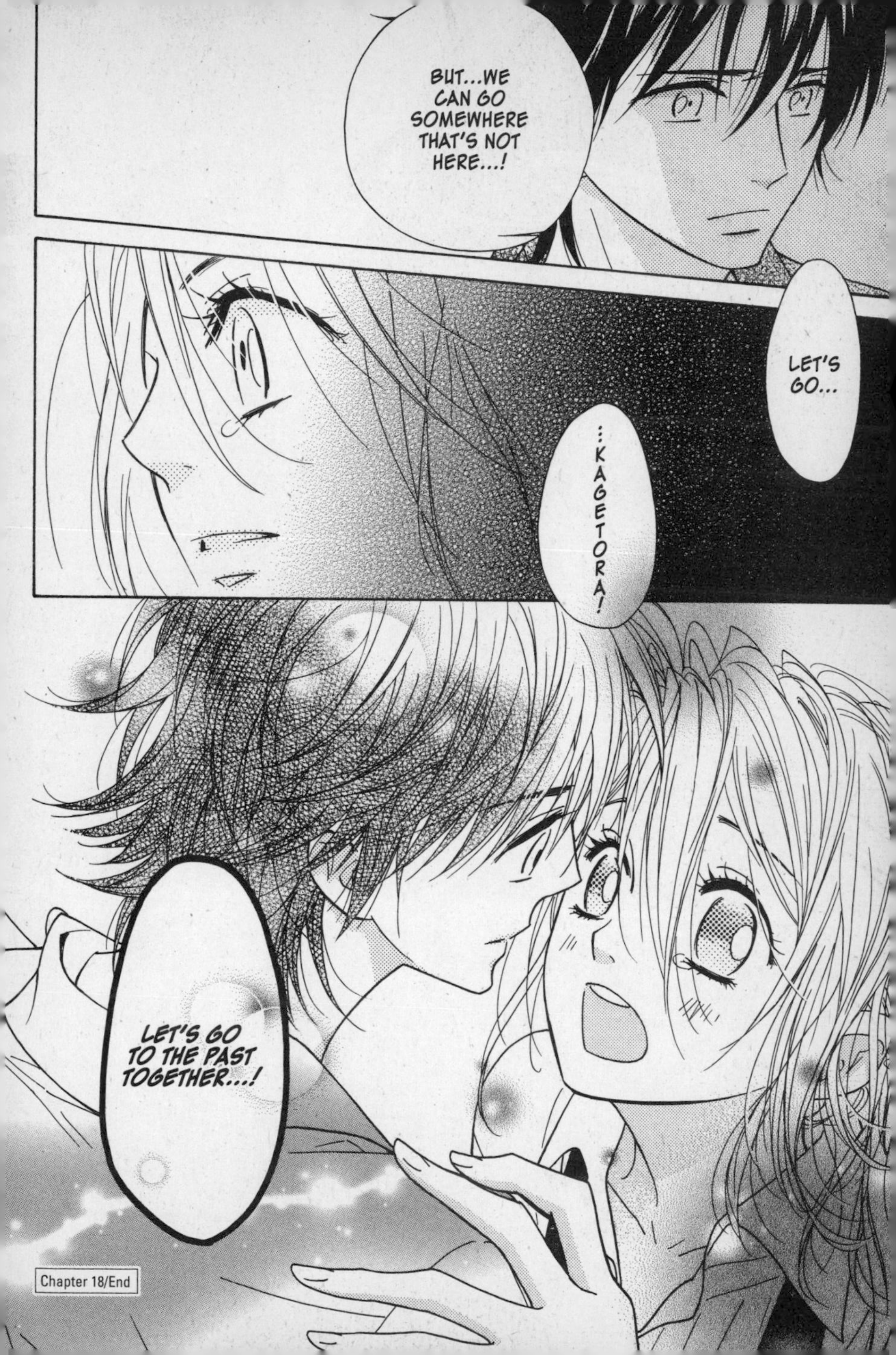
BUT...WE CAN GO SOMEWHERE THAT'S NOT HERE...!
LET'S GO...
...KAGETORA!
LET'S GO TO THE PAST TOGETHER...!
Chapter 18/End

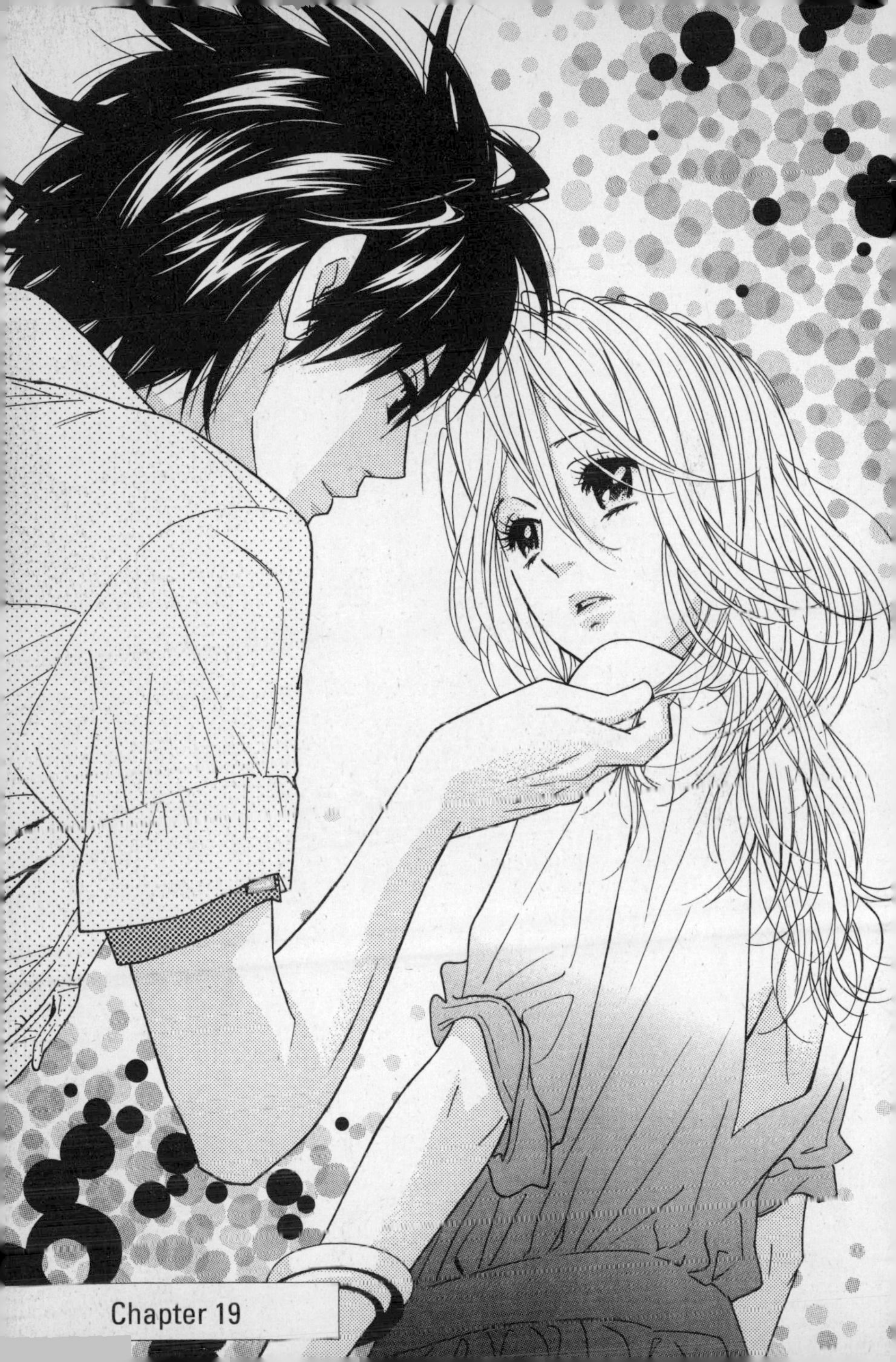

Chapter 19

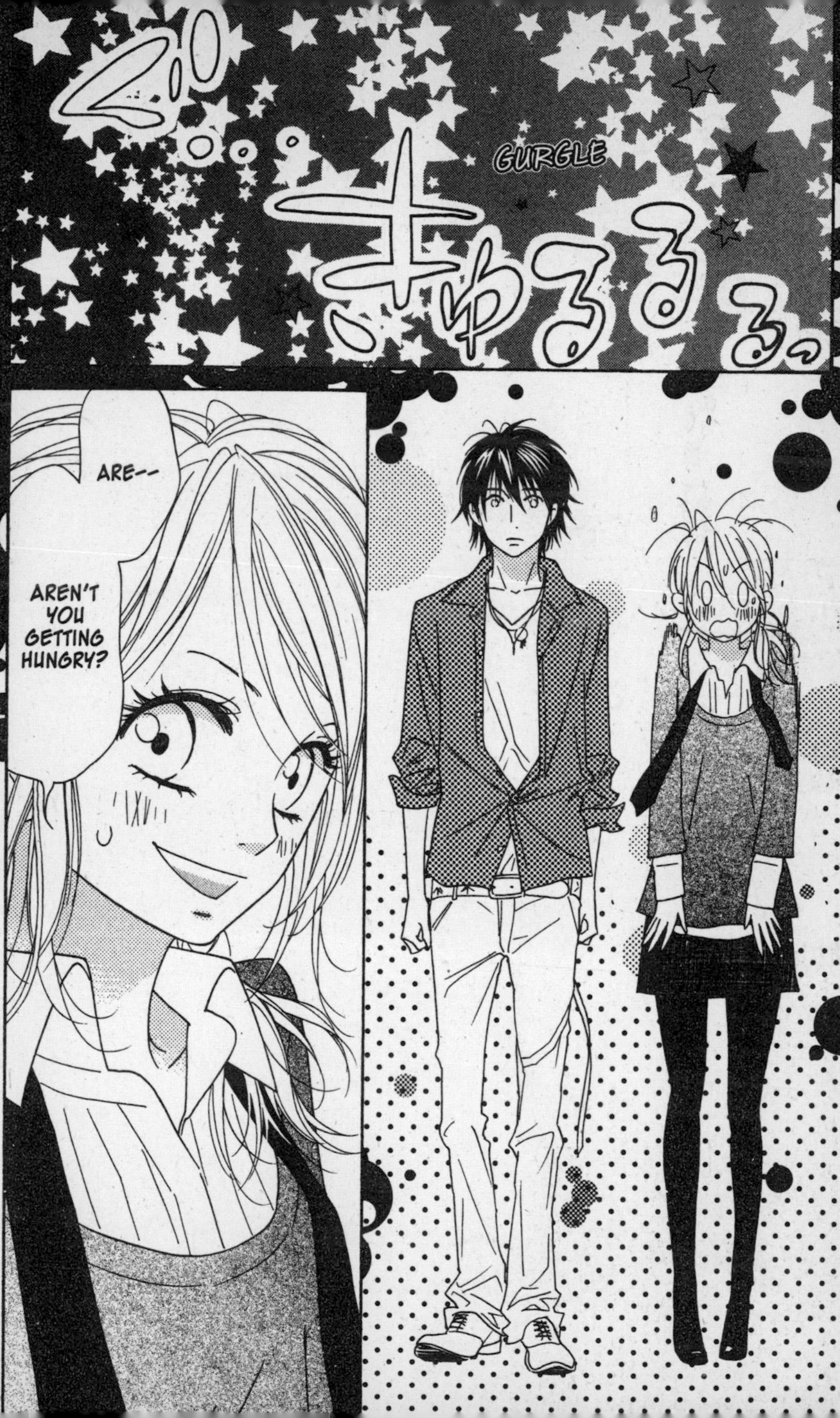
ぐ。。。きゅるるる
GURGLE
ARE--
AREN'T YOU GETTING HUNGRY?

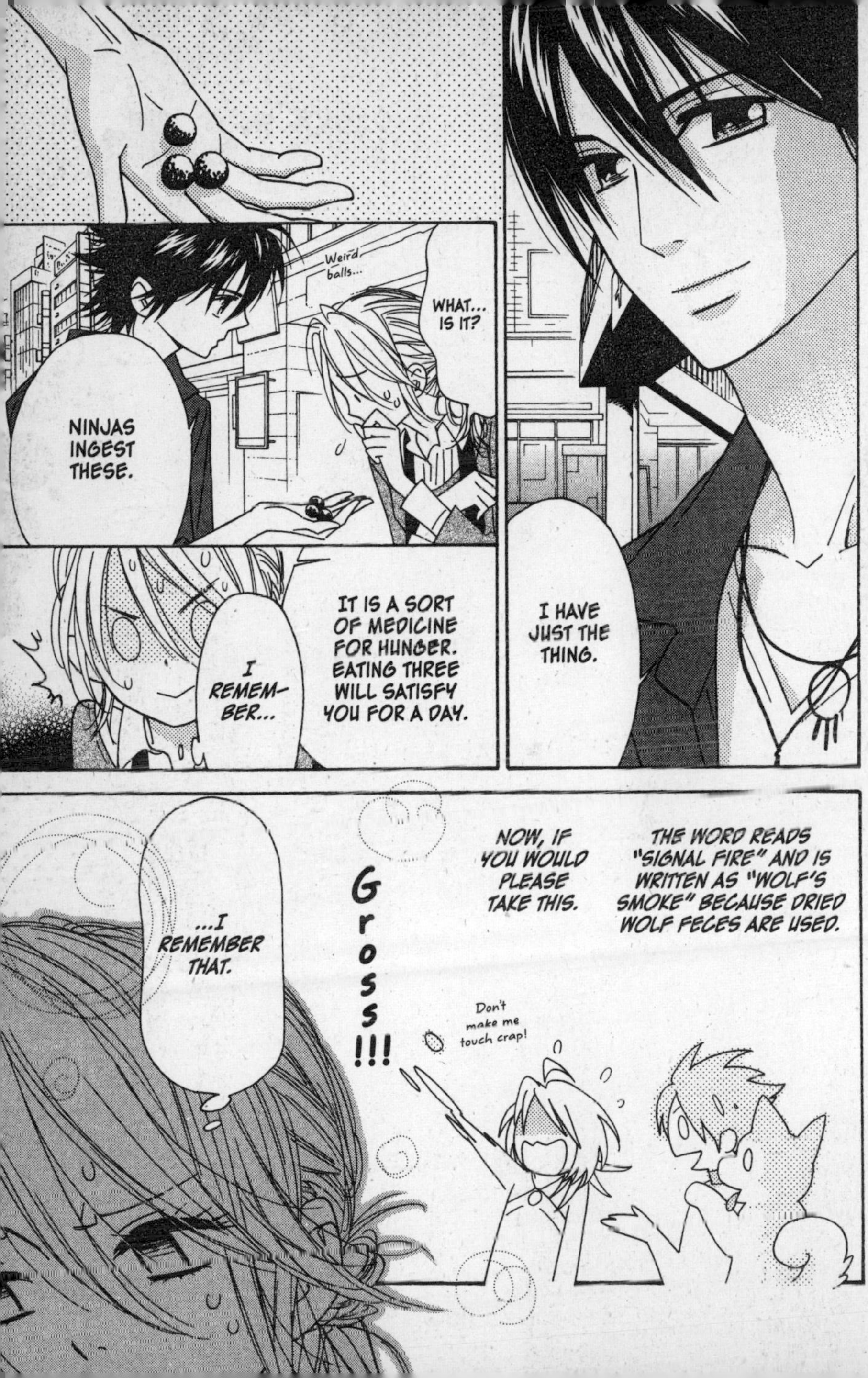
I HAVE JUST THE THING.
WHAT... IS IT?
Weird balls...
NINJAS INGEST THESE.
IT IS A SORT OF MEDICINE FOR HUNGER. EATING THREE WILL SATISFY YOU FOR A DAY.
I REMEMBER...
THE WORD READS "SIGNAL FIRE" AND IS WRITTEN AS "WOLF'S SMOKE" BECAUSE DRIED WOLF FECES ARE USED.
NOW, IF YOU WOULD PLEASE TAKE THIS.
Gross!!!
Don't make me touch crap!
...I REMEMBER THAT.

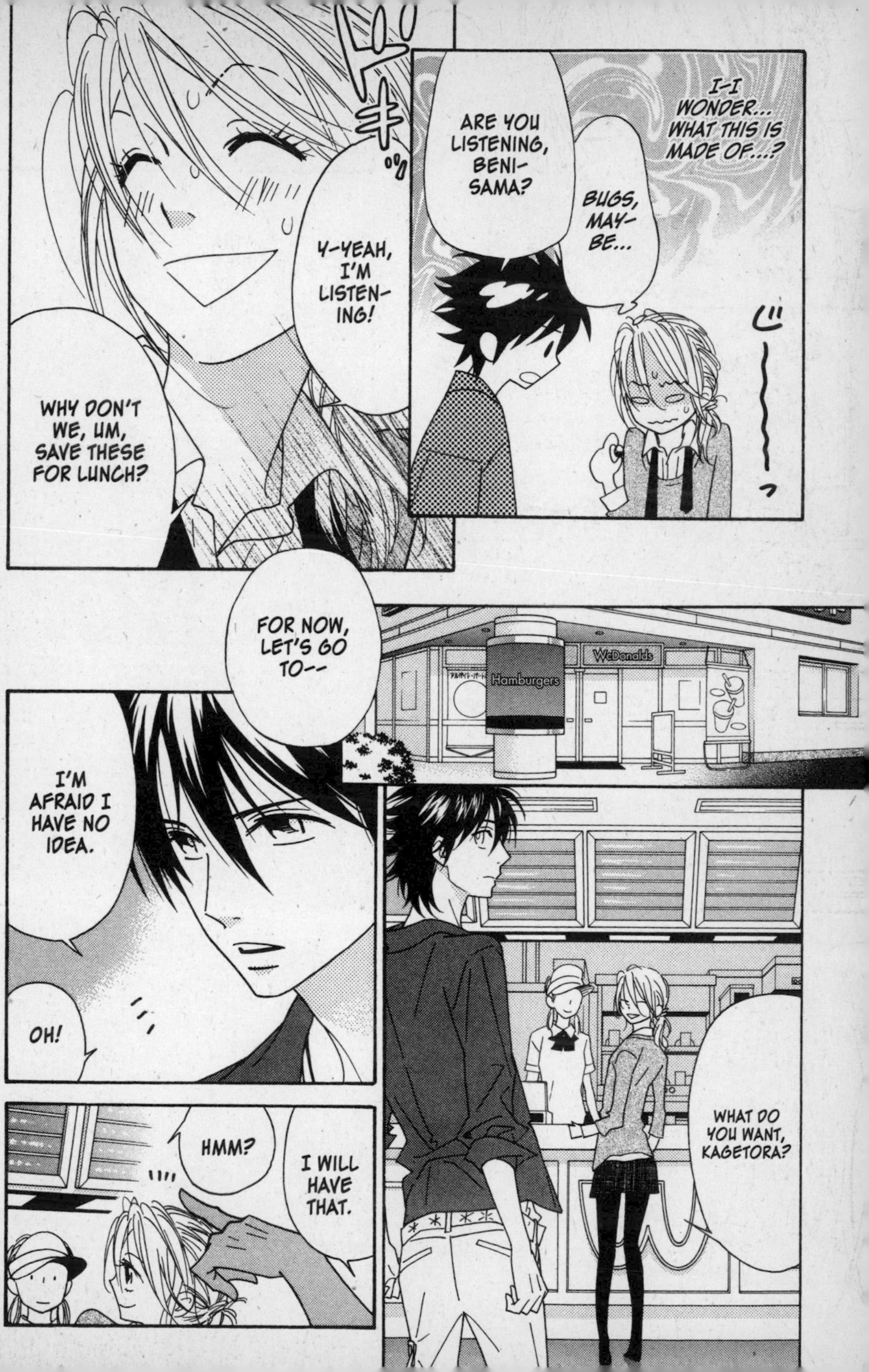
I-I WONDER... WHAT THIS IS MADE OF...?
ARE YOU LISTENING, BENI-SAMA?
BUGS, MAY-BE...
ドキ
Y-YEAH, I'M LISTEN-ING!
WHY DON'T WE, UM, SAVE THESE FOR LUNCH?
FOR NOW, LET'S GO TO--
WcDonalds
Hamburgers
WHAT DO YOU WANT, KAGETORA?
I'M AFRAID I HAVE NO IDEA.
OH!
I WILL HAVE THAT.
HMM?

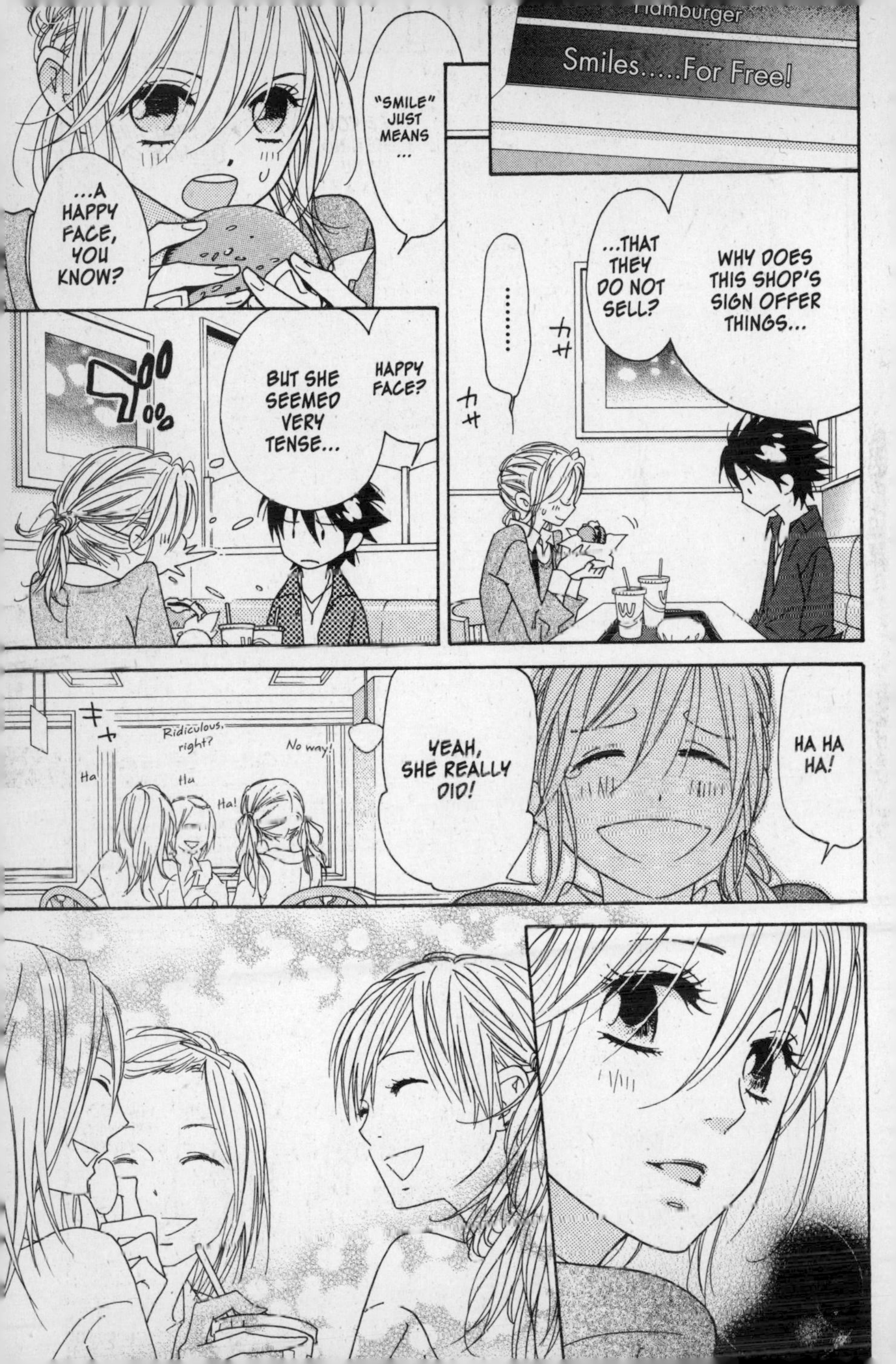

Hamburger
Smiles.....For Free!
WHY DOES THIS SHOP'S SIGN OFFER THINGS...
...THAT THEY DO NOT SELL?
......
キャ
キャ
"SMILE" JUST MEANS ...
...A HAPPY FACE, YOU KNOW?
HAPPY FACE?
BUT SHE SEEMED VERY TENSE...
HA HA HA!
YEAH, SHE REALLY DID!
No way!
Ridiculous, right?
キャ
Ha
Hu
Ha!

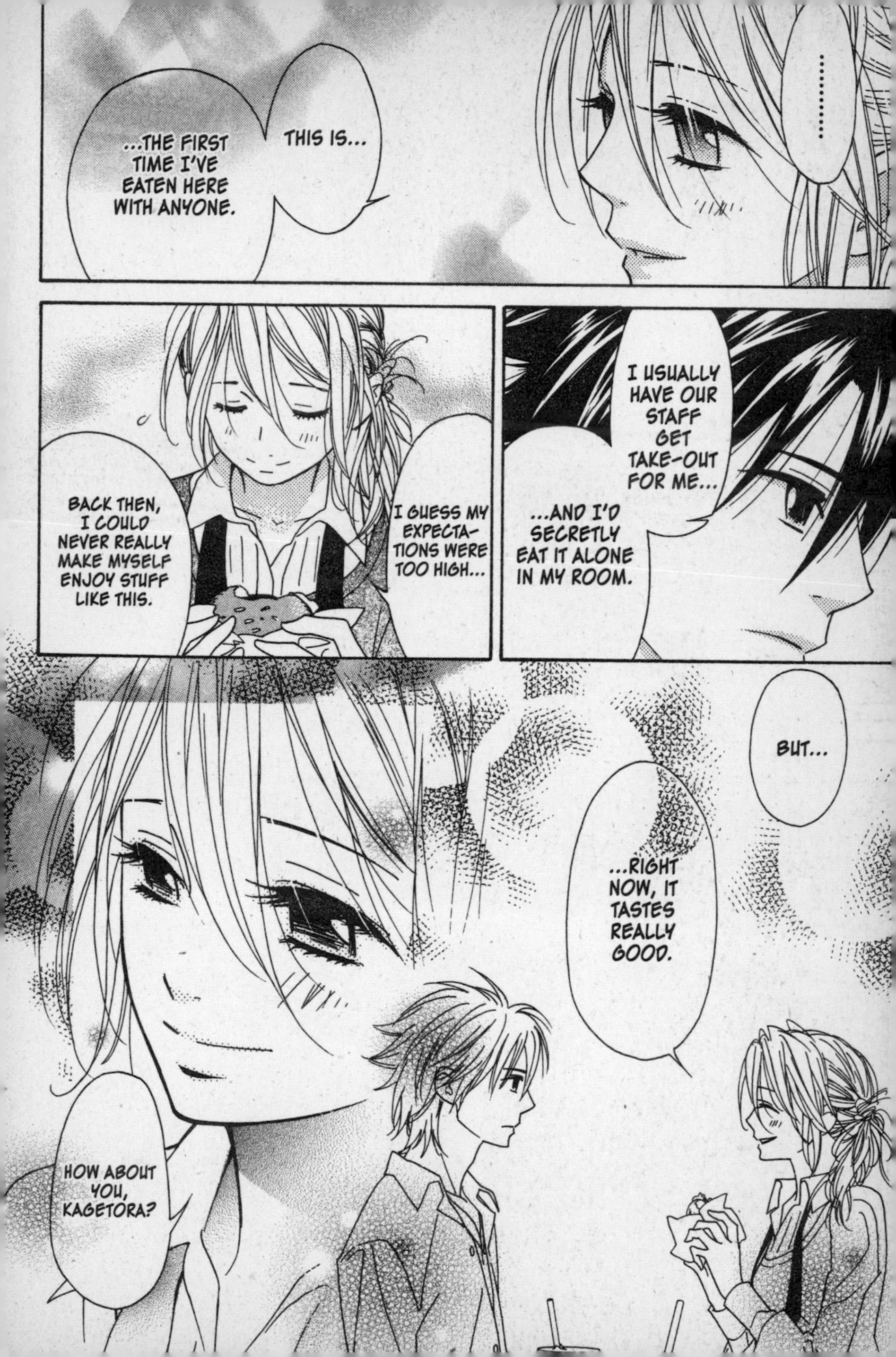
......
THIS IS...
...THE FIRST TIME I'VE EATEN HERE WITH ANYONE.
I USUALLY HAVE OUR STAFF GET TAKE-OUT FOR ME...
...AND I'D SECRETLY EAT IT ALONE IN MY ROOM.
I GUESS MY EXPECTATIONS WERE TOO HIGH...
BACK THEN, I COULD NEVER REALLY MAKE MYSELF ENJOY STUFF LIKE THIS.
BUT...
...RIGHT NOW, IT TASTES REALLY GOOD.
HOW ABOUT YOU, KAGETORA?

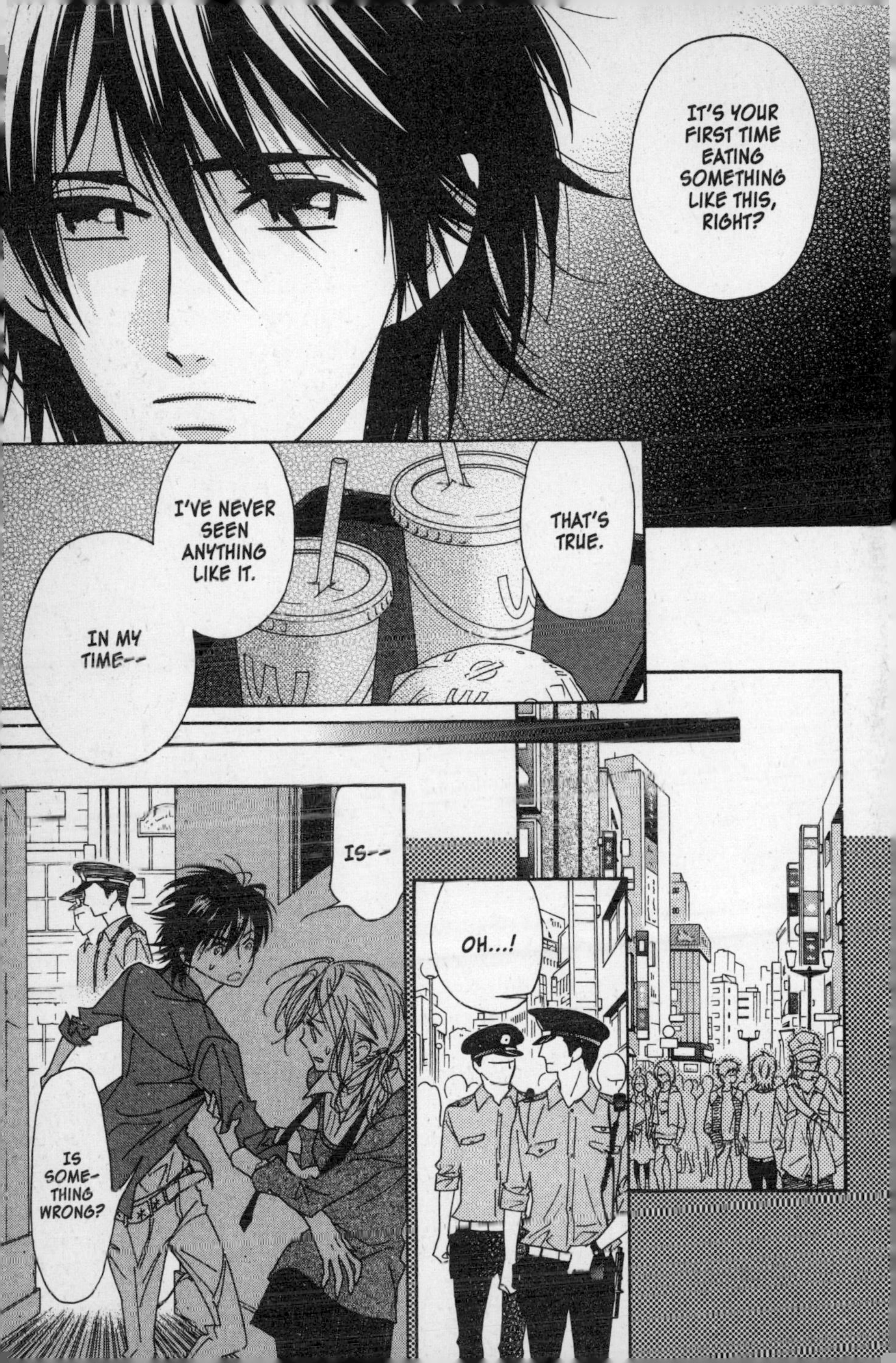

IT'S YOUR FIRST TIME EATING SOMETHING LIKE THIS, RIGHT?
THAT'S TRUE.
I'VE NEVER SEEN ANYTHING LIKE IT.
IN MY TIME--
OH...!
IS--
IS SOME-THING WRONG?

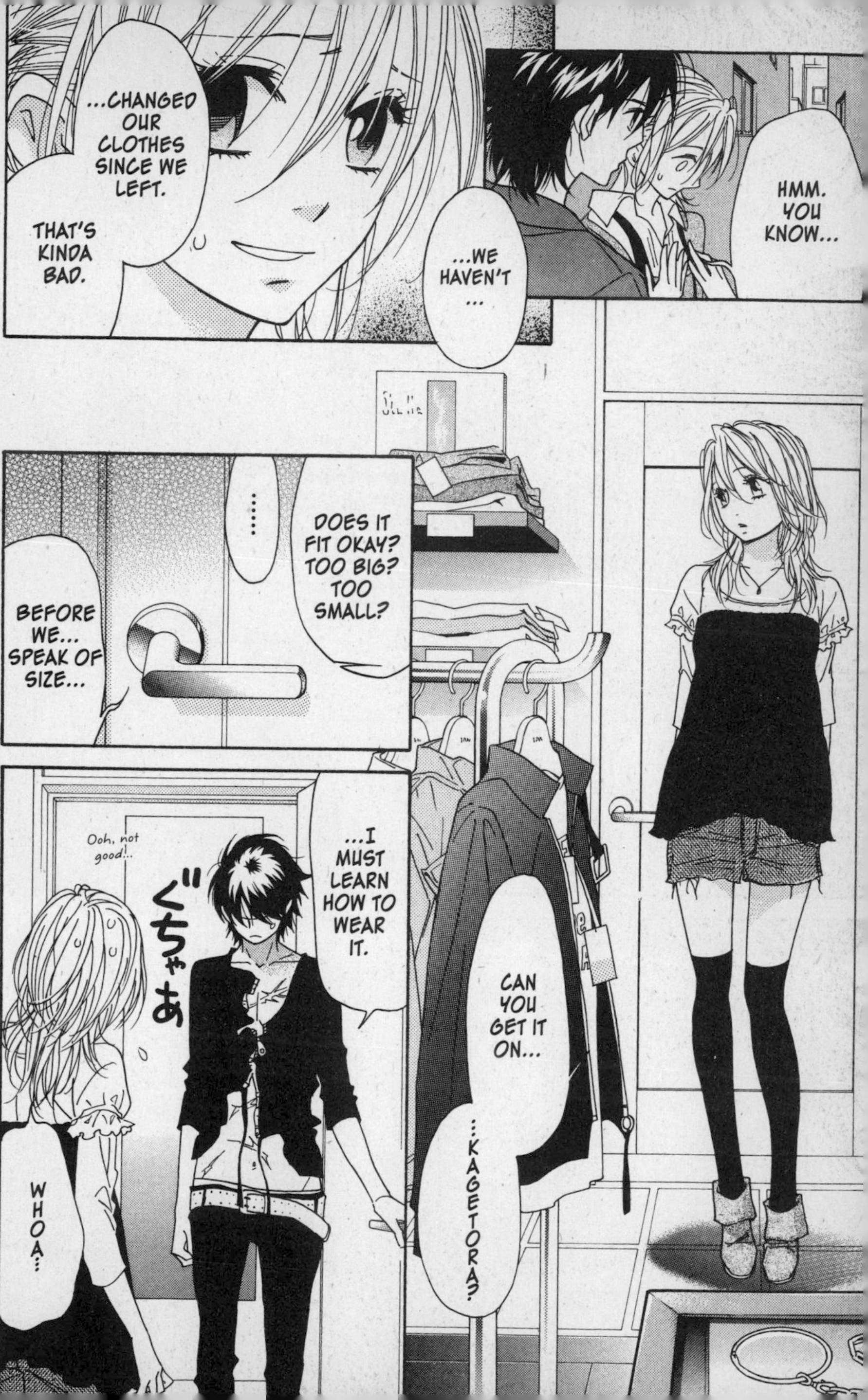
HMM. YOU KNOW...
...WE HAVEN'T ...
...CHANGED OUR CLOTHES SINCE WE LEFT.
THAT'S KINDA BAD.
CAN YOU GET IT ON...
...KAGETORA?
DOES IT FIT OKAY? TOO BIG? TOO SMALL?
......
BEFORE WE... SPEAK OF SIZE...
...I MUST LEARN HOW TO WEAR IT.
ぐちゃあ
Ooh, not good!...
WHOA...

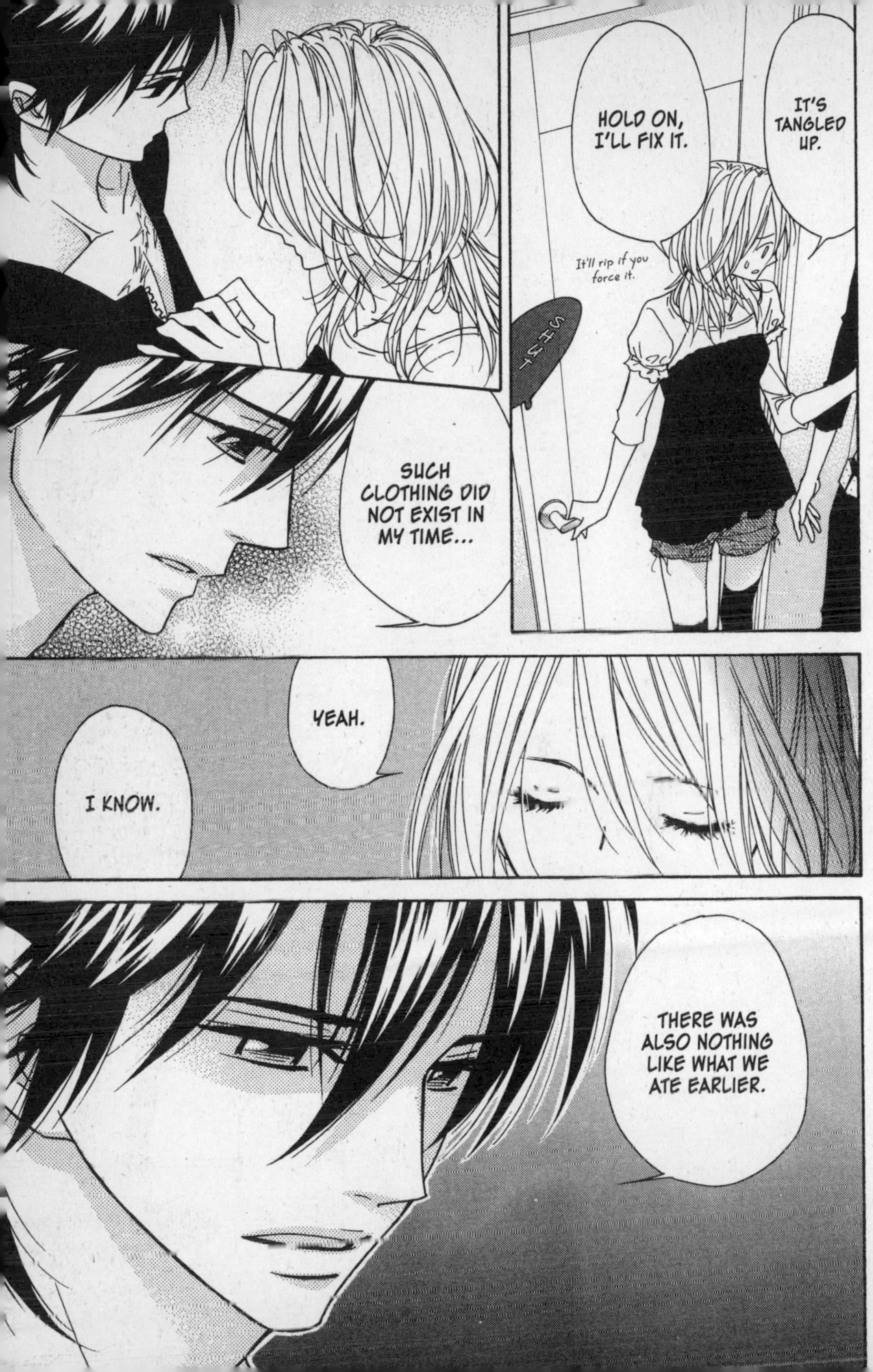
IT'S TANGLED UP.
HOLD ON, I'LL FIX IT.
It'll rip if you force it.
SHUT
SUCH CLOTHING DID NOT EXIST IN MY TIME...
YEAH.
I KNOW.
THERE WAS ALSO NOTHING LIKE WHAT WE ATE EARLIER.

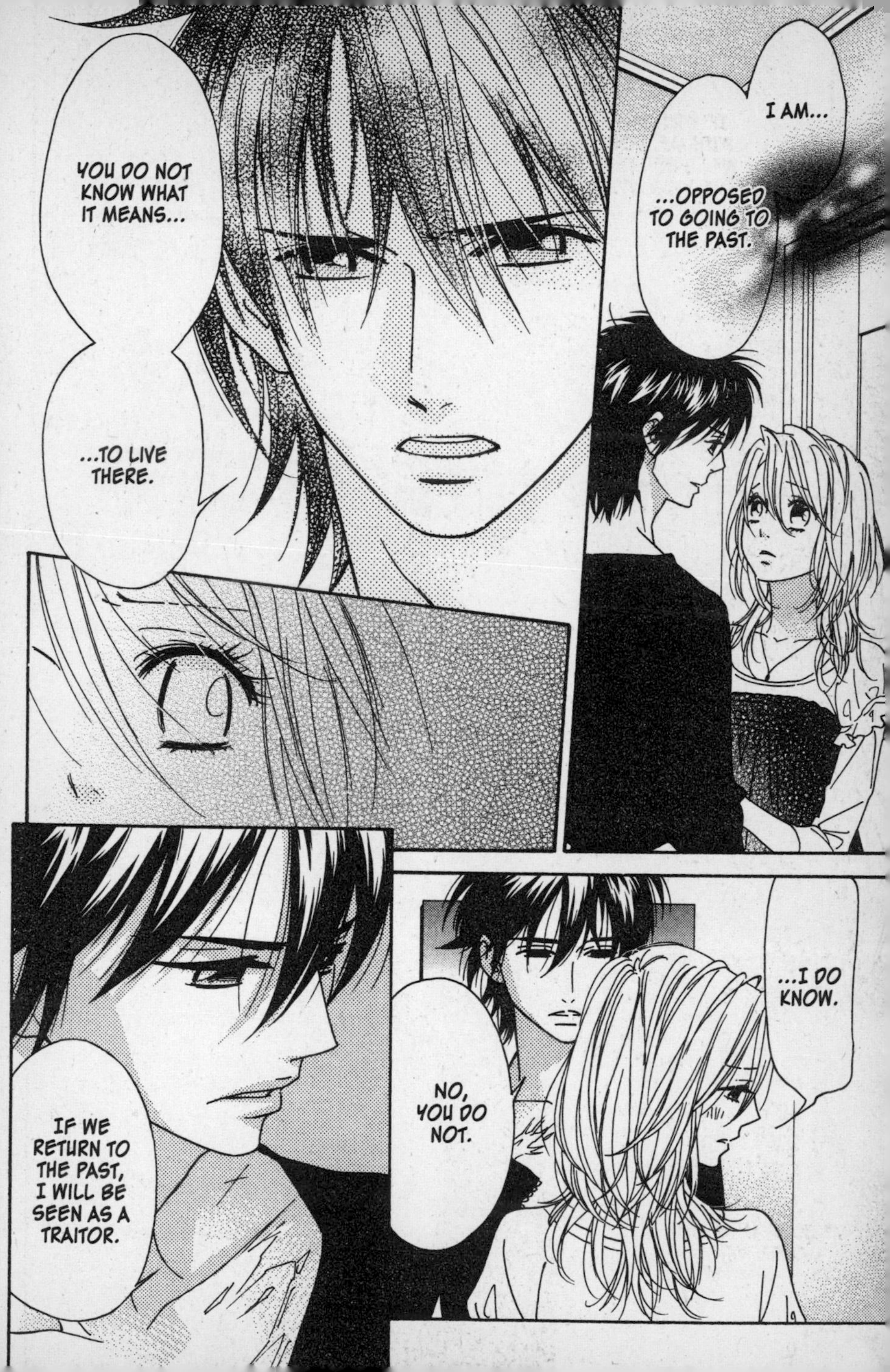
I AM...
...OPPOSED TO GOING TO THE PAST.
YOU DO NOT KNOW WHAT IT MEANS...
...TO LIVE THERE.
...I DO KNOW.
NO, YOU DO NOT.
IF WE RETURN TO THE PAST, I WILL BE SEEN AS A TRAITOR.

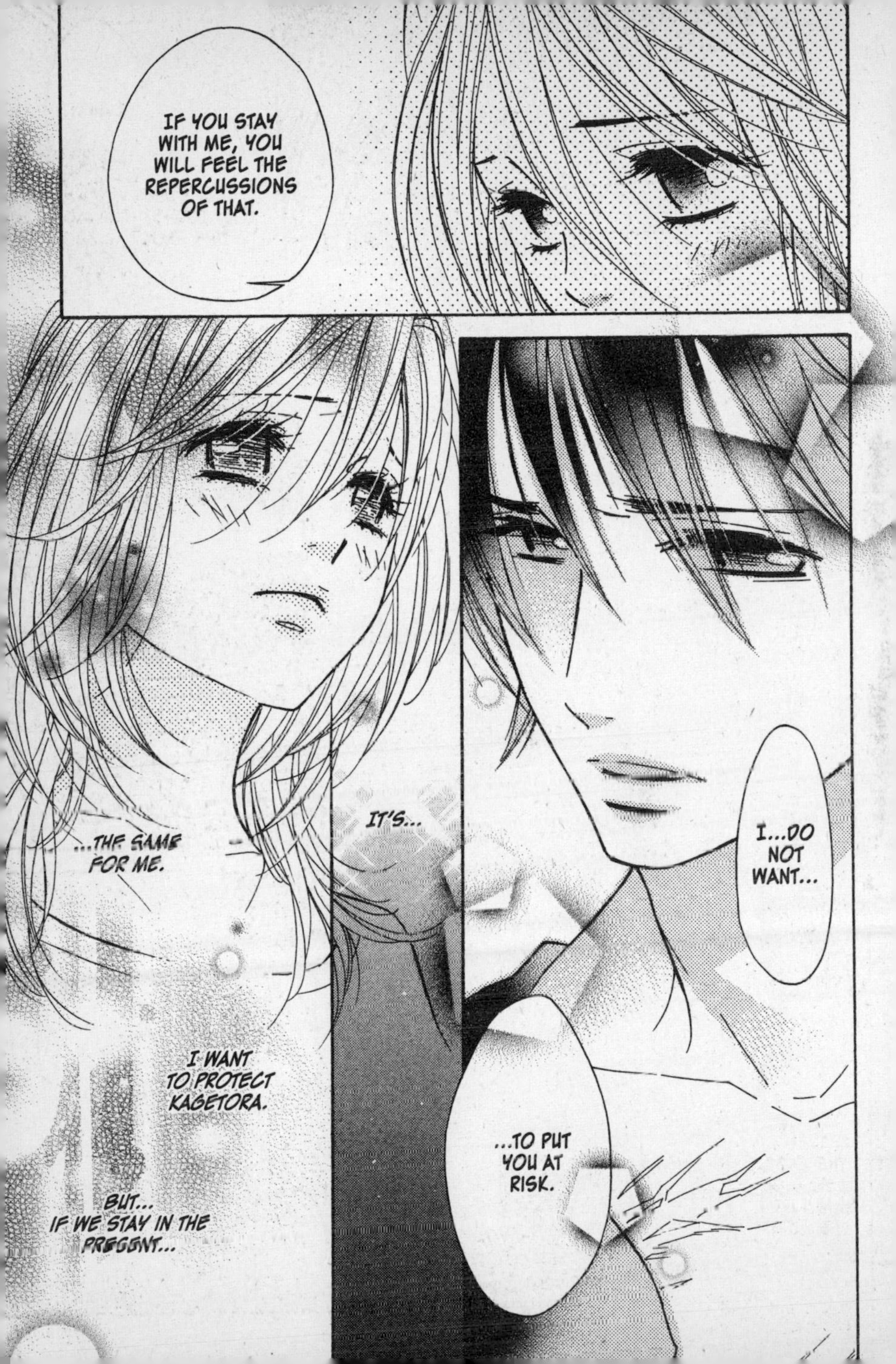
IF YOU STAY WITH ME, YOU WILL FEEL THE REPERCUSSIONS OF THAT.
I...DO NOT WANT...
...TO PUT YOU AT RISK.
IT'S...
...THE SAME FOR ME.
I WANT TO PROTECT KAGETORA.
BUT... IF WE STAY IN THE PRESENT...

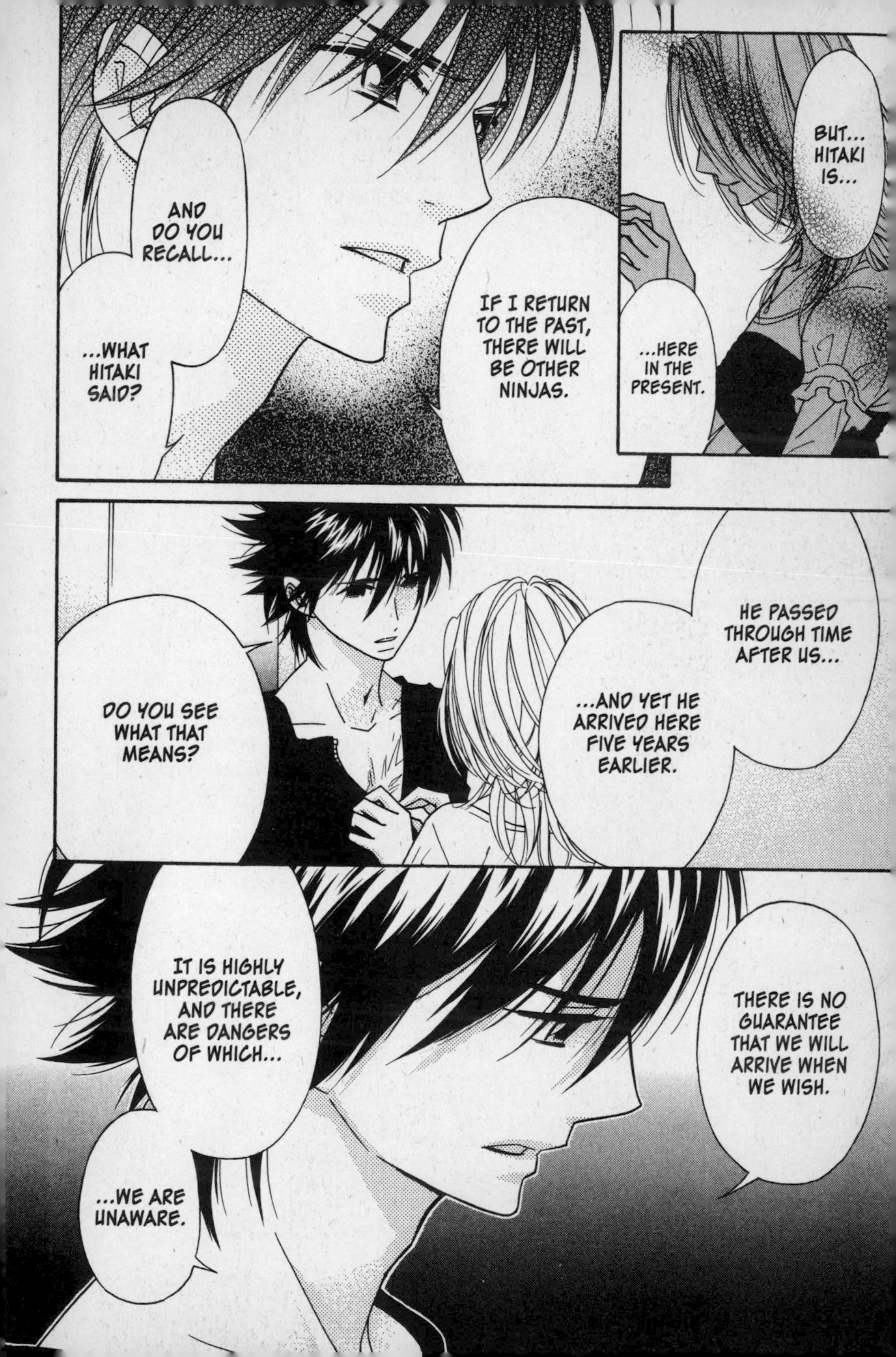
BUT... HITAKI IS...
...HERE IN THE PRESENT.
IF I RETURN TO THE PAST, THERE WILL BE OTHER NINJAS.
AND DO YOU RECALL...
...WHAT HITAKI SAID?
HE PASSED THROUGH TIME AFTER US...
...AND YET HE ARRIVED HERE FIVE YEARS EARLIER.
DO YOU SEE WHAT THAT MEANS?
THERE IS NO GUARANTEE THAT WE WILL ARRIVE WHEN WE WISH.
IT IS HIGHLY UNPREDICTABLE, AND THERE ARE DANGERS OF WHICH...
...WE ARE UNAWARE.

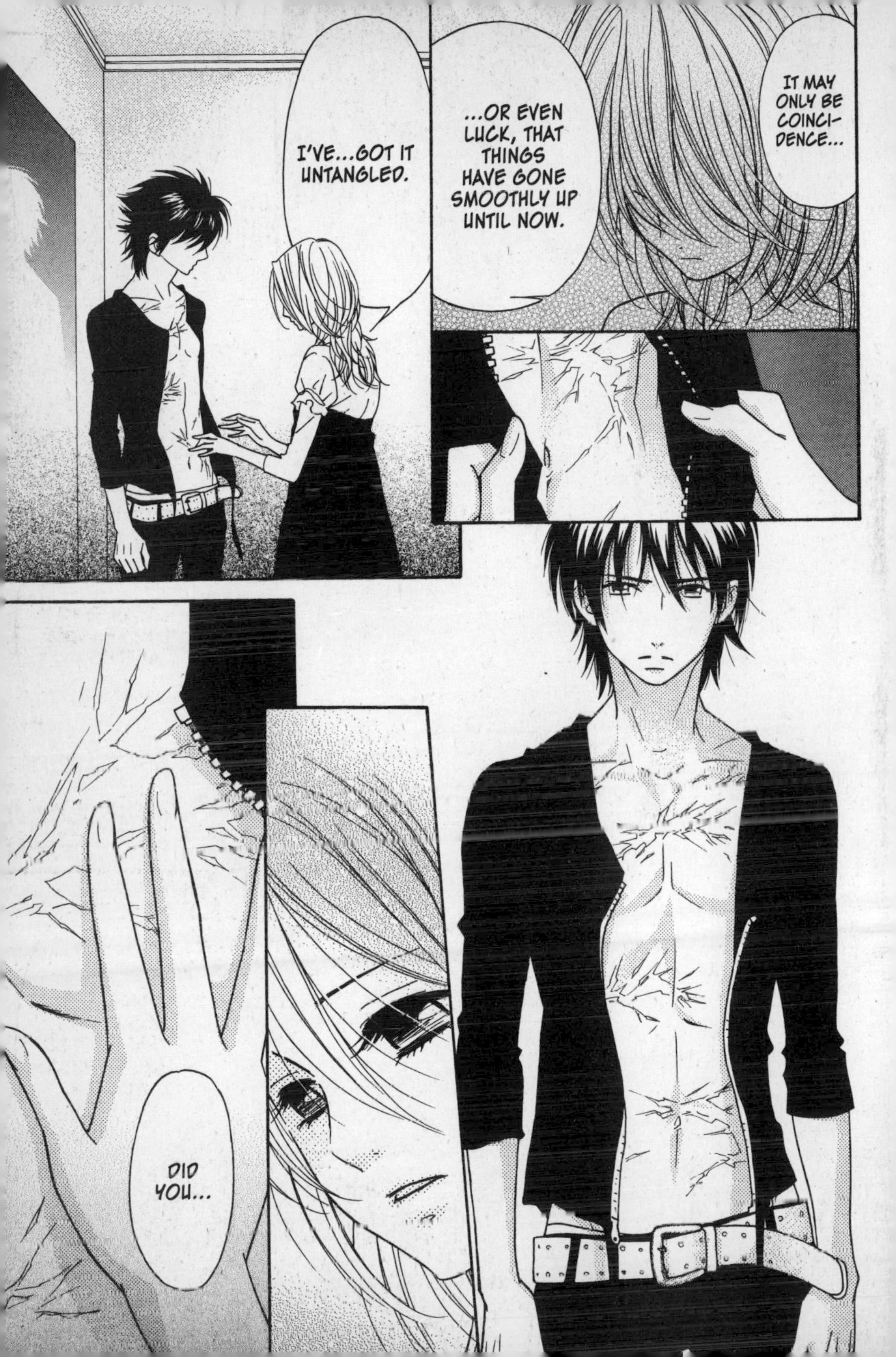
IT MAY ONLY BE COINCIDENCE...
...OR EVEN LUCK, THAT THINGS HAVE GONE SMOOTHLY UP UNTIL NOW.
I'VE...GOT IT UNTANGLED.
DID YOU...

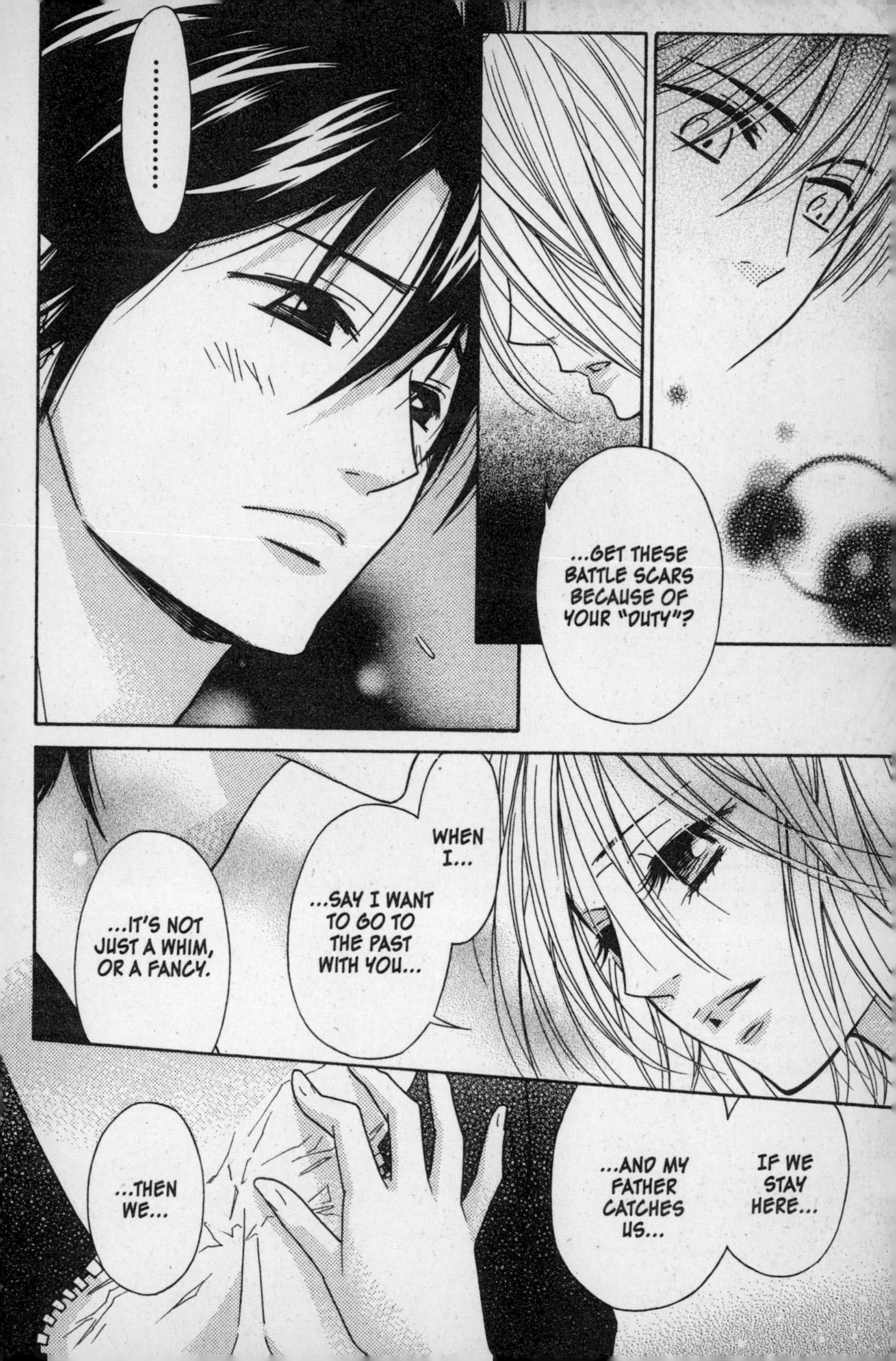
...GET THESE BATTLE SCARS BECAUSE OF YOUR "DUTY"?
......
WHEN I...
...SAY I WANT TO GO TO THE PAST WITH YOU...
...IT'S NOT JUST A WHIM, OR A FANCY.
IF WE STAY HERE...
...AND MY FATHER CATCHES US...
...THEN WE...

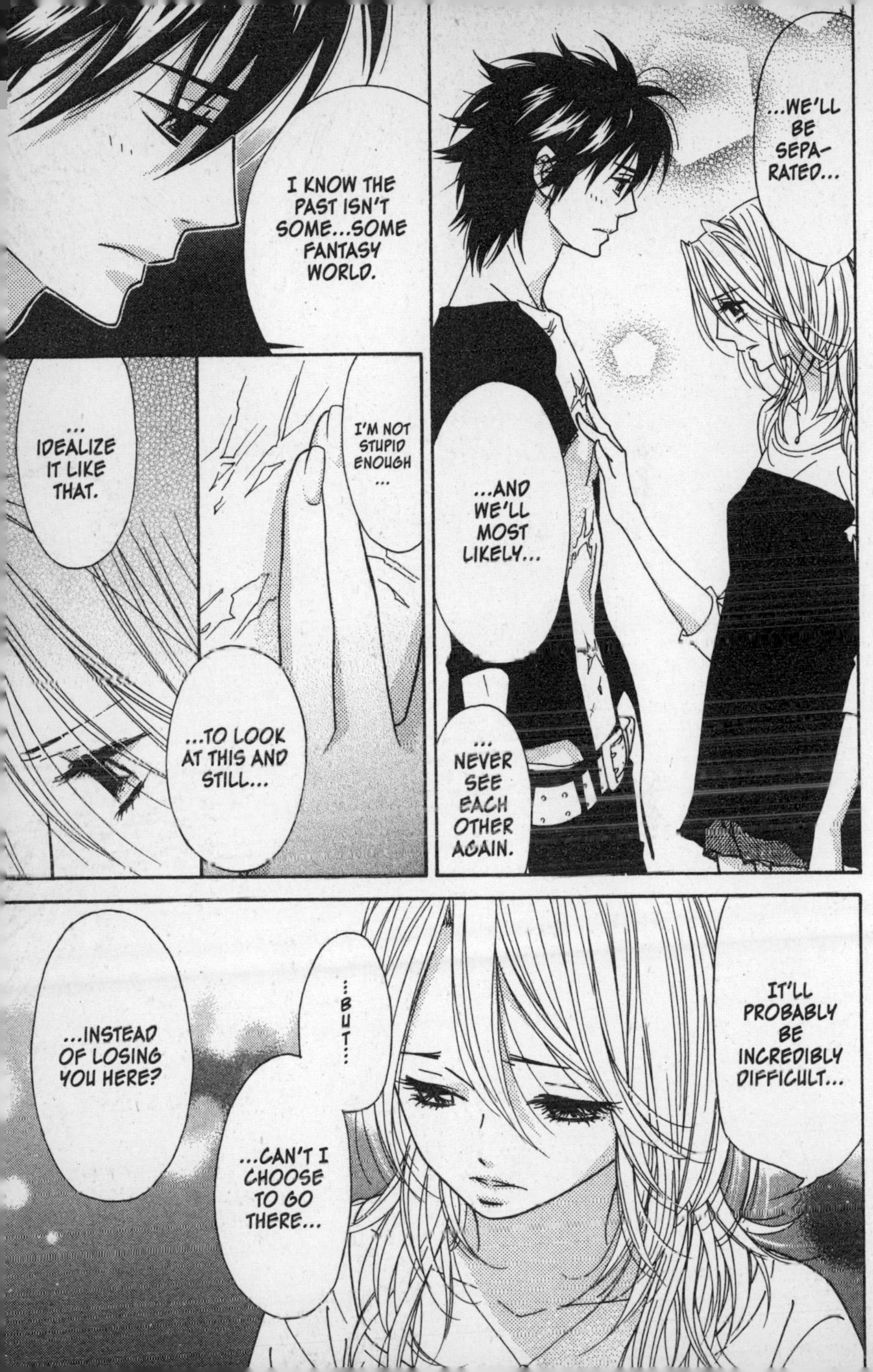
...WE'LL BE SEPA-RATED...
...AND WE'LL MOST LIKELY...
...NEVER SEE EACH OTHER AGAIN.
I KNOW THE PAST ISN'T SOME...SOME FANTASY WORLD.
I'M NOT STUPID ENOUGH ...
...TO LOOK AT THIS AND STILL...
... IDEALIZE IT LIKE THAT.
IT'LL PROBABLY BE INCREDIBLY DIFFICULT...
...BUT...
...CAN'T I CHOOSE TO GO THERE...
...INSTEAD OF LOSING YOU HERE?

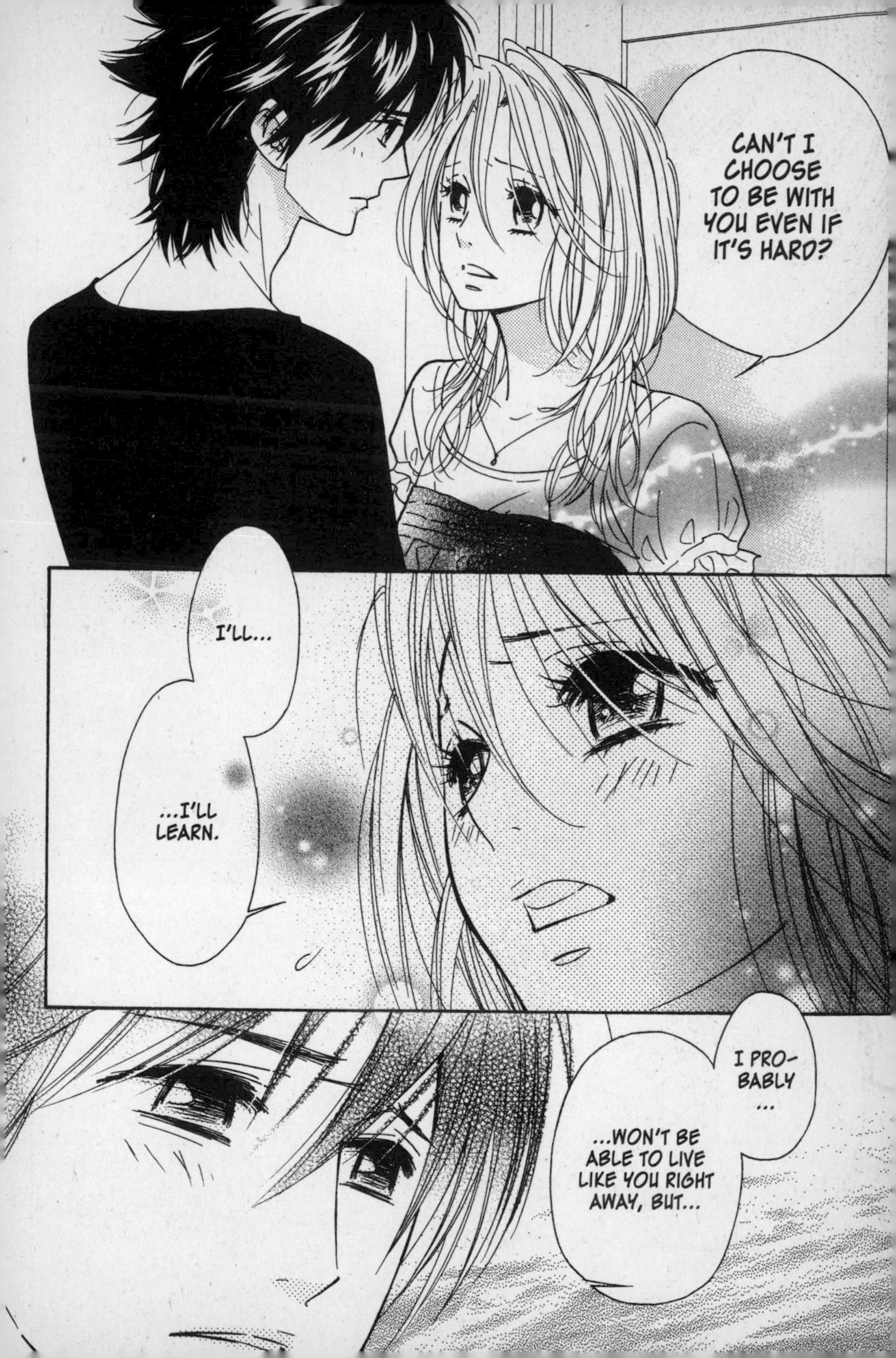
CAN'T I CHOOSE TO BE WITH YOU EVEN IF IT'S HARD?
I'LL...
...I'LL LEARN.
I PRO-BABLY...
...WON'T BE ABLE TO LIVE LIKE YOU RIGHT AWAY, BUT...

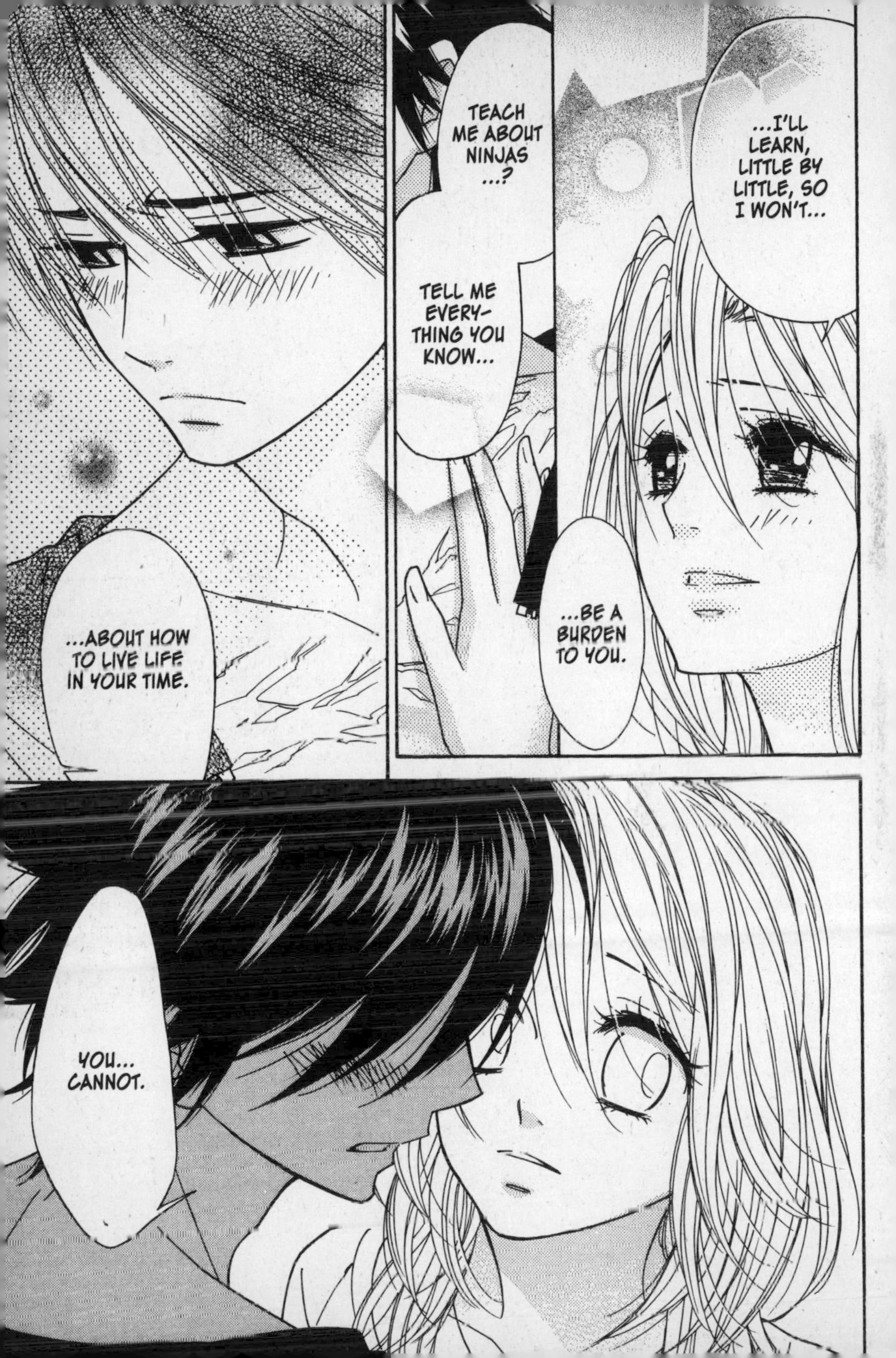
...I'LL LEARN, LITTLE BY LITTLE, SO I WON'T...
...BE A BURDEN TO YOU.
TEACH ME ABOUT NINJAS ...?
TELL ME EVERY-THING YOU KNOW...
...ABOUT HOW TO LIVE LIFE IN YOUR TIME.
YOU... CANNOT.

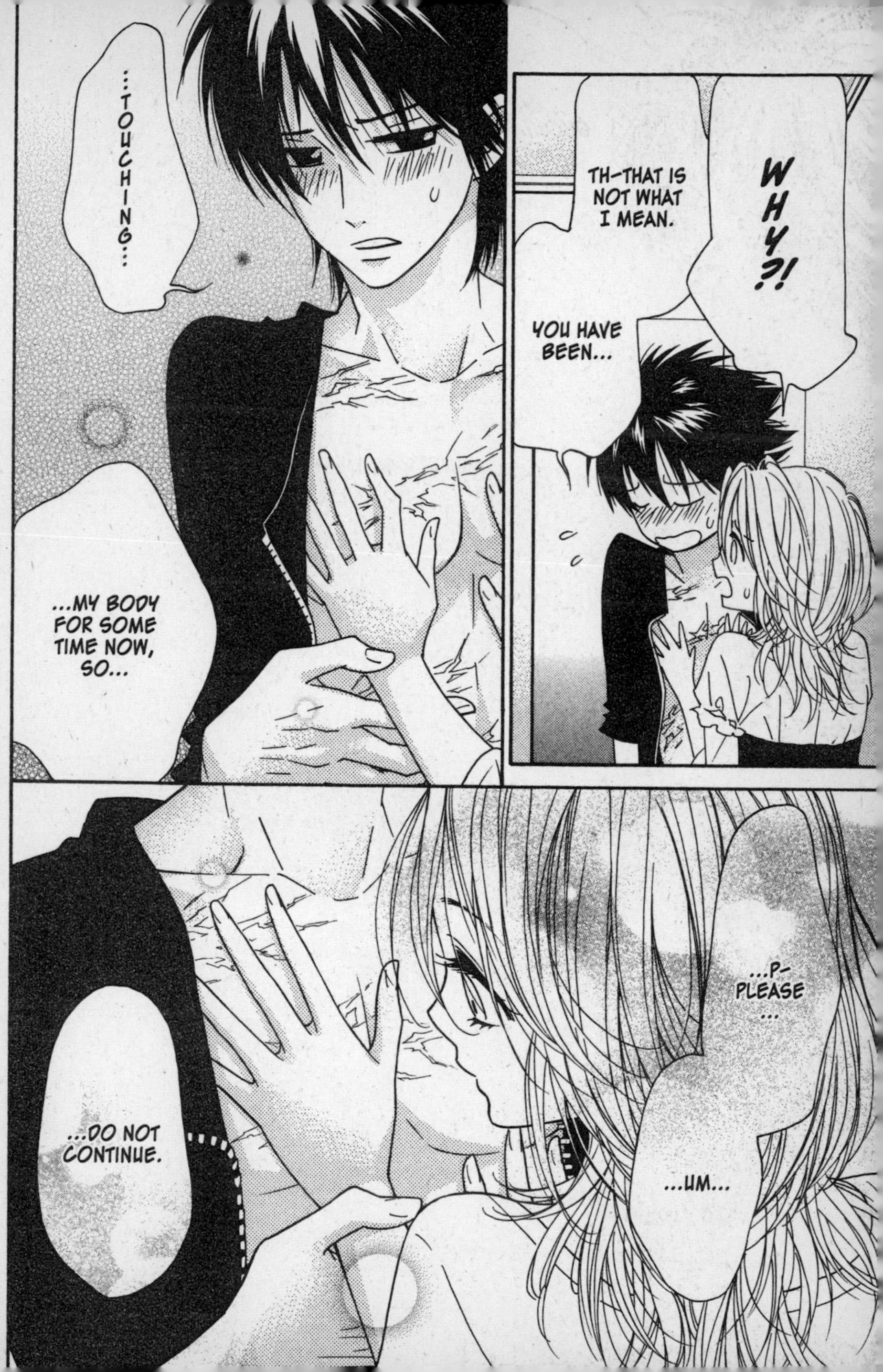
WHY?!
TH-THAT IS NOT WHAT I MEAN.
YOU HAVE BEEN...
...TOUCHING...
...MY BODY FOR SOME TIME NOW, SO...
...P-PLEASE...
...UM...
...DO NOT CONTINUE.

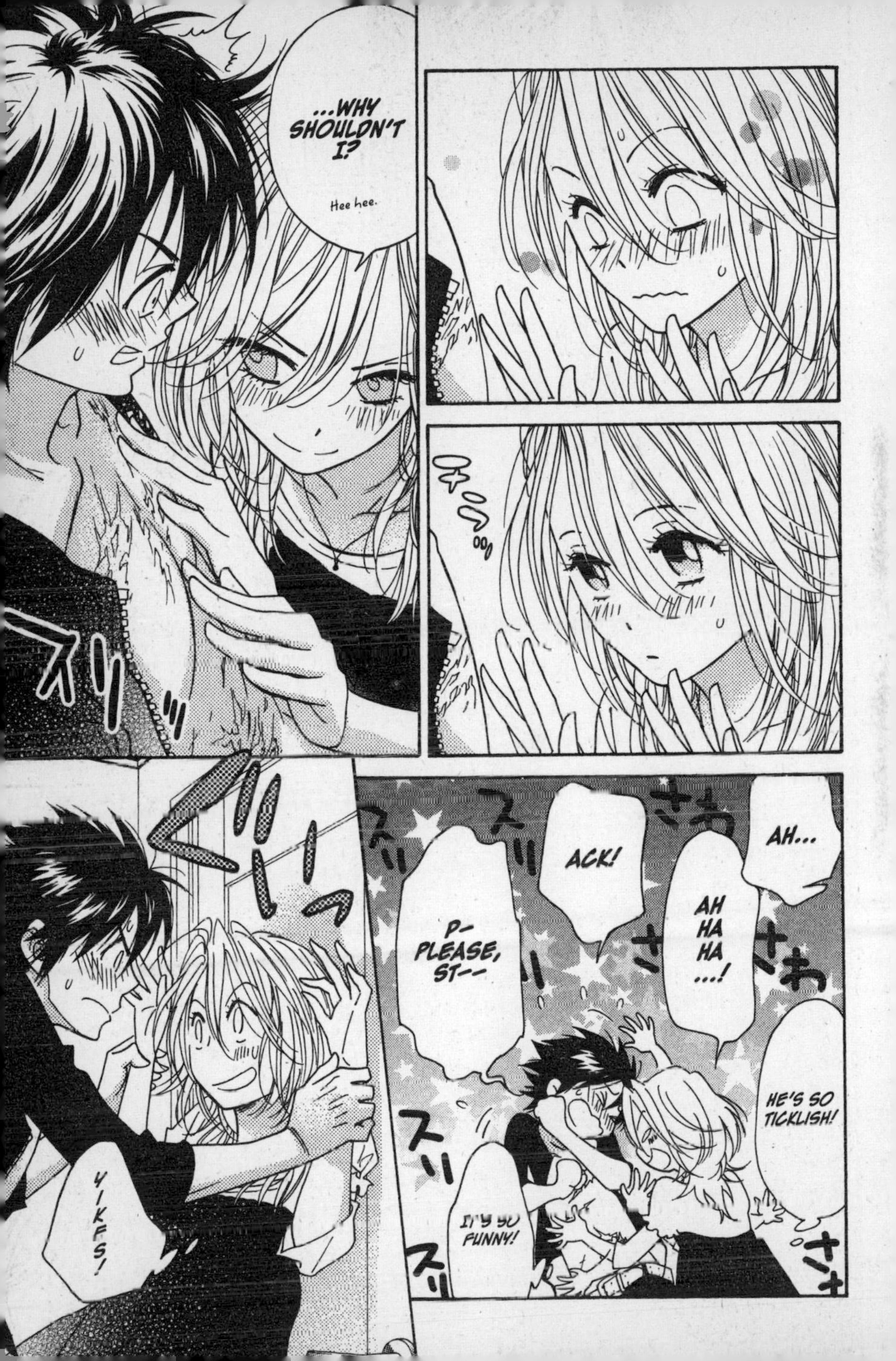
...WHY SHOULDN'T I?
Hee hee.
AH...
AH HA HA...!
ACK!
P-PLEASE, ST--
HE'S SO TICKLISH!
IT'S SO FUNNY!
YIKES!

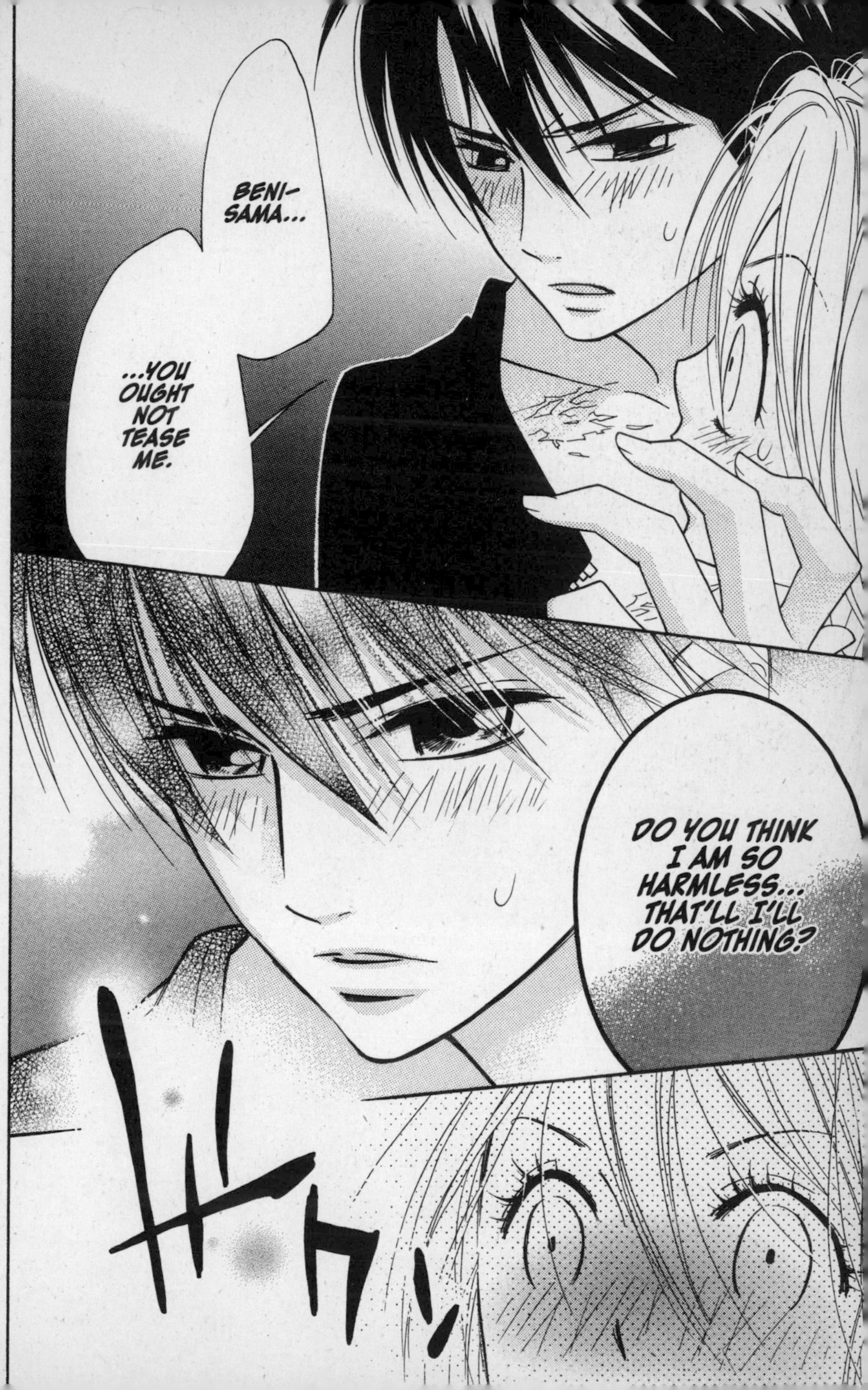
BENI-SAMA...
...YOU OUGHT NOT TEASE ME.
DO YOU THINK I AM SO HARMLESS... THAT'LL I'LL DO NOTHING?

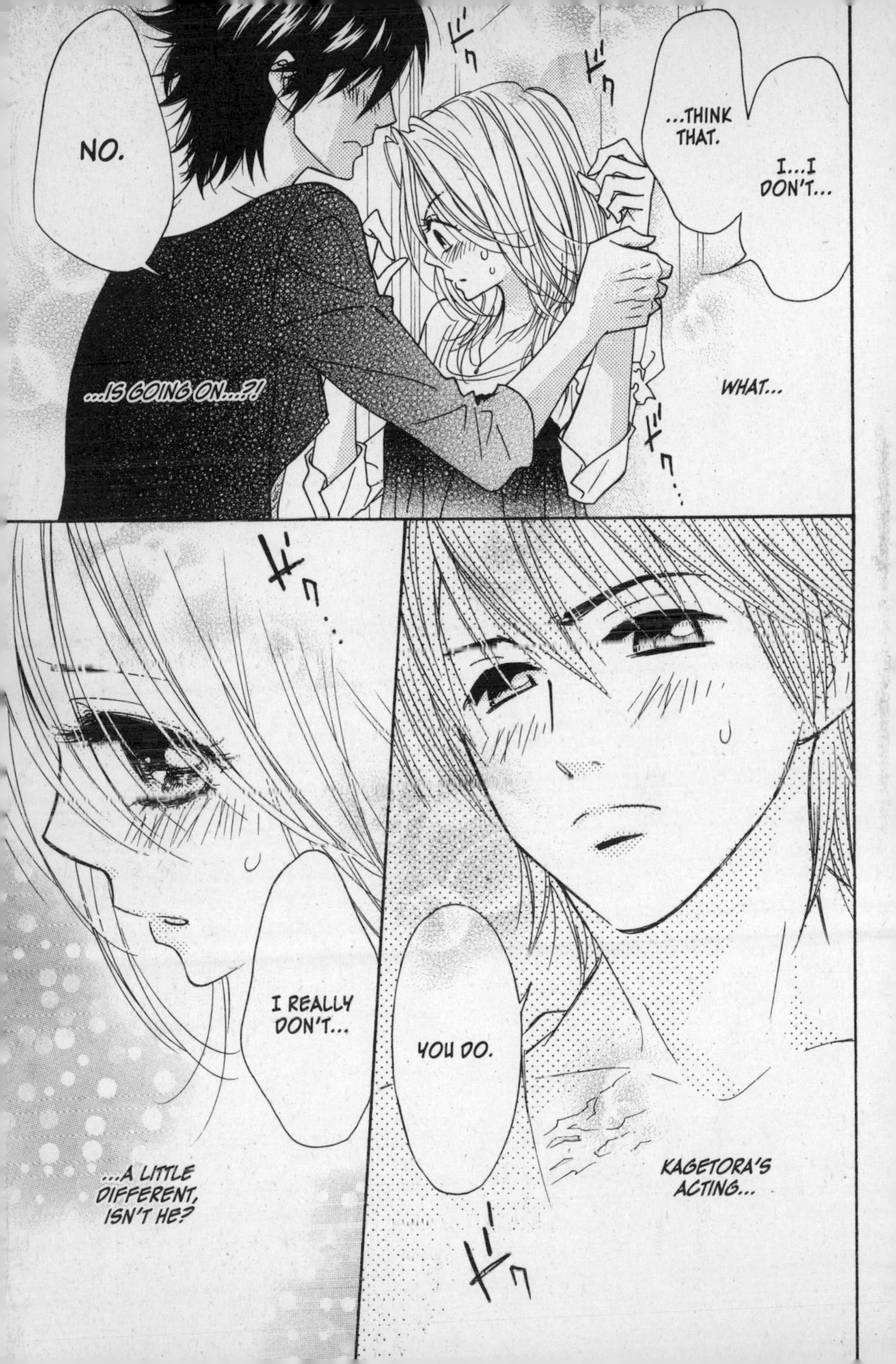
I...I DON'T...
...THINK THAT.
WHAT...
...IS GOING ON...?!
NO.
YOU DO.
KAGETORA'S ACTING...
I REALLY DON'T...
...A LITTLE DIFFERENT, ISN'T HE?

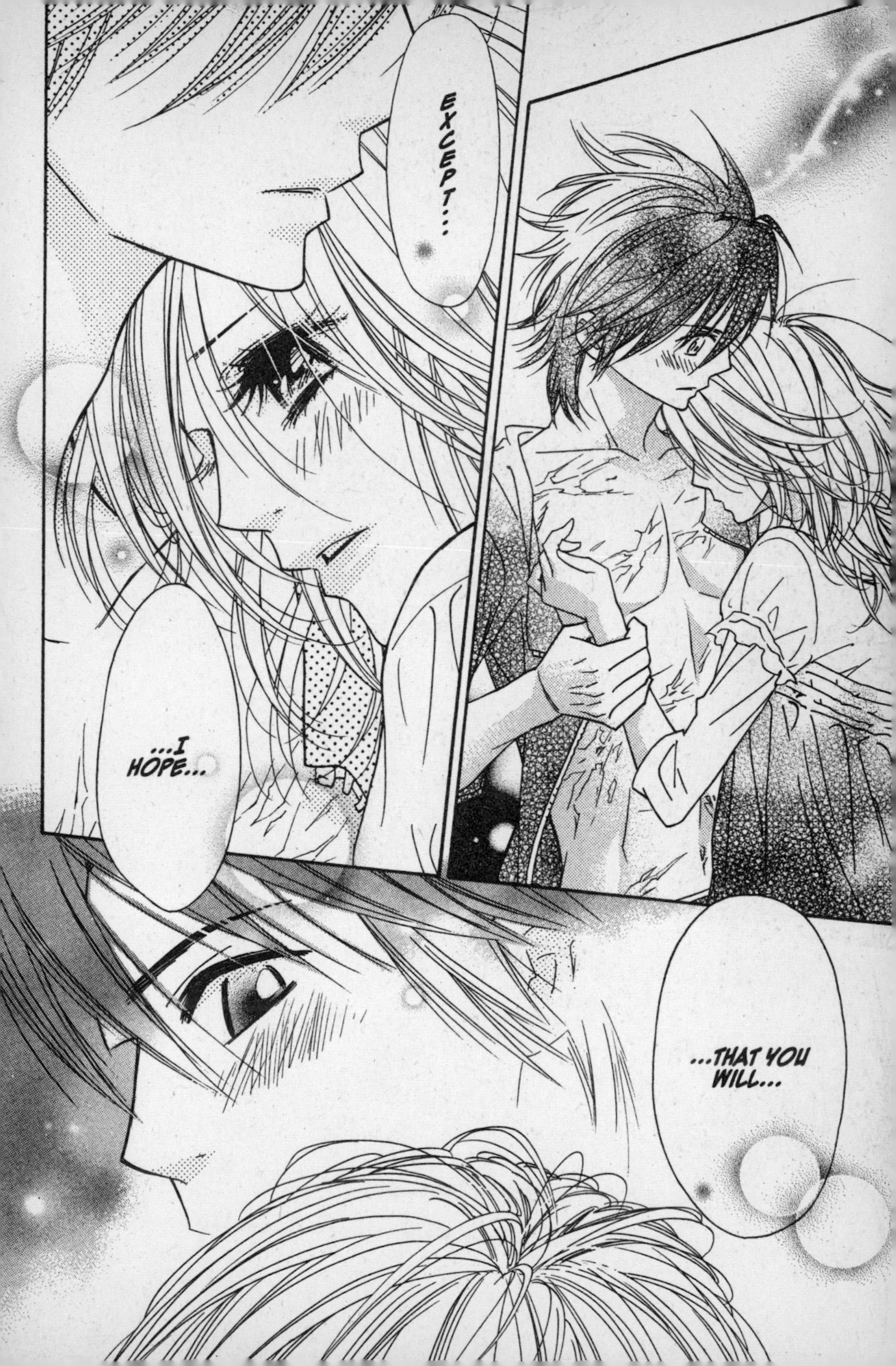
EXCEPT...
...I HOPE...
...THAT YOU WILL...

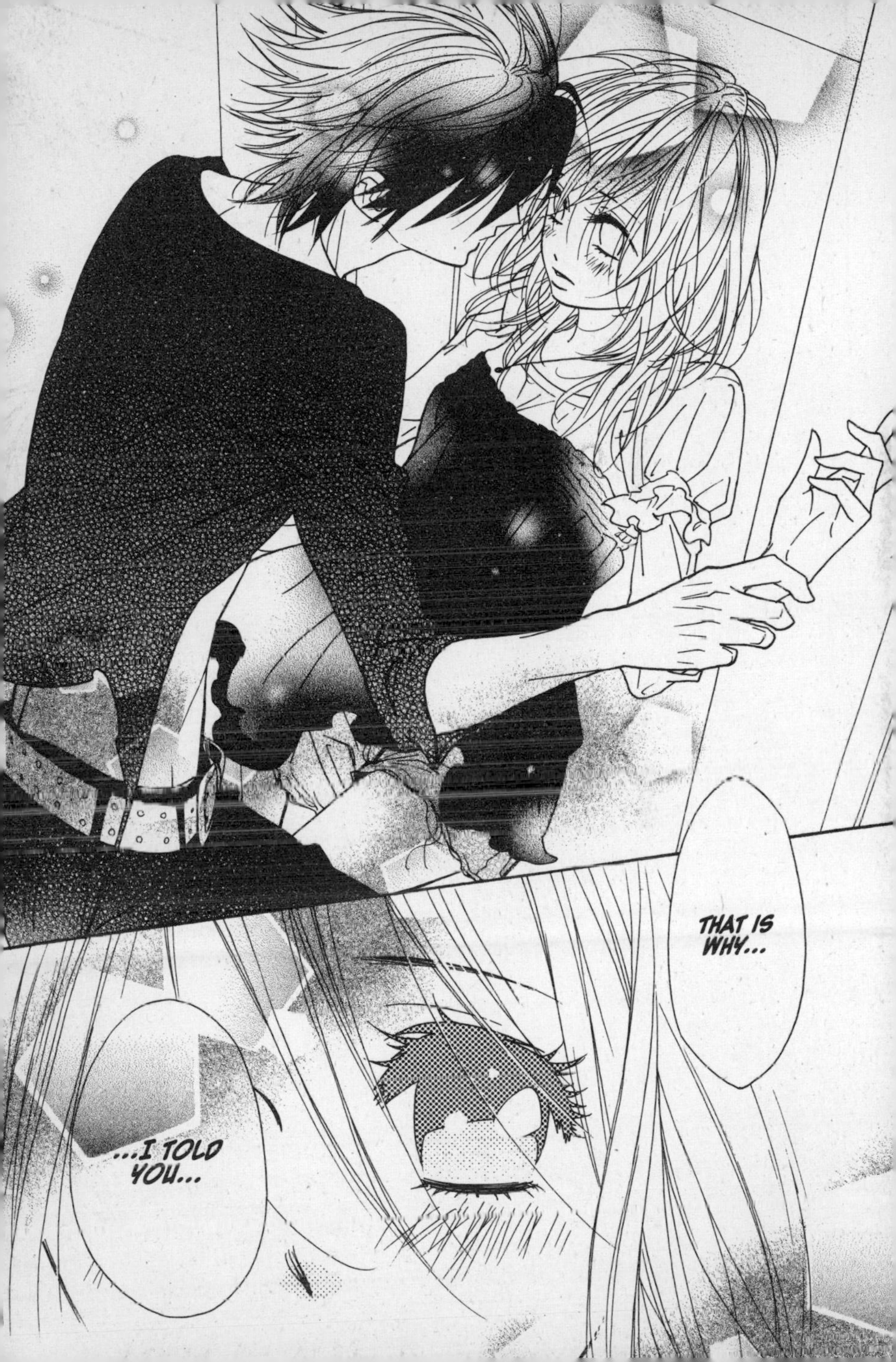
THAT IS WHY...
...I TOLD YOU...

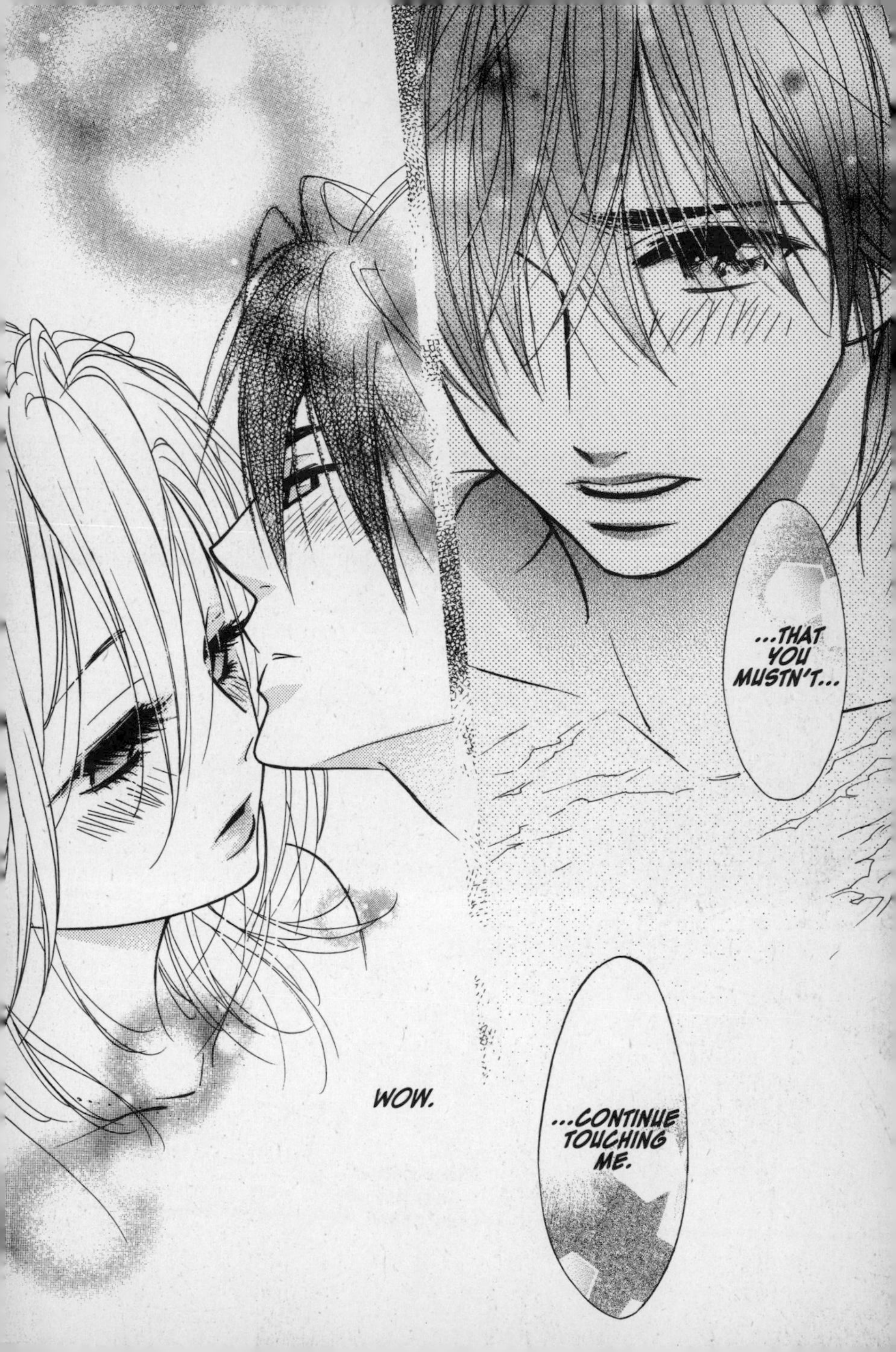
...THAT YOU MUSTN'T...
...CONTINUE TOUCHING ME.
WOW.

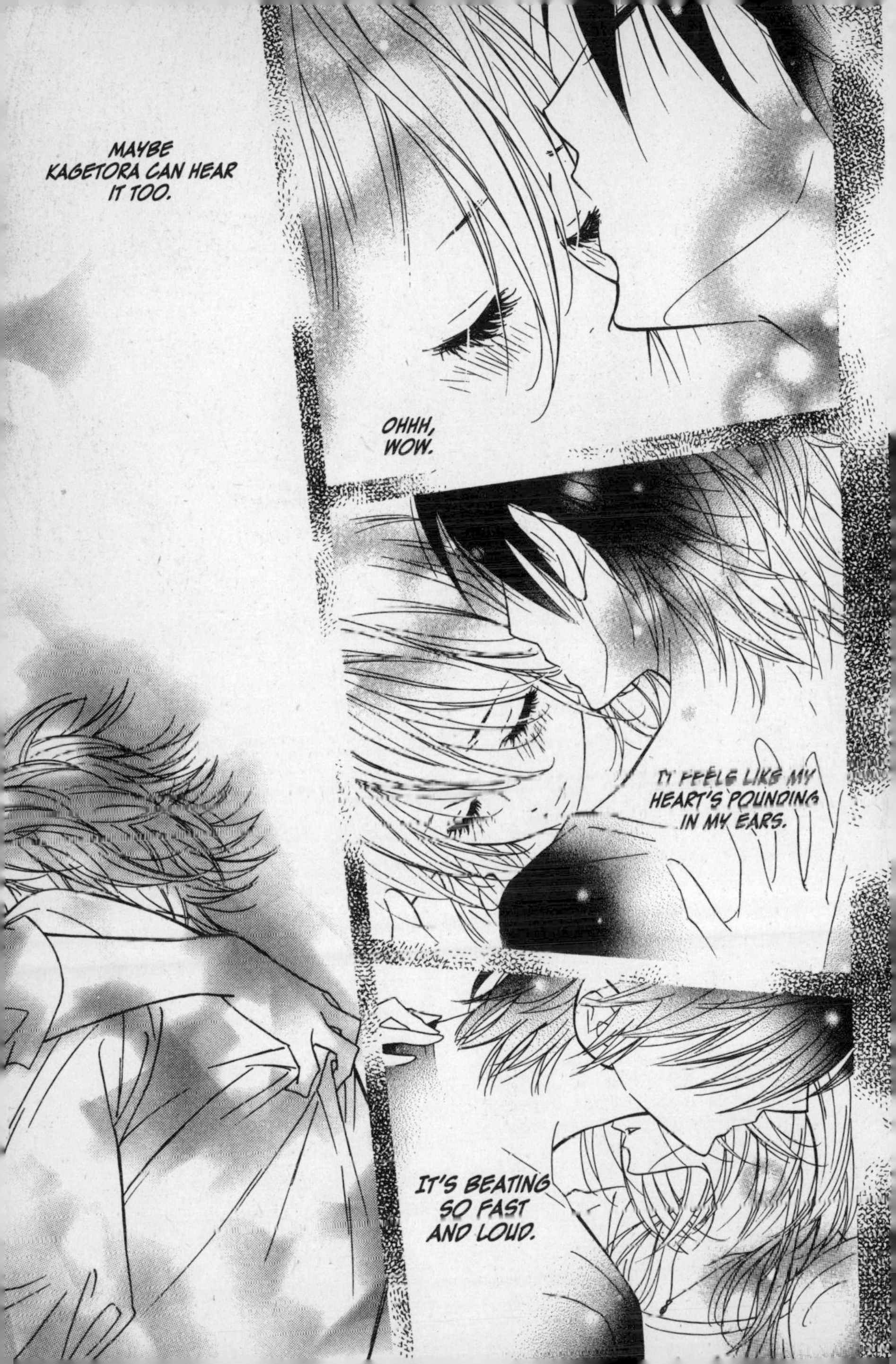
OHHH, WOW.
IT FEELS LIKE MY HEART'S POUNDING IN MY EARS.
IT'S BEATING SO FAST AND LOUD.
MAYBE KAGETORA CAN HEAR IT TOO.

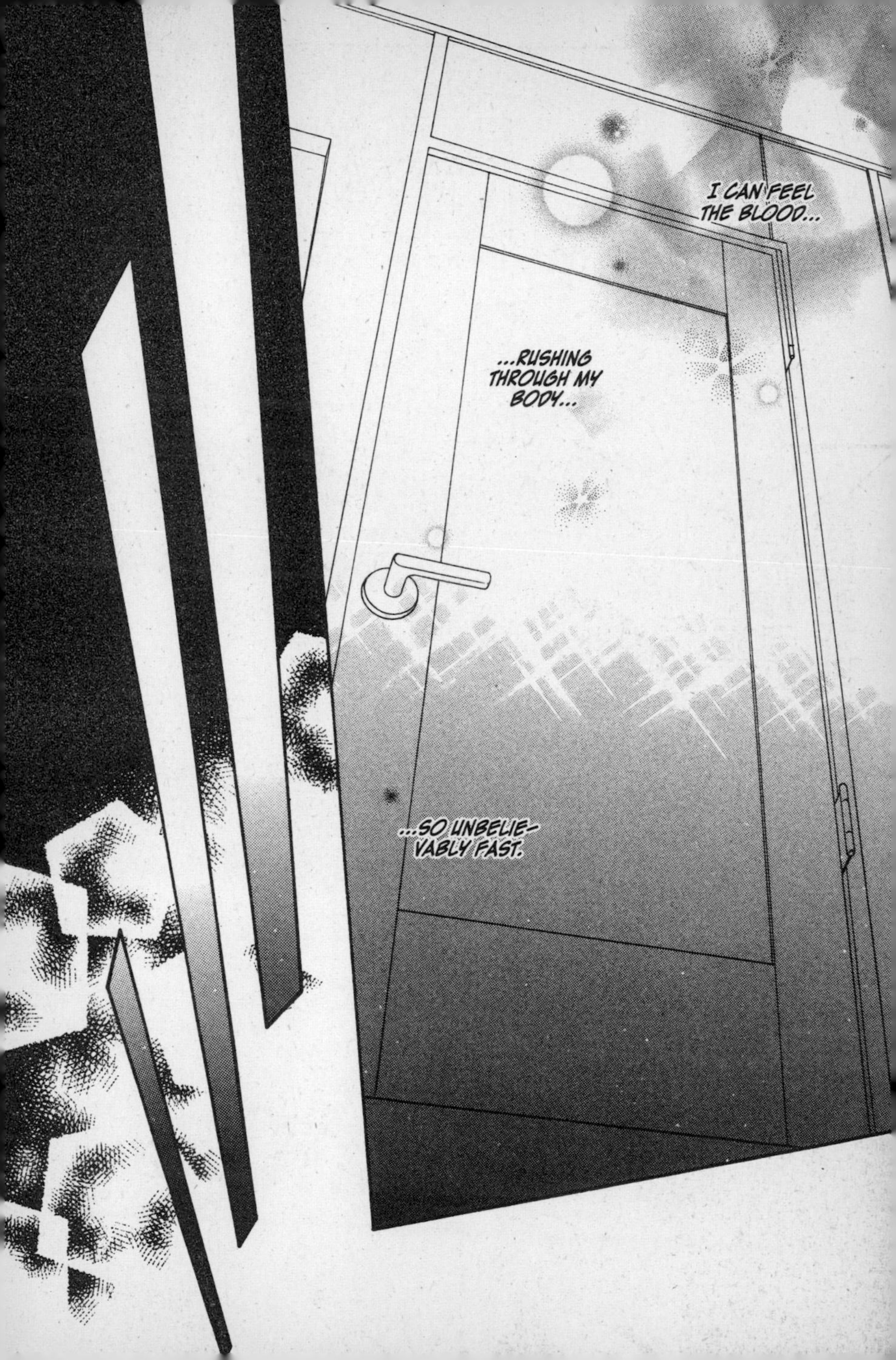
I CAN FEEL THE BLOOD...
...RUSHING THROUGH MY BODY...
...SO UNBELIEVABLY FAST.

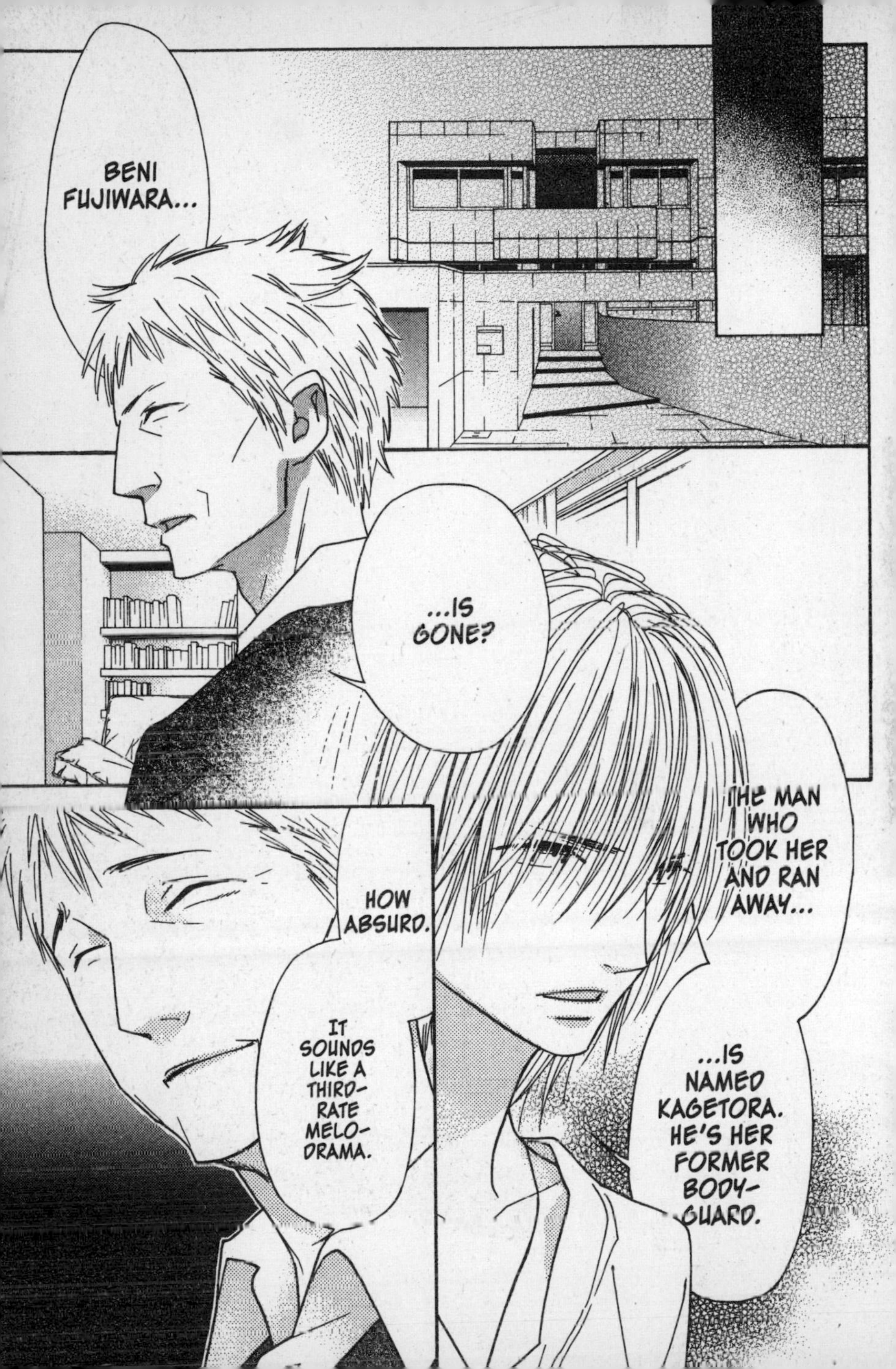
BENI FUJIWARA...
...IS GONE?
THE MAN WHO TOOK HER AND RAN AWAY...
...IS NAMED KAGETORA. HE'S HER FORMER BODY-GUARD.
HOW ABSURD.
IT SOUNDS LIKE A THIRD-RATE MELO-DRAMA.

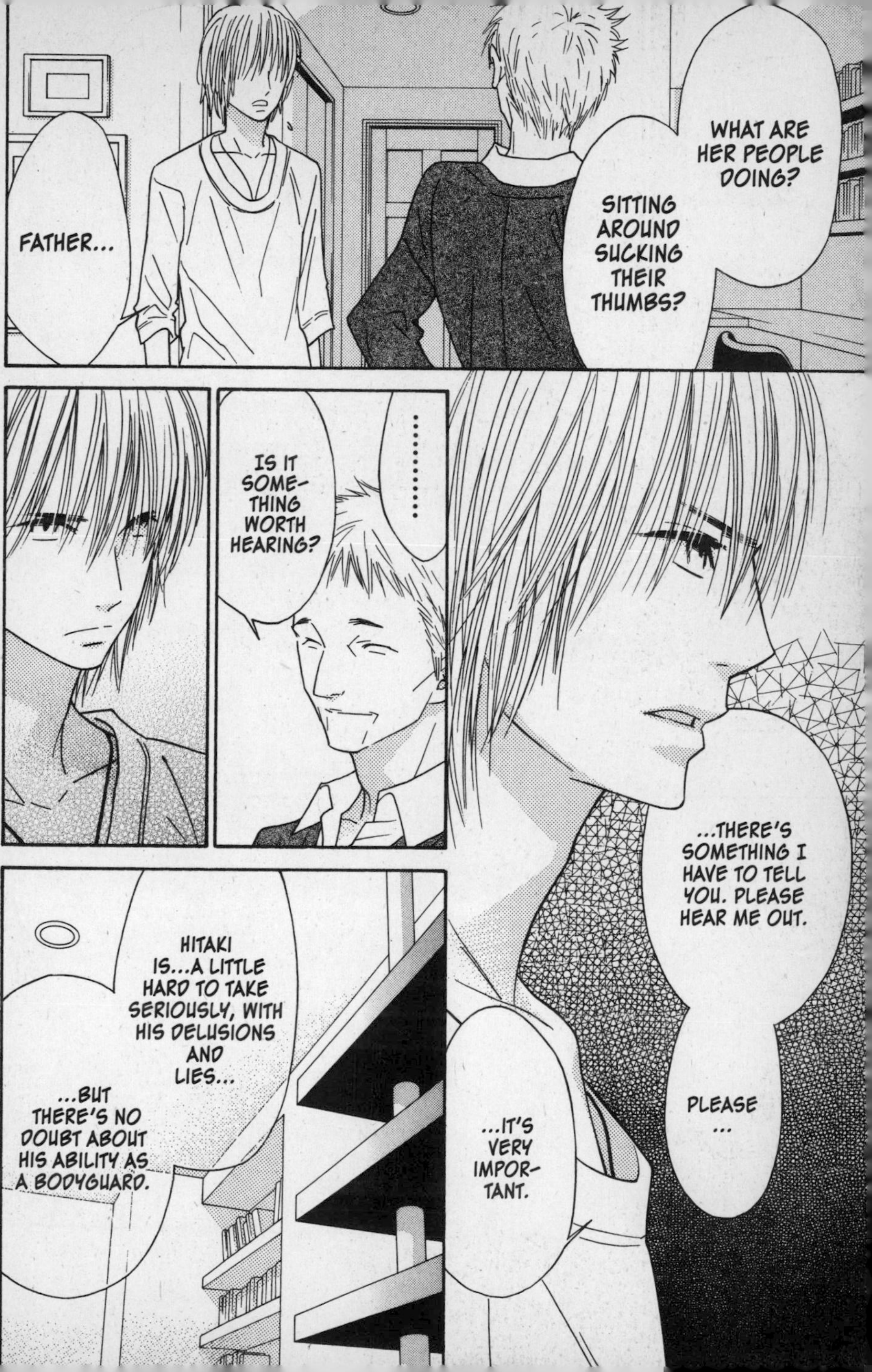
WHAT ARE HER PEOPLE DOING?
SITTING AROUND SUCKING THEIR THUMBS?
FATHER...
...THERE'S SOMETHING I HAVE TO TELL YOU. PLEASE HEAR ME OUT.
PLEASE...
...IT'S VERY IMPORTANT.
....
IS IT SOMETHING WORTH HEARING?
HITAKI IS...A LITTLE HARD TO TAKE SERIOUSLY, WITH HIS DELUSIONS AND LIES...
...BUT THERE'S NO DOUBT ABOUT HIS ABILITY AS A BODYGUARD.

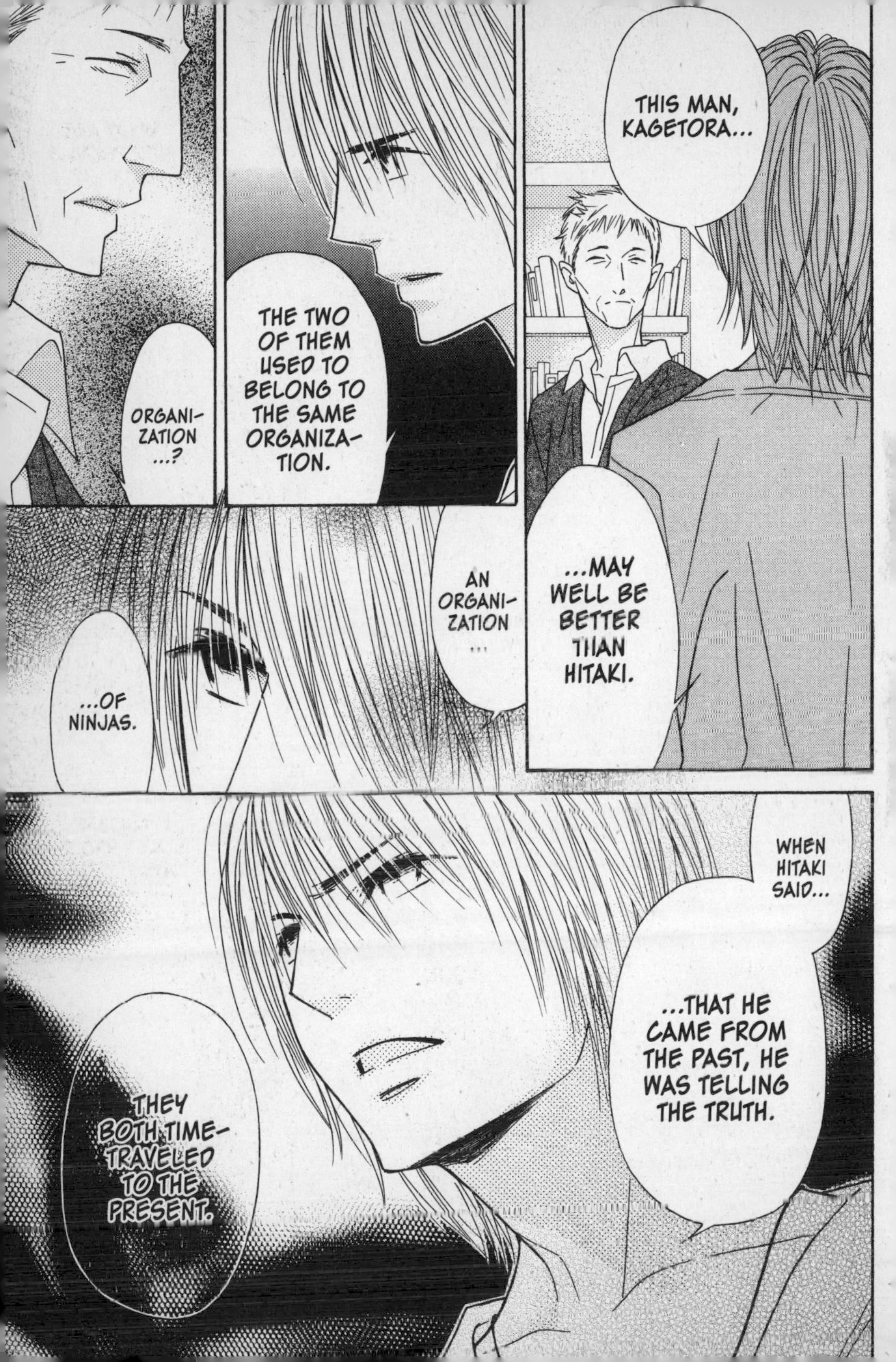
THIS MAN, KAGETORA...
...MAY WELL BE BETTER THAN HITAKI.
THE TWO OF THEM USED TO BELONG TO THE SAME ORGANIZATION.
ORGANIZATION...?
AN ORGANIZATION...
...OF NINJAS.
WHEN HITAKI SAID...
...THAT HE CAME FROM THE PAST, HE WAS TELLING THE TRUTH.
THEY BOTH TIME-TRAVELED TO THE PRESENT.

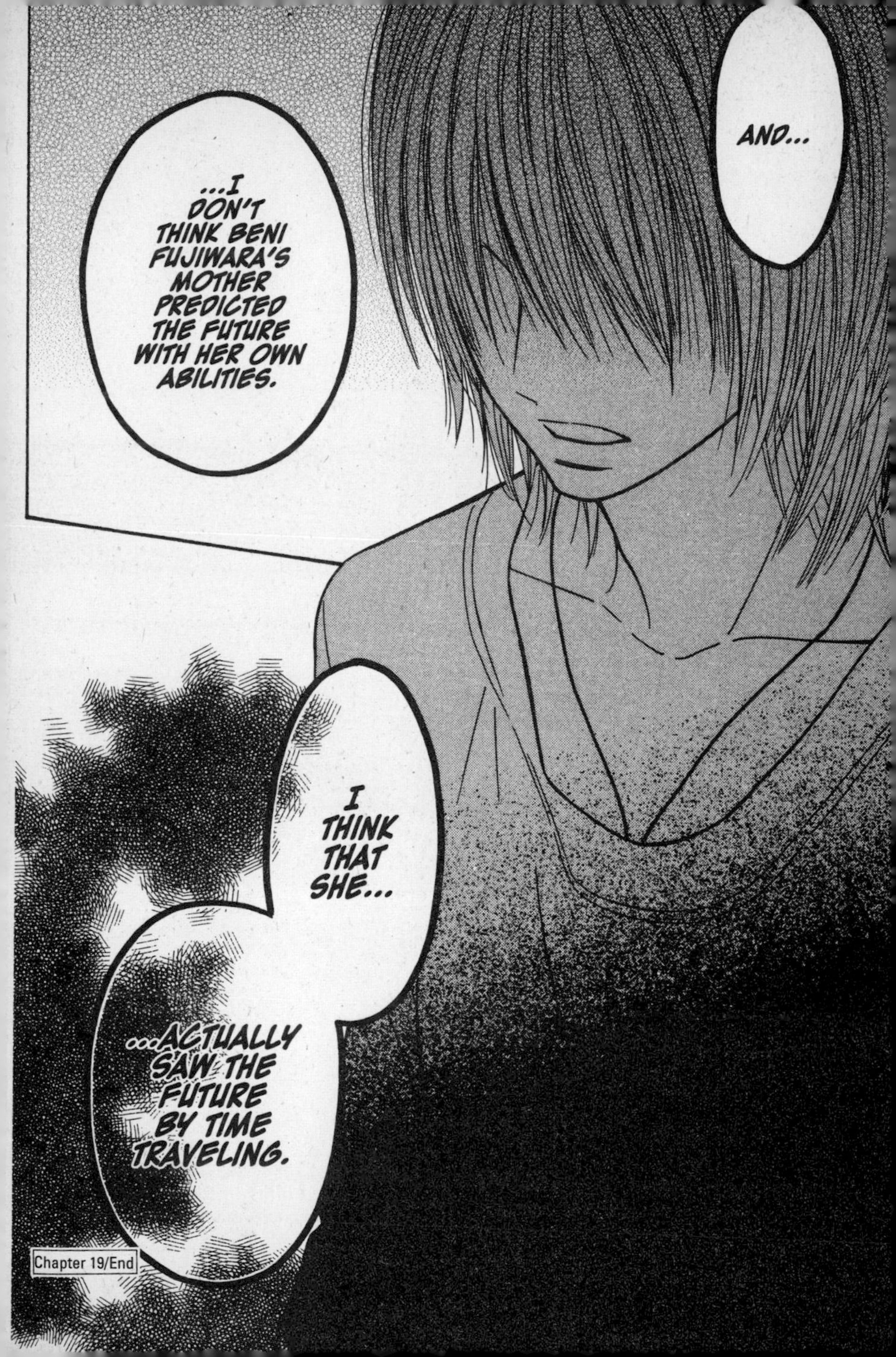
AND...
...I DON'T THINK BENI FUJIWARA'S MOTHER PREDICTED THE FUTURE WITH HER OWN ABILITIES.
I THINK THAT SHE...
...ACTUALLY SAW THE FUTURE BY TIME TRAVELING.
Chapter 19/End

Bonus Manga! Kagetora-kun Hitaki-kun the Ninja!

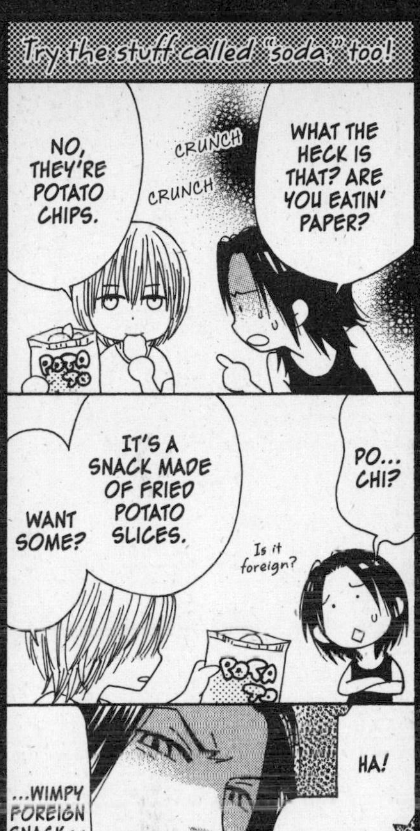
Try the stuff called "soda," too!
WHAT THE HECK IS THAT? ARE YOU EATIN' PAPER?
CRUNCH
CRUNCH
NO, THEY'RE POTATO CHIPS.
POTATO
PO... CHI?
IT'S A SNACK MADE OF FRIED POTATO SLICES.
WANT SOME?
Is it foreign?
POTATO
HA!
AIN'T NO WAY I'M GONNA EAT THAT...
...WIMPY FOREIGN SNACK--
WOW, IT TASTES AMAZING!
CAL-BEE'S THE SALTIEST BRAND.
CRUNCH
I THINK THESE ONES ARE LESS SOUR...
HE'S TOTALLY OBSESSED.
...DUDE, CHILL.
CRUNCH

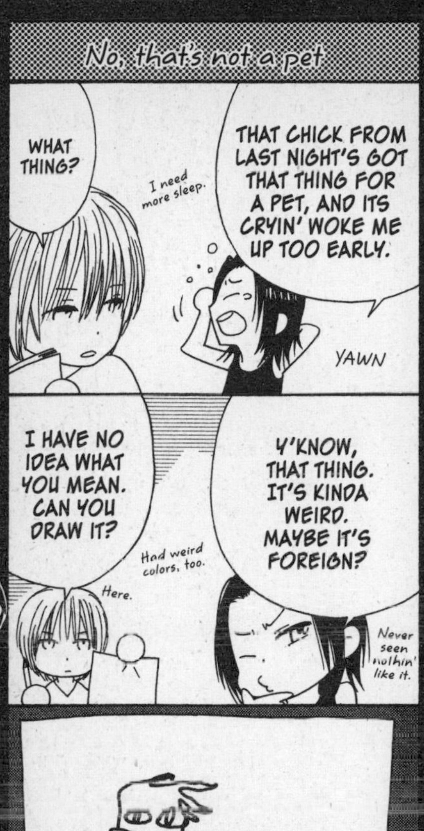
No, that's not a pet
THAT CHICK FROM LAST NIGHT'S GOT THAT THING FOR A PET, AND ITS CRYIN' WOKE ME UP TOO EARLY.
YAWN
I need more sleep.
WHAT THING?
Y'KNOW, THAT THING. IT'S KINDA WEIRD. MAYBE IT'S FOREIGN?
Never seen nothin' like it.
Had weird colors, too.
I HAVE NO IDEA WHAT YOU MEAN. CAN YOU DRAW IT?
Here.
A... CHINESE LION...?
Four legs...
Dumbass!
IT'S TOTALLY A BIRD!

Shinobi Life 4/End

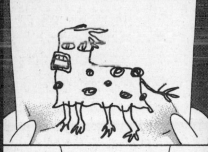

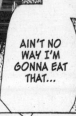

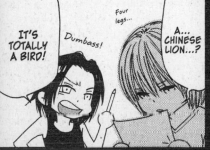

Shoko Conami's homepage: http://conami.cc/
(You can access it with your cell phone too!)

In the next volume of

Shinobi Life ™

THEIR INTERLUDE IN THE FITTING ROOM INTERRUPTED, BENI AND KAGETORA MAKE THE CHOICE TO FLEE TO THE PAST, WITH HITAKI HOT ON THEIR HEELS. BUT WHILE SHE WAS FULLY PREPARED FOR THE CONSEQUENCES OF HER DECISION, BENI'S NEVERTHELESS IN FOR A SURPRISE WHEN SHE ACTUALLY PASSES THROUGH THE TIME WARP... AND IS SEPARATED FROM KAGETORA! WITH A PERVY NINJA AND HIS UNCOMFORTABLY FAMILIAR YOUNG PROTEGEES AS HER HOSTS, BENI'S NEW LIFE IS ABOUT TO GET WAY MORE COMPLICATED...

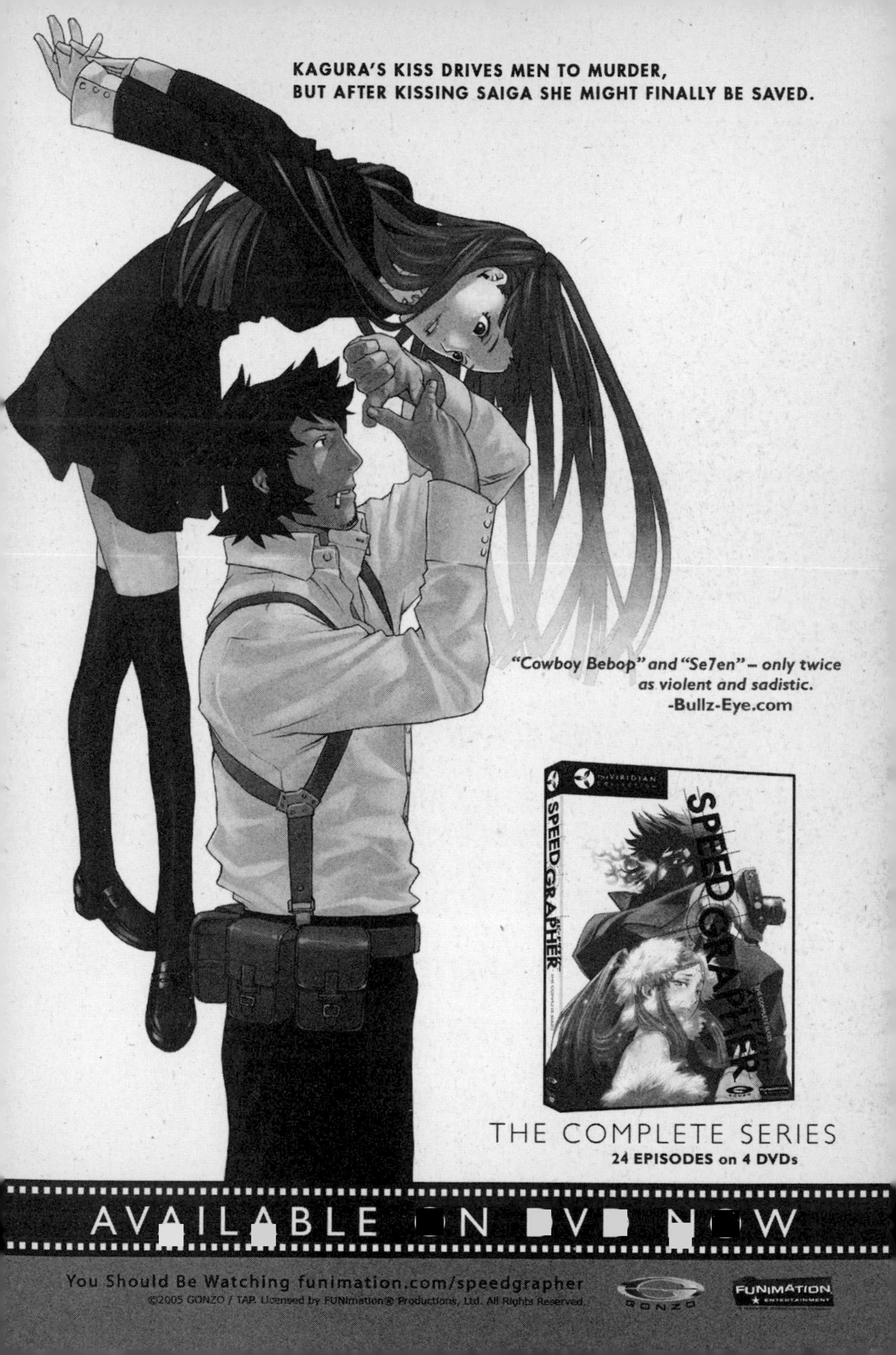
KAGURA'S KISS DRIVES MEN TO MURDER,
BUT AFTER KISSING SAIGA SHE MIGHT FINALLY BE SAVED.
"Cowboy Bebop" and "Se7en" – only twice as violent and sadistic.
-Bullz-Eye.com
SPEED GRAPHER
SPEED GRAPHER
THE COMPLETE SERIES
24 EPISODES on 4 DVDs
AVAILABLE [redacted]N [redacted]V[redacted] N[redacted]W
You Should Be Watching funimation.com/speedgrapher
©2005 GONZO / TAP. Licensed by FUNimation® Productions, Ltd. All Rights Reserved.
GONZO
FUNIMATION ENTERTAINMENT

The second epic trilogy continues!

Princess Ai: The Prism of Midnight Dawn

Ai fights to escape the clutches of her mysterious and malevolent captors, not knowing whether Kent, left behind on the Other Side, is even still alive. A frantic rescue mission commences, and in the end, even Ai's magical voice may not be enough to protect her from the trials of the Black Forest.

Dark secrets are revealed, and Ai must use all her strength and courage to face off against the new threat to Ai-Land. But will she ever see Kent again...?

"A very intriguing read that will satisfy old fans and create new fans, too."
– Bookloons

D·N·ANGEL·

The secret of the Hikari/Niwa curse is revealed!

The time has come for Satoshi to reveal to Daisuke the history behind the Hikari/Niwa curse. How will Daisuke respond when he finds out why Satoshi is destined to die so young? Meanwhile, another fight breaks out against Argentine, sending Daisuke spiraling toward death as he tries to rescue Risa...

D·N·ANGEL·™

VOLUME 13 • YUKIRU SUGISAKI

FANTASY

T
TEEN
AGE 13+

BE SURE TO VISIT WWW.TOKYOPOP.COM/SHOP FOR EVERYTHING YOU COULD EVER WANT!

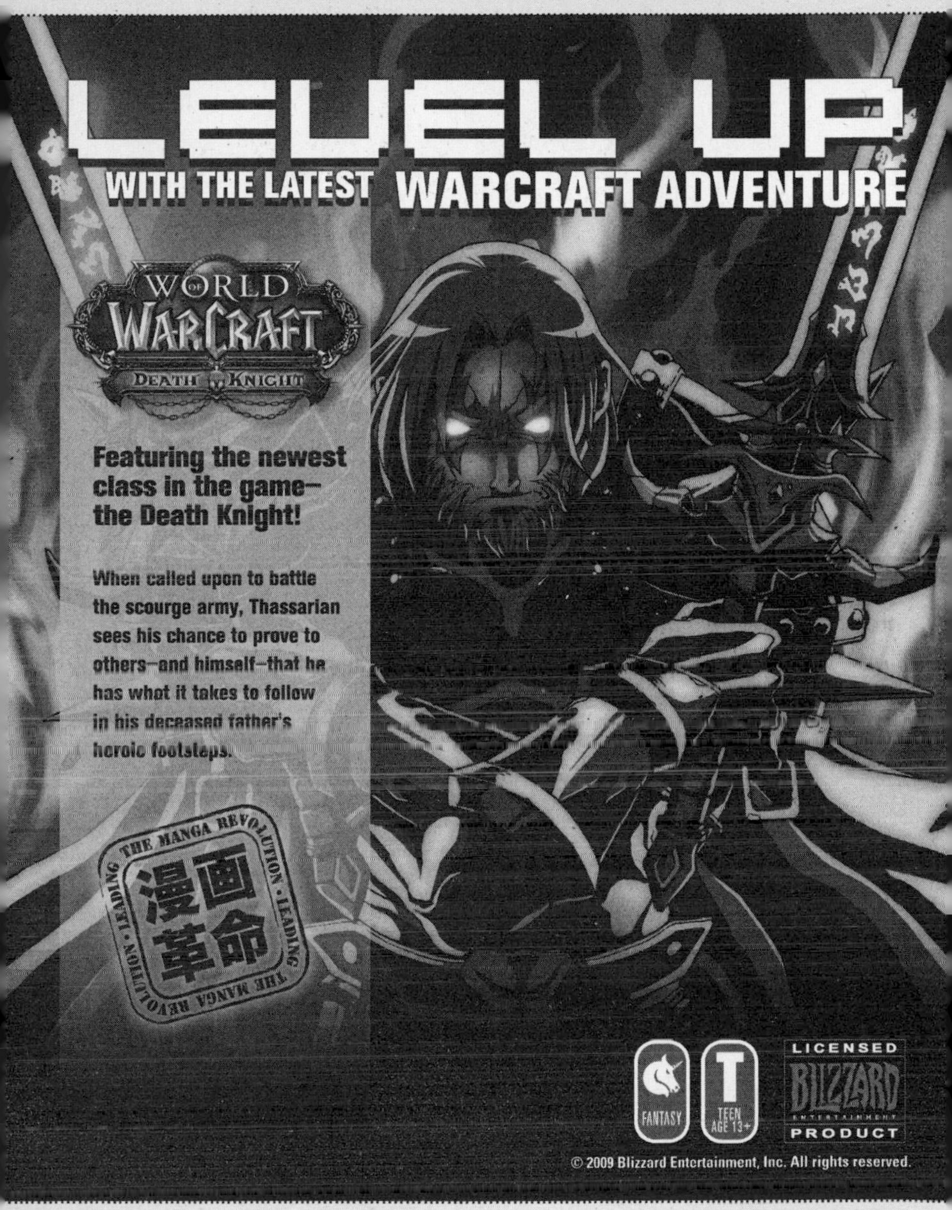
LEVEL UP
WITH THE LATEST WARCRAFT ADVENTURE
WORLD OF WARCRAFT
DEATH KNIGHT
Featuring the newest class in the game—the Death Knight!
When called upon to battle the scourge army, Thassarian sees his chance to prove to others—and himself—that he has what it takes to follow in his deceased father's heroic footsteps.
THE MANGA REVOLUTION · LEADING
漫画革命
FANTASY
T
TEEN AGE 13+
LICENSED
BLIZZARD
ENTERTAINMENT
PRODUCT
© 2009 Blizzard Entertainment, Inc. All rights reserved.

FOR MORE INFORMATION VISIT: WWW.TOKYOPOP.COM/WARCRAFT

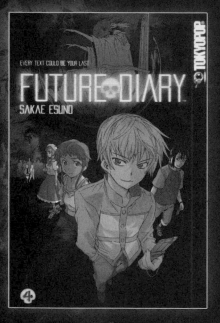

© Kou Matsuzuki

Happy CAFE

Enjoy VOL 1

Today's Specials

Romance, Happiness,
General Wackiness

Uru takes her mother's remarriage as an opportunity to work part time at the Happy Café. There, she befriends Ichirou and Shindou, two of the most unsociable guys she's ever met! To make matters worse, it turns out that Uru is not exactly meant for the waitressing world, as she's a HUGE clutz. But as this hilarious shojo tale unfolds, true happiness—and even true love—lurk just around the corner...

If you like Maid Sama! and V.B. Rose, you'll love Happy Café!

KARAKURI ODETTE

カラクリ オデット

VOL. 2

KARAKURI ODETTO © 2005 Julietta Suzuki / HAKUSENSHA, Inc.

She's a robot who wants to learn how to be a human... And what she learns will surprise everyone!

Odette is now a sophomore at her high school. She wants to be as close to human as she can, but finds out she still has a long way to go. From wanting to be "cute" by wearing nail polish, to making a "tasty" bento that people would be happy to eat, Odette faces each challenge head-on with the help of her friends Yoko, Chris, the Professor and, of course, Asao!

FROM THE CREATOR OF *AKUMA TO DOLCE*

"A SURPRISINGLY SENSITIVE, FUNNY AND THOUGHT-PROVOKING SCI-FI SHOJO SERIES ... AS GENUINELY CHARMING AND MEMORABLE AS ITS MECHANICAL HEROINE." —ABOUT.COM

STOP!

This is the back of the book. You wouldn't want to spoil a great ending!

This book is printed "manga-style," in the authentic Japanese right-to-left format. Since none of the artwork has been flipped or altered, readers get to experience the story just as the creator intended. You've been asking for it, so TOKYOPOP® delivered: authentic, hot-off-the-press, and far more fun!

DIRECTIONS

If this is your first time reading manga-style, here's a quick guide to help you understand how it works.

It's easy... just start in the top right panel and follow the numbers. Have fun, and look for more 100% authentic manga from TOKYOPOP®!

1
2
3
4
5
6
7
8
9
10

THE MANGA REVOLUTION • LEADING THE M